*New Ways of Knowing*

# NEW WAYS OF KNOWING

## The Sciences, Society, and Reconstructive Knowledge

BY

MARCUS G. RASKIN & HERBERT J. BERNSTEIN

WITH

SUSAN BUCK-MORSS · NOAM CHOMSKY
MICHAEL GOLDHABER · EDWARD HERMAN
JOSEPH TURNER

Rowman & Littlefield
PUBLISHERS

ROWMAN & LITTLEFIELD

Published in the United States of America in 1987
by Rowman & Littlefield, Publishers
(a division of Littlefield, Adams & Company)
81 Adams Drive, Totowa, New Jersey 07512

Copyright © 1987 by Rowman & Littlefield

**Library of Congress Cataloging-in-Publication Data**

Raskin, Marcus G.
New ways of knowing.

Includes index.
1. Knowledge, Theory of.   2. Social sciences.
3. Science.   I. Bernstein, Herbert J.
II. Buck-Morss, Susan.   III. Title
BD161.R33     1987     121     87-4492
ISBN 0-8476-7462-2
ISBN 0-8476-7463-0 (pbk.)


91   89   87   88   90

5   3   1   2   4

Printed in the United States of America

*For our wives,*
*Lynn Randels and Mary Bernstein,*
*participants and*
*colleagues*

# Contents

# Acknowledgments

We thank our colleagues at the Institute for Policy Studies, its trans-national affiliate (TNI) and Hampshire College for their participation and support of work on reconstructive knowledge. We have benefited greatly from forthright criticisms and spirited discussions.

We are especially thankful to another group whom we count as part of the invisible college of support. They act in their own lives in ways that make clear that knowledge and affection are linked and important guides to inquiry and action: Ed Janss, Cora Weiss, Peter Weiss, Phil Stern, Ann Janss, Mel Raskin, Helen Hopps, Diana de Vegh, Joseph Duffey, Richard Falk, Rusty Garth, Deborah Gunn, Evelyn Fox Keller, Joseph Leggett, Felicia Lynch, Larraine Matusak, Jack Tooley, Everett Mendelsohn, Harriet Barlow, Sidney Shapiro, the Levinson family, Adele Simmons, Bernard Weissbourd, Gibson Winter.

We wish to thank Ron Gross, Julianne Halberstein, Jill Lawrenz, Rachel Fershko, Robert Neill, Linda McCormack, Roberta Rosenau, Nancy Fuchs. All have helped at critical stages in the preparation of the manuscript and the continuation of the knowledge project.

Finally, we wish to thank our children, who suffered through innumerable telephone conversations between the authors and who urged us onward—some with criticism and praise—all with love. Erika Raskin Littlewood, Jamin Ben Raskin, Noah Annan Raskin, Eden McArtor Raskin, Carolyn Joy Bernstein, Laila Jael Bernstein, and Keith Littlewood.

# Introduction

HERBERT J. BERNSTEIN

Since the late 1970s the principle authors of this volume have collaborated on inventing a new form of inquiry—reconstructive knowledge—by studying the assumptions and practices of modern science, the politics of scientific discipline. This collaboration, together with the efforts of many others, has formed the core of an ongoing project on the analysis and reconstruction of knowledge. Starting from a study group at the Institute for Policy Studies in Washington, D.C., whose main participants included Marcus Raskin, Joseph Turner, Susan Buck-Morss, Ann Wilcox, and me, the project has engendered discussions in other locations. Raskin and the writer helped launch study groups centered at Cambridge, Princeton, and Amherst. A number of journal articles on reconstructive knowledge were published. We convened a series of three conferences on reconstructive knowledge under the auspices of Hampshire College,[1] where an undergraduate seminar and a faculty symposium (in cooperation with the University of Massachusetts and Smith, Amherst, and Mount Holyoke colleges) on reconstructive knowledge have ensued.

Today, the lessons of nuclear accidents at Chernobyl and Three Mile Island, of design flaws in space shuttle Challenger, of toxic gas releases at Bhopal and Institute, West Virginia, make us all wonder if we have "pushed science too far." My experience as a theoretical physicist and policy consultant have led me to question not just the application of science but the roots of scientific discovery, as well. The disasters of a seemingly autonomous technology call for renewed examination of the values embedded in our machines and our techniques. Only such examination will enable us wisely to decide when and where to limit technology. The search for wise limits to technology leads inevitably to questions about science itself. What are the values embedded within the *creation* of modern knowledge? How do they frame and limit the science that is so basic to technology? What characteristics of scientific knowledge and discourse make our best efforts at application seem so often to end in disaster? However far from "pure" theoretical physics, I have come to see these and similar questions as part of the legitimate concerns of a research scientist and university professor. By casting the introduction to this volume in a personal as well as historical mold, I hope to help

1

the reader understand not only how its essays fit together, but what they imply for the expertise we rely upon as a society, as well as why those who produce and those who use scientific knowledge ought to be interested in these subjects. The story begins with my earliest professional experiences.

As a member of Princeton's Institute for Advanced Study, fresh from graduate school in 1967, I recall the impression made on my cohort by its mentors. The physicists who were most respected were invariably also the most active in government consulting. They played a clear social role by using their intellect at the service of the nation, while still being eminently excellent theoretical physicists. Their involvement set an example for my own impulse to do social good. Eventually a leave of absence from teaching and research provided the opportunity for me to consult full time in Washington, D.C.

As an independent consultant, I worked for NASA, the Department of Energy, the World Bank, and other agencies (including the President's Science Advisory staff). I was still the young "pure" scientist, educated as purely as the leading physicists whom I emulated, but I began to see a problem many of them did not. I saw good, expert people in all these agencies repeatedly hindered by the framework of their own scientific and technical knowledge. I began to suspect there were difficulties far beyond those created by imperfect institutions or fallible leaders. My experience started to reveal a problem beyond the sociology or politics of science, a full-fledged "knowledge problem."

For example, as consultant to the World Bank, I reviewed its current water resource projects: three-quarters of all the Bank's loans came under my purview. The World Bank itself was (and still is) the leading institution for large-scale development projects. In almost every field, World Bank development projects set the standard for other big institutions and governments to follow. And yet, starting to work for the Bank, I found myself reviewing project after project where the most excellent engineering called for "pouring concrete" over the lives of people whom it should have served. The Bank professional cadre were an international body of engineers and economists, selected from the top ranks of those trained at the world's best universities and polytechnical institutes. They were experienced economic development professionals, who knew the area they were serving, having visited it often. Their reports reflected such knowledge; the sections describing "the Project Area" gave vivid descriptions of its setting and of its inhabitants' lives. These expert men and women, who understood the people, were (with few exceptions) both sensitive and dedicated to the Bank's helping mission. Nevertheless, they designed massive irrigation projects requiring enormous socioeconomic jumps in the lives of the affected farmers. In some cases they projected moving from a shifting nomadic sow-and-return agriculture to full scale computer-controlled irrigation (modeled after our agribusiness management) in as little as three years' time.

All of this jarred my notions of how to use science to do social good, of how to fulfill the model of my Princeton mentors. Excellent engineering and economics seemed to lead directly to inappropriate projects! For several months I struggled to find a way to present my concerns in writing, concerns which went quite beyond my own expectations and undoubtedly exceeded the bounds of most Bank staff members' notions of their roles as well. Reading Marcus Raskin's classic "Being and Doing," by chance, I was encouraged to address the issue directly.

My final report called for the active integration of social concerns, empathy, and express social purpose directly into the technical design of the projects. I realized that adding social science experts might help, but would not suffice. For their disciplines, too, had been formed with a model of purity which cut off precisely those value questions needed to unite academic excellence with social good. What I wanted was a way for engineers on Pakistani irrigation projects, for example, to use their knowledge of how water is actually divided (with the rich buying high lands to control and resell water), of how on-farm works actually proceed (in family groups, often requiring duplicate tertiary canals where two clans live side-by-side), how marketing occurs (certain age and sex cohorts doing the tasks) and so on, in order to make the projects fit and serve the people.

What prevented this was the notion of engineering taught in all the world's schools: excellence in engineering (and in development economics) required professionals to cast their gaze away from social values towards a technocratic "fix." And this pattern repeated itself in the other areas I consulted, from space research to energy policy: in each case bright, sensitive experts—sociologists, economists, historians, statisticians—reported the frustration of experiencing disciplinary excellence cut off from social good. Some of the most thoughtful had themselves pondered the reasons—beyond the simple analysis of power, beyond even the sociology of science, which shows how power steers research— why their best efforts often ended with solutions at odds with their own values. I began to think of this combination of personal frustrations and the social issues raised by the applications of science as the knowledge problem.

Marcus Raskin's thoughts, as expressed in *Being and Doing* were crucial to my growing awareness. His anticipations (from an earlier era) of much the same ideas fostered and encouraged my own. The test of good design, he wrote, was whether the engineer would actually be willing to "live the project." The application of empathy, as an integral part of the technical process, would prevent highway designers, for example, from dividing communities by "pouring concrete" over them. Here was someone who had foreseen not merely the problems exemplified in my World Bank review, but also the need for empathy in order to escape technocratic traps in solving them. The final sections of Raskin's book called for a reconstructive knowledge: a new process that could help rebuild society while healing the rift between subject and object, between excellence and morality, within the community of scholars, teachers, and experts. I was delighted when Raskin invited me to join the Institute's study group.

Our collaboration continued even after my return to college teaching. It allowed us to approach the knowledge problem by organizing the study groups and conferences for graduate students, scholars, scientists, and practicing policy experts. We found academics, artists, and even government officials reporting their own versions of the same findings. I began teaching Hampshire's undergraduate seminar on knowledge; and I delved into physics itself, where historical evidence showed the quantum revolution of the twenties elevating the technological, value-blind phrase "it works" to replace deeper, wholer understanding as the final arbiter of merit for scientific explanation. We saw this shift reflected in many other fields of modern knowledge, too.

By no means do the physicists and social scientists who have contributed these articles all express one view. Yet taken as a whole, their work sheds light on how different our thinking could become. As a collaborative work, this volume is rather unlike others; it aims to catalyze inquiry towards new and different purposes. As with most collaborations, the reader is free to start anywhere. The central exposition is found in the joint essay "Towards a Reconstructive Political Science." But one might read this quickly on first pass, turning to the exchange it sparked between Noam Chomsky and Raskin as an introduction to the subject. For Chomsky, who has been a friendly critic of the project since the first conference in late 1979, clearly and forcefully takes up many of the points a reader might challenge.

Indeed, stimulating such intellectual dialogue as the Chomsky-Raskin exchange was one of our intentions in writing "Towards a Reconstructive Political Science." Its discussion embodies a mixing of ethics with epistemology that is often considered dangerous. We are well aware that a call for moral determination of what is to be known raises the questions of "Whose morality?" and "What ethics?" That is the thrust of the dialogue which must begin, of the questions which we need to address, and of the sequel or second volume to the current work. For we may be sure *someone's* values underlie everything we do: better that they be visible and chosen than hidden and uncritically accepted. "Towards a Reconstructive Political Science" intentionally goes beyond the easy analysis that frames the knowledge problem as a problem of institutions and their corrections. In this, I suppose it owes a debt to the works of Herbert Marcuse and of Paul Goodman; but in fact our work is a later outcome of the efforts begun by the Washington study group. It was generated by the conferences, discussions, and dialogues of the recent project, activities which have convinced us that our times require more than a safe and easy approach. The ill effects of modern science now can threaten our whole civilization.

Three of the essays—my "Idols of Modern Science", Raskin's "Reconstruction and Its Knowledge Method," and his "Ending the Faustian Bargain"—help trace the development of our approach. The investigations into physics and molecular biology that led to "Idols" showed how political and social influences in our century became *internal* to these supposedly pure disciplines. As interests come to frame the questions and assumptions of science they become invisible, not merely cloaked in the processes of granting money or awarding prizes. In this regard, the work of the European deconstructionists and especially of Foucault's "archeological" approach provides valuable, effective tools for analysis. These tools remain, however, fixed on tackling how things currently stand, how subjects now adhere. And attempting a stance that attacks *all* values as equally arbitrary and unreal only leaves their choice to others; continual deconstruction locates one in an alienated, outsider's stance. What is needed is a process from within science, a continuing reconstruction which is conscious of its history—not merely an external deconstruction, however effective.

Raskin's analysis in "Reconstruction and its Knowledge Method" concludes that our times demand a revision of the very bases of science. He then gives one possible revision of Bacon's founding principles, showing what a basis that allows the needed reconstruction might look like. Both "Idols" and "Reconstruction" are based on earlier journal articles. "Ending the Faustian Bargain," originally a talk at the University of Mexico, also dates from this era and notes the evanescent nature of "facts." It points out the need to develop potential moral axioms—themselves subject to constant revision—from which to tease out the elements of "value" that always adhere to the "facts." Here we can see the grandparents of Raskin's thought in those of the great American pragmatists, Dewey and James. Taken together, these three essays flesh out the foundational analysis in "Towards a Reconstructive Political Science".

The theme of social construction of reality, of the breakdown of subject/object division (indeed of questioning the nature of the knowing subject itself) threads many of these essays. Here there are clear parallels to feminist works, including especially those of Evelyn Fox Keller on science and gender, of Sandra Harding on systemic reality and of Luce Irigaray on signification. Like "Reconstructive Political Science," such essays emphasize the role of desire and power as hidden determinants of knowledge. These determinants are investigated particularly in the essays of Joe Turner and Susan Buck-Morss, works that develop ideas expressed in the original Washington study group and in the conferences they attended.

Turner's essay investigates the social sciences' ability, through the power to name, to determine fates and fortunes. The control implicit in being the knowing subject, and the potential oppression experienced in serving as object of study both let science shape who plays what role—

who *is* what in society—by what they are allowed to know. Just as the Raskin-Bernstein article intentionally departs from linear essay form, Buck-Morss' cinetext, "Semiotic Boundaries and the Politics of Meaning: Modernity on Tour/A Village in Transition," also reaches for a new form to express a semiotic approach to the cultural effects of economic development. It demonstrates how emphasis on the desire and power dimensions can transform what one says and shows in discourse on social problems without losing the personal element.

Finally we have included two essays selected to show the linkage between the realms of knowledge generation and of political direction; most directly, theoretical physicist Michael Goldhaber in his ongoing work, as reported in "The Human Meaning of the Information Revolution." He argues that an altered social relation resulting from the information revolution forces us to choose between the right of expression and the right to know on the one hand and "the right to hold information as property on the other . . ." In other reconstructive knowledge work he has raised the question of what values inhere in the various discourses, of what language might make more transparent the linkage between theory and politics. In project discussions, for example, Goldhaber suggests training physicists to realize that the ubiquitous $X_\mu$ in field theory—denoting a location and time, a point in spacetime—may stand for a specific point and time in the United States, or in the Soviet Union if and when their theories are put to use for weapons.

"The Selling of Market Economics," by Edward Herman investigates one case of a shifting framework of questions. His analysis, including the facts of life of daily working conditions in the field, points out that economics as a discipline is a rule of human organization, not of nature. In all seriousness, Herman shows that the practice of economics itself is derivative of market pressures. This information consciously applied could liberate economists to transform their work. As Raskin details in his new book *The Common Good,* close examination of economics' history brings up possibilities for questioning still more fundamental definitions. What is the meaning of production when it counts nonuseful and life-threatening items even as some go hungry? Must scarcity be the basis of economics? Can we not rather view the abundance of air, water, perhaps even food as givens, with the effect of redefining economics by focusing upon distribution: how to make sure everyone gets theirs, gets plenty, and gets good quality?

It is a long way from actively working, for example, on nuclear and strategic issues as a consultant (for me) or peace activist (for Raskin) to epistemology. The theory of knowledge is in some ways closer to the physics itself or the political theory which we each, respectively, *do*. But it is *not* a long way back when we consider the implications of knowledge on our modern society. This volume attests to the fact that questioning the disciplines, questioning the application of knowledge opens a new alternative path. Not only our intellectual but our physical reality depends upon the choice of direction. As creators and users of knowledge, we may face away from the bleak specter of annihilation to follow a reconstructive course, a path towards a brighter future for all.

## Note

1. For funding the conferences we thank the National Endowment for the Humanities, the Anna and Max Levinson Foundation, the Howard Bayne Fund, and the Blue Mountain Center. I was a Mina Shaughnessy Scholar (1984–1985), and am currently a Kellogg Fellow. I thank the Fund for the Improvement of Post-Secondary Education and the Kellogg Foundation, respectively, for this support.

# 1

# Reconstruction and Its Knowledge Method

MARCUS G. RASKIN[1]

## I

It is now being said, more often than in the past, that the quest for knowledge is no longer leading to "progress" or the betterment of the human condition but is taking us in quite other directions. Since this insight may be right, it is crucial that those who have staked their lives on the importance of reason and imagination for the betterment of humankind should understand that we are at the end of one way of looking at the world—or changing it—and the beginning of another. To put it another way, we are in a conceptual shift as massive and important as the knowledge changes which ushered in the modern age of science and the enlightenment. We have all lived off the capital of those times and the methods propounded by the savants of the past. But this capital is no longer enough. One reason is that it is becoming increasingly clear that political revolution will not yield the results its advocates justly want if the knowledge system remains locked in crude positivism or what I call the colonizing knowledge of the past, or is otherwise faulty and unattached to humane and shared ends. The result will be that a fierce fundamentalism either of a fascist or regressive totalitarian nature will emerge to challenge modern civilization. This fundamentalism, of the kind we see reflected in Ayatollah Khomeini or of the kind hidden in national security and military bureaucracies, could destroy [a world] . . . civilization and its most laudable attributes. Part of the reason that this reactionary direction could take hold is that those of us who favor and champion massive shifts in social, political, and economic relationships are only dimly aware that we must be far more discriminating about the types and methods of knowledge and research that we encourage and develop. Very few of us have ever doubted that knowledge and the process of knowing is a good unto itself. We have not wanted to believe that certain knowledges reenforce oppression, nor have we found adequate ways to relate the powers of our intellectual and artistic work to a coherent and humane purpose.

How to begin? First, we have to recognize that we are in the cave of the shadows. While we sit imprisoned we might address ourselves to certain questions or find approaches to answering them:

What is to be known?

How and through what process are we to know things?

How should the scientific, technical, and social knowledge process change when there is a political revolution whose purpose asserts equality and dignity for all people?

How, if at all, should we determine worth in what is worth knowing?

Is there a knowledge of the spirit or of the unconscious which is separate from what we observe and does it help the project of liberation in acquiring these knowledges?

Can the process of knowledge ever be neutral?

Can there be a scientific knowledge which itself is pristine, unriddled by political or ideological interest, a particular social system or moral intention? And should there be?

Is there knowledge which has guided this period which should dry up, like the demonology on witches of the sixteenth and seventeenth centuries, so that it will not dominate the rest of this century or the twenty-first century?

Can such a change be organized?

What educational and productive concerns now flow from an answer to these questions? And finally,

What knowledges of reconstruction should we emphasize?

I do not propose to answer these questions in this essay, although I do hope to begin the chain of thinking and practice which will help us focus on them. I do not think that these questions are dry or abstract. They beat like the excited thump of lovers' hearts discovering each other for the first time. All we have to do is hear them through a "knowledge stethoscope," and perhaps we will be rewarded. Finding answers to these questions will help in sustaining the common project of humanity, by which I mean its quest for full consciousness and liberation. None of this will be an easy task, first because we are trapped inside the cave and need a relatively pragmatic and immediate way of getting out if we are not to suffocate. This means that many mistakes will be made. And secondly, few of us will want to recognize the role we play in the current productive process—in having made the cave—because its recognition brings the shock that what we do, the knowledges we pursue, are not neutral; these knowledges define the character of modern life and are presently used for colonizing and controlling purposes. Some have embraced the stance of self-betterment, hoping to use Eastern religion and personal knowledge as the vehicle to levitate themselves from the cave. The quiet desperation that these fellow knowledge workers feel is caused by the painful social fact that much of our inquiry system sustains racism, sexism, and classism. Those of us who pursue the seemingly most nonpolitical and fundamental questions about nature, seeking universal principles and "codes," often find our work bolstering brutalitarianism.

Even those of us who seek humane ends directly are personally torn apart because we are doing something wrong. We are often unaware of the matrix in which research fits, or the actual assumptions behind the inquiry we pursue, the way our knowledge is found, or the service to which it is put. There is no nook or cranny of inquiry, even (I dare say) artistic work, which is exempt from this crisis; therefore, no knowledge or art worker should or can be blind to these questions. That this crisis exists is clear. Whether or not we can find a reconstructive method which helps us and persists as more than a fashion remains to be seen.

The process I will describe requires that we begin by exposing our values, rules, and knowledges to critical scrutiny by those outside of a particular discipline—by the nonexperts in a particular field, even those who are not "peers." Our purpose is to refashion the discipline where necessary, to change its direction, and to expose the social and moral deformations which may exist in it without such scrutiny. My hope is that this "political" method will lead us to a unity of knowledge and practice in the context of constantly debated purpose.

We begin, therefore, by seeking new definitions and boundaries that may be entirely different from those we presently think necessary. New boundaries and definitions will help us bury certain knowledges and techniques which we formerly thought crucial to fulfilling either our appetites or those of the colonizing few—for example, the subject matter of criminology, how to make model prisons and model prisoners. Or how the mind is a code and how the universe is a code, and how the mind can unlock the universe for dominating purposes. We may find it necessary to abandon our elusive search for order or rigor as they are symbolized in catechistic religions or logics which deny serial understandings and shadings. Those who insist on one framework for considering questions are deceiving themselves. We should be aware that the supposed clash between rigorous science language and everyday metaphoric description is less real than we may be led to believe by the priests of a particular craft or discipline. All things are forever open to interpretation and shifting meaning.

*This means that the primary concerns of humankind are political action, ethics, and moral discourse just because they are not necessary—that humankind's actions are contingent on what is freely chosen. Consequently, that which is not necessary becomes the only discussion, the only concern. It is the unnecessary which defines the necessary, that is, the material reality.* Neither love, hate, caring, empathy nor justice is necessary. Each may be seen as a "secondary" or "tertiary" characteristic of people. Yet in fact they define our approach to material reality. It should not be a surprise that such concepts and feelings will finally determine whether we have enough reverence for water, oxygen, animate and inanimate nature for it—and us—to continue. It may well be the case that the "secondary" quality of things must now be taken to be as important as the "primary" characteristic. The intangible and the ideal are the ether, or the particles and waves—in a metaphoric sense—which tell us how to handle material things and others.

What should we be conscious of? What once may have been a polite or academic discussion between idealists and realists has grown to a fierce argument, for what is at stake is civilization itself. Civilization will expire with a bang and a whimper, and humankind will lose its preferred position in nature unless we find a convincing way to relate reality to ideal, humane ends and the "ideal" to materiality itself. Even as the world crisis becomes more obvious, the old knowledge methodologies and purposes are hugged. The fact that present socialist paradigms borrow and replicate bourgeois ones merely shows that, in terms of historical institutional power, that is, how the business of nations is run on an everyday basis, the bourgeois paradigm is more powerful. The reason is obvious. The socialist system is mediated through state organizations. These organizational forms are based on the bourgeois paradigm of science *and* social organization, which fails to help a person find meaning or to protect humankind. Unfortunately, it is now the political terrorist who shows how fragile these forms and explanations are.

Perhaps our awareness of this situation makes it possible to transcend the present socialist and capitalist traps by devising and then, through practice, acting on noncolonizing, reconstructive modes that change relationships and social organizations. How can this be put metaphorically? When everyone sits at the table, taking turns or participating in what is eaten, what is to be grown, and how to take out the garbage, the social structure changes with our perceptions and gaze. The fundamental structures of who perceives with whom, what we think we see, and what we decide to emphasize in what we think we see, all change. So, the perception and the gaze itself, when shared, change the political and moral purpose. The modern technico-bureaucratic elite has not found a way to serve this purpose, nor has it found a way to adequately express openness and possibility which invite everyone into a creative and liberating process.*

---

*The technico-bureaucratic elite which holds the key to major technical secrets mistakes automation, efficiency, and delivery of services for liberation. This elite has learned to organize and permit the manipulation of man and nature. Its method is that of problem and crisis management through institutional manipulation. Its adherents hope for a technical institutional system which will generate a way of treating much of life in an automatic way, with the automatic nature defined outside of freely chosen paths. The administrative mechanism seeks to frame our time, space, and consciousness. The technical system also finds a means of organizing seemingly marginal activities such as "paper flow," "appearances," "accounting," and so on, until the process of administration is the only purpose of social organization and society itself.

The technico-bureaucratic elite seeks to organize the time and space coordinates according to rules defined through the institution and single-dimension goals like profit. Such goals may be successful as a dominant purpose of a capitalist class, but they are surely not ones which are shared by workers, artists, or most people because they deny the

## II

All knowledge, rules, and understandings of the world *are freely chosen.* We choose what we want to emphasize, believe, and make. Our descriptions, proofs, and rules often stem from literary and political metaphor. Some rules and knowledge may seem to be truer than others, "scientific" and more obviously necessary because they comport closely with sense impressions which are received by the person from outside himself and then reenforced by the group. To Einstein, it is the "degree of certainty" between sense impression and intuitive connection which "differentiates empty phantasy from scientific 'truth.'" Newton's laws of mechanics appear truer to us than his studies of the occult because our individual sense impressions can be checked against one another and our minds are trained to see similar things. However, it may be that what is "empty phantasy," or Newton's occult, could also have been more fully explored by the society as a whole and our sense impressions would have legitimated the occult interpretation of the world, just as our minds could have been trained to make connections about the world other than those we make. Both could have worked or been integrated as a single coherent explanation of how we live in the world.

We should be wary of those who insist on rigor, for what they are not telling us is that they have a particular framework which for them determines rigor. In daily practice, so-called rigorous proofs give way to literary and culturally determined metaphors which have an existential, physical, and political basis. They ground us in what we see and how we formulate time and space in the description of the world and our place in it. They frame scientific inquiry even though the scientist may like to believe that what he sees contradicts our everyday experience or understanding of the world. On one level, such phrases as "falling behind," "give him a chance," "nothing left to lose," "your words are hollow," "fuzzy thinking," even "time is money," are empty metaphors and empty fantasies, yet they are filled with shared social and political meaning which knowledge and art workers use. These phrases colonize and frighten people, for they are metaphoric statements of people's psychosocial and economic reality which are then applied to nature. The process of "making nature" is an extraordinary and startling form of anthropomorphism. It is no wonder that the owners of means of

multidimensional and richly textured nature of humankind. Our institutions fall hopelessly behind the needs of the person and the people. The result is that the technico-bureaucratic actors, the "decision makers," are overwhelmed, and their knowledge system, which for them translates into their status and the cash value in the market, turns out to be worthless. Nevertheless, this elite's judgments, myths, and unconscious desires become determinative. They engulf the time and space axis which technical man now controls to order the world and humankind. But this objective fails because such an elite (moving to its own self-consciousness) lacks independent purposes no matter what its claims. It is like the noisiness of *Apocalypse Now* which surrounds us with zooming, murderous helicopters and ends with a Mussolini-like character who tells us that the will of the Übermensch is more important than helicopters and western technology. But we do not have to choose either.

production seek to control or guide how we think and feel through the use of slogans in their advertising, curriculum development, and the like. It is not only slogan control which is so important.

Foucault and Simone Weil have stated that the person's fundamental power is that of directing [the] . . . gaze. But it would seem that our gaze is subordinate to our sense impressions. They cannot be denied except through a conscious effort of will to rationalize or explain them away. When we deny them, we either repress them or lie about them to ourselves and others. Immediate sense impressions can be inhibited through memory of previous sense impressions or through forgotten sense impressions which are hidden (the unconscious) under the surface of our collective or individual consciousness. Often these sense impressions are memories of fantasies of past events which are stronger than our present sensation. In other cases, we consciously dismiss our present sense impressions because we have accepted political, social, and economic rules—whether from our teachers, parents, colleagues, jailers, or advertisers—which are so strongly felt that we are not to sense what we could (or momentarily do) sense. We censor ourselves like the holy man who punishes himself for fear that his present sensation of lust will overwhelm him.

G. E. Moore taught that the direct apprehension of a color or of heat is a form of "dispositional" knowledge which is kept in our memory. In other words, after the apprehension of the color or the burning, we have merely an image of the event. And how are images shaped by us? They are framed by us with other people in mind—those to whom we tell the experience or describe the moment. Therefore, the chosen rhetoric shapes the common understanding of the individual's sensation and the image itself. No social system can obliterate our sensations. They can either be legitimated or denied. And consequently, even our sensations are social. *Because this is so, and because our perceptions are legitimated by others, a moral and political sentiment is always present in our scientific endeavor, our gaze, and our sense impressions.* There is, invariably—although it may be hard to find—a direct moral and political correlative to what is seen, studied, and acted upon once we consciously look at and report or seek to change nature. Experiments, like experience itself, have powerful moral and political components. The free gaze, therefore, is only a moment which itself is unmeasurable. Once something can be measured or calculated, we are able to work back from the quantification to ascertain the various components that "make up the numbers," that is, the scientist's reductionist description. We are then able to discover its moral and political components, once we drop abstract notions of scientific rigor and moral purity. We may seek a "pure" substance or "pure" understanding, but these are romantic illusions, just as the thrust toward clarity is also misplaced. Perhaps, as Marxists say, clarity may only be achieved by knowing the whole. But what is the whole? All questions are framed by "impure" or sloppy political and moral considerations which in fact are related to supposedly isolated acts—before, during, and after they are performed. They are framed in situations and through "tacit" understandings which may be far more important than any conscious or planned activity. Consider the enterprise of the scientific experiment: At each step of the way, people inside and outside of particular scientific roles determine the nature of the experimental process, from conception to the development of machinery for the shaping of present technology; from guessing or gazing at nature to making it fit with conclusions and understandings of past experiments, including the mythology about them; from acquiring funds and people to work on the experiment and reporting it in a way which fits with ongoing hopes and presently shared paradoxes, to dissemination through journals, media, and other forms that have their own ritual, and the replication of their conclusions, if not in practice at least in mythology. It is obvious that there is a continuous interaction of different forms of knowledges and attitudes, all of them impinging on each other. The experiment is not hermetically sealed. It is based on the social relationship of good faith and truth telling. But such predication is no longer enough, because faith and truth are not abstractions. Their meaning and validity are determined outside of immediate experiment. Reporting an experiment and understanding its results are the beginning of communication and are, therefore, of varying interpretations. Scientists themselves accept the conclusions of experiments without doing the work leading to their conclusions. Thus, they understand stories, conclusions, and then myths about the experiments, just as we understand myths about events that take on symbolic lives separate from the phenomena—such as that which really happened at the Munich conference in 1938 as opposed to what was said about it. The process of saying things, of publishing, of editing, invariably changes meaning; the presentation of conclusions through literary metaphor, including the description of what is happening within the laboratory through literary or common-language metaphor, is a statement of what we think and what we want to think is happening. The process of mediating our understanding of scientific conclusions through institutions, be they universities, scientific societies, or families, makes the scientific enterprise no different in its process from any other, once bourgeois, technical, scientific principles are meant to govern all activities. As has been noted by Gurvitch and others, the bourgeois knowledge-structure is meant to rearrange the external world in terms of certain geopolitical concerns. This means that markets, political and colonizing modes of investment, types of minerals to be found, and industrial corporations to be encouraged are not neutral matters. They tend to dominate all activity. We may recall that the decision to make the atomic bomb started as a letter to the Queen of Belgium from Einstein (drafted by Szilard) to control the uranium in the Belgian Congo so the Germans would not have access to it. Political attitudes are crucial to experimentation and research. When we think of political knowledge and attitudes as defined by struggle, we know that racist and sexist attitudes, or their reverse, change how we see and what we see. We believe certain people over others, accepting what they say over others. And we do so on the basis of *appearance* and status.

When we think of rules, categories, and experiments in scientific matters, we usually think of that which is truthful. The truth is not a scientific matter. Where truth's use is not a logical game (like that about Epimenedes the Cretan, and so on), it is an existential experiment, a method in which people say what they think they see or feel about a moment, event, or thing, not fearing that others may feel or say otherwise. But in both cases, they must say what they feel or think; otherwise, the serpent of bad faith corrodes communication and truth disappears.

It is true that the language we use to describe, observe, or feel can only approximate. There is no difference, therefore, between abstract and concrete language when they are honestly spoken. What *seems* accurate is that what evokes understanding in one person toward another—or in one type of society—may not do so in another. It seems true, however, that the sensitive can hear others and know that they are describing the same phenomena. A Tibetan doctor's description of a heart patient may be poetic and seemingly nonreferential, although it may be as accurate of the patient's condition as that of the leading American heart surgeons, with both groups reaching toward the other in understanding the same phenomena.

The technical or specialized languages of "precision," as in physics or biology, describe experiments in aesthetic terms, such as "elegant." We are told to imagine relationships between unreal things in which we are to assume that both have a didactic *and* existential reality relating our experience to abstract matters. Listen to Feynman, the Nobel laureate, teaching a physics class at Cal Tech on the conservation of energy:

Imagine a child, perhaps "Dennis the Menace," who has blocks which are absolutely indestructible, and cannot be divided into pieces. Each is the same as the other. Let us suppose that he has 28 blocks. His mother puts him with his 28 blocks into a room at the beginning of the day. At the end of the day, being curious, she counts the blocks very carefully, and discovers a phenomenal law— no matter what he does with the blocks, there are always 28 remaining! This continues for a number of days, until one day there are only 27 blocks, but a little investigating shows that there is one under the rug—she must look everywhere to be sure that the number of blocks has not changed. One day, however, the number appears to change—there are only 26 blocks. Careful investigation indicates that the window was open, and upon looking outside, the other two blocks are found. Another day, careful count indicates that there are 30 blocks! This causes considerable consternation, until it is realized that Bruce came to visit, bringing his blocks with him, and he left a few at Dennis's house. After she has disposed of the extra blocks, she closes the window, does not let Bruce in, and then everything is going along all right, until one time she counts and finds only 25 blocks. However, there is a box in the room, a toy box, and the mother goes to open the toy box, but the boy says, "No, do not open my toy box," and screams. Mother is not allowed to open the toy box. Being extremely curious, and somewhat ingenious, she invents a scheme! She knows that a block weighs 3 ounces, so she weighs the box at a time when she sees 28 blocks, and it weighs 16 ounces. The next time she wishes to check, she weighs the box again, subtracts 16 ounces and divides by 3. She discovers the following:

$$\text{(number of blocks seen)} + \frac{\text{(weight of box)} - 16 \text{ ounces}}{3 \text{ ounces}} = \text{constant} \quad (4.1)$$

There then appear to be some new deviations, but careful study indicates that the dirty water in the bathtub is changing its level. The child is throwing blocks into the water, and she cannot see them because it is too dirty, but she can find out how many blocks are in the water by adding another term to her formula.

Is Dennis the Menace more or less real to the students, to us, than the law of conservation of energy? Feynman is teaching through the Oedipus complex and mass culture. Does this story mean that at all times we must see the interrelationship of the "unconnected?" We are taught that the organization of things, the assessing and fostering of rules and regularity, is superior to and more important than disorganization. And we assume or search for such order and organization until a breeze blows through us which upsets our equilibrium and structure. Yet that is not how we understand or explain things to each other.

Nevertheless, if we are not great scientists, we believe as part of our package of received notions that "terse" and "economic" descriptions are better than long-winded or magisterial ones. We want lives and things, books and nature to have a "point" which we can "buy" or understand, rather than rest content with a process of reasoning or practice which includes the supposedly irrelevant—those things that Saul Landau would insist we do comprehend even though we may have rejected them, putting them in ash heaps, wastepaper baskets, or on the cutting-room floor.

Because the sense impressions which we choose to emphasize to make rules and conventions are themselves products of struggle and imagination around class, race, age, sex, occupation, and the tricks of the mind, there can be agreement of a fundamental reconstructive nature on what we think we observe and feel, if we are prepared to examine what frames or controls that which we sense inside and outside of us as individuals. For reconstructive knowledge, there is no discrete thing or event which cannot be studied as part of a process or motion. There is no rule or convention which cannot be seen as part of a process, motion, or institution. Dennis the Menace, blocks, imagination, mother, houses, and metaphors are all mixed together. They are part of an interrelated series of things that do not appear to have a relationship. We have to read scientific and social endeavor accordingly: there is no scientific rule which does not itself reflect social structures and which does not itself, in turn, define what social structures are to be or become. There is no scientific rule which is not a product of judgment that seeks to explain away the "shadings" of things, or that which is supposedly unrelated.

Since the scientist must use "Dennis the Menace" or "mother-child" relationships to *prove* a point, those engaged in the "enterprise" of reconstructive knowledge may cross-examine science, criticizing it by methods that are not bound by the particular discipline or mode of discourse that the discipline may ordinarily use to "build a foundation." Scientific activity is open to inquiry about itself from other perspectives, just as other activities which are "political" or aesthetic must be open to those forms of questioning and inquiry that locate the activity within the social process. This aspect of reconstructive method is meant to confront directly those who believe in the separation of scientific endeavor and experiment. It is meant to confront the hidden political, economic, and moral assumptions with another set of assumptions and propositions which are to be more clearly understood, debated, and, in the service of human purpose, which have well-articulated moral ends. This rule repudiates the fanciful notion that scientific experiment and endeavor are formulated without political and moral concern. Instead, scientific work is to be framed and understood according to rules and contexts outside the "necessary" aspects of the experiment itself. The scientists' own internal rules are to be judged in terms of what they describe, the place the specific object holds in the totality, what the rules do to distort the object, and so on. The rules of the experiment are to be examined for hidden propositions which should be exposed and debated. *It is now necessary to recognize the obvious. There is no interruption in our consciousness or belief system (what we see and want to see and report) from one side of the laboratory door to the other side. The only question is whether the system of belief, and the system which puts on the experiment, can be held to account.*

There are many hidden or "tacit" rules within science—as Polanyi would say—that link subjective sensibility with universal principle. But these rules may be highly political or quite incomplete. They may be adopted for aesthetic reasons or because they conform to mathematical propositions which are intuitive; that is, they feel correct and are not necessarily provable. Here the mind (subjectivity) and the world become one and, therefore, no proofs can be offered or are necessary. They are, as the phrase goes, "self-evident." This highly praised notion of self-evidence, by which the thing or relationship "out there" in nature is to make sense in terms of its "self," is the foundation of mathematical proof.

It seems that a proposition of certainty is not proven unless it is felt. That which is felt may be open to explication, but not to "rigorous" proofs. Proofs are predicated on closed systems. What is felt is more open than proofs, for it comes from many stimuli. Consequently, a reconstructive method would rely on feeling because it disdains closed systems. The reconstructive process never denies the subjective, which means opening one's mind (and heart) to seeing, acting, and calculating in original ways. It begins from the rational, which is based on individual sensibilities. A reconstructive analysis, however, also begins with the assumption that, if exact existential proofs may not be communicated very well, they nonetheless exist. The empathic sensibility is such an existential proof when it is set in motion through discovery and discourse with the Other. "I feel your toothache." When it is not released, and it is hidden or consciously repressed by the social system or the discipline, we lose this capacity for fundamental proof and moral action.

*When we say that our rules and understandings are freely chosen, we are really burdened, for it means that we are free.* There are no external constraints on us except through those conventions which themselves may change, or which we can change, whether in science, morals, music, or politics.

When we state our freedom, it means that we can act and risk because we understand that much of the world could be different. We could describe what we see in other ways, as, for example, the Indians, Tibetans, and Chinese do. An artistic description of the world could predominate, rather than a theological, scientific, or technical one. How would Feynman's story be read by Kabbalists, Tibetans, or psychoanalysts? As I have said, all principles about nature and civilization are invented and changeable; facts themselves are invented, valued here and disparaged there, according to the knowledge system chosen. Does the freedom to choose force a moral grounding to our actions? Do we then become responsible, in the direct and consequential sense, for what we see and say, choose to see and say, for who gets to join us in what we see and say, and finally, for who we are? (Freedom is a linked conception which must be tied for its vitality to caring, truth, and power.)

The anarchist breeze eliminates questions and processes which by their nature are pathological; that is, they fit no natural sensibility. The moral and political purpose which it seeks to reflect must mature into the joint efforts of a civilization to distinguish the living and renewable from the dying and doomed. In the physical world we may speak not of the death of things but only of their change of form. Humankind, however, conscious of itself, can hardly be so cavalier. We are compelled to be far clearer in our judgments about what is ending and what is pathological even as we are finding the need to be more provisional in our judgments of what nature is, or what is "out there." Tragically, the twentieth century has not been the best teacher in eliciting moral precepts from ourselves to define purpose and limits.

We invent cover stories for power, like sociobiology, hoping in this way to evade moral and political discourse and rearrangement toward liberation. Instead of the colonizing knowledge system, there is another way to understand directly the human purpose and action. We become conscious of how we see and what we see, and how we report what we have seen, and the manner in which we do so, and that which I choose to call empathic invariance—what each of us sees, identifies, and reaches out to in the other. It is obvious, as we have said, that all such activities are predicated on the social relationship of good faith and truth telling. But such predication is no longer enough, because faith and truth are not abstractions. As we have said, their meaning and validity are determined outside of the immediate experiment, but they are always present inside of us because the experiment is a human and social endeavor. This fact is more important than what is discovered or understood about phenomena through the experiment.

# III

What are the points which can be made from what I have said? They tie to formulating a *novum organum* significantly different from that of Bacon. (The first fifty numbers are reconstructive answers to Bacon's *novum organum*.)

1. Humankind is part of nature. Often man's observations are what he wants to see and what he assumes to be important; what is assumed to be important comes from that which is outside of what is observed.

2. In modern times, since Bacon, it is assumed that neither the "naked hand nor the understanding left to itself can effect much." But without our bodies and our minds, which include passion and affection, the instruments we construct have no grounding in humaneness, human purpose, or conceptualization.

3. We know cause and effects by results which themselves are their own moments. Each moment is new, in absolute terms, and this is what makes for the freedom of things and humankind. But each moment requires a history and time, as Levinas would say, "for its appearance" to be made.

4. Man makes artificial things, and in that he changes himself and nature. The paradox and tragedy for modern times are that what he should control he does not, and what he should not, he does. This is the central problem of our present ideological formation, which has lost the relationship of means to ends, and which rebels at subject-to-subject relations.

5. We study more and more pieces of nature, bringing forward our modern scientists, systems analysts, and whomever. But our success is only great in gathering particulars which seem to slide away from us into more particulars and more mysteries. Our codes seem little different from Aristotelian essences.

6. The only means we have at hand is our imagination, which seeks to achieve a different order of things, and, we hope, an empathic sentiment of living in the world.

7. It is true that we know very little more than we have always known and that what exist are variants of notions long accepted or assumed.

8. It is questionable if science is anything but chance and experiment.

Our inventions are freely chosen but dictated through the social process, now as then, in the future as in the past, as long as man is man.

9. We are mistaken when we extol the powers of the human mind without understanding that the mind itself is *in* the world to be attached to cumulative wisdom and judgment, themselves molded by ethical and passionate precepts, which see humankind as naked and trembling.

10. Our senses and understanding are part of the natural order and, therefore, it is mistaken to talk of nature as being more subtle than our senses or our minds. Yet, with or without minds, nature cannot be engulfed by mind.

11. What is the moral premise behind logic? If logic is an empty form without moral premise, it can never help us generate reconstructive knowledge, which must be predicated on moral understandings.

12. Logic docs not clear away conceptual cobwebs, as Carnap might have hoped. It has reduced itself to verbal games that do more harm than good. Nor did clean logic save us from fascism.

13. No syllogistic construction can encompass the inside and outside of the thing. It can only present us with relational utilities. But these are not trivial.

14. True induction, as it is called, can never be rigorous, for it is only partial by definition. Therefore, it should not be surprising that any superstructure constructed from induction will be limited in value.

15. That we should not be able to define and comprehend the meanings of heavy, light, dense, rare, moist, and so on, or quality, action, passion, essence, or not consider them as terms equally valid as those we seek to measure, denies everyday experience, the hand, and the heart. This is diastrous for science and humankind.

16. All language, all concepts are "wanderings." And no "proper rigorous methods" can escape language which constantly changes boundaries and meanings.

17. All ideas begin as notions which may appear as fantasies. The notions are screened and it is here that we must be aware of what and by whom they are screened. For some notions of the world cannot be heard because they are such an attack on what is the current state of institutional reality that they are dropped or forgotten.

18. "Vulgar" notions are the basis for scientific work. And vulgar understandings of the scientific induction or experiment are understood in that way by virtually all, even those within the scientific community, who themselves do not perform the experiment. Their understanding remains a myth about the original experiment and takes on a new myth about nature.

19. Truth is a changing attribute discovered, verified, and then changed through a social process. Sometimes induction is used, other times deduction is used. But truth itself is also a *method* by which we say to others what we think we see *out there* or within us. We do not lie or fool the Other. Truth is trust of the Other and integration of the self, so that neither the self or the Other is deceived.

20. Our understanding and our minds must now leap to levels of higher generality and disdain those experiments which do not seek to explain more than the particular. Within each experiment, its method and results, we should find general rules. Such generalities have within them the germ of the civilization humankind now needs.

21. The understanding *(Verstehen)* is the primary instrument for making moral judgments, for acting prudently, and for distinguishing sense data.

22. Useless and abstract generalities are as likely to grow out of experiment and gradual steps as they are to grow out of mere fantasy or the unrestrained imagination. Almost everyone does nothing but accept received information about experiment and, therefore, what they understand is abstracted and usually "misapplied."

23. There are no true signatures, nor are there empty dogmas which apply only to humankind and not to God.

24. Argument is the primary social means by which we discover new connections. Argument is a mode of proof. It is used in all human institutions and in all endeavors. Standards for argument may vary, but not so much that we do not use everyday language and metaphor to prove a point in so-called "rigorous" science.

25. We cannot encompass any more "particulars," for they are crowding our minds and institutions. We set up institutions for every new particular discovered or thought to be there in nature, or for perceived social problems. We have created a mechanical and organizational jungle of particulars out of disembodied "fact."

26. What is thought at some time to be a conclusion about nature is at other times thought to be an interpretation and hypothesis about it. The mode of reasoning is both conscious and unnoticed (sometimes thought to be unconscious) and, therefore, we can only confuse various ways of analyzing and concluding.

27. In both cases argument is used. Depending upon the fashion and the place, that argument will include calculations, statistics, *music*, authority, appeals, and whatever else is thought to be at hand or useful to win the argument.

28. The fact that we establish relationships does not mean that we have established causes. Often our descriptions help us to conclude that certain things have no relationship. They are often made to appear unrelated by the categories, educational and social systems we adopt. Institutions and specialization mask the connections of natural and social phenomena we might otherwise see and which are there.

29. One wishes we had not demanded that we master things, but merely get others to accept our arguments. But getting others to accept arguments seems to relate to the mastery of others and things themselves. This can be changed through the way we argue.

30. Every step of the way we have conclusions. And we find them in slow and patient work, hidden, but there. The wise of all ages have known that conclusions are a fact of our lives and our mode of looking at

the world, as we think about it from our position of everydayness. For better or worse, it is what creates ideological coherence and habit. But where that coherence no longer exists, we are reduced to sleepwalking.

31. There can be no advancement in reconstructive knowledge without recognition that a different framework is needed, with different categories, modes of judgment, standards of proof, and modes of acquiring resources, with ways of saying no to certain directions of knowledge because they take a dubious path. What we mean by "new foundation" or "progress" is inextricably linked to the survival of civilization in a humane form.

32. There is little choice but to challenge the types of knowledge produced through present institutions, to investigate the research process, and to inquire why certain forms of knowing are thought *better* or more praiseworthy than others, why one path leads to understanding and the sustaining of civilization and the other does not.

33. New methods will be found in the process of challenge. And these methods will have their own mode of proof and standards. In this we are required to start fresh, for certain ideas and questions, certain proofs will be exposed and dropped, certain knowledge that might be acquired will be thought of as beneath collective human interest.

34. We all use the ruling language and we are all trained in a system, whether it is called capitalist or technocratic, whose assertions of the way of doing things we internalize. It remains to be seen how many of these ways must be directly and forcefully rejected, or whether only their social implications are to be rejected.

35. It is no less a struggle when we seek advancement of reconstructive knowledge for liberation seeking to end the rush to disaster than if the struggle was one of naked political power. It appears that too much of present learning, colonizing knowledge, leads back to the old context: man conquering nature, man dominating other men and women.

36. What is one person's particular is another's generalization. We must look *through* and into the particular to see its generality. But as important, we are to see the particular as a whole in its general relation to Other.

37. Those who think there is no way of reaching certainty are proved right by modern science. The senses and understanding give us approximation. But certainty is an important myth to perpetuate, for it gives limits: To feel probable consequences as certain should deter us from certain acts. In practical action we put into place what we know of probable consequences. We do so as if the uniformity of nature and the uniformity of social organization are the same. And in one sense they may be, for both are dependent on our acting as if they were uniform. When a prisoner is led to the gallows he assumes that the hangmen and guards will fulfill their social role. He does not tell them to organize *against* their social role. He is as sure, or more so, about the inability to win over the guard, the minister, and the hangman, as he is that his neck

will be broken and he will fall downward according to physical laws of stress and gravity.

38. The idols and false notions we now face come from applying traditional narrow notions of cause. They are not fundamental to comprehending the frame of our situation. We are enamored of those causes which appear obvious to us and which can result in a quick fix, as if those were the actual framing systems for what occurs. Knowing that one particular is precedent to another particular is not understanding either of them fundamentally. And believing in the operational effectiveness of particular cause-effect systems, whether in nature or in social organization, now both intertwined often beyond distinction, merely shores up an incomprehensible and destructive dynamic for civilization.

There are the Idols which are meant to reenforce foolishness and misery, which detach one person from another and deform relationships. And there are now social sciences which can be used to mask this situation. The error of modern knowledge is that it assumes a revolutionary technical order in the service of an unchanging social order which concentrates power and understanding in the powerful upper 5 percent of the population. To the extent that this is politically possible the knowledge generated is colonizing knowledge either in its formulation or use. Government reports build on such assumptions and prejudices.

39. What are the modern Idols which beset us and which should be moved aside by social reconstruction and by reconstructive knowledge? The first is the Idol of colonizing knowlege; the second is the Idol of capitalism; the third is the Idol of militarism; and the fourth is the Idol of order.

40. There is no way to escape these Idols except through understanding directly our existential interest in what we see and what we do, in the laboratory and in our social roles. The false mirror through which we see things is the one which asserts a distance between ourselves and our work, our lives and our computations. We can only see and understand things partially. To know this should make us humble.

41. It is true that some of us are governed by our own Idols, our own personal neuroses and peculiarities, and our own secret idiosyncracies. But these may be spoken to and spoken about in enriched and multilayered I-thou and I-we relationships. There is no rule or proof which eliminates them from consideration. They must be factored into what we think we perceive to be out there.

To the extent the secret self is not present in these relationships, our socially shared understanding is distorted. To the extent that we seek uniformity through calculation and quantification in our social ordering, we sustain the process of hierarchy and, finally, authoritarianism. Those who seek to escape everyday language for the more rigorous language either of quantification or form, for the format language of social organization, help deform and destroy the more liberated, noncolonized language. Therefore, it leads to the destruction of the person. Language must open doors to understanding. It does so when we realize that language speaks to our many needs and moods, changing its meaning through interaction with others.

42. The public marketplace cannot escape language. It seeks to determine, however, what is important. It seeks hegemony through the control over media, government funds, the consideration of what is to be discussed, and what is assumed to be the altar at which all must pray.

43. We sit in the cave of the shadows where people do not think they exist until they are told they exist . . . and so objectified, wherein they think that celebrityhood is authentic and can only be known through media, governed in the traditional way, be it corporate or state power.

All words are worlds of our own creation and they intersect with the "real" world. Is Disney's world now real or fake? Is it less real than the existence of nuclear weapons and the horror of nuclear war which has only occurred once?

44. There may be less regularity and order than one would suppose in the world. And yet one must marvel at Einstein, who discovered uniformity through deductive reasoning where others saw very little but the wrong order of "mistakes." Nevertheless, if all is approximation, then we know that approximation includes judgment, and judgment itself must include fantasy and moral understanding.

45. It is important that we study failure. But failure must be judged in terms of ends, which themselves are invariably open to question. What do we mean by a failed social system? Is the Nazi system a failed social system? If we state that we are to *prove* truths, it is likely that in terms of social systems and the natural order we are still able to judge the truth of things only upon the good faith of one person to another. While we seek uniformity and proof of the positive, there is no doubt that in modern times we are skeptical and do not want to believe, except in that to which we have become already habituated, in which case we accept anything that buttresses what we already know or want to believe. Political rhetoric is fashioned to obtain this end. Our system of knowledge discounts what we do not want to accept.

46. It is a terrible thing that in our time we can conceive of an end or limit to the world, at least to humankind's place in it as guide. We may guess at how we got where we are, but there is precious little thought given to how human understanding will be drafted to teach us how to get to another time. The desperation of our present condition is that we have not known what limits to place on what we do, and what limits should come from our understanding in the practical sense. Nor have we understood that humane limits require knowing what can and must be changed to secure more than the mixture of misery or fascism that now prevails in the world.

47. The will and affections are not to be denied their rightful place as informing and indeed framing human understanding (*Verstehen*). There

is nothing to suggest that affections and even the will are less useful than human understanding detached from them. It is human affection which points us to our own modesty and the difficulty of knowing nature, but it is not true that sober thoughts deny hope, nor is it the case that common opinion is not found in that which is "uncommonly" believed as true. If we forbid our affections to "color and infect the understanding," we will be left with no capacity to feel and no moral ability to reject. All will seem the same. "Everything can be known" and therefore, many think, everything can be made. And so we have Albert Speer and Robert McNamara as the symbols of modern man. Behind their computer or slide rule, beneath the coldness of their exterior, is the death of human-kind. Even the word "understanding" is detached from anything but a cold positivism and empiricism which misses what happens and what moves.

48. Power, freedom, and what we feel and understand through our bodies and senses are inseparable. The knowledges which we are re-quired to form must grow out of our attempts to bring these attributes of life together within the situation in which we find ourselves. If we are conscious of our purpose, by which I mean assessing and changing our fundamental conceptual and value ground—doing so with grace, under-standing, and empathy—we will be able to reach to the common sense of humanity, the sole basis (discounting good fortune and God) upon which civilization can move to a measure of peace with liberation.

49. By power I mean the set of relationships which allows for a person or a group to frame the situation of another. The meaning of power can only be understood from *inside* a situation; those who seek to understand power from the outside, rather than from the inside, can deal only with their inferences from behavior. The reviewer or writer perceives or "manufactures" the perception for his own purposes. thus, historians tell us myths, or stories, happenings and moments they call "events." They teach us their lessons about events, not the events themselves, which are known only through reconstruction about them. They are one step removed from the event. Events themselves cannot be known.

50. By freedom I mean the capacity to act on another, to frame, and begin acting against, for, and with other people. Freedom, therefore, must include empathy, power, and knowledge, for it is in the knowledge system in the modern world that those with power decide what and whom to control, what standards to protect, what people to incarcerate, what things and phenomena to look at. Conversely, it is through the knowledge systems that we decide whom, how, and what to be free of; how standards change and are dialectically formed; what, if any, institu-tions systematize freedom; what we should or should not study.

51. Two major forms of knowledge have been used since the eigh-teenth century to assert, acquire, control, and maintain class power for one group over another and one person over another. This colonizing knowledge is meant to ensure classes and pyramidal control of top over

the bottom, of one over the other, eradicating what is natural and obvious. Henry Kissinger is the modern purveyor and exemplar of colonizing knowledge and its practice, for he speaks and represents the vain, ambitious, and cynical in diplomacy and geopolitical manipulation. Unfortunately, there are examples of those more noble in intent, who are less cynical, but no less mistaken. They are more painful to recall because they were meant to contradict a colonizing arrangement. But they only repeated it.

52. Since the eighteenth century, the most powerful partner of colonizing knowledge has been scientific knowledge, the formulation of rules from empirical observation, and mathematics, which give a modest level of understanding about the interaction of things in nature. I couple scientific knowledge with technical knowledge. Even Einstein's science required technical forms and instruments for their proof. And technical knowledge itself requires the invention of instruments and organizational processes that are meant to reinforce political control from the top, ensure moderate levels of convenience for certain classes, and help scientific workers frame their experiments through the use of machines (although their particular machine may be thought of as handmaiden rather than dictator).

53. When we consider what it is we feel, we find that we are concerned with the rush of sensibilities and sentiments that overtake us in a moment of excitation, passion, and contemplation. Those feelings can only be repressed or excluded from the scientific or knowledge enterprise at our peril. Instead, we must consciously consider them as teaching us about the past moment for a future one. I do not intend to suggest that one moment "causes" a later one. These moral determinants of our actions are constantly challengeable: they are pressures and precedents, but not inevitable patterns. Thus "repression," if there is such an attribute, becomes a matter for public scrutiny and debate. Its contents must be demythicized.

54. We have been trained to believe that to prove there is truth, falsehood must exist. So it is we have to believe that absolute prescriptions require control, repression, and penalty, for if there is no way to enforce a "no," there can be no absolute "yes." The task of social control advocates is to assure the sanctity of this principle. From Erasmus and Alberico Gentile, however, we have heard voices who have said otherwise. Reconstructive knowledge and knowledge for social reconstruction assert that, because knowledge of any *event* is part real and part linguistic statement referring only to itself, there can never be an absolute knowledge (except that one) because it, too, is a partial description. There are only shadings of no's into yes and, therefore, we must always question any penalty, for it assumes no mediations. Our further trouble comes when we establish institutional structures and controls, as if there can be absolute understanding of events, causes, or destiny. Institutional structures established to solve "objective" problems will seek means of control

through knowledges found and made to justify the power of those who have them. They may be manipulative knowledges as in the cases of testmakers and statesmen, observational knowledges as in the case of scientists, numbers and columns knowledges as in the case of accountants, rules knowledges as in the case of lawyers and natural scientists, who seek codes for purposes of replication and understandings of the "out there."

If they are social knowledge workers they find themselves involved in a Sisyphean task. They are charged with securing a knowledge and power system to create a tomorrow like yesterday, and so they try to predict, plot, and enforce their version of our tomorrow. If they are scientific and technological workers they are charged with the responsibility of securing natural knowledge rules that do not challenge social and economic institutions, but merely extend them. Because they are in the wrong critical framework, knowledge discoveries cannot meet Martin Buber's challenge: "The graver the crisis becomes, the more earnest and consciously responsible is the knowledge demanded of us; for although what is demanded is a deed, only that deed which is born of knowledge will help to overcome the crisis."

55. We should remain intensely skeptical of "fundamental explanations." When we think about rules and laws of the natural world we should not be awestruck and assume that such statements are invariably statements about the "natural order." That something operationally works may be a product of luck and its misunderstood aspects. That something is *out there* and acts according to certain laws may be correct, but it may be acting according to its laws, not ours. The natural world is as animate as we are: The kidney knows more than the urologist about its workings, the brain than the brain surgeon, just as a planet or atom knows more about itself than our physicists know about it. And this disturbing fact causes biologists, physicists, and technologists to believe that if they can build and replicate things (nature), they then understand them, thinking that they know more than the thing or atom or cell they construct. We now are required to formulate laws between "us" and "it" or "them." If this sounds strangely mystical and animistic, it is only to make clear that we had better think again about the limits of what we know and what *they* know about themselves, including our relationship to "it" or "them." That they cannot make us does not mean that they cannot destroy us. In this matter we have the painful lesson of the Golem.

56. Quantum mechanics was the way in which scientists sought to accept that they knew less than they hoped about the real world, by stating the Heisenberg principle, wherein "the uncertainty of the momentum and the uncertainty of the position are complementary, and the product of the two is constant . . ." or to put it another way, we "cannot know both where something is and how fast it is moving." But surely this is not the only thing we don't know about the relationship between light,

speed, and place. This law is delivered to us in such a fashion that scientists and nonscientists alike come to believe that we "know" everything else about speed and place. There is a political aspect to this question. When we speak of societies as a whole, who gets to use such rules and how do they shape our general consciousness? Is there an operational value to them for the powerless?

57. So that we may keep ourselves, humankind, in the center of what we can do, we should remember what we are trying to escape. It is the Cartesian split which separates out the living person from feeling (empathy), whether as experimenter or experimented upon. It is, therefore, an attempt to achieve a radical objectivity which takes into account the situation, the inside and outside of it, and the actors in it. But such a knowledge requires bridging the internal and the external. It means that the knowledges which we have presently devised are elegant but limited. As Gödel and Heisenberg have shown, we are unable to prove mathematical or physical rules by logic or evidence from within mathematics or physics. Like rules about other phenomena, such rules are constructions and intuitions of our minds. We must finally accept or reject them, or both. We can only know aspects of things, measuring and weighing them without knowing their internal purpose and motion. This being the case, what we know is a world of appearances, a passing show on the wall of the cave. The image in the lens of a camera is not the thing itself. It is the image of a thing and we cannot know it in the conquering or possessing sense of "knowing." How foolish and degrading it is to attempt to control what we cannot know. How much more important it is for us to know that we can choose our rules of convenience and behavior, if we are prepared to pay the consequences. What we can only know is a moral and political lesson. It may be fashionable to say that man is no longer in control of his unconscious, or that the earth is no longer the center of the universe. But all people live—and correctly so—as if the earth were the center and there were no unconscious.

58. I have mentioned coding. Do codes inhibit or liberate us? In music it was thought that Schoenberg's code liberated the musician and composer, because recognition of limits plus decentering meant that music itself was only a convention. But music has a structure and a code of what is within us (even as we recognize that there are accidental musics), each helping to expand what we hear and, therefore, feel and think. Such musical codes *free* us and help to tell us something else about ourselves.

59. How important the empathic sensibility becomes, for when we are decentered by physics, particularly when we think about quantum mechanics, we are aware that there is no code or rule of the natural world. We are not, according to Feynman, able to "predict exactly what will happen in any circumstance," because large (Newtonian) bodies and atomic bodies act according to different rules. No code of nature can exist. And if this is true of atoms, and we know that atoms make up cells,

how can we talk about a genetic code? And once we understand how limited our knowledge is, it should become obvious that genetic engineering, for example, is foolish on its face. We do not know and therefore cannot be aware of the consequences. All we can know is a political or ethical question, namely, do we want to tamper with what we cannot know or control because we do not like what we presently are?

60. It is not true that replication is central to experiment in the physical sciences and that each experiment in its own way is unique within a range of approximations. But this then is exactly like politics or language of art, where ambiguity allows for a *range* of meanings about anything. The degree of precision, as Aristotle says, depends on one's purpose. But even this is mistaken if we think that there is precision at all. Sartre wrongly believed that it was literature which gives many meanings, but philosophy could be written "precisely" one way.

Modern life teaches us that nature and humankind are more complicated than the dialectical notions of the nineteenth century supposed. Life is a series of shadings, say, between black and white which double back on each other, as Karlheinz Stockhausen and Karl Worner have pointed out. Anything can be mediated. The consequences of such notions are of great importance.

Once the idea of mediation has been grasped, then nothing should be excluded from its scope. Its conceptual principle is a principle of organization to establish a scale between extremes and then to construct a series having determinate proportions. . . . Universal mediation constitutes the first basic idea of serialism, but there is also a further idea. Everything connected with a structure and requiring formulation should be included in the form on a base of equal participation. This principle, too, is related to a general principle in modern thinking."[2]

It is the principle of equality in which everything when it appears must be given its due.

61. We have different knowledges because we have different social roles. We believe that these knowledges and roles are unrelated. Gurvitch argues that certain knowledges take precedence over others given the goals of the society. He tells us about the history of philosophical or theological knowledge, commonsense knowledge, scientific knowledge, perceptual knowledge of the world, and knowledge of the Other. He claims that each social organization from feudal society to managerial society, from empire to decentralization and city-state, all emphasize particular modes of knowledge as against others. But his otherwise attractive argument assumes that each epoch does not have a unity of knowledge.

Without prejudice to Gurvitch's position, we will find that knowledges of whatever kind are intertwined. There is no "pure" scientific knowledge or political knowledge or mythical-theological knowledge. If, after breaking open each "hard and stubborn" fact or datum of knowledge, we come to see that each partakes of politics or perception as mediated through particular class structure and using everyday common understandings and metaphors, the question will come down to whose knowledge, whose perceptions? The use and understanding of the fact and datum will come down to the form of *ethics* or moral purpose to be found in the situation that produced and used the "fact." This means that we are required to analyze the situation of those who make the fact. In other words, we may take a particular situation and "know" it in particular ways, thereby creating and reinforcing particular types of human relationships—patriarchal, colonizing, or otherwise. Suppose we are psychoanalysts or priests, father confessors listening to people confess their sins. What sort of control knowledge and symbol manipulation is created to make such an unequal relationship continue? But suppose that I share with another my fears and hopes, and he does the same. What is new that is created between us? Or what is the new knowledge that is created beyond ourselves? Or suppose that we look at particular phenomena of the world, creating a set of experiments which by their nature are part of a human social situation. Should they be eliminated from consideration, or by doing just that are we in fact falsifying data?

62. All this means that reconstructive knowledge should first define the social situation and clarify for all what each member's role in that situation is. This definition should also include the particular experiment which is to be performed, the logistic activities within the experiment, and the unseen social support which is demanded either explicitly or implicitly by those performing that experiment. Thus, who supplies the mice? How are they manufactured? Which class or gender does the basic work in a laboratory? Does this affect the nature of the experiment? But then what is required is another understanding. Let us call part of reconstructive knowledge *political* in that it requires reaching out within a situation to satisfy others *without* destroying the situation of the participants. We undertake a subject-to-subject dialogue by which the unequal relationships of expertise, mystery, and the like are dispersed. This type of political knowledge includes an empathic understanding of the Other. By this I mean a nonjudgmental acceptance of the Other. The empathic sense accepts the Other within his role as well as outside of it. The Other, like the "thou" or the "I," includes many layers. Our acceptance of the Other is not enough without moral sensibility, for it requires us to first accept the Other in the empathic sense and then to judge ourselves and the Other in the situation.

Judgment leads to action. Often, it is moral judgment which may require us to act against our situation. Moral judgment plus empathy tell us what we want to know and why we want to know it. They generate a philosophy, politics, psychology, ethics, and, I dare say, theology that seek a new understanding of the universal and particularly the "abstract" and the "concrete." This will change the scientific enterprise.

As Gurvitch has pointed out, it was thought in the age of enlightenment and since then that one could be a scientist without being a philosopher, but never the opposite. For one dealt with truth in the testable sense and the other dealt with that which was barely useful and not very explicative of the world, even man's place in it. The Marxists Nizan and Gramsci criticized these philosophers for being tools of ruling classes who wanted only instrumental knowledge or seeking to represent fundamental truths without taking into account people's lives. Now most philosophers abstain or flee from either fundamental truths defined as "soul," "transcendence," and so on, or the material world in which we live and struggle, and which we attempt to tame.

In mandarin debates philosophy protected science against theology, but science never returned the favor. Indeed, to protect its own position, philosophy had to begin sounding only like the formal categories of science (logic). Perhaps the gang-up will now be the other way, as technology and science are unable to deliver practical things, betterment of humankind's lot, or explain the world more clearly or comprehensively than the old philosophers of whatever stripe.

63. The twentieth century has taught us about the limited ethical value of the division of labor wherein both work and responsibility are split up, wherein people are alienated from their actions and situation because they do not have responsibility for the situation—or so they think—or are able to influence or affect or be held responsible for actions not defined as their job.

Of course, no culture is able to live without the division of labor, just as no nation is able to sustain itself without machines and technical knowledge. Is it possible to fulfill the Marxist hope of liberating man through technology? Before this question can be answered affirmatively, a conscious effort must be made within technology to address the present problems caused by technology and machines, including the problem of alienation and our uncaring irresponsibility with regard to the machines we do create. The types of machines we invent and what we produce through them should lead to integration of the machine process in a noncolonizing way. It need not result in a situation of increased alienation for the person. This is accomplished by introducing the principle of I-thou and I-in-we in the industrial process itself, worker-community control, and subject-to-subject relations. Like insurance, technology is sneaky. It encourages us to prepare for the future, for disasters and possibilities which may never come. But what does inevitably occur are the social and systemic changes which are necessary to make or use the technology. Political liberation recedes as technology and science require security systems for their continued experimentation, and as security systems soon use and require science and technology to reenforce the role of the powerful, the military, and so on. We are left with no deliberation and liberation, but merely security systems which are meant to order the society and the people into colonized and broken-spirited roles. Consider the computer in our situation. What is striking about it is that it reenacts the division of labor through circuitry. One would have hoped that this result woud have allowed man to become whole again, thereby finding it no longer necessary to embrace the division of labor and the factory as instruments of liberation.

We can agree with the Marxists, who believed that technology is not an independent variable but instead is dependent on the nature of the social and economic system. But this insight is characteristic of all modern states, including socialist ones. They seek "progress" through integrating man and the machine. Progress soon takes on the connotation of denial for the next generation, or protection against present enemies, or perpetuation of bureaucratic stability and orderliness. Unless there is clear understanding that technology should be integrated into "I-thou" and "I-in-we" modes of knowledge, the technology will end up as a brutal controlling form.

The "I-thou" and "I-in-we" are discovered through the dialogic method from the assembly line to the consumer so that the industrial mode is open to constant examination by the entire society. Even where the questions asked appear foolish and offpoint, or the dialogue on a particular subject appears wrong, answers through other problems will be found.

At the university, in the laboratory, and at technical school, scientific research and inquiry is to be judged on the basis of criteria *beyond* the particular discipline and beyond so-called peer-group review. Each discipline and mode of criticism must actively include the "I-thou" and "I-in-we" sense of the project. The emptiness that the modern person feels has caused deformations which show the importance of finding ways to understand the "I-thou" and "I-in-we." Where attempts are made to strategize and technicize the form of defining one's relationship to others, or where people lose or avoid any reference to themselves as a group beyond their "encounters" in group therapy sessions, finding no way to relate the material world to what they know or should know or feel, one form of colonization and alienation replaces another. No activity, person, or thing can be understood in isolation from the situation that it creates by its existence and that the existence of other activities, persons, and things creates for it.

We may state, therefore, that there is no value of things unto themselves, not because individual things have no value, but because there are no things unto themselves. Once someone discovers, makes, or conjures up a thing, that thing at the very least has a relational existence to its discoverer or maker. When the troubled person says" Leave me alone," that person seeks to break the bond of relation because the relation has become deformed. It is not a statement of withdrawal. "I-thou" and "I-in-we" relations begin from recognition of the unique value of the person unto himself or herself. The principle of personal uniqueness does not deny a relational perspective, for it is through relationships that we are able to recognize the uniqueness of the person. Uniqueness within relations causes us to formulate a set of moral and political premises. These moral and political premises are to inform and be informed by the type of empathic knowledge which gazes on the Other.

64. In the world of "one thing at a time," political, theological, and aesthetic knowledge often take the form of unexamined assumptions or frozen dogma. They serve as the unexamined or hidden ground inside a scientific discipline. For example, mathematical and physical conceptions may in fact be predicated on aesthetic conceptions of elegance and concision when other principles may be far more important.

65. What are the modes of knowledge which we find critical to strengthen? And can they be taught? Moral philosophers once wanted to teach virtue and, indeed, they looked for principles within society or people to ensure virtue, skill, and goodness. But they are easier to attain than to talk about. Socrates talks of Pericles—if one is to believe that he was a virtuous man—who had ne'er-do-well sons. Other philosophers find that they end up believing in rules and, therefore, in force to ensure that those rules are followed. How else to explain Plato? Invariably, the mechanism of social control and "intelligent" application of scientific method becomes a means of saying what is right and wrong and reinforcing the moral right. Needless to say, this system can be used to advantage by those who hold power to frame questions—and people. The reenforcement of colonizing knowledge rules has a further degenerative effect on knowledge development and the social system. A comprador field of inquiry soon emerges, whose subject matter is only techniques and means. It takes for granted that technical considerations will make issues of value and ends. The politically powerful are quite comfortable with this approach. But beyond awareness of this phenomenon, is there a way to confront and change it? Certain notions come to mind that may have the desired effect.

The primary mode of social knowledge should be examination of "I and thou" and "I-in-we," as each relates to the other on a variety of levels. In practial terms, this means that subject-to-subject dialogue, mutual and joint exploration, is the primary way of doing social research. Indeed, social research which does *not* include the subject of research as a dialogic equal is research that should not be conducted. This radical point of departure means that we are required to examine the assumptions and methods of most psychologies, of most social experiments that are performed on others, of manipulative techniques, of systems of educational testing which hold knowledge as private property, of social experiments and researches meant to control behavior categorizing and labeling for social control. It is taken as a given in modern times that political knowledge begins with specific attainable ends. We make explicit our purpose, we define who the "we" is, and the limits that are set beyond which we do not go because we would change the character of what we seek and who we are. Yet we recognize the unlimited nature of our intellectual and humane task, transcending disciplinary boundaries which distort the overall purpose of the society. What we are struggling to do is define the central spirit of our time as one of decency, liberation, and caring, which are related to the ground of our being, of who we are in the world and in the universe. Our political knowledge begins, therefore, with recognition of the self and the Other, seeking means of bringing those in relation to each other in egalitarian interdependence. We are to find those political knowledges and that set of activities which strengthen natural bonds and affection and which assert that the roles of the Other and the self, of brother, sister, mother, friend, comrade, are to be mediated through a new understanding of what is human and humane.

Reconstructive method seeks to treat people as subjects, and assiduously avoids the distancing and placing system of colonizing knowledge. Reconstruction, by its nature, must depend on the dialogic relationship which brings forward what is unspoken, inarticulated to the conscious level.

We screen when we choose, and we may do so though conscious unawareness. This conscious unawareness is meant to close off the important from the unimportant. We then arrange our dessicated understanding into rules or laws, whether of the mind, of nature, or of social existence. But if what we understand and see is limited, we must also know that our understanding constantly changes with what we see or choose to deem important. If this is so, there is no progress in what we know, no building blocks and foundations, but merely the fact that we address other problems and questions or articulate them in different knowledges and belief systems at different times and places. That there is no progress in the usual sense because much of life is cyclical and since there is a continuous need in the history of philosophy to rethink old questions, I have no interest in disestablishing the social fact that there are colonizing and pathological modes that demand our confrontation and rebellion, whether they are in the streets, the laboratories, the factories, in families, schools, or churches.

When we recognize felt oppression that is socially caused and the dialectical tension of living in many different *times* within any particular moment or event, because each part of our body relates different to a particular moment, we should not be overwhelmed by our sense of being condemned to alienation. This understandable dread does not relieve us of the responsibility for dealing with what we can do. The world's competing ideologies are drowning in reality and, therefore have missed what was necessary—a revised understanding of what we do with the unnecessary, the ends and purposes for which liberation is brought into being.

There is a second consideration. We want to accomplish certain ends. But our project includes ourselves as part of the subject-object field. It is an attempt, therefore, to bring together political action and one's personal responsibility. The process of reconstructive knowledge and knowledge for social reconstruction is not a passive activity. Thus, for example, the fashioning of *knowledge-events* is of importance. Imagine if at Yale University there were students and researchers who picketed the building where the Milgram experiment was to be carried out, stating that the experimenters are lying to the "subjects" who are really tested as objects. Would this commitment to truthfulness have changed that experiment sufficiently so that it would not have been performed? For if truthfulness in science is crucial, truthfulness must also be present for the subject-object. Otherwise, a very false form of research will go on. Educational testing, for example, is based on categorizing and labeling in a competitive educational and job market. What is being sold is a specific form of indulgence to students through the testing system, for if the person scores well in competition with others, he or she will be able to enter the elite institutions. But suppose we say that knowledge is shared and that the end to be obtained in the social world is the continuation of that sharing. Shouldn't we praise those who develop ways to end the testing system, for example, by printing the answers and giving them out to those being tested, or insisting that tests should be developed that are cooperative in purpose—in other words, group tests? What should be emphasized is the group and shared nature of the knowledge process, the fact that it is shared property, and that it must be predicated on truth telling. This process is the educational process as against other modes of communication which for better or worse may be predicated on lying, bad faith, or silence. When we consider these questions, we are seeking a shift in focus of what is to be considered primary, as well as the way in which research is to be done in the social and natural sciences.

I have stated that there is an integral relationship between what is taught, what we look at, how we learn, and what we think important, with the type of society we inherit or fashion. This seems an unassailable truth. We are also aware that only the breeze, sometimes gentle, sometimes very windy indeed, of different forms of knowledge and ways of looking at that which we do in the world will change the doomed course that civilization seems to be following.

The techniques of the physical sciences and the human sciences should be the same; that is, they should have the same root. But the present forms of knowledge—both their ends and their means—are not wise ones. This conclusion is predicated on what modern knowledge has not done for society. I start from the principle that scientific endeavor and artistic activity should be part of a system which seeks greater coherence of the world for the person, a grounding for that person, and a way in which that person will no longer feel thrown. To achieve anywhere near this end we are required to surrender compartments of knowledge and ways of looking at questions that do not have direct bearing on these purposes. We should not have to wait for war crime trials to explain to us what sort of research should not be conducted. If we can agree broadly with the framework of this view, it is then quite reasonable for us to disagree on the meanings we ascribe to long-term ends. What we need to be in agreement about are the immediate structural effects of developing certain knowledge forms, forms which may rip people asunder, torture them, abuse their spirit, or cut them into segments like a boarding-house pie. It is not even that we have to reach for immutable principles "which will never exhaust experience, or be themselves exhausted by it." It is that knowledge systems are to be seen through a new prism, with a new attribute coming to light. If this attribute does not come forward to point us out of the cave, a way in which we can determine what to do, we are lost as a people and civilization.

The practical intellectual task, therefore, is to integrate modes of knowledge into those values which will nurture liberation, collective participation, individual dignity, sharing, and relative peace. Once we are past "I-thou" knowledge we may ask what types of political knowledge we need in our quest to reach beneath institutions to change them and bring them into congruence with natural feelings and sentiment. And we must change our natural scientific discoveries and notions, both in the way discoveries are made or formulated and in the way they feed back into the society to contradict our humane purposes. Is this not the intellectual project we need to formulate and organize to shed the horrors of the twentieth century?

## Notes

1. This essay was originally printed in *The Journal of Social Reconstruction* 1, no. 1 (Jan.–Mar. 1980), pp. 1–25, © Earl M. Coleman Ent., Inc.

2. Karl H. Worner, ed., *Stockhausen: Life and Work* (Berkeley and Los Angeles; University of California Press, 1973), pp. 83–84.

# 2

# Idols of Modern Science and the Reconstruction of Knowledge

HERBERT J. BERNSTEIN

## Introduction: The Many Worlds of Science

Most of us believe that the well-understood, firm, true universe of science is both unshakable and expanding in all directions. We may even picture the region of knowledge as a bright volume in a vast space of darkness, the darkness of ignorance. New experiments are performed each day, and the boundaries of science advance. Configurations of phenomena never yet explored are being put to the test of "nature under constraint and vexed." Scientists use *control* of nature to manipulate special situations that can cast more light on large areas of related phenomena. As a result, while certain questions receive more attention than others, so much is being investigated that virtually every possible direction receives some scrutiny and has some light cast its way. So it seems that we inhabit a shining sphere of scientific knowledge, with perhaps a dimple or two where progress has not been very rapid, but where expansion in all directions is the rule rather than the exception. Unfortunately, in actual practice, our science does not work that way.

In their quest to extract consistency from nature, scientists relentlessly pursue very particular and specialized knowledge. The strategy of control means that science starts attacking conceptually simple, albeit methodologically difficult, problems—with a tendency to reduce away the complexities which make the subject interesting in the first place. As a result, most pieces of scientific knowledge are highly specific. Much of the detailed knowledge of human cancer metabolism, for example, stems from research on cultures named HeLa, after Helen Lane, the pseudonymous patient whose cancer produced a cell line which would replicate under laboratory conditions, as most other human cells will not. Subnuclear particles appear only when teams of specialists use gigantic high-energy machines to create them in complete isolation from normal matter. Nerve conduction is understood best in squid axons because these giant cells are large enough to permit easy manipulation. The visual-perceptive tract was mapped out almost entirely in cats anesthetized nearly to death (lest their eyes wander, or blink, or be distracted from the experimenters' controlled stimuli). And almost all molecular genetics was discovered in the simple bacterium, *Escherichia coli.*

Thus, what looks to us like a sphere of scientific knowledge more accurately should be represented as the inside of a highly irregular and spiky object, like a pincushion or porcupine, with very sharp extensions in certain directions, and virtually no knowledge in immediately adjacent areas. If our intellectual gaze could shift slightly, it would alter each quill's direction, and suddenly our entire reality would change.

Picture two different configurations of such an irregular shape, superimposed on each other in space, like a double exposure photograph. Of the two images, the only part which coincides is the body. The two different sets of quills stick out into very different regions of space. The objective reality we see from within the first position, seemingly so full and spherical, actually agrees with the shifted reality only in the body of common knowledge. In every direction in which we look at all deeply, the realm of discovered scientific truth could be quite different. Yet in each of those two different situations, we would have thought the world complete, firmly known, and rather round in its penetration of the space of possible knowledge. As a result, we can hardly conceive of how many possibilities there are for what we call objective reality. Our sharp quills of knowledge are so narrow and so concentrated in particular directions that with science there are myriads of totally different real worlds, each one accessible from the next simply by slight alterations— shifts of gaze—of every particular discipline and subspecialty.

We are only now beginning to see how this works. Clearly one of the mechanisms for picking a reality is the sociohistorical sense of what is important—which research program, with all its particularity of knowledge, seems most fundamental, most productive, most penetrating. The very judgments which make us push narrowly forward simultaneously make us forget how little we know. And when we look back at history, where the lesson is plain to find, we often fail to imagine ourselves in a parallel situation. We ascribe the differences in world view to error, rather than to unexamined but consistent and internally justified choice.

Consider the astronomical "Events of 1054."[1] As a new and changing star, the Crab Nebula supernova was seen all through the east. Chinese and Japanese astronomers watched each night with great interest. In Europe, however, the scholastic teaching that perfect heavens never change provided a different social environment. No astronomer in Europe *saw* the supernova or rather, recorded it, even in private notes. Could it be that Europe was clouded over for months and months? No. A physician in Constantinople reported the new star; for there they had a plague, and mutability in the heavens served to explain the physicians' inability to halt the virus.

With empathy, we can understand the European astronomers quite well. Their morality made it important to press forward the nightly search for regularity in the heavens, in relentless pursuit of further evidence of God's perfection. This notion extended from the savants down to the common folk; except, of course, in those places where the deranged order of things below made certain mortals seek astral evidence of God's wrath. No matter how spectacular the phenomenon, to scholastics a new star was what we would call *Drekeffekt* ("noise"), the random glitch which so often appears in experiments signifying nothing but meaningless bad data to discard.* Judgments like these, parallel to medieval judgments, define the world we know. Today's noise becomes tomorrow's facts.

Indeed, even the historical order of discoveries helps determine our conceptual universe. Though it is execrable history, students are sometimes asked to speculate on what physics would have been if Hamilton, in the eighteen hundreds, had taken the single step Schrödinger took only in the 1920s: to quantize the action variables of mechanics. Long before the complete development of field theory, we might have understood quantum mechanics and developed the philosophical views of complementarity. Fields that could not be formally quantized could not readily be introduced, and gravitational theory might not seem anything like what it is today. Our universe might not have any black holes or "big bang" or final collapse—our view of the real world would be quite different from its present state.

But we need not restrict ourselves to hypothetical discoveries. In cosmology, the case of the Copernican revolution provides a surprising example of the historical nature of our real world. We all know the story of Galileo's trial: the struggle of religion against Copernicus's scientific truth that the earth revolves about the sun and the scientist's political demands of independence from the Church. Few of us realize, however, that Einstein's general theory of relativity overthrew precisely those notions of absolute space and time which made the Copernican description true and the Ptolemaic false. In General Relativity even an accelerating body, like the earth, may be chosen as the center *at rest* from which all other motions are described. In principal, the geocentric picture of the universe is mathematically as good as the Copernican one and, therefore, just as true. After Einstein, any frame of reference, even one moving with the earth, is as good as any other. Science has not bothered to correct our common notion that the earth revolves about the sun because that description is the simplest.[2]

How strange. So much strife and power were exerted over whether it is the sun or earth that really moves. Yet today we know that this cosmic reality comes from the undefined and human-based criterion of *simplic-*

---

*They doubtless reasoned that the phenomena were "sublunary," or beneath the moon, where atmospheric imperfection allowed such irregularities. The celestial sphere, their true concern, occupied them totally—especially over and beyond temporary sublunar displays.

*ity.* It is true the earth goes around the sun; that is real, but only because belief in mathematical simplicity has replaced literal religious faith in defining our world.

Nor is this an isolated case. Modern science records a history of intellectual constructs becoming the world, virtually as real as palpable everyday objects. Until this century, many scientists referred to atoms only as "the atomic hypothesis." Yet every possible consequence, from the gas law to potential biological events, even to seeing individual atoms in real (microphotographic) pictures, actually occurs. At first a scientific construct may be introduced ad hoc. Later it explains other unexpected or seemingly disconnected phenomena. Finally it predicts phenomena that never could have been conceived before its introduction. Atoms have gone through all these phases.

Because we have supported the research teams to investigage them, to observe their consequences in every possible circumstance, to "see" them with electron microscopes, and to assemble the necessary rare materials and special high-vacuum conditions that isolate their behavior, atoms are now part of our real world. But they are not tiny hard balls or miniature solar systems. Nor are they ultimately indivisible. In fact, they do not really behave exactly like any macroscopic object. The construct "atom" really summarizes all the precise laws, all observed and predicted phenomena, and all the mathematical description which science has adduced about these ultimate building blocks of things.

Scientists partly understand the nature of such a constructed reality, for they use the freedom it provides as a tool in both experiment and theory:

Physicists sometimes admit to a little fantasy that goes like this. One day they have a bright idea for an experiment. They write a proposal, gather their friends and their funds and build complicated equipment. At last all is ready. They lead the pulses of energetic particles into the midst of their apparatus and peer anxiously at their instruments. At that moment God convenes a conference of angels.

"Seen what those people are doing now?" He demands.

"Hey!" the chief angel says, looking down. "They're crashing those dinky bits with 3 GeV at the centre of mass. And they're watching hard this time."

"Well don't look at me," says the Lord. "It never really came up before."

In the thoughtful pause that follows, one of the angels pipes up impatiently: "We've got a million collisions already, and I don't know what to do with them."

"We'd better take a vote then," God declares. "All those in favour of granting them a new particle please raise a wing. . . ."

Back on earth, the counters start registering the result of the vote.[3]

None of us can possibly comprehend all the choices, all the trade-offs and political decisions that enter our scientific world view. And yet we have a few good examples of how two widely different scientific views might exist, each as valid as the other for explaining observed phenomena:

SIMPLICIO . . . consider the electromagnetic field. Faraday suspected it, Maxwell discovered its laws, Hertz measured it, and a large industry is based on it. We produce it in power stations, transport it, and sell it for good cash. Anything that can be bought and sold seems to me real; sometimes I almost suspect that these are the only real things in the world. Salviati, what do you say to this?

SALVIATI: Indeed, it is an excellent example. Let me ask you, Simplicio, do you think a theory of electromagnetic interaction is possible without supposing the reality of the electromagnetic field? . . .

One does exist. It is called *the theory of action at a distance.* It has only particles as real entities and it uses no field. This theory is in complete agreement with the other theory which you know and which we all use, but it is a bit more complicated. Hence it is less familiar. However, its fundamental ideas are as easy as they are significant.[4]

The alternative action-at-a-distance theory, which Jauch cites, appeared eighty years after the concept of the electromagnetic field.[5] Men and women have probably been thinking about nature for hundreds of thousands of years. Since that which we consider science is only about three hundred years old, the fact that we already have such examples of alternative descriptions, alternative realities, has deep implications for the nature of our firm, true, and unshakable knowledge of the world. How many more such worlds—fully scientific, verifiable, and real— would be possible if all the alternative theories were known, or if alternative human social, political, and historical conditions surrounded our quest for knowledge?

Indeed, in three centuries, scientific rationality has had remarkable achievements. Science, with its apparent solidity, has become both leader and model of all intellectual activity. But is it the best model? In particular, is it the best for using our minds to do good? This is the larger question I wish to address, a question raised by understanding both the contingent nature of scientific knowledge and the dangers it poses.

Recall that the modern science model is the source of our technocratic urge to rationalize decision making, to reduce complex social choices to mere technical problems, to mathematize the social sciences. Today many crises facing society seem to come directly out of supposedly value-free technical choices; all too often the only cure proposed is the application of *more* technique. Energy supplies, for example, derive from technologies that seem increasingly hazardous, possibly endangering the environment for entire ecosystems. And expert technocracy sees only one way out—increasingly centralized new techniques and bigger, more abundant sources of energy, technical fixes for quantitative problems. Similarly, our economic theories have guided us to periods of chronic slow growth but rapid increases in prices, alternating with widespread deprivation of gainful employment. Unemployment, we are told, is the necessary cure for inflation. In hundreds of smaller problems, too, objectified analysis is suggested to rectify the evil "side effects" of the initial value-free, technical approach.

Under the circumstances, we must examine quite scrupulously our model of firm, true wisdom; especially for its hidden value assumptions, never forgetting how specialized is that kind of knowledge which can be called scientific. To perform that examination, we have the professional study of science, including such fields as the philosophy, history, and sociology of science, each with its own methodology, approach, and corpus of work, embodied in its own professional literature. But as disciplines themselves, these fields form part of the modern rational world view which we propose to scrutinize. They should be very important to our search and useful in the reexamination of science by all of us—scientists, nonscientists, professional scholars-of-science, and concerned, thoughtful, outsiders—but only if we also scrutinize their values, as well.

As a physicist, I began this essay with critical self-examination of science as a particular form of organized human behavior. In this light, one aspect stands preeminent. The scientific study of the world upholds experience as the final arbiter of knowledge. Not any experience, but only the specially controlled and preconditioned experience of experiment. Science entails as much creativity, originality, and as many "free inventions of the human spirit"[6] as other intellectual activities (like art, poetry, philosophy, or social studies), but always inventions which can be checked against the experience of nature; not direct, emotional experience like smelling a rose or hiking to exhaustion in the High Sierras or "psyching out" the answer by intuition, but rather as stylized, conventionalized and, indeed, bizarre behavior which traps nature and emphasizes its regularity. Think of the most ordinary scientific operation, such as finding the length of this page with a ruler. You use an instrument of great complexity, with a straight edge supplied by a brass strip held in the fine groove of a specially stamped and printed piece of wood, calibrated against an arbitrary standard. For more detailed knowledge of the world, science obviously goes beyond the simple rule, but note how value-laden even that device is: could any but an industrialized and commercialized society provide so many millions of brass and wooden copies of a central arbitrary definition of length, or the training and attitudes needed to use it correctly?

After dealing with "Experimentation as Bizarre Behavior" (section I below), we will consider the moral implications of maintaining large, hierarchical subsocieties of scientists and knowledge workers (section II). At a deep level such structures allow the interests and ruling forces of society to choose directions of inquiry. These choices have *defined* the sharp disciplinary "quills" of knowledge, thereby defining reality for all of us. Individual natural scientists, social scientists, and artists feel the moral effect as a contradiction between disciplinary excellence and social good. Science as a whole no longer serves Francis Bacon's original claim to moral purpose.

Section III, "Towards an Archaeology of Modern Science," exhibits two particularly fundamental cases in physics and biology: the probabilistic interpretation of quantum mechanics in the mid-1920s, which first elevated manipulative rationality to a defining principle in science and cleared the stage for nuclear physics and the 1947 selection of a potentially dangerous organism as the defining example of molecular genetics. This specialized knowledge contains a delayed danger inherent in the choice of *E. coli*—a choice conditioned by encouragement of personal ambition over social good and by the circumstances of post-war research.

In section IV, "The Current Situation," we see the circle closing. Modern practitioners of Big Science—heirs to the glamour of quantum mechanics and molecular biology—now find themselves in dehumanizing situations. Moreover, the logical circuit has also closed: specific proof of the limitations of investigation has been given in many fields. Realization that we *create* reality has proliferated from science to the arts and social sciences. Those who accept the moral obligation to direct the inquiring gaze so as to humanize the process of discovery are inventing reconstructive knowledge—knowledge which reintegrates personal motivation, intellectual power, and social good.

# I. Experimentation As Bizarre Behavior

## *Diversity of Method and Motivations*

Consider the extremes to which physicists now go. Obeying Francis Bacon's dictum that "the nature of things betrays itself more readily under the vexations of art than in its natural freedom,"[7] scientists assemble highly specialized instruments, with exotic materials of pure tungsten, copper, and gold, specialized compounds, man-made plastics, and glass. Then they produce unusual conditions like high vacuum, low temperature, or high concentrations of energy all in an effort to discern that regular behavior of nature whose knowledge is science. In a way it is a gigantic charade, for much of experience is reduced away, disallowed. A detailed example from modern physics will help to clarify these points. I have chosen one which is clearly related to strategies used since the turn of the century; namely, to investigate properties of matter in the small by seeing how energetic bits (atoms, particles) scatter from a target containing many of the objects under study. This technique, rather like a minute game of marbles, has grown into a burgeoning industry in current high-energy physics. The most famous early prototype scattering experiment by Rutherford demonstrated the existence of the atomic nucleus by bouncing alpha particles off the atoms in gold foil.

The next four paragraphs describe a more recent "marble game." The important point to remember is that each technical detail implies a corresponding social web of prescribed behavior: the personnel have all been selected through tests and interviews, after training for years in specialized subjects; the institutions they work in have their written and unwritten rules; every material and part comes from elaborate systems of suppliers and manufacturers. The hierarchy of their own social organization parallels that of our national society as does the local hierarchy of the laboratory.

To measure how protons of specific spin interact, scientists at the Argonne National Laboratory prepared both the target protons and the ones to be accelerated. Starting as hydrogen gas, the source protons are processed through several indirect steps in order to make a beam whose spins are all in the same direction. A New Zealand firm constructed the polarized-proton source. Like many high-technology scientific devices, it uses rather extreme conditions to achieve its results: high-vacuum chambers, rare materials found only in certain parts of the globe, very specific electric and magnetic field configurations—all maintained by selected crews of students, technicians, and control-room operators. We scarcely glimpse the extraordinary aspects of this endeavor when taught its significance in a popular account:

Hydrogen molecules are dissociated into atoms, which emerge as a beam and enter the nonuniform fields of a sextuple magnet. All the atoms whose electron spins happen to be oriented down are drawn toward the periphery of the field and are thereby eliminated from the beam. In the remaining atoms all the electron spins are up and the proton spins are oriented randomly, half up and half down. The atoms are next exposed to radio-frequency radiation tuned so that it can be absorbed only by atoms in which the electron and proton spins are opposite. The absorption of the radiation flips both spins, an event called a hyperfine transition. After the double spin flip all the proton spins are up and the electron spins are random (half up and half down). Finally the electrons are stripped away and the resulting beam of polarized protons is reflected through a 90-degree angle [by an electrostatic field] so that the spin vectors are perpendicular to the direction of beam motion.[8]

The target end of this experiment was no less elaborate than the beam source. Tiny beads made of ethylene glycol carefully "doped" with a precise amount of chromium impurity were frozen (rather ironically, since ethylene glycol is automobile antifreeze) in a flask held in a magnet whose field was 25,000 times as strong as the earth's. A very precisely tuned microwave field used electrons in the chromium to line up the spins of the protons (hydrogen) in the ethylene glycol molecules. Refrigeration required two isotopes of helium, each with its own gigantic vacuum system, to produce evaporative cooling to one-half degree above absolute zero.[9]

Between source and target lies a three-stage proton accelerator, itself a marvel of vacuum chambers (the protons must not collide with a single atom during their entire one-hundred-mile trip), bending magnets (they must circle a five-hundred-foot ring at an energy twelve times their rest mass'); and hierarchical social organization (crews of engineers, scientists, and technicians keep the machine working twenty-four hours a day for weeks on end, at times serving dozens of simultaneous experiments).

Clearly we are in the presence of very specialized human behavior. Virtually all normal experience is discarded in favor of the highly particular effects of experiment. And much knowledge is rejected, such as that of everyday life, of handcraft, of nature lore, of farming or virtually any other hands-and feet pursuit. But what is left is as powerful (*vide* modern technology), inspiring, and ultimately satisfying to the intellect as *verifiable* "free invention" can be.*

The insistence on verifiability and the criterion of experiment as arbiter require a precise definition of terms—a universe of discourse as well as a community of discourse. This often makes specialized and counterintuitive use of common words, such as the physicists' mass, energy, speed, work, dimension, and unit. Scientists often use the strategy of operationalism, wherein a course of actions is prescribed— such as setting up metersticks and clocks or manufacturing instruments and reading their dials—to define a construct by defining the process used to measure it, at least in principle, to avoid the inherent ambiguity of words. To validate all of this strictly prescribed behavior, the other scientists must also be involved. They must agree to define terms the same way, to adopt the same conventions (including the rules of logic which they share with all men and women), and they must ultimately be able to verify one another's results.

From my perhaps idiosyncratic emphasis upon experiment as the arbiter of verifiability, and measurement as the characteristic distinguishing experimentation from other human behavior, it becomes clear that Truth cannot be the goal of this endeavor. Rather, science seeks consistency. One cannot claim more than that, for many things that are not scientific possess their own Truth. Examples include our practical skills, common sense, and intuition; at another remove, they include the mystic knowledge of God, the universal comprehension suddenly gained from psychedelic experiences, or the wisdom of traditional understanding in supposedly primitive cultures. Indeed, the specially circumscribed criteria of experience allowed by science even rule out some phenomena; to science they simply do not exist.

This search for consistency specifies science's goal, but not its method. In the creation of science—that is, the invention of verifiable propositions which are later found to be experimentally consistent (or the invention of the experiments themselves)—there is as much variety of method as in any other creative endeavor. The brilliant idea may strike a

*I am reminded that "verifiable" had a technical use for some philosophers, as a criterion for meaningful statements. Its use here (and throughout) signifies only confirmability or consistency with experiment.

prepared mind while eating, swimming, relaxing, thinking hard, or making love. As for the way to prepare one's mind, some people work best in spurts, others steadily; a few perhaps are inspired by poring over mounds of data, while others attempt logical a priori attacks. Certainly there is no prescribed Baconian ritual induction. There are at least as many scientific methods as there are scientists, perhaps even as many as there are scientific problems.

That which drives people to become scientists shows as much variety as their methods. Often early childhood experiences, personality needs, and passionate motivations toward mental exercise (and excellence) seem decisive. A brilliant young astronomer cites the gift of a star chart at age seven. Einstein, at six, was captivated by the magnetic compass and later wondered, "Would a runner's hand mirror suddenly become blank at the speed of light?" The paleontologist whose family took him weekly to the American Museum of Natural History recalls his strong happy emotions. I still remember the Friday night during my seventh year when father asked me, "What is heat?"—instructing me not to look up the answer for a week—and my delight at fifteen to find that the most beloved parts of science were all called "physics."

Beyond early childhood experiences, the emotional wellsprings of science continue throughout one's productive life. Today specialization has gone so far that God-given curiosity, or that childlike wonder about the world which a scientist may preserve in his or her passion for learning, no longer connects directly with the particular morsel of inquiry at hand. "It is fortunate, then, that the thrill of *discovery,* as much as learning, motivates the researcher. Nor can we ignore the motives of competition for prestige and for material rewards that help label scientists as human."[10]

But if the motivation and processes of creativity are varied and emotional, regularity reigns in the creations. One element pervades all these results: rationality. The rules of doing science require that predictions, theories, and interpretations must each be logical. The passionate and nonrational roots of scientific work must issue in the growth of a rational, consistent and, hence, predictive understanding. As a result, incidentally, scientific papers are frequently more obscure than other professional literature. The emphasis on logic and rationality leads to a conventional suppression of the true motivations for the work. In its place appears a dry report of the methods, narrowly defined—that is, the operations used in experimental work or the mathematics applied in a theoretical piece.

Even the rational results of science cannot reconstruct a perfectly firm and true knowledge. History and philosophy of science have done a great deal to show that data require interpretive theories; that *facts* arise from the shared interpretation of the community of scientists; that verification and consistency of theories rely on meeting standards which are communally held and constantly (slowly) changing; and that ultimately there is no strict logical necessity to the picture of the world which science manages to project by combining the wonderful effects of individual researchers.[11]

### *Paradoxical Aside: The "Unreasonable Effectivenes" of Mathematics in Physics*

Physics shows as much variety of method as any science. Indeed, the first attack on a new problem is to try all the tricks that previously worked; conversely, every new trick is quickly applied to all the currently interesting problems if it succeeds on any one of them. There are always new techniques and new approaches being invented. But some form of mathematics always appears, so we might attempt to deduce a general method from this fact. At least one eminent theoretical physicist, Eugene Wigner, has marveled at the "unreasonable effectiveness" of mathematics. He was referring to the fact that physical theories utilize mathematics very extensively, and that mathematical elegance and newly created mathematics are often guides to new physical theories. It is as if Nature herself were secretly, somehow, mathematical . . . and man's creation of mathematics mimics nature's creation of phenomena.

But from the present point of view, it is rather bizarre behavior of experiment which projects consistency onto nature. We are, in effect, making phenomena appear rational for our own intellectual and emotional pleasure. Current scientific data are the result of manipulations of natural objects with the specifically numerical outcome of measurement. While doing scientific experiments we do not assemble those rare substances and produce those unusual conditions in order to "groove on the vibrations." Men's and women's minds invent facts of science through their intellectualized, and mathematized, perceptions of phenomena. It is not at all surprising that the highly similar invention of mathematics—with its emotional, nonrational, and unconscious motivation, its own search for consistency as opposed to Truth, and its insistence on producing a rational outcome—has great power and relevance in science. Out of the vast range our minds possess, mathematics and science seem to have tapped the self-same mode.

Asking why the world turns out to be so mathematical is almost like wondering how vegetables come to be so well-suited to feeding animals. Nature's construction of all the organic forms (we now know) is of a piece; of all the various ways to combine elements on earth, only certain carbon-based molecules, controlled by extraordinarily similar genetic codes, form the compounds of all life. Compatibility is no mystery. What sunlight streaming through the biosphere has done for animals and plants, nonrational inspirations flowing into the human mind have done for science and mathematics. What seems most marvelous in this is the "unreasonable effectiveness" of emotions in producing rationality both in mathematics and in physics.

To summarize: Science is a strange, highly specialized human social activity designed to create and expand a rational understanding of the universe as revealed by consistency with results of experiments which measure phenomena.

## II. Moral Implications of Science as a Social Activity

### Surface Relations

In addition to being a social activity, with its peculiar institutions, hierarchy, and traditions, science has an important bearing on the larger society, and vice versa. An age pervaded by technology, based upon science, peopled by the survivors of the first nuclear war and their progeny, and faced with innumerable technical crises hardly needs to be reminded of the power and importance of science. But we sometimes forget the consequences of that power. If the typical scientist were an individual seeker of externally given Truth, an isolated genius working alone on his or her specialized problem, then perhaps the moral implications of scientific work would be mitigated. Indeed, the dispensation of knowledge could then be closely controlled by its inventor, and the act of publishing would more fully bear the moral weight. But as we have seen, however, modern science must always be pursued in the context of a scientific community; that subsociety is supported, nurtured, and utilized by the larger society or by its ruling elite for reasons far from those motivating scientists themselves. Indeed, there is often dissimulation involved in this support, as when medical, consumerist, and economic benefits are adduced to justify work which is really motivated by military considerations. Government seems to have a simple desire to maintain liaisons with, and to make dependent, as many scientists as possible so that they or their work may be more readily recruited when necessary.

The scientific community, in fact, is a privileged subsociety, distinguished by its role and training. In America today, for example, the scientific community is largely male and white, as is the ruling elite. It can provide vast powers to society, yet it is hardly politically independent. Perhaps it is too paternalistically structured for effective political action; perhaps its members are too apolitical. At any rate, this community existence is necessary both to science and to society, though for different reasons. And, partly as a consequence of its existence, doing science cannot be considered amoral. The diversion of resources from other potential uses is, in itself, sufficiently weighty as a societal moral issue. No one can decide the moral questions posed except the person facing them. We can, however, point out that even the purely intellectual study of science (and surely the potentially powerful fruit of its cultivation) is *not* morally neutral. Sometimes the moral choices are not initially clear, nor even easily seen as such, but they are there.

The point was personally impressed on me by a story my mother delights in telling. She describes by father's great relief when, in 1944, the rumors reached the National Bureau of Standards that the Manhattan Project was in reality an atomic bomb project. According to the story, my father came home beaming—joyful that several years earlier he had rejected an offer to join the Oak Ridge group as a staff physicist. Apparently my parents had been suspicious of the secrecy, the unnatural community conditions, and the disruption of the group's ties to their families. In the end, it was an intuitive rejection, partly based on distrust of physicist Edward Teller's attempt to recruit my father, which made him stay in Washington. He spent the war working on lights for landing strips instead of on nuclear weapon manufacture. I cannot help but feel it was part luck, part moral instinct at work in this particular case. I hope and believe that all of us are more sophisticated now about the implications of secrecy and of military work than scientists were before World War II. But we must remind ourselves that even open, peaceful science is done at the expense of money, time, and effort which might be utilized in other ways. How can one find moral guidance?

The first step is analysis which attempts to be value-free and rational. But this may have severe limitations confronting the byzantine social complexities of today's science. To such an approach it always seems that science is noble and pure when internally directed, but both powerful and precious. The good resides in brilliance, in technical superiority, in excellent science. Evil forces or social errors seem to gain control only when politics, outward direction, or even application to technology come into play. Some liberal critics have even gone so far as to question the entire science-government connection. Bronowski put it quite baldly:

> Scientists can no longer confine their qualms to the uses and abuses to which their discoveries are put—to the development of weapons, or even to the larger implications of an irresponsible technology which distorts our civilization. Instead, they are face to face with a choice of conscience between two moralities: the morality of science, and the morality of national and government power. . . .
>
> The time has come to consider how we might bring about a separation, as complete as possible, between science and government in all countries. I call this the disestablishment of science, in the same sense in which the churches have been disestablished and have become independent of the state.[12]

He calls for an eventual block-grant for the entire international community of scientists and complete divorce of their funding decisions from government agencies; scientists alone are to determine what research is to be done and by whom.

Such dreams of reinstating the supposed lost purity of science reflect deep care about the uses of knowledge. "We are scientists second, human beings first. We become politically involved because knowledge implies responsibility. We fight as best we can for what we believe to be right. Often we fail."[13] But people who care deeply may still make rather strange moral choices. One nuclear physicist who began World War II as a radical pacifist, ended as a committed weapons designer. His major postwar work was designing smaller and smaller miniaturized "nukes"—

to make nuclear war so possible and so horrible that it would (of course) be outlawed. He left his military work when it no longer held technical or political challenge. A more recent moral decision was to make public how unclassified information could be used to steal the materials, fabricate the device, and assemble a working nuclear explosive. His reasoning: This would dramatize the need for major security precautions in order to prevent nuclear terrorism, fuel diversion, and proliferation of weapons.[14]

The problem is that any analysis based solely on our scientific notion of rationality reflects the historical, political, cultural, and economic values which selected that particular notion of reality. For example, in explaining to a reporter how the site was chosen for our largest particle accelerator, a physicist decried that "President Johnson eventually intervened after months of bitter regional fighting over the lab's proposed construction site."[15] And a team of scholars studied the entire issue, seeing high-energy physics as failing to live up to its professed ideals (let alone larger social goals) without ever noticing the clear analogy between the pyramids of power within the discipline and the nation as a whole. Their book describes the events and effects, but leaves the mechanisms whereby ruling interests were served as murky as ever.[16] An analysis of those mechanisms would reveal the roles played by actors deep within the governing structures. It would help scientists go beyond a version of decision making based on intervention from on high and might help reveal the human side of their endeavor. This in turn could profoundly open the scientists' own understanding of how science serves particular interests in society. It might also empower them in future, similar political embroilments, as might soon arise with physicists' proposed $1.5 billion superconducting supercollider, the latest particle-accelerating scheme.

Even when the analysis is about an application or technology at one remove from science itself, we hardly ever hear empathetic description of the people most directly affected. After the Three Mile Island nuclear accident, for example, much was written about machine failure versus human error. Much was made of the fact that operators twice turned *off* the emergency core cooling system (ECCS), eventually causing the core to be uncovered. But (until the operators themselves gave carefully worded testimony for the Kemeny commission) no one described how it felt in the control room around 4 A.M. of that fateful day: it is lunchtime on the graveyard shift; only three months of operation for the new reactor, so there are probably still plenty of bugs to iron out—here's the emergency cooling system going on again!

If we see it from the operators' point of view, the story may reveal that the ECCS actually triggered itself quite frequently and was routinely overridden. For there probably was at least one experienced operator on hand (the other reactor unit had been producing electricity for several years); and like a driver with a new car whose temperature light keeps going on, we can imagine the equivalent of pulling off the road, tapping the light until it goes out, and driving on.

What is more, we can see there is something right about the attitude. The operators must have an intuitive sense of their apparatus or the system is likely to fail *us*. We only want electricity for our lights and comforts, not to take the risks of an astronaut in the hands of a highly trained space pilot. We certainly should not like to be dependent on "more automated" systems—computers are notoriously inflexible and often subject to their software errors in ways which make it difficult to effect a quick cure. And the solution of a highly trained "nuclear priesthood" only pushes our society ever closer to a regimented Orwellian future. The case of the 1986 disaster at Chernobyl in the USSR may also require empathic analysis for complete understanding. It certainly underscores the need to analyze moral implications of science and science-based technology, whatever the political or administrative system.

But I have belabored the point: standard surface analysis of morality in scientific and technological issues tends to mimic the outlook of the enterprise it wishes to examine. Whereas such analysis may be necessary, it cannot be sufficient for want of the human and introspective dimension. At best it describes the external effects of society on science, the sociology of grants and the like. Such a sociology of science generally produces one of three predictable stances: a rationalization of the status quo, a "technical fix" to some identified social dysfunction, or an anti-science verging on faith. To use the porcupine-quill analogy, the effort may help explain how science steers the tips of quills in minute and fluctuating deflections. But it does not get to the question of how the central axis of each quill is aimed; nor to the implications of understanding that our seemingly spherical world of knowledge consists of quite specialized and disjointed quills.

### Deep Connections

Scientists are not ordinarily encouraged to go deeper than the sociological level in their analysis of science-society interactions. But their growing employment as consultant-advisors, as think-tank staff, and as policy analysts has opened the bureaucratic world to a wider (and younger) spectrum of scientifically trained professionals. To anyone sensitive, bright, and on the spot, all of these rather more political than academic intellectual settings reveal science clearly developing a dual role. First, it becomes the ultimate source of all "technical fixes"—from new methods of doing things (the technology we live by) to new methods of analysis or ways of arguing a case. Second, it consolidates its function as the model epistemological base, the sine qua non for true understanding and, hence, correct action in the world—in effect replacing the role of authority played by Church, Monarch, and Divine Revelation in bygone days.

The second role generates a pervasive need for manipulative rationality in the human world, exactly parallel to its role in scientific inquiry into nature. Little wonder that the hidden ideology of manipulation helps propagate dehumanizing and dangerous uses of technical knowledge. At a deep level, the unexamined epistemology becomes the crucial moral issue. Is the peculiar, specialized, hierarchical scientific approach the best way to go about knowing? How will its narrowing, restricting lens affect our ability to see the wider range of phenomena we need to see when we seek to deal with the world outside the laboratory? And perhaps most important, how will it serve us when we later turn our minds from creating reality to creating social good?

To Francis Bacon, there was no doubt of the answer. In establishing the topics and methods for human inquiry, Bacon intended his new experimental science to serve God's ultimate good. The scientific truth about the world would reveal its Creator's handiwork, and *therefore* the moral object.[17] Bacon's *Great Instauration*, fragmentary and unfinished as it stands, bears witness to this view. Thus, in the *Advancement of Learning* Bacon sets out a hierarchy of topics, those "deficiencies of knowledge" which the scientific revolution was supposed to remedy through logical (inductive) investigation. The topics progress from observational and experimental work through the "Georgics of the mind; or the means of procuring the true moral habit of virtue," to "the true use of human reason in the business of revelation."[18] They pass on beyond our value-free definition of scientific knowledge, right up to interpretation of scripture and discernment of the Good.

And in exhorting to the search, Bacon seems almost prescient in his warnings. He admonishes those who search out knowledge to take care

that they consider what are the true ends of knowledge, and that they seek it not either for pleasure of the mind, or for contention, or for superiority to others, or for profit, or fame, or power or any of these inferior things; but for the benefit and use of life, and that they perfect and govern it in charity.[19]

As we have lost any universal, absolute religious faith somewhere along the line during our pursuit of inductive knowledge, we have likewise lost the original connection between scientific truth and social good; we have refined moral concerns out of the process.[20]

This lack of moral inclusiveness does not except the men and women in fields other than science who, as "knowledge workers," apply intellectual creativity in their professions. In its acute form, the difficulty appears as direct conflict between accepted standards of rigorousness and a sense of the common good. Professionals in many fields have reported feeling such a conflict. As my experience and research began to demonstrate to me the situation in physics, my conversations unearthed resonances in other disciplines. Engineers working on economic development find that basic human considerations are almost automatically excluded in the design of projects. Economists note that definitions and theories which cannot be verified by the data and which no longer confront current realities are nevertheless applied as rigorous science. Sociologists realize that knowledge of interactions between the observer and observed is not used to help the subjects, nor entirely honored as restriction, but instead shapes the "experimental design" in sociological work—thereby further dehumanizing the people being studied. Even artists find that the social structures, both entrepreneurial and managerial, which have grown up around their work, redefine art and reduce it in essential ways.

In every case, the motivating human impulse—the childlike wonder of the scientist, the playfulness of the artist—is enlisted for some moral purpose and social good: satisfying people's material needs, organizing our society openly and equitably, even delighting our aesthetic sense. But in each case the disciplinary rigor, that very assumption of what defines good value-free work, obstructs the higher social purpose and frustrates the personal motivation of the scientist, social scientist, or artist.

Thus, the structure of their work, the conditions of support, and the ultimate use of their creativity—all external considerations—channel and define the discipline. Not surprisingly, the very interests and political forces of a society, including their biases and judgments, enter into the definition of "good science," of disciplinary rigor, and of internal standards and merit. Yet the superficial level of analysis stops short of connecting the steering of intellectual activity with the determination of its own definition.

Ultimately, we must suspect a deeper connection, and ask some pointed questions about the vanguard natural sciences and their current specific directions of expansion: Why does technocratic problem solving, modeled on physics' search for firm, true knowledge, seem to produce inequitable and domineering systems? Indeed, why are so many of the worst potential horrors direct offshoots of our most prestigious sciences: nuclear war, various energy doomsdays including the runaway greenhouse effect, environmental pollution, and nuclear energy disasters from physics; genetic engineering, monstrous new life forms, and uncontrollable pathogens from molecular biology?

The search for answers yields intriguing conclusions about our definitions of science, the human organization those definitions require, the particular nature of the scientific world view, and the moral and political implications of science as a social activity. The next section of this essay traces some of the deeper connections between the moral dimension and the fundamental definitional moves in modern science. The examples of physics and molecular biology seen as parts of an intellectual archaeology of the twentieth century help tell the story of a world view which has avoided potentially valuable openings to the combination of choice and social direction *within* science. The connection to other fields is discussed, leading to consideration of our current situation as one ripe for a new synthesis of scientific problem choice and social good.

## III.  Toward an Archaeology of Modern Science

Our inquiry must be more archaeological than historical;[21] connections between widely varying fields, parallels between arts and sciences, and similarities of limitations in different endeavors are as important as the intellectual history of any one discipline. At times it will seem that other scholarly distinctions are being lost, or glossed over. We consider science and technology to be intertwined, though it is clear that they are conceptually independent. For only recently have practical men and women turned to intellectualized and systematic descriptions of nature as primary sources of information to help "get the job done." Art, (design) experience, and common sense are all still important inspirations; but science in this century often pleads its case on the technological power it can deliver. Without requiring perfect prescience or a crystal ball, where purpose intended justifies the search, purpose attained is a legitimate measure of the moral implications of today's science. And while scientists do not believe they steer their research toward production of technology, they are quick to seek new technologies for use in their experiments. Often such choices of technology, no less than the choice of a problem, a mathematical framework, or a model system to be studied, become intrinsic defining characteristics of our science. Scientists promote technologies related to their subdisciplines; they even work as straight technologists to develop usable forms of their knowledge. The kind of product our knowledge brings measures science as well as society.

Our story of two crucial developments in modern science, quantum mechanics and molecular genetics, is far from a full-scale archaeology in Foucault's sense. But it demonstrates the possibility for a more complete analysis of underlying assumptions, cross-linkages, and thought-determining conditions. We begin to see the shift from contemplative to manipulative rationality as internalized results of scientists' *moral* choices. The history of physics shows that the interpretation of quantum mechanics derived more from the cultural, social, and ultimately political milieu than from any compelling logical necessity. And the choice of *E. coli* in biology introduced heightened potential danger for humans, not entirely by accident, but from causes inherent in the research of the time including neglect of science's wider purposes, encouragement of ambition over social good, and post-World War II funding conditions.

The tale begins with quantum mechanics. All nuclear science is ultimately predicated on this revolutionary new work produced by German-speaking central European scientists in the 1920s. The decisions they made within theoretical physics have been traced to popular postwar disaffection with mathematical physicists, as exemplars of the approach which drew Germany disastrously into World War I. Paul Forman has argued that an essentially antiscientific *Lebensphilosphie* dominated the Weimar academic milieu. He further asserted that the quantum theory, particularly its interpretation renouncing causality, represents in some important sense an adaptation to that milieu.[22]

This idea strikes introspective theoretical physicists of our time with great force. As undergraduates confronting quantum mechanics, many of us recall the remarkable difference in our instructors' attitudes from that in classical physics. Quantum mechanics is presented as effective, consistent, and correct; but *not* as a simple generalization of common sense. Our courses teach, in effect, that naive truth or falsehood in physics was superseded at the atomic level with the advent of quantum mechanics in 1925 and 1926, and its subsequent probabilistic interpretation (proven two years later)—superseded by the phrase "it works" applied to explanatory propositions and theories—dropping the goal of understanding the world in favor of being able to calculate, predict, and control. And the eventual world-shaking application underscored the power of this intellectual shift. A poet conversant with modern physics put it retrospectively as follows:

> The mathematics and physics men
> Have their mythology; they work alongside the truth,
> Never touching it; their equations are false
> But the things *work*. Or, when gross error appears,
> They invent new ones; they drop the theory of waves
> In universal ether and imagine curved space.
> Nevertheless their equations bombed Hiroshima
> The terrible things *worked*.[23]

The story of this shift in the framing assumptions of physics is a fine example of social influences shaping the very definition of a discipline. In the years 1921 and 1922, virtually all theoretical physicists who spoke before popular and general audiences announced their belief that atomic physics would require the overthrow of causality. This was, as Paul Forman points out, four to five years

before it was "justified" by the advent of a fundamentally acausal quantum mechanics. I contended, moreover, that the scientific context and content, the form and level of exposition, the social occasions and the chosen vehicles for publication of manifestoes against causality, all point inescapably to the conclusion that substantive problems in atomic physics played only a secondary role in the genesis of this acausal persuasion.[24]

Moreover, Forman argues that physicists were responding to political climate and social pressure, rather than the serious philosophical precedents expressed by *Lebensphilosophie*.

Some scientists reject aspects of Forman's interpretation, challenging his characterization of Weimar culture. Others see a weak link in his reliance on physicists' private reactions to popular works. For, at least in the present, physicists think nothing of spicing their colloquia and general talks with all sorts of political or topical nonsense, simply to generate audience interest. Nevertheless it is remarkable that for quantum mechanics enunciation of the interpretation preceded the entire theory (and some of the facts) on which it was based.

That interpretation brought with it a metaphysical debate which remains unresolved to this day. Einstein's later publications show that the real meaning of the move was not to introduce indeterminacy so much as to effect a fundamental redefinition of physics from studying the real world to studying what one can know by *measuring* the universe.[25]

To Einstein, the good of physics resided precisely in its objective ability to comprehend reality, not to manipulate it. Only contemplative rationality could serve the morally commendable goal of pure knowledge. In the light of Forman's analysis, Einstein's choice was to reject the standard science, with its hidden acceptance of political pressure, in favor of older values of objective realism. He would not have put it this way; he did not identify the Copenhagen (acausal) interpretation with world politics, but simply with an epistemological error in science itself— namely, confusing study of what we know with a study of what actually is.* But most physicists could conveniently relegate such issues to philosophy. They substituted their own construction, knowledge of the universe, in the place of the real world itself as object of investigation *without* taking full responsibility for the power of making real that which they would choose to know. The quantum physicists hoped to banish unverifiable analogies and fictions. But moral visions are also fictions, images, and analogies. In bypassing them (as in ignoring the question of *what* to make real) they excluded this whole realm of thought. Without addressing any moral implications, they took quantum mechanics and its interpretation as the very definition of disciplinary excellence.

The consequent events were extraordinary. Quick to apply the "best" new theories to nuclear puzzles (once they solved those of the atomic electrons), physicists hurtled us willy-nilly into a new age, fraught with powerful new dangers. In 1928, barely two years after Born invented the statistical interpretation, Gamow applied quantum mechanics to nuclear physics;[26] in fact, his data on alpha decay happened to start from Uranium-238. In the thirties, experimentalists discovered fission, presaging nuclear energy; the Manhattan Project, triggered by a letter from

*Some new experiments have pushed the limits of Einstein's objections to the level of empirical demonstration (especially those of Aspect and his collaborators in France: cf. *Phys. Rev. Letters* 49 [1982]: 1804.) To me, and to many physicists including coworkers, Anton Zeilinger and Michael Horne, they show that our current understanding is very close to claiming that quantum mechanics fundamentally describes *information about* microphysical systems, rather than the systems themselves. Of all possible macroscopic analogs, information alone behaves like the constructs described by the quantum forumlism. Thus, the last half-century may show us that quantum mechanics is here to stay, but it also underscores the framing questions raised by Einstein.

Einstein to Roosevelt, eventually made World War II our first nuclear war. After the war, we emerged in a world where the physicist-government connection was firm: both Big Physics and Nuclear Power ("safe, clean, too cheap to meter") were born.

Many physicists, looking for new challenge, joined the life scientists in creating molecular biology. Consider Leo Szilard. He first conceived of the chain reaction (reportedly after reading H. G. Wells's prophetic *World Set Free*) in the early thirties, and later discovered neutron multiplication during fission—the effect which makes such reactions possible. His secret patent of the chain reaction (assigned to the British Admiralty) stands as a clever resolution of a scientist's obligation to publish and the human desire to retard Nazi A-bomb development. The invention itself, however, was not obscure enough to make this ploy effective. And his proposed research moratorium foundered when Joliot-Curie refused to suppress French publication of work on uranium fission. Szilard drafted the famous 1939 letter urging President Roosevelt to fund A-bomb research, correctly gauging the prestige and impact of having Einstein, a pacifist, sign it.

During the war, Szilard worked with Enrico Fermi as part of the reactor team who first demonstrated sustained nuclear fission. He later recalled: "There was a crowd there and then Fermi and I stayed there alone. I shook hands with Fermi and I said I thought this day would go down as a black day in the history of "mankind."[27] With Germany's defeat, realizing that the pressing moral reason for the Manhattan Project was gone, he organized those physicists who were not caught up in the final stages of the A-bomb assembly (mainly the Chicago group around him) to urge restraint in its use. His report promoting a "demonstration" went as far as Roosevelt's desk, but the final decision passed to Truman when FDR died.

At war's end, Szilard, who clearly always felt the delicacy of moral decision on the uses of pure science, was one of the most eminent physicists to change fields, study bacteriophages, and help launch molecular biology. His often futile struggle with the morality and politics of nuclear science shows us the possibility of awareness at crucial decision points.* His career, curiously enough, links us to another subject whose technological consequences currently loom large—recombinant DNA.

One of the most disturbing aspects of recombinant DNA experiments is the inherent danger of using *E. coli* bacteria. The choice of this most common human symbiote as the "model system" for genetics carries the moral burden of increasing the risk that deleterious human genes, employed for pure research, may escape the lab in the body of a technician, scientist, janitor, or student and dwell in our midst, inside our bowels. But this organism is actually a virulent pathogen, at least for

*Indeed, part of Szilard's uncanny prescience for the flow of money and prestige into scientific fields probably came from his exquisite elitism—elitism that was perhaps one of the reasons his ethical political actions often failed.

women. Up to 90 percent of urinary infections are caused by *E. coli*, and such infections are a major cause of illness in young women. Yet the most rigorous microbial genetics can be done only in *E. coli*—it is the one organism that molecular biology has studied for forty years. Excellent science requires the control afforded by using a system whose known properties are as extensive as possible when probing the unknown. How did we end up with disciplinary excellence requiring work on such a potentially dangeous subject? (Or equally bizarre—a gaggle of biologists attempting to prove that the scientists' strain, K-12, cannot possibly live or transfer genes outside the lab.)

*Escherichia coli* was the first bacterium shown to have rich "genetics" to study; it was many, many years later that scientists developed recombinant techniques for splicing genes into bacteria. In all those years, every step was taken by researchers motivated in good measure by a wondrous curiosity about life. Still no one investigated the crucial decision— choosing an organism that carried this potentially dangerous development from the outset. How was that choice made?

As a bright, ambitious, medical student at Columbia, Joshua Lederberg conceived of experiments to prove that bacteria exchange genes. He wangled a short-term (elective semester) job in the Yale University laboratories of Professor Tatum shortly after World War II. With the decrease in scientific funding, few large new undertakings could be launched in most departments. Indeed, little equipment and material were left from wartime bacterial projects at the otherwise fruit fly- (and bread mold-) dominated laboratory. Luckily, Tatum had just moved from Stanford and was receptive to expanding research. Lederberg was given a chance at this tedious, rather remote-payoff experiment using the available strains of common human gut bacteria. He was bright, diligent, and lucky, so he found the spectacular result—the *E. coli* K-12 strain seemed to exchange genes just as if they had (rather infrequent) sex!

Lederberg may have been somewhat brash. In any event, he evidently had not perfected all the single-cell techniques he needed when he presented his results as discussion at one of the summer symposia (on quantitative biology) which also served to introduce physicists to molecular biology; a kindly participant apparently took him aside to explain those techniques which his critics implied were necessary.[28] Lederberg did the required checks, submitting his report, and proceeded without hesitation to start mapping the genes of *E. coli* K-12,* pushing the field of bacterial genetics as far and fast as possible in his career path to the Nobel prize.

---

*This is the crucial juncture. As James Watson put it in his text *Molecular Biology of the Gene*, the original reasons for choosing *E. coli* are essentially accidental. Once serious work had started on *E. coli*, however, it obviously made no sense to switch to another organism. But if the externalities which help define excellent science were moral rather than competitive drives, serious work might have started by choosing the right organism.

Only five years later did he pause to publish a survey of possible organisms for bacterial genetics. Several researchers had experienced difficulty in verifying his results on other species and strains of microbe. Lederberg showed in 1951 that his original results were nevertheless valid by demonstrating that his first experiment had worked because, compared to most bacteria, *E. coli* K-12 was quite profligate at sharing genes—it was *prone* to recombination.[29] So part of the reason we now face the danger of man-made recombinant DNA in a human symbiote can be traced to Lederberg's original "good luck."

But this story has a moral dimension too. Knowing the significance of choice of model system, the early bacterial geneticists—Lederberg himself—could have slowed down and done a variant of the 1951 experiment *first*, to search for the best organism. If all the considerations and ultimate purposes of biological research had been weighed, perhaps we would all be safer now. Molecular biology could have defined itself with the paradigm of some plant parasite, or ostrich symbiote, or whatever in the judgment of scientists would serve the highest common good—not merely publication speed or personal striving. By omitting the moral dimension in choosing a model system, the pioneers of molecular biology set the stage for society's current concern over biotechnology. The current debates about safety, regulation, and environmental effects of recombinant DNA research—debates which by now span a decade or more—all come back to the defining moves that established the discipline and chose the organisms to be studied.

In the case of quantum mechanics, the defining shift from "it explains" of classical physics to "it works" inspired a different sort of debate. For many years Einstein argued that quantum mechanics was physically imcomplete, that there were elements of physical reality which it could not represent. Bohr argued that only the actual results of experiments could be considered real—and these results all obey the probabilities given by quantum mechanics. Both Bohr and Einstein realized that physics had discovered a limit to its own knowledge of reality. Neither of them realized that this limit posed questions or moral dimensions: not whether we were slipping from an old morality of objective (and omniscient) knowledge but new questions, questions about knowledge that works: "Works for what?" "For whom?" "Knowledge to what end?"

All of these questions arise because the quantum revolution entailed not merely abandoning a priori definitions of reality (upon which Einstein seemed to insist) but adopting a new direction of gaze as well—one which is self-reflexive of the fact that it involves a choice. Jauch compares the phenomena of nature to random messages, waiting to be deciphered by scientists:

But since the code is not absolute, there may be several messages in the same raw material of the data, so changing the code will result in a message of equally deep significance in something that was merely noise before and *conversely:* In a new code a former message may be devoid of meaning. Thus a code presupposes a free choice among different, complementary aspects, each of which has equal claim to *reality,* if I may use this dubious word.[30]

That physics has found itself selecting a reality may seem striking. For our archaeological approach, however, the cross-linkage of parallel developments in several fields is even more important. We might even say the analysis could only be correct if the realization that we create reality were reached simultaneously in many aspects of modern culture.

And so it is. Contemporary artists now see the present stage (and modern history) of art as focusing onto its role as definer of perception:

There are in aesthetic experience potentially as many "arts" as there are encounters with its incidences in the world. In confusing the art/object of "art" with the subject of art, we objectively tried to hold to the idea of one transcending art. While there is no one transcending "Art," there is one infinite subject: The subject of art is aesthetic perception.[31]

A group of economists speculate that their discipline's mathematical formulations (such as the relationship of unemployment to inflation) are far more freely chosen than previously suspected.[32] In sociology, the fact that obsrvation itself produces some of the phenomena has become quite apparent, *vide* such named interactions as the Hawthorne Effect. Finally, many of those in powerful "thinking-doer" roles (planners, bureaucrats, policy makers, and governmental and corporate decision makers) now realize that most often only the self-fulfilling prophecies, of all their pseudo-mathematical calculations, turn out to be correct. In a very literal sense, the criteria of success for any of their models is "it works."

This self-reflection occurred first in physics. It came into the theory along with the first decisive limit rationality had discovered to its own powers. The Heisenberg Uncertainty Principle acknowledges the circumstance that different—but each perfectly reasonable—experiments on the same atomic system require mutually incompatible measuring apparatus, and treats this situation as a framing postulate. The fullest development of quantum theory then calls each pair of incompatible-to-measure quantities "complementary properties," and reinterprets physics—deleting its original contemplative goal, and with it omitting crucial questions of purpose.

SALVIATI: . . . You will notice that your experimental results being based on immediate facts, are not contradictory by themselves; they *become* so only if you take these facts as evidence for the existence of a *real* property which is supposed to be present independent of any observation and whose existence is only *revealed* by the observation.

SAGREDO: . . . We should thus call them complementary properties which exist only in relation to a detecting instrument. . . . And this is not due to our lack of ingenuity, but it is the very essence of the physical law we are trying to discover.[33]

The state of the universe is unseeable; only the knowledge of an observer becomes accessible. Yet quantum mechanics goes on as though physics had always been only about measurements. The physicist fails to pose the central moral issue: "Since my mind is running into its own scientific limits—not just the limits of heart, soul, and humanity which I know are there, but true limits to knowledge of the world: Can I appeal to the rest of me to restore the program to its original Baconian intention—the urge to match intellectual power with moral outcome?"

This question persists today. Indeed, it extends to many other fields, as they *in turn* discover the theorems and proofs of the limits of scientific intellectuality: Gödel's Incompleteness Theorem for mathematics, the Church-Turing Theorem for automata (computers), Arrow's Theorem for utilitarian economics, Marcuse's analysis of classical sociology,[34] certain postminimal explorations in art.* For each realization of the manipulative possibilities inherent in Reason's gaze, there is a corresponding understanding of the intellect's inherent limits, and for each limitation the deeper moral question of what to investigate next (and how).

We sense ourselves at a discontinuity. Though it has taken three hundred years to strip away the notion of pure inquiry as much as established religion and ancient superstition, we are finally forced to contemplate ourselves and our institutions of knowledge, as Bacon fully intended at the outset.[35] In the next section a start is made: we examine the current situation. Choices made in the very definition of modern scientific fields have also by now shaped the conditions of work. Under those conditions, researchers find themselves arrayed in hierarchy, acting with only part of their full capability and often feeling, or living out, the inherent contradictions caused by the initial omission of moral concerns.

## IV. The Current Situation

Their defining scientific choices inevitably helped shape how physics and modern biology have developed as Big Science. Today, corporate social structures define and limit the human potential of researchers, while the technological offshoots multiply rapidly. Quantum mechanics is basic to all the "high-tech" applications, ranging from nuclear power to polymers to microprocessors, that are shaping our lives as well as our views. If one had to characterize the modern scientific view of our world in a short sentence, "Everything is made of atoms, whose constituents obey quantum mechanics" would be a fair summary. But along with these advances in technology and in world view, the unaddressed moral issues have come back to affect science itself.

---

*David Antin points out that art, like science, has its contemporary manipulative methods as well. The relation to knowing and to morality of artists and of "the work they exhibit and distribute is conditioned solely by the circumstances of exhibiting and discourse." 1980, private communication.

High-energy nuclear physics—heir to the quantum theory—provides some fine examples of the effects of disciplinary rigor as an extreme instance of an advancing "industrial" model of scientific research. Theorists (especially new graduates) face dire prospects for pursuing their craft: few jobs for the present, little hope for long-term career slots, and tremendous danger of having their quest for knowledge converted to a product, weapon, or technology of destruction and dehumanization. Experimentalists work in tight social structures, like that of the team needed to perform the proton scattering described above.

In experimental groups of the 1960s graduate-student wives and older well-educated women reentering the job market after raising their families were frequently employed as scanners to look at photographic tracks of elementary particles. Often they had little knowledge of the experiment or its significance, but only because the levels "above" them—graduate students, postdoctoral scholars, research scientists, and professors—neglected to include them. Among researchers, division of labor became increasingly real—group leaders spending more time procuring grants than ideas, younger professionals finding varied niches as managers of equipment, people, or computing machines. Of course, the sense of alienation from the total "product", of competition and self-aggrandizement overriding knowledge as a goal, and of frustration over lack of recognition all grew.[36] Even the full professors at the top of their miniature empires felt unfulfilled—one went so far as to file suit contending another had used his ideas to win the Nobel prize.[37]

Clearly, in such an environment people increasingly treat each other as objects and impediments—intelligent men and women with rich life histories end up serving menial functions: when automated techniques increased the amount of data one could manage, the lower-level jobs (still largely occupied by educated women) became manual labor—pulling electrical cables into place. So dehumanization of work goes along with the increasing hierarchy.

But what are the effects of such knowledge production? Is this ultimately worse for humanity? The self-aggrandizement and glorification puts theoreticians at a high level—they justify and magnify the importance of their own schemata, *and* are not-so-subtly influenced by the experimentalists' desire for bigger machines, more direct "power."[38] Thus the biennial alternating experimentalists' and theoreticians' ("Rochester") conferences have seemed to embrace open searching for justification for new machines by experimentalists, alternating with theoreticians promoting schemes that need higher energy to check.[39] Addressing the accelerator designers and builders, an experimental physicist joked about it this way:

We work hard in mutual stimulation. You make the machines and we try to use them so well that the need for more machines becomes self-evident. Both of us, of course, working so Gell-Mann and his [theoretician] friends become more and more famous.[40]

And many physicists have pandered to less affirming branches of government: Quarks are promoted as possible future bomb ingredients; accelerators themselves are studied for application to missiles' interception; prominent physicists seek advisory positions (the JASON group during the war in Vietnam); policy-level science advisers, who so fear loss of credibility, provide suggestions (and ultimately thoughts) of distinctly Establishment stripe.

Moreover, the "pure" fundamental laboratories themselves become models of little secret research plants with barbed-wire fences, uniformed guards, and identification systems—not merely as a holdover from war research or the Manhattan Project, but on new installations like the Stanford Linear Accelerator Center as well. Note that both critics and supporters of recombinant DNA techniques have called for increased security measures (and in some cases special, concentrated national facilities) for this research. It seems quite the rule that as hierarchical structures grow, laboratories become less open, free, and penetrable.

The recombinant DNA debate revealed further effects of fossilized social values embedded at the base of modern science. Proponents of relaxed guidelines on these techniques suggested that they could easily guarantee the purity and containment of their experimental bacteria; yet the standard sources of *E. coli* K-12—keepers of the *scientific* duty to maintain a pure strain—now include a note, with samples of one original line, stating that certain extra-viral genes have entered the organism by some unknown event at an uncertain time. Even the supplying laboratories have not been able to prevent gene transfer in the crucial "model system" for recombinant DNA.[41]

The battle over physical containment guidelines also underscores how pressure to release science from safety constraints can undercut prudent procedures. The class of experiments allowed in moderate containment (P2) facilities was broadly expanded when the guidelines were relaxed. In fact the move to relax them was approved by the National Institute of Health's Recombinant DNA Advisory Committee—approved, at what was the first meeting for a sizable number of new members (some of them unaware that important matters might be discussed), on the basis of what critics consider to be insufficiently novel or decisive scientific evidence.[42]

*Implications for Science and Creative Intellectual Work*

In the introduction to this volume, I indicated that my experiences as a policy adviser revealed that many knowledge workers feel quite personally the conflict between disciplinary excellence and social good. How can the reintegration which they desire be achieved?

In each current field and discipline, those who feel this conflict must examine the most fundamental locus for recombining values into the discourse. The proven limitations to knowledge may provide an opening for such recombination. As we have seen, physics finds itself creating reality precisely in those interactions which investigate physical phenomena—measurements. Similarly, the numbers in Gödel's Proof are used as coded representatives of proofs about the number system; the social scientists of Hawthorne study a system within a system—the plant under investigation and the social interactions with themselves that come along with such a study. Perhaps this self-reflection is the proper place to seek an entrée for values. Precisely where a discipline begins to analyze itself it must analyze its purposes and the uses to which it is put.

Fortunately, science provides areas of *current* interest where the issues of limitations to knowledge can be addressed. With understanding that all knowledge, however theoretical, may have its eventual applications, with the right social relations to one's coworkers, and with attention to the image of reality that one is constructing, working on something related to self-reflection or limitations to knowledge may begin the reconstructive process. Consider again quantum mechanics, where the problems of measurement theory remain unresolved after more than fifty years: How much does the experimenter control reality? What attributes of the experimenter are relevant for the exercise of this control? How different would physics be if *more* of the experimenter were allowed into the science, if more of the motivations and societal connections were considered part of the experiment itself? These are some of the questions that can now be posed within the discipline of physics.

One theoretical physicist, Asher Peres, has even gone so far as to publish his thought that the decision of which property to make real—out of two complementary properties—can be determined by experimenter choice even after a measurement has been made.[43] This requires, he says, merely that the proper precautions be taken not to lose any initial information; according to Peres, such percautions can be taken in principle, only if the experimenter (read *society* or *the funder*) is willing to pay enough! This suggests a rather nice research program, right in my branch of physics, touching very directly upon the widest implications of a constructed reality.

Indeed, each of us can begin to consider the questions to address, the avenues for reexaming values which frame inquiry directly within our work. We may begin to form cross-disciplinary groups to discuss the issues raised by knowledge which "works," and to bring those considerations back into the laboratory, workshop, or studio. In every field, the task of reuniting personal impulse with social motivation begins by taking responsibility for one's daily life, one's own little subdiscipline. The struggle to connect ultimate purposes with normal work will prevent obvious inhumanities, while it confronts the larger society. We need friends (not competitors) to do science if the reality it creates is to value friendship; our coworkers must be equals if we really prize equality; all must be involved who are touched by our thought, if our ideals are consensual. And we must all examine the specifics of scientific experiments, research programs, and collections of research programs: Do they set examples for a truly free, nonbureaucratic, nonpolice-dominated, or nonsecurity-dominated future?

Faced with some of the dangers spawned by science, our civilization must ask these forgotten questions—perhaps we can use the proven limits to an older, simpler view of knowledge finally to fuse our great technical skill with equally great ideals of openness, humanitarianism, and benefit to all the peoples of the world. To contemplate the alternative is such a bleak endeavor that we must hope new wisdom, from new ways of knowing, will soon become developed.[44]

## Notes

1. This eponym was suggested some years ago by Professor J. Needham in private conversation.

2. J. M. Jauch, *Are Quanta Real?* (Bloomington: Indiana University Press, 1973), 58.

3. Nigel Calder, *The Key to the Universe* (New York: Viking Press, 1977), 97 (hereafter cited as *Key to the Universe.*)

4. Jauch, *Are Quanta Real?* 59.

5. J. A. Wheeler and R. P. Feynman, "Classical Electrodynamics in Terms of Direct Inter-Particle Action," *Reviews of Modern Physics* 21 (1949): 425–34.

6. Albert Einstein, in *Albert Einstein, Philosopher-Scientist*, ed. P. A. Schlipp (LaSalle, Ill.: Open Court, 1970), 392 (hereafter cited as *Albert Einstein.*)

7. Francis Bacon, Preface to "Novum Organum," in *The New Organon and Related Writings*, ed. F. M. Anderson (New York: Bobbs-Merrill, 1960), 25 (hereafter cited as *The New Organon*).

8. A. D. Kirsch, "The Spin of the Proton," *Scientific American* 240 (May 1979): 72.

9. Ibid. 77.

10. Joshua Lederberg, "Research: The Promethean Dilemma," in *Hippocrates Revisited*, ed. Roger J. Bulger (New York: Medcom Press, 1973), 164.

11. Cf., e.g., Imre Lakatos and Alan Musgrave, eds., *Criticism and the Growth of Knowledge* (London: Cambridge University Press, 1970), references cited therein; and certain works of Scriven, Hanson, Coppi, and Margenau, among many others. The notion of science (indeed of scientific fact) as human creation has by now reached to popularizers' works. Consider Gunther Stent's *Scientific American* article on creativity or prematurity in art and science, or the following quotation from Douglas R. Hofstadter's engaging book, *Gödel, Escher, Bach: An Eternal Golden Braid* (New York: Basic Books, 1978), 695. "My feeling is that the process by which we decide what is valid or what is true is an art; and that it relies as deeply on a sense of beauty and simplicity as it does on rock-solid principles of logic or reasoning or anything else which can be objectively formalized."

12. Jacob Bronowski, "The Disestablishment of Science," in *The Biological Revolution: Social Good or Social Evil?* ed. W. Fuller (New York: Anchor, 1972), 311, 314.

13. Freeman Dyson, *Disturbing the Universe* (New York: Harper & Row, 1979), 5.

14. This remarkable career summarizes one detailed in John McPhee's *The Curve of Binding Energy* (New York: Farrar, Strauss & Giroux, 1974).

15. Philip Hilts, "Lord of the Rings," *Science 80* 1 (January 1980): 55.

16. Theodore Lowi & Benjamin Ginsberg, *Poliscide* (New York: Macmillan, 1976).

17. I first learned of this intriguing connection from the text of a lecture by Thomas K. Simpson, "The Scientific Revolution Will Not Take Place," given at St. John's College, Annapolis, Maryland, on 27 January 1978.

18. Francis Bacon, *The Advancement of Learning and Novum Organum* (New York: John Wiley, 1944), 306–7.

19. Bacon, *The New Organon*, 15.

20. Some philosophers see the great scope for creation in science and still call for a union (or at least cohabitation) between religion and science. See, e.g., Mary B. Hesse, *Science and the Human Imagination* (London: SCM Press, 1954), 161.

21. Cf. that "Archaeology of the Human Sciences" written by Michel Foucault, *The Order of Things* (New York: Randon House, 1973), especially in the Foreword of the English edition, pp. xi–xiv.

22. Paul Forman, "Weimar Culture, Causality, and Quantum Theory, 1918–1927," in *Historical Studies in the Physical Sciences* 3 (1971): 1–115 (hereafter cited as "Weimar Culture").

23. Robinson Jeffers, "The Beginning and the End," as quoted by H. Arthur Klein in *Physics Today* 30 (January 1977): 85.

24. Forman, "Weimar Culture," 110.

25. A. Einstein, B. Podolsky, and N. Rosen, "Can Quantum-Mechanical Description of Physical Reality Be Considered Complete?" *Physical Review* 47 (May 1935): 777.

26. G. Gamow, "Zur Quantentheorie des Atomkernes" ("Quantum Theory of the Atomic Nucleus"), *Zeitschrift fur Physik* 51 (1928): 204–12. In the same year, A. E. Ruark proposed nuclear double-gamma emission as a "Critical Experiment on the Statistical Interpretation of Quantum Mechanics," *Proceedings of the National Academy of Science* 14 (1928): 328–30. The theoreticians' impulse to apply new approaches is underscored by the fact that even the basic constituents of nuclei remained unknown until the discovery of the neutron in 1932.

27. R. Weart and G. W. Szilard, eds., *Leo Szilard: His Version of the Facts* (Cambridge: MIT Press, 1979).

28. André Lwoff criticized the apparent loophole of nongenetic transfer of biologically active products in Lederberg's experiments. Dr. Max Zelle actually instructed Lederberg to do the single-cell isolation work necessary. Private communication of memoirs from Lederberg, 1976.

29. Joshua Lederberg, "Prevalence of *Escherichia coli* Strains Exhibiting Genetic Recombination," *Science* 114 (1951): 68. This experiment checked whether a mutated K-12 variety could exchange genes with strains from chickens (1 in approximately 40 did) and from human urine cultures (8 to 16 out of 100).

30. Jauch, *Are Quanta Real?* 64.

31. Robert Irwin, "Notes Toward a Model," in *Robert Irwin Catalog* (New York: Whitney Museum of American Art, 1977), 31.

32. L. Rapping and J. Crotty, private communication. Briefly, they contend that the actual data are insufficiently precise to fix a relationship between any two variables. Moreover, which data to collect is under partial control of the discipline; and the provision of a large research budget (coupled with good will of the economics fraternity) in time would be sufficient to establish alternative, equally well-founded, theoretical interdependencies.

33. Jauch, *Are Quanta Real?* 81.

34. E.g., "in Weber, the analysis of bourgeois reason negates itself in its consummation." Herbert Marcuse, *Negations* (Boston: Beacon Press, 1969), 221.

35. "He vigorously called attention to the lack of verified and verifiable knowledge about the whole realm of nature, and he made it unmistakably clear that the realm of nature included man and man's institutions." Hugh G. Dick, Introduction to *Selected Writings of Francis Bacon* (New York: Random House, 1955), xxi.

36. Stories of jealous recrimination and undercutting have been current in particle physics, as in most prestigious endeavors, for many years. At present, however, such behavior is becoming part of the popular folklore of the field. See, e.g., Calder, *Key to the Universe,* 102.

37. Charges that Owen Chamberlain would not have discovered the antiproton without Oreste Piccioni's ideas apparently were dropped in 1974. The last of three court hearings led to a finding that the legal time for remedy (for an alleged wrong committed circa 1955) had passed. Acknowledgment in the prize winner's acceptance speech (one of just two design suggestions named in the text) stands out for its specificity and mildness: "The use of magnetic lenses was suggested to us by Dr. Oreste Piccioni, who pointed out that a greater number of useful particles would pass through the system if lenses were employed." Owen Chamberlain, "The Early Antiproton Work," in *Physics Nobel Lectures* (New York: Elsevier, 1964), 494.

38. A few years ago, *Physics Letters* impressed me that the role of theorist in justifying new equipment has spread to all branches of physics. A mere hint by my coauthor (of a paper on neutron interference) that experimentalists interested in very slow neutrons had found our paper useful as argument for an Ultra-Cold Neutron Interferometer helped convince the journal to publish our work. Before that, he had been exchanging comments inconclusively with the referee for several months.

39. Fuller analysis of such alternation would make a wonderful study. Primary sources include issue number 3 of alternate volumes of the IEEE *Transactions on Nuclear Science,* e.g., NS–18 (1971): 46; NS–20 (1973): 1045, etc. The justification for higher energy machines also reaches a general scientific audience (cf., e.g., D. J. Miller, "Longer Perspectives in Neutrino Physics," *Nature* 280 [1979]: 192) and in subtle ways informs wider public dissemination (as in the final paragraphs of Sheldon I. Glashow's "The Hunting of the Quark," *New York Times* Magazine, 18 July 1976, 37). Andrew Pickering's *Constructing Quarks* (Chicago: University of Chicago Press. 1984) begins the job of showing how social construction of physics' reality proceeds.

40. Leon M. Lederman, "The Next Step: Accelerators Versus Storage Rings," in *Proceedings, Ninth International Conference on High Energy Accelerators,* 650.

41. A. M. Reiner, private communication.

42. Bruce Levin, private communication. The report of committee "packing" made its way to our scientific community via Roger Lewin's columns in the British journal, *New Scientist.* As for compliance with guidelines, by now several cases of corner-cutting (impossibly quick publication after a moratorium ended, leaving one university post for another where enforcement was lax, etc.) have become public, often via *Science* magazine's coverage.

43. A. Peres, "Can We Undo Quantum Measurements?" *Physical Review D 22* (1980): 879.

44. My thanks for helpful discussions go to all who were involved with the

conferences on reconstructive knowledge, especially Marcus Raskin, Robert Irwin, Mary Bernstein, and Evelyn Fox Keller. Special thanks are in order for criticism, suggestions, and discussion of particular topics to Eleanor Dube, Paul Forman, Everett Hafner, Anton Zeilinger, Leonard Rapping, Anne Truitt, Helen Smith, Michael Horne, Jack Schaar, Allan Krass, David Antin, and Jan Raymond. Despite all this help, whatever errors remain in the work are mine. I gratefully acknowledge the support of the National Endowment for the Humanities Chairman's grant, and a Mina Shaughnessy Scholarship (Fund for the Improvement of Post-Secondary Education). I prepared this essay for publication during my Kellogg National Fellowship (Kellogg Foundation).

# 3

# Toward a Reconstructive Political Science

MARCUS G. RASKIN & HERBERT J. BERNSTEIN

Knowledge workers are the linchpins of modern society. Their tasks relate to taking bodies of information, other people's insights, words and analyses and applying them in ways which create new insights, information, images, and ideas. Knowledge workers may find themselves in a bureaucracy, university, or scientific laboratory, in a newspaper office, or a law firm. Their subject matter itself could be virtually anything.

To say what knowledge workers do is to recognize that they create the basis of modern life. Whether in the laws we write, the psychological categories we accept, or the attitudes and perceptions we have towards others not directly involved with us face to face, whether in the inventions of destruction we fear, the information we receive on how the universe and economy appear and work, knowledge workers have spun the web of our consciousness and belief world. Their knowledge web shapes our material reality.

Since knowledge workers exist in the context of a power matrix, they are usually responsible to and responsive towards an "employer" or some seemingly autonomous institution that sets the framework in which they perform their tasks. In many circumstances knowledge workers, whether lowly bureacrats or Henry Kissinger, usually articulate or rationalize the desires of the powerful. Scientists also are similarly "determined," although there is less willingness to recognize this situation.

The unwritten assumption of modern science is that scientific knowledge workers could actually escape the framing conditions of their work by their "pure" discoveries which would add to progress and understanding. This situation has never obtained. One reason that scientists and technologists have not been wholly successful in getting their own agenda is their requirement of capital. The more capital the scientists needed for their work, the more intertwined these knowledge workers became in the prevailing power system.

Today the social division of labor reflects the system of knowledge generated by knowledge workers. Marxist analysis of the capitalist division assumes that the knowledge process derives from the social division of labor, which is itself grounded in society's material conditions. But as the Ehrenreichs, Andre Gorz, and others have maintained, there is a shift in modern society's material conditions. They recognize that the traditional Marxist view of class structure must change, because the division of labor is now based on knowledge power as well as physical power. The result, of course, is that the new class of knowledge workers could have direct positive effects in the shaping of modern life.

For this to happen there must be self- and group-consciousness beyond usually defined views of economic interest or personal ambition. By consciousness we mean knowledge workers gaining moral awareness of what they do and political awareness that they do not have to be dependent on aggregates of violence or capital. Knowledge workers can be more than hired brains. They can reach out to manual workers and to the dispossessed once they comprehend what is required to change their situation. They can transform the laboratory, university, the "defense" establishment, and the business corporation in ways which have positive, life-affirming results,* for the work of this class frames the future. Consequently, they (and all of us) need to recognize that the social organization of modern life can be reconstructed through ideas and the radical critique of ideas. This transforming, creative work we call political science, with an intentional play on words. We mean to address both political theory *and* the political dimension of modern (scientific) knowledge.

In the sense of political philosophy, reconstructive political science recognizes the centrality of the relationship between politics and science. Although supposedly independent, the two are intertwined, currently moving us toward unprecedented disaster for humankind. Yet science remains the paramount avenue for great intellectual advances; and politics is the arena for potential social reconstruction. So those with political consciousness must reexamine science, and scientists must work with greater understanding of politics.

To put it quite plainly, knowledge is thoroughly political itself and crucial to social decisions. Power and knowledge are virtually synonymous. Practically every issue requires investigation not merely of the scientist's object of study (or of the technologist's production) but of the entire relationship between the knowledge worker and the object. Every

---

*When finance and industrial capitalists claim that there is a "capital shortage," when they seek more funds for their personal enjoyment or their business schemes, they are projecting a double fear. In this regard, the Reagan administration has reflected the business sensibility. The first fear is that there is a shift of power away from their own class to a new class, which is not a working or dependent class in the old sense. Second, they fear the bureaucratic role, which, for example, extends social welfare or education funds thereby denying capital to the rich for their purposes. Politically, the short-sighted bourgeois fear that those with a surplus of consciousness will join together with those who have a surplus of pain. This is not a farfetched fear. Suppose social workers began—as they often have—to see their concerns politically and professionally standing with welfare recipients rather than as social control agents. Suppose inner-city educators took the empowering goals of Freire and Dewey as their aims, in place of tracking, maintaining discipline and training for nonexistent or demeaning jobs. Suppose economists asserted that scarcity is *not* the central principle of modern relationships and that distribution *is*, thus embarking on a rethinking of the moral premises of their profession.

"event" or "phenomenon" or "datum" replicates a broad social and historical determination; and each such socially constructed event shapes future consequences. Our essay calls for a science suited to this historical condition.

The *political* science we favor is one which will help the practitioners of the disciplines realize their power and the ethical-practical effects of the world view—the reality—they consciously or unintentionally create. The advance of science must be upheld, rather than discarded. Scientists bear responsibility to make their creations (both technologies and concepts) nurture humankind, rather than destroy it. This political science is to be continuously and dialogically involved in moral inquiry. There are no questions which are divorced from moral and ethical concerns— or from concerns of power. Even the most abstract of thought today reflects questions about power and moral relevance. As Davis and Hersh put it in *The Mathematical Experience.*

One began to hear it said that World War I was the chemists' war, World War II was the physicists' war, World War III (may it never come) will be the mathematicians' war. With this there entered in the general consciousness the full realization that mathematics is inevitably bound up in the general fabric of life, that mathematics is good or bad as people make it so, *and that no activity of the human mind can be free from moral issues.*[1] [emphasis added]

Without knowing the right answer or knowing in advance the correct ethical proposition to apply to particular cases, one still must recognize that each activity of the mind has an ethical and political dimension which must be teased out for its implications and consequences. The proposed political science would build on certain invariances, notably an *empathic invariance,* which sees oneself in the eyes of the Other, and which therefore secures limits and boundaries for human action. It would begin the difficult task of transforming social roles and organization for the recognition of the Other.

The tools for such a task implicitly exist in a variety of current discourses. The deconstructionist method now so prominent in the humanities holds one key. It breaks open "stubborn, irreducible" facts to comprehend their value assumptions. This method gains epistemological-ethical force when combined with social scientists' insights on the social construction of reality.* This continuous social process, which transforms values into facts, in turn requires anthropological analysis of knowledge production.

Such an analysis would allow us to see science and technology as a ritualized process, mythologized, serving human and organizational purposes, some doubtful, others laudatory. Simultaneously, the reconstructive analysis reveals the places where a new moral impetus may

---

*Quantum mechanical experiments of the past few years have also revealed the nature of reality construction in microphysics. In testing predictions of quantum theory for pairs of correlated photons, scientists have shown that their own measurement choices create a strongly interconnected reality on the microscopic level.

move; they are located at historic branch points, in fundamental assumptions, and in the social structures of the disciplines.

Political science must understand the "local" and "global" framing questions of scientific inquiry set against ethical axioms which themselves are constantly analyzed. This encourages people to become aware of the questions they refuse to ask or are unaware of, as well as those socially (but foolishly) defined assumptions which divide one discipline of knowledge from another, including political science itself. Its reformulation goes behind the distribution of power to the relationship between science and politics. That relationship will determine whether dignity and liberation are possible or merely another costly shattered illusion of a humankind fated to an unrelenting tragic destiny. Ironically, ambiguity may be our ally in avoiding such a destiny, once we recognize the mythical and cloudy nature of our most rigorous thoughts.

In 1908 Arthur Lovejoy pointed out that there were thirteen different definitions of pragmatism; a similar situation holds for reconstructive knowledge. When searching for new intellectual and political routes there must be toleration of a variety of approaches to the same insight in service of common purpose. Coalition is an essential ingredient in the discussion for new insights into knowledge; ambiguity can help build coalition among knowledge workers who are alienated from the root assumptions or from the social organization of their disciplines. Groups of workers who begin reconstructing knowledge together will also make coalition with broader social movements whose impetus towards liberation constitutes, in fact, the same cultural transformation as that of knowledge.

Discussion, indeed dialogue, is the natural form to explore coalition and reconstructive knowledge. This article reflects that generative process. It means to be an exhortation as well as an essay on a new political science. Its discontinuities and juxtapositions to the effect of a meditation or of conversational leaps, intentionally depart from the ruling methodology of linear exposition. We hope the following synopsis will help the reader sufficiently guide his or her thoughts to understand our own:

The first section begins with the current analysis, namely the philosophy of science, supplying some of the needed political links. We question some of the framing postulates of the philosophy of science, especially pointing to the problem of its "apolitical" approach to the bases of knowledge. In this section, we pose a fourth option to the three other positions in the philosophy of science: the skeptical, demarcationist, and elitist positions outlined by Imre Lakatos. Of necessity, our analysis parallels these schools'. Yet we do not consider our work to be (nor would our critics) a philosophy of science. Our purpose in this essay is more general. We would suggest however to philosophers of science that an analysis of objective knowledge and epistemology should be expanded to include analysis of belief, political power, and ethics. Studies of science must make explicit their own historicity. This we believe is the only way now available to fulfill Bacon's and Descartes' hope that science would lead to happiness and progress for humankind. Our time requires philosophers themselves to analyze what metaphors and myths are built in support of science, what interests are served, and what values promoted. And they must instruct a political science to do the same.

The present essay holds to this standard, too. We do not view ourselves as solely engaged in naming, describing, and understanding. We therefore explore the values upon which we base our thoughts. The section on values is followed by a discussion of method: this shift within our paper—in effect from the "high ground" of abstract philosophy to the "lower" mode of lived values—is an object lesson in reconstructive methods. We suggest that personal issues and motives, to the extent they can be known, are integral parts of knowledge generation and its accompanying power/desire dimensions. A new political science will colocate these motives and personal issues in relation to the actual scientific and epistemological formulation. Everyone's value cards must be laid on the table.

Because the reconstructive mode recognizes myth and belief elements as central to scientific inquiry (especially in its explanations and in the reasons that it ascribes to causes for things and actions), the method of a reconstructive political science is one which includes self-awareness and consciousness. Such awareness necessarily leads to a continuous open critical examination of the direction that knowledge inquiries move: Why are certain things "seen" and not others? What are the class, sex, and race biases and implications of certain forms of knowledge? What are the possibilities of distortion in practice of certain inventions and "discoveries"? What is the language system of metaphor and the power system of domination that feeds and is sustained by present science? Why does current science favor reductionism rather than wholism?

As part of this set of questions, some stated, others implicit, we discuss the myths of new ways of knowing, including traditionalist, feminist, and highly critical modern mythic interpretations of science. We conclude this section with the myth of reconstructive knowledge—one which goes beyond the reassembling of given pieces, to incorporation of the human good which we believe to be intertwined with a nonstatic egalitarian interdependence. This, we argue, is compatible, indeed, congruent with a rigorous moral epistemology, which brings us back to our starting point—the need for a political science that can help everyone analyze and transform his or her situation.

We ask you, the reader, to help by continuing a chain of creativity that will give all of us the knowledge, insights, and ideas to move beyond our deteriorating social crisis. If you are tied to a discipline you must begin to reconstruct it. If you are not, you must look for a new locus of concern, something beyond even interdisciplinary work, which in the final analysis merely adds together the individual deformations and paradoxes of current disciplines. One last point. It is time to be hortatory, analytic, rigorous, emotional, insightful, and dialogic. In other words, human.

## I. The Analysis of Science

In thinking about reconstructive knowledge we must consider two types of knowledge. One we may refer to as colonizing knowledge. The other we may refer to as deep knowledge.

The first calls for a thorough reconstruction, an act of dismantling and reassembling the research results which justify domination of the few over the many, of white over nonwhite, and of man over woman. The second requires, in addition, a more far-reaching change; the reconstructive knowledge of our title would generate knowledge in new ways. It would be dedicated to self-examination and continual reconstruction.

Thus, when we talk about the reconstruction of colonizing knowledge, we are concerned with those areas of life which are already framed by "rational" decision and the hidden hand of bureaucratic authority whether by the corporation or state. For example, recent works by Philip Green and Stephen Jay Gould have begun to reconstruct an important but intellectually questionable area of thought, namely, psychological testing. Through them one understands the attempt to rationalize behavior, pigeonhole people, and assign them proper places in the social hierarchy.

Reconstruction goes beyond analysis of the use of knowledge; it shows how—in the way that certain questions do *not* get asked, thought about, or researched—attempts are made to control the future for the same institutions, forces, and vested interests that have brought humankind to a near collapse. Colonizing knowledge, perhaps best reflected at its most sophisticated and distorted form in the so-called policy sciences, is employed to rationalize institutions and behaviors in such a way that political, ethical questions (as well as questions of power distribution between people) do not have to be dealt with. For example, deterrence theories of defense, clothed in mystery and quantitative data, make it possible not to question their fundamental foolishness, nor the irrationality and bias of the social system which created the theories. Denominating antivivisectionists as "kooks" smothers in advance the qualms of novice and graduate students about destroying hundreds of living creatures for each footnote. Children rebellious of authority are now labelled hyperactive, assuring that such a label becomes a usable category of description in the psychological sciences. Such labels and theories are deployed with the end of keeping authority and the distribution of power intact.

Another, if more mundane, purpose of colonizing knowledge stays hidden, namely the reinforcement of hierarchic power. As Marcuse has pointed out, this notion may be applied to technical reason itself:

. . . the very concept of technical reason is perhaps ideological. Not only the application of technology but technology itself is domination (of nature and men)—methodical, scientific, calculated, calculating control. Specific purposes and interests of domination are not foisted upon technology "subsequently" and from the outside; they enter the very construction of the technical apparatus. Technology is always a historical social project: in it is projected what a society and its ruling interests intend to do with men and things. Such a "purpose" of domination is "substantive" and to this extent belongs to the very form of technical reason.[2]

The rationality of domination, reflected in the way science and technology are made, is an approach which also permeates deep knowledge, knowledge which is usually thought of as reflective of the actual way the world—and universe—work, irrespective (as far as possible) of man's footprints on them. But it cannot be easily denied that the way man has approached thinking about the universe has had its roots in man's need to dominate or conquer. And here we intentionally place emphasis on those male social structures that define the public social space which themselves assert conventionally male patterns of behavior. This situation is not accidental, as Evelyn Fox Keller has shown; and it results in the skewing of understanding.

The question which has puzzled some philosophers (and which is no longer a question for the few) is whether there is another way to "do" science and technology in order to escape the problem inherent in the notion of conquering nature. There are those who believe, as Habermas points out, that social emancipation "could not be conceived without a complementary revolutionary transformation of science and technology themselves." He analyzed Marcuse as seeking a new, nonpower-oriented science "familiar in Jewish and Protestant mysticism of the 'resurrection of fallen nature.' "[3]

But if Marcuse's insight is correct, namely that it is the link of technology and science to established power which produces autonomous forms of domination and exploitation, then the ability to break the hold of domination can be found through the analysis and reconstruction of science and technology—a task which the German idealists, namely Heidegger and the Frankfurt School, did not undertake. The thoroughgoing reconstruction of which we speak moves beyond inquiring into the social determinants of science and technology; through such reconstruction deep knowledge is also to be relocated, both for its own sake and as the means to catalyze reconstructive social processes.

While the technical and scientific system may be legitimized by power in the first instance, in the second instance the results of science and technology tend to transcend the social system from which they were spawned. The result is that the social system itself changes radically. This apparent autonomy of technology can spur demands for control. Thus, for example, in the United States various technicians and scientists may favor Right fundamentalist causes and a stable social system as the answer to the social turbulence and dislocation created by science and technology.

But the Right's attempts at social reaction are doomed precisely because productive and intellectual forces of science and technology generate change. These forces are strong enough to shape a social system that conforms to them, making it all the more important to reject the "imperative" that scientific and technological work be autonomous. Instead, such work should concern itself directly with ethics and political consequences in all its aspects. But today this is not done: neither in scientific and technical work nor in the traditional disciplines studying science.

Such disciplines as the history of science, philosophy of science, and sociology of knowledge are themselves part of the structure one must study. *They,* like their subjects, the current natural and social sciences, more nearly represent the raw data for reconstruction than the tools of analysis. Moreover, the questions that are fundamental to understanding ourselves and the universe cannot fall into a single discipline *at a time.* One feels this quite immediately when a child asks (in a myriad of specific questions), "What is the stuff of the universe?" Any answer in a particular discipline is too short; such questions can only be approached by escaping the currently imposed boundaries and by avoiding reductions of knowledge—whether for a child or for an entire civilization.

And yet we cannot avoid traditional approaches, for we cannot escape history. We must, if we *reason,* relate to these current modes of discourse. We seek to show why certain utterances and moves are taken to be valid—ironically, this will be classified as touching exactly those disciplines it most seeks to surmount. But if our work delves into the present modes, it is also accompanied by self-reflections and emerges with a different perspective.

One way to proceed is to enumerate, along lines that a philosopher of science might have enunciated a few years ago, several different ways of looking at the sciences and/or social sciences. The reader may wonder why such categorizations are anything but trivial academic concerns, games that intellectuals play.

Our view is quite the contrary. These categories have profound implications for the organization of modern society and the relations among people. Each way of organizing and *viewing* the knowledge process could either slow down, speed up, or ensure humankind's end within the period of a century. We do not believe that the first three views that we shall describe speak satisfactorily to this overriding problem. It is our belief that the reconstructive mode has such a chance. Each mode reflects a different way of organizing society and relations among people. Each has profound political implications. The three standard views can be found in modern societies, with the second and third being dominant.

We refer to the three as skeptical, demarcationist, and elitist positions.

To these we would add the reconstructive. In our view, *it* is the one whose process and purpose is necessary to assist the reconstruction of society. Conversely, social reconstruction is necessary if a new reconstructive knowledge is to continue and thrive. Here are capsule summaries of these four views with names of philosophers who exemplify them. We are indebted to Lakatos's work for this schema.[4]

1. Skeptical (Feyerabend). Any knowledge method, any investigation, any world view or descriptive system is as good as any other. This is analogous to an ACLU/New Left political position: "Let 1,000 flowers bloom, including the weeds." Under this dictum astrology is as good as astronomy; alchemy as good as chemistry; and racism, if it adopts "rigorous" standards of proof, is to be supported in social research (like that on heritability of IQ) as well as nonracism. In other words, there are no communal standards, whether of a moral, political, or scientific nature. Feyerabend holds the traditional anarchist view about political power.

2. Demarcationist (Popper, Lakatos). There are special rules of proof and procedure which distinguish science from all other human activities. These separate good science from bad science. They distinguish astronomy from astrology, the flowers from the weeds, and put the imprimatur on astronomy and flowers over astrology and weeds. The demarcation criteria are known to scientists but appreciated by nonscientists. The demarcationist need not believe, but must assume that there is a reality and a definite, unchanging rational way to know that reality. To be understood, reality must be cut up into problems. The demarcationist position appropriates the moral terms Good and Bad for this supposedly objective way of doing things. The demarcationist asserts willingness to be proved wrong in his or her theories—if conventional, "accepted" methodologies are used to do so. While scientific results may be questioned, the methodology of science is doctrinal.

3. Elitist (Polanyi). Only scientists can know good science from bad science and appreciate the criteria for distinguishing between the two; indeed, only they can truly understand the methods or results of modern specialized fields. One reason a scientist-philosopher's name appears in brackets is that scientists alone (and good ones at that, who are of course too busy with important science to do philosophy until later in life)[5] are competent to make these distinctions. In the United States science is administered as if position number 2 were correct, for it maintains a science bureaucracy, which in turn uses position number 3 ("peer review") in order to distribute grants and prizes.

These three positions govern the flow of resources from political bodies to knowledge workers. They also have political implications for the distribution of power in a society. The first asserts a social world of anarchy without addressing the uneven distribution of power and the danger that certain ideologies and myths of reality have for human destruction when they are linked to power. The latter two views—

demarcationist and elitist—also have profound implications for the nature of society.

Both accept the principle of expertise. From family relations to traffic flow, from missile command to social policy, there are appropriate experts, with special expertise, to whom one invariably defers. Both also assume an Aristotelian and Platonic view. That is, they accept an antidemocratic theory of statecraft in which there are political experts with "technique" whose task it is to "harmonize" and "orchestrate" the different elements of society.[6]

These experts all serve established interests, in effect adding management of democracy and management of nature as separate branches of expertise. And each branch of expertise relies upon the proliferating store of accumulated knowledge, a store provided by the enterprise of dedicated knowledge workers.

The present division of knowledge assumes that wisdom and ethics are neither in the democracy (the people as a whole) nor in work roles, whether they be those of the shoemaker, the nuclear physicist, or the builder. To the extent they are thought to reside anywhere, it is with men of established power, who supposedly act for the whole. But in modern life there is virtually no one who considers the whole, or even tackles the issue of "objective knowledge" in the social context: what are the consequences of knowledge or "information"? Who has it, how is it stored, and does it have any liberatory meaning?

Such attempts as are made, through systems theorists, also end as justification for established power. And those with established power, whether the industrialists, or the landed gentry, or bankers, act out of interest against the whole. They help to arrange the structure of society in such a way that the appearance of democracy exists, and the common good is applauded. But at heart such democracy is ornamental, to serve the few, their needs and purposes. Knowledge is pursued for power and its traditional distribution.

4. Reconstructive. The fourth view seeks to transform the concerns and boundaries of science by returning it to a humanistic activity and by analyzing its roots either in faith or political power. The reconstructive view holds that scientific work is a project like any other activity. To the extent that science seeks power, separating any specific explanation of natural or social phenomena from meaning without acknowledging human attributes (such as love, happiness, despair, or hatred), the scientific and technological enterprise will cause profound and debilitating human problems. It will mask more than it tells us about the universe and ourselves. In rejecting the idea of "purity of science," we as adherents of reconstruction ask that inquiry begin from the heuristic that scientific descriptions of the world and universe be recognized as social and rhetorical myths of persuasion. Therefore, because they are social constructions and because they construct our image of the world, they may be judged ethically. (Ethics itself becomes a "tool" which can be

dialogically and critically examined for its consequences: in other words, we take a pragmatic view of the good or bad effects of the objects men and women make and the myths they create.)

As such, reconstruction tests the proposition that all knowledge has cultural functions; and the most needed and important knowledge in our present crisis is that knowledge which simultaneously informs and helps people to center themselves. Presently, the character of such centering, where it is attempted, is too limited or itself deformed. The public interest community, for example, currently works in conventional categories, wherein the powerful and the wielders of traditional assumptions of science define the problems. This points to a clear distinction between liberal programmatic reform and real reconstruction: the latter always considers as variable the framing postulates which reform accepts as given.

On the other hand, the Maoist and Bolshevik projects to make science fulfill particular social goals of production can only end in misery. The communist view has been that while science is or can be autonomous, it should be turned through social organization (or in its methodology) to social good by overall police control of society. We believe liberating social reconstruction rules out such instrumentalist *direction* of science and technology as if they were entities separable from society.

In our own society, the most dangerous partial truth about science and technology is belief in their neutrality. This is especially obvious in technology, for the act of making things is laden socially with import.

From this point of view, the common position that technology is neutral logically requires the prior stance that it is autonomous of the personal and social intention which produces it. Only by ignoring the web of connections binding us together in modern times can instruments be divorced from intentions. And only by considering aberrant and intended uses on the same plane can instruments seem to be morally neutral.

Each completed object made through human endeavor embodies a set of accumulated ethical principles just as it embodies accumulated labor. Hence, one type of deformed knowledge is a technology with built-in contradictions to its ethical use and producer's intention. The kitchen knife has a range of normal or intended use. Within that range, it may be an embodiment of moral knowledge—good knowledge. (Even vegetarians would presumably accept the kitchen knife as a tool for cutting celery.) But outside the normal or intended range, where it is used to murder, even the kitchen knife can represent a deformed knowledge, an object of questionable and possibly evil purpose. People immediately recognize an aberrant situation when a technical implement is used against its intention and function.

*On the other hand, the production, preparation and use of nuclear weapons reflect by their nature an immoral embodiment. There is no right or wrong way to use nuclear weapons. The abnormality inheres in their social production. Such weaponry is a prime example of embodied deformity of knowledge—physical evidence of knowledge workers and other workers performing immoral action.* Yet turning away from these activities may be simpler than one ever imagined. The history of ideas records major shifts—shifts which seem, for all their contemporary turmoil—to amount to a shift of gaze, a changed focus. Even that terrifying cold warrior, John von Neumann, had his doubts: "The interests of humanity may change, the present curiosities in science may fade."

### Relocating and Changed Focus

That the questions change and knowledges dry up or are moved to the margins is hardly news. This does not necessarily mean that the question or problem is resolved. Paul Feyerabend has pointed out that:

Problems are not solved, they are dissolved. Examples are the problem of an absolute velocity of the earth, the problem of the trajectory of electrons in an interference pattern and the important problem of whether incubi are capable of producing offspring or whether they are forced to use the seeds of men for that purpose. The first problem was dissolved by the theory of relativity, which denies the existence of superluminal absolute velocities. The second problem was dissolved by the quantum theory, which denies the existence of trajectories in interference patterns. The third problem was dissolved, though less decisively, by modern (i.e., post-sixteenth century) psychology and physiology, as well as by the mechanistic cosmology of Descartes.[7]

In the past, many questions, disciplines and myth languages of persuasion which were supposedly central to people's understanding of reality dried up or were drastically altered. This is what we think must happen again. That the persecution of witchcraft is no longer a fundamental discipline of the universities and the churches, and therefore does not hold society enthralled, we may count as a positive good. That the type of scientific and technological inquiry which leads civilization to its demise is now the dominant knowledge form suggests the importance of changing the epistemological *location of concern.* There is no way that such a change could not be counted as an affirmative, life-giving activity for world civilization. Refocusing should not be taken as either frightening or a plea for irrationality, right-wing fundamentalism, or production-oriented socialism. Quite the contrary. Refocusing, and therefore change, is the hope of humankind.

Unfortunately, our most pressing problems cannot be dissolved or transformed in our dominant institutions because of the limiting forms of rational discourse which they engender. In the United States, these problems are now being reinforced by new arrangements which tie defense establishments, universities, research laboratories, and corporations even more closely together. The way the computer is used also results in tighter "binding" of these establishments and the society as a whole through a limiting language dictated by the logic of programming. Coincident with this social process is an epistemic one. The knowledge worker's understanding of any one piece of information or insight becomes deformed because he or she narrows the focus of concern to a "particular" without seeing its relationship to other "particulars." This methodology fits well with hierarchically defined corporate systems. As knowers, we are trapped in the bureaucratic-epistemic framework of "one thing at a time." In order to measure, to quantify the outer mapping of the "particular," we all change the nature of who we are as human beings. Current knowledge systems and their rewards encourage us to restrict ourselves to social roles that reject concern with anything beyond the measurement of appearance. But this is an unnecessarily restrictive response to the lessons of modern science. The proof of limits to inquiry contains the seed of a reconstructive transformation.

Werner Heisenberg has taught that the interaction of observing things, measuring them at the molecular level, changes the phenomenon itself. Modern psychology also teaches this, for the therapist is affected and changed by the analysis he or she may be conducting. The result of interaction, therefore, changes the location and meaning of the inquiry. Scientists must be aware constantly of refocusing. And they must be prepared to refocus on the basis of ethics and needs of human liberation. This is the reconstructed concern. It calls for a wider focus, one appropriate to *using* the effects of observer interaction. Questions seemingly far afield should be incorporated to transform the original experiment and the scientific enterprise itself. As we have argued, that enterprise contains hidden social, economic, and psychological aspects. Once these are brought forward, we may generate a method that concentrates on a conscious series of choices for the experiment in which more than the scientist and funder participate. The shift of focus which *includes* the framework of knowledge unequivocally raises issues of moral values.

## II. Values

We are all taught implicitly to conflate rationality with so-called value-free technological choices. Nevertheless, need for the belief in value-free knowledge, so important as an academic shield of protection in a highly tendentious period, has decreased. It is now virtually commonplace to say that value-free knowledge is a contradiction in terms. This belief suggests a deeper and potentially healthier approach than continually solving the technical puzzles which sprout from technique itself, especially given that these "technical puzzles" are deep value issues. It would make more sense to reexamine rationality and knowledge, relocating them and therefore redefining them, without feeling one thereby violates the "truth" of the universe. We may ask: Who is served by certain forms of rationality? Who is hurt? How are questions validated and separated from "metaphysical nonproblems"? What sort of society is modelled and molded by the lives of researchers and technicians?

Knowledge workers produce both explanations (of phenomena) and myth systems (of concepts, theories, and methods). The explanations *and* the everyday activity of scientists rest upon their myths. For myth is far more than fiction and anything but falsehood. Myths are the narrative of the fundamental beliefs and codified rational constructions of science. The values embodied in both the explanations and the myth systems of persuasion cannot be divorced from judgments about good or bad. Scientific judgments and myths can be evaluated pragmatically: How will they eventually affect people and nature? How do the people who will live with the ultimate effects of applying that science perceive the likely effects of current inquiry? Through a dialogical process, involving as many of those affected by the inquiry as possible, we could see many concerns which would otherwise remain invisible. How do scientific judgments stand up under continuous participatory cross-examination? Even this process of participation, explication, and dialogue cannot foretell the future. It cannot yield a truth beyond that of a process, a process which we must continually reinvent to prevent it from becoming mere formality. We must ask and re-ask, even of ourselves, the question drawn from Kierkegaard: Does this critical-rational creative work decrease our strength as human beings? Otherwise we are talking only of blind ritual, an added cosmetic step like the preparation of an Environmental Impact Statement.[8]

Indeed, even this essay's analysis, so well intentioned by its authors, must be subject to evaluation. Perhaps there might be deleterious effects of the very essay you are reading now. There is no sure calculus of future consequences. And actions all have consequences. *Our* proper action is to live up to the thoughts we are enunciating; let us lay out a few values, our methods, our myths—insofar as we are consciously aware of them.

Something of our values has already appeared. We believe in the spirit of liberation which infuses the scientific enterprise. The revolutionary character of that spirit attacks and transforms institutions today. We realize that it lies at the historical root of all modern institutions, and in some sense it can penetrate even those arrangements which cause domination, colonization, exploitative hierarchies, and deformed technologies. We wish to sustain this spirit of liberation, always present like lava in a volcano, but too often quiescent. We see the promise of science as ally and intended champion of liberation. But to sustain liberation, we should build on the sentiment of complementarity and of empathic bonding. This sentiment will lead us to understanding and joining in common social organizations to pursue collective goals, including those of dignity and equity.

If truth must be established by repetition or replication of experimental results, then a universal truth must be in principle replicable by all. All of the people who work on a particular project should be able to participate in doing the experiments, planning them, and deciding when to repeat for confirmation. How can we expect closed, secret or private experiments to produce knowledge for openness, honesty or equity? In other words, truth telling may require the radical socialization of the knowledge workplace, so that new questions and insights may be considered.

Truth telling amounts to being aware of what you see or measure, sharing and reporting that to others, allowing everyone interested to check what others sense against what you perceive. In any case, truth telling operates well only to the extent that everyone involved understands its fragility; it is human, it is fallible, and it is political—either ethical or unethical—to the core. It is predicated on convention and social agreement. But to violate this social agreement is to cause enormous havoc. Authoritarian and hierarchic structures deny the validity of truth telling because they locate truth in a very few. The rest are thought not to know—therefore their "truth telling" is irrelevant.

There is a disturbing question to keep in mind, and the followers of Polanyi and Popper will be most quick to point it out. Why do we have to tell the truth of our knowledge of the universe if, according to the reconstructive view, what we say is never the actuality of the universe or of how things are? We tell the truth about the myths we perceive or conjure because it is a human obligation of affection to one another. That is to say, the obligation to tell the "truth" of what we think is out there is an emotional bond between us.

Perhaps the best analogy is to childrearing. We would reject an adult as sadistic and mad who told a child learning to talk and recognize objects that a table is a horse, or a mirror is a car. Whether for a child or adults, all are in the curious position of having to trust one another and to generate modes of social agreement.

As noted by Imre Lakatos, in the present knowledge system, the further a subject of investigation is from human beings, the more accurate the science is thought to be. When knowledge is forced by its own limits to introduce some reflections of the process, as with the role of the observer in modern physics or in sociological investigations, the method is thought to be more accurate, truthful, or "scientific" if *less* of the observer is introduced. We reject the view that the less the human being is introduced, the less these interactions are allowed for, the better.

The epistemic principle which values the remote and unlivable as the highest of knowledge must be overthrown, since what little knowledge we have of the future—of applications of our knowledge work—comes to us *mainly* in answer to ethical questions of our own daily practice. These can only be thought about by us as human beings in history and in the context of the current human situation.

The ethic of reconstruction grows out of the actual concrete conditions of our life; it is not utopian. It is a lived, shared, evolving set of values, bonding across position and function. It joins us as authors to you the reader, and shapes the message we can share. We are related through the manuscript and the publisher, each in our own way, and linked by the private realities of joy and sorrow. It flows from an insistence on participation; the certain knowledge that no one can escape potential error, especially ourselves, and that only dialogue contains the essential corrective of full personal presence. This means active involvement in the development of ideas as well as participation in defining the objects and events which shape the world.

It also means tackling the question of experience itself and the inequality of opportunity for experience. The construction of the subject—who we are, which roles we have been brought to play, what "outposts of the Establishment" we have nurtured in our own consciousness—all immediately become problematic. For by participation, we understand the full-fledged acceptance of every man's and woman's role as subject-actor in history.

Neither demarcationists nor elitists can accept this point of view. It means ending the socially stratified nature of who gets to think about what.* Openness conflates the classes and creates a continuous dialogic relationship between all those who want to take part, irrespective of what they supposedly already know. This view should not be thought of as particularly shocking. There are revolutions every few years in the dominant modes of science which undercut the knowledge, education, and training of those who elect not to keep up. The proliferation of knowledge potentially provides opportunity to anyone considering virtually any research, not in terms only of its consequences, but of its processes/methods and purposes.

"Opening up" the knowledge process to everyone will result in greater clarity of purpose and a set of "moral axioms" which could apply to the project of inquiry. Indeed, we are tempted to invent the phrase "moral fluxioms" to emphasize the continual process of finding these limits, and the need for them to change. The original Greek meaning of axiom—that which is thought worthy of value, that which recommends itself for belief[9]—together with the modern lessons of non-Euclidean geometry and axiomatic math, argue for retaining "moral axiom." For one now knows that axioms are *not* self-evident. Several different sets of axioms are equally possible, equally consistent.

For example, in Euclidean geometry it is an axiom that only one line parallel to a given line can be drawn through an outside point; non-Euclidean spherical geometry postulates that no parallels exist; and hyperbolic geometry assumes that an infinite number can be drawn. Therefore, we know that the prevailing axioms change within history— just as Euclidean geometry ruled (in physics) until Einstein showed that time and space are united, whereas hyperbolic non-Euclidean geometry

---

*The present specialized disciplines of studying knowledge do not help us understand the whole of the "external" values which define the discipline. Nor does interdisciplinary work help us; for this system, as well-intentioned as it might be, merely brings the contradictions and flaws of any specific discipline together with other flawed disciplines, causing not a corrective, but an additional series of distortions in analysis.

has governed spacetime ever since. Just such evolving and testable "axioms" are what we need for limits to knowledge today. And even these fundamental values must never be specified from *on high*, but form themselves in the mold of discussions—among as broad a group as possible—with those whose lot it befalls to transcribe their growing consciousness. In this way we may begin to find some guides, "fixed limits" that make obvious, necessary sense for our civilization.

## III. Method

In rethinking the knowledge enterprise to offer an alternative direction, one must be sure that the alternative set of questions and assumptions themselves can be examined and laid bare; this too can best be done dialogically. The modern dilemmas our culture faces demand forms of inquiry related to oral communication. Books, articles and computer results arrogate to themselves a certitude which usually vanishes under the scrutiny of direct conversation. Talking together allows for seemingly unrelated matters to be introduced, which in a book or essay may appear to be off point, but nevertheless are quite relevant. Just as there is "body language" between speakers which counterpoints the content and must be received for successful communication, so there is the "mind language" of free association which clarifies concepts but is thought not relevant in written exposition.

    We should be aware of two types of ambiguity that are ineradicable. One stems from the historical nature of proof. Since nothing can be proven forever, whether in mathematics or any other science, the foundations of our most "rigorous" disciplines are ambiguous. The nature of mathematical proof itself has become an issue. Ever since the turn of the century, when the Constructivist and the Intuitionist schools championed different schema for mathematical proof, what constitutes a proof has been a matter of some controversy. In our day two new developments highlight the issue: (a) Certain published theorems now require hundreds of closely reasoned pages to prove.* Practically, they cannot be checked. In some cases the checking is complicated by having another closely related, equally long but not completely concordant, proof published at the same time. In these cases, only time, or the development of far simpler approaches, can resolve competing claims of proof. (b) Other proofs reside only within the operation of a computer program (such as the recent demonstration of the four-color theorem by

---

    *Examples include many theorems in number theory such as finding all the integer solutions (modulo 37) to the equation $x^n + y^n = 1$. In fact, even to solve this modular Diophantine equation for $n$ equal to the first few integers is a gigantic task. And such problems are merely subproblems of the famous named theorems, in this case, the still unsolved Fermat's last theorem that $x^n + y^n = z^n$ has no solutions for integer $x$, $y$, $z$, and $n$, if $n > 2$. Fermat's theorem is a generalization of the pythagorean theorem; to find the integer right triangles, that is, to find sets of three whole numbers $x$, $y$, and $z$, which satisfy $x^2 + y^2 = z^2$.

examining several thousand particular cases). The proof amounts to claiming that the computer program actually does what it is designed to do; that it actually did run through all the possible cases, in effect showing that of all the planar maps which might be drawn, *none* required more than four colors to distinguish adjacent areas. In the current situation, it seems that proofs and their definitions are no more than highly socialized concepts. A series of logical steps which convinces the professionals constitutes a mathematical proof.

The second ambiguity inheres in the profound hidden and external facets to any knowledge; facets which are classed as irrelevant, but which may be controlling of one's inquiries.

Bernard Williams, in his introduction to Isaiah Berlin's book of philosophical essays, makes the point that interest in ideas forces one to jump disciplinary boundaries. The most natural way to do this is through *parole,* or oral communication. As a critique of current disciplinary knowledge, the reconstructive effort obviously best allies itself with the dialogic method. It ferrets out and seeks to comprehend the fundamental contradictions in values, methodology, and purpose in the disciplines.

This process parallels that of a jazz improvisation, wherein the audience is part of the chain of creativity. The hearers shape the work through the enjoyment, taste, call and response, participatory listening. Indeed it is taken for granted that in the system of interrelationships among the musicians there is a close and dialogic relationship. Improvisation and intuition operate together. At a later stage this dialogic relationship is systematized through books on orchestration and composition.[10] But systemization, the development of rules, can either close off relationship and empathic excitement in jazz, or allow, as in the case of Schoenberg in modern music, an opening for new modes of intuition and aural understanding. So too when we think about reconstruction in scientific inquiry. The only "rules" to which it conforms are those which increase the bonding and affections among people. One can view the inconclusiveness of the debate among mathematicians on the nature of proof as a reflection of this principle. However imperfectly, mathematicians are coming to realize the social or interpersonal nature of their "pure" inquiry. The language of description is predicated on metaphor and persuasion; the social relation of proof to truth, even in mathematics, is quite palpably present.

Greek culture in the time of Plato, Socrates, and Aristotle made much of the relationship between "correct" harmonies and hierarchic social bonding. Musicians were thought to have the same problem as statesmen, for both were concerned with "the proper ordering of unequal parts in a complete whole." In other words, harmony established a hierarchy of importance between the notes.

Until the twentieth century, harmony and tone centers in polyphonic music reflected this structural hierarchy. With Schoenberg and with modern jazz, musical compositions have become decentered and non-hierarchic. In modern music an equality (really an egalitarian interdependence) now exists between notes and phrases. There are clues here which may benefit those concerned with political operations of a society, just as there are political clues for us from the dialogue of jazz improvisation.*

## Why a Political Philosophy of Knowledge
## Is Possible and Necessary

Once we *want* each person to be a subject-actor in history (or "her-story"), playing his or her tune in concert with others, we are also stating an objection to the philosophy which has dominated Western thought since Socrates, Plato, and Aristotle. These gentlemen believed in an aristocratic model of society and hoped for the overthrow of democracy. We should take cognizance of what Kant said so that we understand how limited the conception of citizenship has been in Western thought. Kant tells us that there are "associates of the State" who cannot and should not be thought of as citizens because they exercise no independent choice. They do not exert the dictates of their own will. As Kant puts it, "the following examples should serve to eliminate any confusion" between the active and passive citizen of the community. Obviously, it is the active citizens who "matter."

The errand boy in the employ of a merchant, the factory worker, the servant who is not in the service of the State, the ward, all women, and generally speaking, whoever is forced to provide for his needs, not according to his own lights, but in conformity with the commandments of others; all such individuals lack a civic personality and exist merely as adjuncts, as it were, of other people. The woodcutter and overseer of a farm, the Indian blacksmith who goes from door to door carrying on his back the anvil, the hammer and bellows with which he works the iron, as well as the joiner and the European marshal; the tenant farmer and the domestic tutor, as nothing more than administrators of the *res publica*, because they must be given direction and protection and consequently, do not enjoy true civic independence.[11]

The return to an aristocratic model can be found in works of conservative political theorists who write in the pages of *The National Review*. Attempts are being made, under the guise of individual choice, to destroy the fragile erratic attempts at democracy which were made in the United States from 1865 to 1980. It is established values that are under attack. We see the results of the Reagan-conservative attack in cultural propaganda, emphasis on free enterprise economics, and most importantly, in the realization by the Right of the nonautonomous nature of both science and technology.

In political terms, this last circumstance opens three alternatives. One

*Another tradition has begun to reassert itself in modern music. It is the music like that of Philip Glass, who seeks to recenter humankind through mantra-like musical repetitive playing of notes and phrases that show differences in everything reproduced.

is to shore up the myth of value-free research. This is the path most promising for the Center—and the one that most laboratories and scientists will take in hopes of avoiding direct attack. They will embrace the notions of Polanyi and Popper. Another is to concentrate on the confrontation with the types of knowledge (and their likely consequences) developed by the Right and Center. The Right's attack partakes of an extreme "skeptical" position in its initial stages. It counsels the fertilization of weeds. For example, why shouldn't racist research be done at the university? Or why shouldn't creationism be given a chance to compete with Darwinism? The tactical purpose is clear. They are intent on asserting the authority of antiscientific fundamentalism. The Center defense is likely to become highly "elitist" in philosophy, with the confronting Left becoming sophisticated "demarcationists" almost by default. They will seek to hold onto the ideology of reason, rationality, and objectivity as a safe haven against attack from racism and Armageddonism. The virulence of the attack on science shows up in such confrontations as the recent trial of "Creationist Science." The onslaught will help to clarify the moral or value position of those who rush to defend particular sciences.*

The defense of science and technology cannot be accomplished by an unwillingness radically to rethink the project of knowledge acquisition. It will not be enough to think of knowledge as a kind of edifice to which we add rigorously and solidly made knowledge bricks. Works such as those of Stephen Gould (on IQ testing) and Philip Green (on inequality research in general) show how one might begin to ferret out the special interests behind particular branches of current knowledge, their histories, and their applications, while showing how so-called "specialized" questions frame and distort the process of liberation. Once scientists move to correct the direction of the work of other scientists by seeing the methodology of particular disciplines as class, race, or sex biased or intentionally false, it is then that reconstruction will emerge. But one should never assume that this correction, either by using counterexamples, or showing flaws in someone else's argument or proof—whether in mathematics or social science—secures the foundation of any discipline of knowledge as ultimately provable.

Viewed from this prism, reconstructive knowledge is political. It seeks to *decode* the various languages of classes and specialties to show their values and premises. As a result of decoding, a different type of science will emerge. For the disciplines may be seen as a set of varied languages. In some tongues there are concepts which could never be expressed

*One curious question that may begin this process: Did the scientists who testified in defense of evolution swear on the Bible that its teachings were unscientific? Did the judge in essence find that the (presumably) atheistic scientists were telling the truth against the word of noble and honorable creationists who may even have believed (having sworn on the word of the Holy Scripture) that they would be struck dead if they lied? Such situations and questions will force people to see their own moral positions. Indeed, one may even ask: Would the scientists have sworn on *Origin of Species* (as the character in *French Lieutenant's Woman* did)?

easily in ours (for example, the Inuit's seventeen words for snow; the intriguing complexities of tenses in certain African languages of the Eastern coastal regions; Navajo's four distinct verbs, according to number and gait, meaning 'to move' for animate beings), and yet we are able to understand them, albeit with circumlocutions. Disciplines viewed as discourse, like languages, are not truth. They are social conventions.

Wittgenstein points out that our firmest knowledge, such as arithmetic,—for example, $2 + 2 = 4$—has the logical status of enforced social convention. Thus, in human terms, the languages of the sciences are languages of rhetorical persuasion. Language provides a method of negotiating a particular cosmos—it may be special or shared, reductionist or open, and so on. These characters are important precisely because language is a mode of persuasion serving both expression and communication, containing both emotion and reason. As the theoretical physicist Geroch puts it, speaking of his own discipline:

One might very well be left with the impression that the theory itself is rather hollow: What are postulates of the theory? Where are the demonstrations that all else follows from these postulates? Where is the theory proven? On what grounds, if any, should I believe the theory? I can only answer these questions with my own opinions. It seems to me that "theories of physics" have, in the main, gotten a terrible press. The view has somehow come to be rampant that such theories are precise, hightly logical, ultimately "proved." In my opinion, at least, this is simply not the case—not the case for General Relativity and not the case for any other theory of physics. *First, theories, in my view, consist of enormous numbers of ideas, arguments, hunches, vague feelings, value judgments, and so on, all ranged in a maze. These various ingredients, are connected in a complicated way. It is this entire body of material that is "the theory." One's mental picture of the theory is this nebulous mass taken as a whole.* . . . In one's own approach to the theory one makes no attempt to isolate a few of these points to be called "postulates." One makes no attempt to derive the rest of the theory from postulates. (What, indeed, could it mean to "derive" something about the physical world?) One makes no attempt to "prove" the theory or any point of it. (I don't even know what a "proof" could mean in this context. I wouldn't recognize a "proof of a physical theory" if I saw one.)*[12]

One way of looking at the proliferation of knowledge, then, is as a kind of tower of Babel; new branches of discourse open up, new wings and parapets of the edifice are constructed, eventually whole areas are abandoned and finally torn down or discarded. In the current situation, specialties and fragmentation abound, as each major discipline grows. It is staggering to contemplate but in that most abstract of fields, mathe-

*Throughout history, languages of rhetorical persuasion have succeeded one another and civilization has taught itself each new language in turn. These tongues are so many and varied that one sometimes forgets even their names; demonology, alchemy, astrology—all have faded away as a dominant language. A new rhetoric of language persuasion has come in the form of computer language, a language that shapes our social organizational structure. If the sciences are languages of persuasion, it follows that a society may choose in a group-conscious manner which languages best serve its values, its own sense of social worth. What, for example, are the political and moral implications of such computer languages as FORTRAN and LISP and PASCAL? How do they differ from each other?

matics, there are at least two hundred thousand new theorems which are proven each year. Indeed, the process of expansion and specialization, while making every practitioner narrow, has the effect of feeding the expansionist tendencies of the established leaders of whole fields. They have no intention of changing their own specialty or its assumptions and premises. Each different discipline begins by attempting to provide framing principles appropriate to incisive discussion of a restricted set of phenomena, but fully capable of investigating practically anything if pushed far enough.

### The Limits of Language

The modern language theories applied to scientific disciplines put emphasis on subject and predicate objects rather than verbs. David Bohm has pointed out that the end result of the language method is to misunderstand the process of becoming, the wholeness of the universe, and oneself within them. Furthermore, one actively fragments in one's language, thought process, and in the way one sees reality;

A cursory examination shows that a very important feature of this kind is the subject-verb-object structure of sentences, which is common to the grammar and syntax of modern languages. This structure implies that all action arises in a separate entity, the subject, and that in cases described by a transitive verb, this action crosses over the space between them to another separate entity, the object. (If the verb is intransitive, as in "he moves" the subject is still considered to be a separate entity but the activity is considered to be either a property of the subject or a reflexive action of the subject, e.g., in the sense the "he moves" may be taken to mean "he moves" himself.)

This is a pervasive structure leading in the whole of life to a function of thought tending to divide things into separate entities, such entities being conceived of as essentially fixed and static in their nature. When this view is carried to its limit, one arrives at the prevailing scientific worldview in which everything is regarded as ultimately constituted out of a basic set of particles of fixed nature.[13]

In precisely such a vein, with the intention to resolve the puzzles of perceiving the political nature of knowledge, we believe that a political science of the world starts with a *political* science of knowledge—works of knowledge, science, and art need not be read as "physics," "biology," "economics," "videoart," and so forth in the historical future they will all be part of the same field of study. They will be read as sources— essentially as world view, literature* to which anyone has access.

*Thus the 1935 Einstein-Podolsky-Rosen paper is not just Einstein's position vs. Bohr's within the discipline of theoretical physics, within the historical context of a world-shaping intellectual discovery "revolution." It is equally about why a good liberal and brilliant human being, Einstein (constrained in our terms to the reconstruction of knowledge at best and at worst to the staunch ACLU-like insistence on an objective world out there and an objective platform from which to view it) sensed something wrong with the introduction of a *corporate* observer in physics, the fundamental science of the world. The effects of placing science (and knowledge) in historical context, and the insights gained from such a move, are fundamental to the important work of Cornelius Castoriadis, e.g. *Crossroads in the Labyrinth* (Cambridge: MIT, 1984).

To do this well requires a new style of rigorous knowledge. It is associational and analogic, tending to the type of thought which sees in each event or problem new aspects of the whole. Knowledge reconstruction of this kind recognizes the importance of *framing* conditions for any problem. Society has foolishly left many concerns unexamined because of the belief that science and its method is rigorous and all else is flabby; and that what is not involved with us in our totality as human beings can be isolated, focused, and separated from ourselves as stinking, loving, and puking human beings. With a new method of inquiry, knowledge workers can now reverse course so that the questions investigated and the methods used can integrate human concerns beyond that of the operation of the experiment.

How to proceed? When looking at who benefits from a particular line of investigation, when one questions what the effects are for personal liberation and for the project of human liberation, one must begin to question the arrangements within the experiment and research program. Are the workers treated equitably? Is participation in workplace direction a feature of the laboratory? Has the public helped to shape or decide the direction of the work? How does everyone (who is everyone?) determine the relationship of scientific work to a common good? Participation and health are more probable products of ultimately derived knowledge if they are hallmarks of the process which generates it in the first place. We are unaware of any social or institutional "alchemy" to turn the scientific method of elitism, mystification, and privilege into the good ends of human progress—their opposite—for the larger polity.

Consider what the simple step of expecting complete participation by laboratory workers, administrators, research assistants, and general staff would do to change scientific practice. Demystification, education for the uninitiated, would be essential. The methods and means of research would be guided by a different, wider set of concerns; the outcomes would necessarily serve a wider set of interests.

If we seek to relate reconstructive knowledge's definition of honesty to rigor there is no choice but to include currently outside-the-discourse considerations as part of our understanding. The closer we get to understanding why certain topics are chosen, and the more open about these considerations, the closer we approach a rigorous search for *good* outcomes. We are able to judge who is affected, what are the motives, and what probable consequences might result. We are also able to judge in immanent terms the socially good or bad result of a particular action.

Take the example of Einstein's famous 1939 letter to Roosevelt, urging the American government to pursue an atomic bomb program. Let us first stipulate that Einstein and Szilard were frightened and concerned about the military application of German nuclear science and they sought a deterrent to it; a deterrent, parenthetically, which *failed* because it was used against Japan for the purpose of intimidating the Japanese and Russians. However, under the rigor-as-honesty rules, this plea to engage in A-bomb research was incomplete. For Einstein actually signed a letter drafted by his friend Leo Szilard, in part motivated by Szilard's personal needs.

Szilard was working on *his* uranium research, as a refugee with no official academic post at Columbia University. He needed a few thousand dollars for his investigations, without which he might lose even the small laboratory space granted by the physics department. How different that letter might have been if the style of research decision making, or even of business correspondence, accorded with the virtue of personal honesty; instead of a billion dollar weapons effort, we might have started with a few thousand dollars in supplies and a chair for Professor Szilard.[14]

Or consider the effect of gossip on today's grant-giving and peer review committees. Personal ambition, academic politics, and sexual intrigue fill off-the-record talk, in corridors and over coffee. How would decisions be affected, especially in marginal cases, if the conversation hinged on dedication to social good, concern with public participation, and efforts to incorporate humane values in the research, to say nothing of frank admission of individual human need? It now seems obvious that we cannot begin to understand humankind and the fantastic myths it concocts without comprehending that its scientific understanding is the product of its sufferings, actions, needs, and thought—that these define its nature and its view of the world.

A reconstructed political science and philosophy must take to itself those questions of nature which have been thought of as ceded to specialized scientific disciplines precisely because they cannot be answered adequately or satisfactorily within the nineteenth- and twentieth-century definitions of science, and because they cannot adequately address consequential effects on human beings and nature. The "facts" of a particular discipline need to be reexamined and relocated, for their meaning will surely change when other questions are asked of them. "Facts"—characterized so frequently in metaphors as "stubborn and irreducible" (Whitehead) or as firm, solid, and true—are conditioned by the theory, experience, and social framework in which the original investigators and their successors operate.

In questioning "facts", we hold to our ethical method: Whom do they serve? What view of reality, or the incomprehensible total flow of reality and thought, do these particular categories enforce? As David Bohm has said, the need to make distinctions, to think, never transcends the wholeness of the universe. The facts, even the categories of observation are all abstractions, things taken from a web of interconnections by construction. One must always be aware that the act of creating knowledge creates the furniture of reality.

As we conclude this section on method, note that both the possibility and necessity for a political science have impressed themselves. To do good with our intellectual capabilities, new knowledge must incorporate an understanding of science as a branch of human history and comprehension. The values and purposes of creativity must fold back upon themselves, rather than be cast aside.

Perhaps the key lies in the self-referential nature of twentieth-century knowledge; limitations of the established disciplines have themselves become part of their subject matter, beginning with Heisenberg's uncertainty principle in physics. We think of Gödel's Proof, Arrow's Theorem, the Hawthorne Effect (and other, better verified observer-subject interactions), and the Church-Turing Theorem in (respectively) mathematical logic, welfare economics, social research, and computer theory. When knowledge incorporates the knower, it seems to find limits; it *proves* that it is creating rather than discovering. This realization implies responsibility for the results; responsibility in fact for those results to serve the greater good—a conception which itself emerges from the dialogic and participatory approach to moral axioms.

How to use the modern self-referential discoveries of limits to knowledge is a critical question. To use them as an excuse, introducing as *little* of the knower as possible (in particular as little of the knower's moral and value sense as possible), is to demean and reduce knowledge workers. Such moves discard the crucial opportunity for liberating and reconstructive knowledge. If we introduce only the morally vapid observer, only the neutral and obedient participant,* is it any wonder that the knowledge produced contains the seed of morally deformed application, of banally evil action?

We must, on the contrary, inquire how much of the knowledge enterprise may be changed to a project of liberation through creativity. How many of the disciplines now contain self-referential results? Does self-reference and self-limitation always require reexamination of the meaning of the "field"? How can one use these discoveries to introduce the missing moral components? These are the leading questions of a reconstructive knowledge method. And they suggest a course of action. The essential act is the first one, choosing a topic and group to work with and a method of working day to day—a method which upholds the possibility of future moral application even while it embodies its values in the present. Each question and its answer is framed in social reality, not in a "discipline."

Clearly, the view from within the disciplinary enterprises is that each has its own peculiar shape. But it would be more accurate to say that from each of them the entire field of all the others—the entire discourse therein, the entire set of activities and relations of its participant-constructors—becomes DATA, grist for analysis or synthesis, for play and rearrangement, for consanguineous embrace and transformation.[15] The more useful mode, perhaps, is that of the archaeologist of ideas,

---

*To paraphrase Michael Goldhaber, the banality of a neutral participant is really that of Corporate Man, a completely replaceable, de-individualized human being. As the perfect observer in quantum physics (since it was theoretically necessary to introduce the observer), this seemed the most objective.

Michel Foucault, who crosses time, space, and disciplinary boundaries at will in search of those determinates of particular disciplines that become, as discourse, an active formative process of what our world is.

## IV. Myth

The special freedom of knowledge workers (if they are willing to accept it) to shift their gaze—to choose a direction of creativity and research—gives rise to new critical ways of knowing. As current knowledge suppresses its two key irrationalities, it promotes a "will to truth" which foolishly refuses to admit to the existence of the root impulses: desire and power. One can only move to correct this by revealing the situation, facing it, and beginning anew. Both the psychological-individual motivations (for example, curiosity, playfulness, and personal gratification) *and* the social-moral (cooperation, welfare, and human understanding) must be released. Their suppression in publication, elimination from discussion and denial in even casual comment—as in the example of corridor gossip by granting committees cited above—stand as a fundamental dishonesty of a system supposedly valuing veracity above all else.

The reconstructive program would turn "thinking about the unthinkable" back upon itself. We would rather *share* the unthinkable—openly admit the arational to analysis and admit to its being part of the source of our thought. When this is done, one can begin to face the problem in oneself of desire and power. And this is the starting point of our myth: the ability to change what is known by changing what is looked into.

We hold that all knowledge, even the "hardest" of sciences (once again to use the metaphor of a sex-linked language about a largely male-dominated activity) is quite socially conditioned. We believe therefore that the current apolitical, amoral myth is nearly expired; that the project of knowledge will build new myths that are more in keeping with the process of human liberation and socially constructed reality. Of course, it is necessary to retain the kernel of the current myth system which is pragmatically useful: that one *may* indeed observe and think about things with positive effect for progress. This must be upheld, even promoted, lest the interjection of values be confounded with an upsurgent irrational thrust against knowledge itself. Yet how can we deal with such a self-conscious mythmaking exercise in an age of disbelief?

One possibility is to admit that there are and always have been alternative potential mythos, modes, and heuristic principles lurking about, waiting to attain or regain prominence. Consider a few of these with us in the following pages: old ways of knowing; modern science as the analog of paranoia; feminist myths; and, finally, the myth of an empowering, reason-preserving reconstructive knowledge—one which refuses any a priori definition, for it seeks by open process to come closer to the total flow (the Wholeness of Bohm's recent writings) than any set procedure or demarcated enterprise could; a reconstructive knowledge which embodies and promotes liberation as it prepares the knowledge basis for social reconstruction.

## Four Myths

*Old Ways of Knowing as New Ways.* The modern view of ourselves is as a biogenetic construct, but other cultures have seen individuals as related both to the group and to nature. This may be medically and ecologically more valid; in any case, it is both more pleasing and more useful because it promotes reverence for the Other by seeking wholeness between self, universe, and the Other. It crosses temporal divisions as well. Traditional cultures have ways of knowing which violate the dichotomies of modern practice. Poet Gary Snyder's "The Old Ways" reminds us, "We live in a universe, 'one turn' in which, it is widely felt, all is one and at the same time all is many."[16] He discusses the relevance of preserved natural wisdom to modern ecological crisis.

The Amerindian life system incorporated a great deal of what modern science only lately teaches: that life processes form a whole, crossing supposed species boundaries and supporting the relatively few (humans) whose privileged position grants them potential to preserve or destroy it all. Snyder ends with the Coyote stories of the Native American trickster, totem of shamans. In such tales, the world as locally present becomes codified—knowledge fits to felt patterns, to historical and geographical variation, to social custom. Experiential learning becomes theory and literally grounds praxis.

Similarly, various religious groups and individuals (like Waskow in modern Judaism) have recently turned to ancient doxological and exegetical practice for progressive answers to modern problems. Everybody is trying to find relation of self to cosmos to save themselves and humanity. One cannot afford not to examine all the sources. These efforts continually pose the question: Have we mistaken narrowness for rigor? Have we not been culturally biased, to our own detriment, against certain possible knowledges? These biases are perforce ending. Science can no longer afford to be split off from other modes of human inquiry (understanding). Many of us now make the personal choice to see Chinese acupuncturists and other practicioners of wholistic medicine. As Dr. James Gordon points out, work on traditional and "indigenous systems—including the Tibetan, the Indian, and particularly the Native American—suggests that there are other ways of conceptualizing and, indeed, of curing illness."[17] Thus even the oldest ways of knowing can be used to rid science of error; or better yet of approaches that the physicist Pauli called "not even wrong"—indicating that an entire concept somehow misses the effective point. To denigrate the knowledge of a place or the practices of long resident peoples is to risk shutting off precisely the kind of centering new knowledge must now provide.

*Science as Paranoia.* Physics has served as both basis and model for modern science. Its mode of analysis, as we have seen of all disciplines, has gone far beyond the initial realm of application. But, in turn, this means that each discipline may comment on the others. For example, Freudian psychoanalysis might identify physics as paranoid. We may learn from the analogy, despite the possible error of taking individual (Freudian) psychology as a valid commentary on modern physics.

The physicist's world is one of unseen forces. A few decades ago, the mystery was centered on the nature of atoms. What could possibly hold these ultimate bits together? What could keep them from eventual collapse? Now the same questions are addressed to the subatomic world. What all-pervasive, controlling force or interaction explains the protons and neutrons? Or their constituent particles (now even postulated to be *in principle* unseeable and unseen) quarks?

Note that the forces in question are always the ones which control all phenomena and dominate the world, for they always are those which operate at the unexplained margin; they are the ultimate constituent, controlling (no longer determinate, that would contradict the quantum mechanical understanding of our microscopic parts) and dominating outside influences. Everything that happens can be explained by their action, for they explain how the smallest parts—of which all else is made—behave. The system is robust. It cannot be shattered, absent the end of all science, since the progress of the enterprise continues to open new questions. New details, sublevels of mechanism, ever finer correlations will be sought once the latest mysteries are solved. And since the deeper levels will always explain, nay, control, the previous level, we *expect* to face unseen—or at least unknown—controlling forces every time we unmask our current quarry.

If scientific "truth" were merely inventions of a single, ordinary mortal mind, we might find the persistence of unknowability, of all-pervasiveness, of dominating importance attributed to the ultimate recently discovered forces, signs of a particularly virulent and tenacious pathology. The symptom of harnessing rationality to the production of ever deeper levels of conspiratorial and controlling influences should clinch the diagnosis. Even the libidinal energy, the sexual or Freudian explanations fit: erotic paranoiac reactions involve a repressed homosexual motive which could describe, with very little change, the largely male enterprise of science.

Is modern physics classical paranoia or are modern psychological categories crazy? As one text puts it,

Classical paranoia is only an extreme, complex, paranoid reaction which may grow more extensive with time, but does not diminish . . . in contrast to schizophrenia, there are no hallucinations, there is no disorganization and there is little or no desocialization . . . The explanation seems to lie in an encapsulation of the delusional system which leaves the rest of the personality free to operate with relative normality.

 . . . Whereas obsessive speculation vacillates, and stops short with doubts, classical paranoia goes on from one "certainty" to another, building speculation into a delusional organization which seems to the patient to have greater reality than the world as others see it. The patient characteristically expresses hauteur and contempt for any reasoning that contradicts or questions what he believes . . . To give up a paranoiac delusion would very likely be to give up ego integration. This is probably why the condition is usually found to be untreatable.[18]

If we consider the patient to be an entire culture ("Western"—that is, Northern, civilization) and take an extreme skeptical view of the nature of scientific proof—so that calling the theoretical structure a delusion becomes possible—the entire excerpt fits physics rather well. There is a political effect to all of this.

Indeed, mild paranoia in the mind of not-so-ordinary mortals creates reality and escapes classification as pathological. The crucial element of nonordinaryness is power, a property of modern science (and science-based technology) as well. When a president believes that Russian military planners will build all the nuclear weapons and missiles they are technologically capable of acquiring, he is not considered deluded. Not even if he goes around proclaiming his belief in public. In his February 1983 "Star Wars" speech on national security, President Reagan sought to reaffirm the science-state connection by calling on scientists to find a defense against nuclear weapons. What is most important about Reagan's call is that he is speaking to physicists who believe in the conquest of unseen forces, just as his counterpart Edward Teller sees in international politics the need to control and conquer enemies of the United States throughout the world. The vision of power and fear is the same. In fact, the whole national security and science connection fosters both belief and actions based on delusion which may be sufficient to create the reality feared and imagined most.

Reductionist science may be viewed as a paranoid reaction which constructs a reality and then a culture around its world view. Ever-expanding, incurable, and encapsulated in that corner of the "personality" of the culture which explains how the world works, it "leaves the rest of the personality free to operate with relative normality." In this analogy, to effect a moral epistemology would be nothing short of curing the psychopathology, whose rareness is no consolation (especially in a powerful "patient") for its incurability. The synthesis of modern physics and paranoia is complete in the development of modern methods of military warfare, nuclear weaponry, and strategy; indeed, an entire culture *is* developed.

What could suit particular powerful (and perhaps personally slightly paranoid) interests or classes better than a system of understanding the world constructed along paranoid lines, brilliant but absolutely mad? Under the ensuing world view, the simple giving of favor and promotion, the ordinary control of grants, perquisites, prizes, and the like could easily help pick and promote particular men of genius. Particular paranoid men of genius, whose personal delusions and madness coincided with the political aims of the powerful would be especially helpful. Their madness would not disqualify them—indeed, it might even enhance their brillance.

The paranoia might even appear as super-brillance; to their peers they would seem the brightest men in the world. Under the guise of unfettered search, of value-free inquiry, and of ever-expanding truth, the desire for domination or rabid hatred of communists (in a capitalist country and vice versa) might become a prime motivating factor in the entire scientific enterprise. For no easy distinction could be made between the cultural paranoia of the science and the individual psychopathology of the genius, the paragon of science, the leader and director of intellectuals. Interest in inherently dangerous, even inherently destructive sorts of knowledge might be quite simply identified as the "cutting edge" of inquiry. Surely proclamations of the future direction of science and technology would be inextricably woven with the policy directions most fitting the biases and assumptions of exactly those particular interests who selected and promoted the scientific leader in the first instance. Power politics would define science, or rather, its direction; that form of science could define reality in clear-cut and in metaphoric consonance with a class interest position. Such paranoia is then structured into the system itself so that initiates and specialists do not question it. Participants no longer realize how crazed the enterprise is. Its assumptions are the hidden frame for the supposedly "objective" decisions or experiments.

Perhaps the case of John von Neumann can serve as an illustration. Von Neumann, who was crucial to the development of thermonuclear weapons, intercontinental ballistic missiles, and the Atomic Energy Commission, founded much of today's paranoid military science and mathematics culture. Von Neumann, it will be recalled, prided himself on being an objective researcher. His reputation among physicists and mathematicians continues to this day as "the smartest man in the world" of his generation.

But how does one begin to question the myths and mathematics of a military-scientific culture that Von Neumann generated? At the very least, there must be a community of "others" who engage the difficult task of arguing through the social construction of an alternative scientific reality and who disagree with those who hold to the present system. Perhaps this community already exists in nascent form among scientists and theologians and others who believe in the importance of a wholistic and ritualistic approach to the universe. As we have noted in our comments on method, these knowledge workers must include other co-workers and "support staff" as well as those especially affected by the new knowledge. If we rely upon the view from one particular race, class, or gender, the ensuing political and social action entails great peril. Knowledge must be considered neither reconstructive nor vigorous unless it incorporates the realization that others are human, while building upon the insights born of historic oppression.

*Patriarchy, Ethnocentrism, and the Official Myths.* Many of the lessons to be learned from the metaphors and myths of current world knowledge views come quite directly from feminist critique. The compilation of writings on biology by Hubbard, Henifin and their colleagues, *Women Look at Biology Looking at Women;* the work of Susan Griffin in *Woman and Nature;* and especially the investigations of Evelyn Fox Keller all show how metaphors and images of male domination permeate the myth of objective knowledge and can be used to explain and characterize many of the most egregious consequences of its application. Indeed, the feminist myths go directly to the heart, or more accurately, behind the scenes of the world of the pompous "wise white father figures." In so doing, this new effort has power to strip away certain gender-related metaphors which are out of place where we adhere to the principle of liberation. The metaphors of the old white father no longer allow us to see afresh, to make the kind of stride taken in the origin of scientific practice—indeed, without the thrust of feminism they tend, through total familiarity, to be invisible:

by virtue of their invisibility, they maintain an old vision of the world. Their invisibility lends that vision the status of fact, prevents us from seeing it as vision. And of all metaphors, few are as powerful as the metaphors of gender. It is our work as feminists to expose these, to make them and the functions they have served visible—therein lies a critical power with revolutionary potential.[19]

The feminist effort converges even in detail, with our efforts at reconstruction of knowledge. From discussion of experimenter bias,[20] through focus on language and the insights on the political nature of science in its daily endeavors, to even the choice of fundamental sources, the work on reconstructive knowledge parallels work on feminism and science. One of us (Raskin) has done a rereading of Bacon (see chapter 2 above), quite as Evelyn Fox Keller has examined the depths of sexual imagery in the same source *(Novum Organum)* for the *Philosophical Forum.* Susan Griffin's word play—and for that matter Mary Daly's in another field—opens eyes to the same power of metaphor to infiltrate and inform daily life, carrying with it the dominating purposes of the original speakers, that our essays on knowledge and science have stressed throughout the works on reconstruction.

That feminists have noted exactly the same entre of dominant root power for the elite brings new understanding to reconstruction. The disenfranchised urge to do good makes common cause with disenfranchised peoples of the world. If the indigenous wisdom of the Old Ways and the *prima facie* equal yet ignored (even disdained) wisdom of the "Second Sex" are both left out of a knowledge base constructed by white males, is it any wonder that such knowledge works to further inequity and to support the biases of the powerful?

Moreover, the feminist reconstruction of a myth and ideology gives hope to the cause of reconstructive knowledge. For the ultimate goal is in both cases not merely to revise what has already been compiled, but to move in a new way. What would science have looked like with a different nonclassist or antisexist bias? This question inevitably leads to others: What will a reconstructive science look like in the future? What parts of it can be formed today?"

The most advanced feminist criticism refuses to cede objectivity (at least the place of objectivity in a masculinist science) to the action of oppressors, rather:

. . . the task of a feminist theoretic in science is twofold: (1) to distinguish that which is parochial from that which is universal in the scientific impulse, reclaiming for women what has been historically denied to them, and (2) to legitimate those elements of scientific culture which, by virtue of being defined as female, have been denied to it. In short, rather than abandon the quintessentially human effort to understand the world in rational terms, we need to refine it. To do this, we need to add to the familiar methods of rational and empirical inquiry the additional process of critical self-reflection. Following Piaget's injunction, we can become conscious of the features of the scientific project which belie its claim to universality.[21]

*Myth of a Reconstructive Knowledge for Social Reconstruction.* We frankly admit that reconstructive knowledge is itself a myth for generating social reconstruction and teasing out implications of present dominant modes of thought. We also believe that the open dialogue of reconstructive knowledge will ensure continual questioning of our own biases and help us to focus on the moral implications of the problems we choose to study. We believe that such recognition of what we are doing is necessary to the regeneration of civilization.

Social reconstruction occurs only with self-consciousness. Because we are aware that we are unable to escape values and bias, we reject the notion of value-free mythology, and proceed as if the antidote were simply to be conscious of the influences upon us and the consequences of our myths or models. We deal with the skeptical impulse not by elevating doubt to a firm basis for founding knowledge, as Descartes attempted (with the historic result of divison and self-denial inherent in our world view today) but by acknowledging continuing doubt, continuous cross-examination in the public space and in the laboratory, as part of our process. The model of plural realities from various groups and the interior voice of conscience speak toward modesty, honesty, and breadth of vision.

Those human concerns which seem improper for "scientific" discourse but are in fact dominant in the very definitions of knowledge, of the compartments and perspectives taken as real or (in Bohm's terms) as relevant, must constantly be introduced. Our methods of honesty, of focus on the current practice, and of inclusivity; our redefinition of rigor to include examination of ambition and personal motivation; our attempts to see ourselves as conditioned by the old order but struggling to emerge—all these become the basis of a myth. Since knowledge workers must begin to do better, to combine themselves as thinkers and doers, as knowledge producers and ethical-political beings simultaneously, we tenaciously hold to the possibility of wholeness.

We find ourselves in the anomalous position of using both implications of myth: the contemporary implication of narrative combines with the classic notion of deep belief, of underlying structure. In effect "rational understanding", which utterly infused social belief, must be brought to the service of human liberation and social responsibility. This can only happen if the myth itself is both lightly held *and* is one which the society as a whole can participate in making and changing. Unlike the pragmatism of dominant science and technology, which is committed to explanation, to numerical "truths" without regard to culture or place, our view is that all science (and technology) is mediated through human language, things, and institutions. It is limited and defined by the profane actions of mankind. One knows enough now to see that the totality, the complete flow of both what is stated to be "out there" and the thoughts which comprehend the "out there," is essentially unknowable.[22] Scientific induction is built on a logical leap of faith, beholden for its power to social and individual judgment. This being so it is more useful, in this time of grave peril, for outsiders to enter the world of science and redirect its focus of concern. Enlightened knowledge workers will approach the implications of their work with practical scrutiny, with an awareness of their work in terms of its effects on humanity, the power-ethical relationships created in their daily actions, and the effect their inquiry has on human liberation. Their imagination, language, and modes of discourse are now called upon to construct those structures, institutions, and myths which will transform material conditions, what is produced, and how we see ourselves in the universe.

We are too far along in the twentieth century not to realize that it already has a *political* science, comprised of political physics, political agronomy, political biology, political economics, as well as a very political "political science." This is both the social and epistemological condition of knowledge. The only question is the choice which human beings take in creating knowledge and in their inquiries so that a reconstructive political science in all its branches will come to replace the present enterprise.

A political science which puts the question of human dignity and liberation as an integral part of intellectual work and practical action can be the way of guaranteeing a future for humankind and a more correct understanding of the past. Knowledge workers—or anyone—need not surrender the purpose of the knowledge project, to produce human progress. But the *current* task of humankind is to find ways of sustaining its existence. This means that the approach one takes to power, to description of the universe, to the construction of institutions, to the process of empathy and dignity, to the things that are made, to the question of participation of one with another—and to the relationship of all these questions to each other—is the stuff of a new political science. Knowledge workers will seek to transform their "disciplines" once they realize the limits of what can be known through them, but see that knowledge can play a central role in sustaining life and building a world civilization.

## Notes

1. Philip J. Davis and Reuben Hersh, *The Mathematical Experience* (Boston: Houghlin, Mifflin, 1981), 96.

2. Herbert Marcuse, *Negations: Essays in Critical Theory* (Boston: Beacon Press, 1968), 223f.

3. Jürgen Habermas, *Philosophical-Political Profiles* (Cambridge: MIT Press, 1985). ("social emancipation could not be conceived without a 'complementary revolutionary transformation of science and technology themselves.' Marcuse seeks a new, non-power-oriented science familiar in Jewish and Protestant mysticism of the 'resurrection of fallen nature.' ")

4. Imre Lakatos, *Mathematics, Science and Epistemology* (Cambridge: Cambridge University Press, 1978), chaps. 1 and 2.

5. Often, even this option is not open to them. They must hustle grants in their old age to keep their labs going.

6. Karl Popper's strong attack on Plato as elitist in no way means that Popper is either antielitist or a democratic theorist.

7. Paul Feyerabend, *Against Method* (London: New Left Books, 1975),274–5.

8. Environmental Impact Statements EIS must be distinguished from the other effects of environmental laws, which gave conservationists and other local groups opportunities for intervention in significant decision making. The EIS, on the other hand, quickly became a cynical instrument for additional enrichment of experts protecting particular interests. Every major government-funded project would hire consultants to write, at great length, about its *lack* of deleterious effect on the environment. An industry of turning out such reports serves only to debase the relationship of ecologists and environmental scientists to the public.

9. The compact edition of the *Oxford English Dictionary* (New York and Oxford: Oxford University Press, 1981), 150.

10. As, for example, in William Russo's book on jazz orchestration.

11. Kant, *Rechtslehre:* quoted by Paul Nizan in *The Watchdogs* (New York and London: Monthly Review Press, 1971), 143.

12. Robert Geroch, *General Relativity from A to B* (Chicago: University of Chicago Press, 1980), 182–83.

13. David Bohm, *Wholeness and the Implicate Order* (London: Routledge & Kegan Paul, 1980) Chapter 5, pp. 110–135.

14. Conversation between Marcus Raskin and McGeorge Bundy on October 7, 1986. According to Bundy, there appears to be further research on these questions to suggest that the Roosevelt administration initiated the nuclear bomb programs independent of the Einstein-Szilard letter.

15. The diagrams of high-energy theory appear as images on gallery walls; a Nobel prize–winning physicist announces to the American Association for the

Advancement of Science that only physics requires description in incomprehensible mathematics—all other sciences should be reduced to daily newspaper level of descriptive exposition; literary critics with a penchant for deconstructing texts consider social scientific discourse, like Orientalism, as narrative in order to reveal an ideological foundation.

16.  Gary Snyder, *Old Ways of Knowing as New Ways* (San Francisco: City Lights Books, 1977), 9.

17.  James Gordon, "Biomedicine and Wholistic Medicine," an essay prepared for the Conference on Reconstructive Knowledge, Hampshire College, 1981.

18.  Sigmund Freud, "Some Neurotic Mechanisms in Jealousy, Paranoia and Homosexuality," as interpreted by Norman Cameron in *Development and Psychopathology* (Boston: Houghton, Mifflin, 1963), 221–32.

19.  Evelyn Fox Keller, *Nature as "Her"* (unpublished, 1982).

20.  For example, see Naomi Weisstein's "Adventures of a Woman in Science" in *Women Look at Biology Looking at Women*, ed. R. Hubbard, M. Hanifin, and B. Fried (Cambridge, Mass: Schenkman, 1979), 198.

21.  Evelyn Fox Keller, "Feminism and Science," *SIGNS* 7, no. 3, (Spring 1982):589–602.

22.  Modern physics has recently investigated experimental consequences of fundamental quantum mechanics, effects like those highlighted by Einstein in his critiques nearly fifty years ago. The results are remarkable. Einstein had claimed, on the basis of presuppositions about reality, that quantum theory was deficient, that it was incomplete. But quantum mechanics has passed the tests. Instead, from these experiments something new emerges. Their results teach us that reality itself is either *constructed* (by our own measurements) or so highly interconnected that, in any case, a morality of what one chooses to know and how one reports it has become inescapable. Either way scientists are responsible for the knowledge—the reality—that they create.

# 4

# Exchanges on Reconstructive Knowledge

BETWEEN NOAM CHOMSKY & MARCUS G. RASKIN
OCTOBER 1983 TO FEBRUARY 1985

October 1, 1983

Dear Marc,

Have read the two papers* with interest, and, to be frank, with
unease, of different sorts. As for the arms control paper, I think
everything you say is correct, and the proposal is impressive to the
rational mind. But the fact, as I'm afraid you agree, is that in the real
world where rational factors are of limited effect, no such proposal has a
ghost of a chance of being considered, at least for institutional reasons—
neither the US nor USSR could survive it, with the systems of power and
authority reflected in them—and maybe because of more fundamental
biological defects of the species, quite possibly a highly transitory one
from a biological point of view, an evolutionary dead end. I frankly
don't see any reasonable hope of avoiding a major war, hence nuclear
war, over the next couple of decades. It seems to me that the most useful
thing to do is to concentrate on reducing the probabilities, which means
piecemeal work on particular cases, hoping that somehow, some now
unimaginable change in consciousness, and with it in institutional structure, will come about on a worldwide scale.

About reconstructive knowledge, I'm afraid I remain an unrecon-
structed unbeliever. I think there are many shrewd points in your
discussion—no doubt, the actual decisions and choices in science are
institutionally biased, culturally biased, and conceivably (though here I
remain skeptical) related to "male" ways of thinking, etc. This is worth
exploring and worth pointing out. All of these are factors that we
recognize as departures from a commitment to rationality, and we know
why. I think we also know fairly well what rationality is, though we learn
more about it as understanding progresses. With all the sophisticated
problems that can be constructed (and I don't demean the enterprise—
it's an interesting one) concerning value elements in science, still there is
a chasm that separates any part of the natural sciences from, say, Freud.
To believe what Freud asserts is, essentially, to adopt a religious stance;
you believe it because he says it, or because it "rings true" for some

*Chomsky was sent two papers: a proposal for general disarmament not reprinted here,
and "Toward a Reconstructive Political Science," with different introductory paragraphs.

104

unintelligible reason. In fact, when you look carefully, no further reasons are given. In the case of explanation in the natural sciences, this is simply not the case. Reasons are given, evidence is given, arguments are given, ways of challenging the reasons come to mind and can be explored, etc. It is quite true that no science, not even physics I suppose, comes anywhere near an ideal that can be stated in terms of true formalization—neither did geometry until Hilbert—but we understand pretty well what the ideal is and why it is an ideal to be striven for, and how steps can be taken to approach it. It is a serious misrepresentation, I think, to describe scientific discourse as merely a kind of mode of persuasion, like a lawyer conning a jury. And similarly, it seems to me that the pragmatic line espoused throughout is a kind of vulgarization, which eliminates the humanly most significant elements of science, namely, the search for intelligibility, explanation and insight into natural phenomena. Increasing bonding and affection among people has absolutely nothing to do with this, nor should it. It's a worthy goal, but commitment to it is only one part of a truly human life (the search for understanding is another), and in that part of one's life that is devoted to extending bonding and affection, it would be a complete waste of time to be engaged in science, in my view; there are other, vastly more significant and appropriate means to advance these ends.

Throughout, I have the feeling that there is a kind of confusion between considerations relating to the nature of knowledge and institutional structures. Take the question of the alleged value-neutrality of technology. Your argument to the contrary I think misses what is being asserted, which is that quite commonly the technology in itself is neither pro-human nor anti-human, etc., and in fact is entirely neutral in the sense that its human significance will depend on the institutional framework in which it is embedded. Take, say, current information-handling technology (computers, etc). It can be oppressive or liberatory. It can be used to "Taylorize" work or it can be used to provide each worker with relevant information about global questions in real time so that workers, not just managers, can make reasonable decisions about investment, organization of work, etc. The technology itself can serve either function and in this sense is neutral. The institutional framework, however, is far from neutral; as things now exist, the new technology will be used to centralize management and increase the remoteness of the worker from decision-making. It would be a serious mystification, however, to attribute this fact to the technology. I think there are many similar examples throughout your discussion. You raise the question at one point whether the "reconstructive" approach may not bear dangerous fruit, despite the intentions of the authors. I think it may, in deflecting attention from the real problem of institutional structures to what in my view is largely a pseudo-problem: the nature of knowledge (masculine, elitist, etc.—I can't make any sense out of any of this, frankly).

Maybe I can make my uneasiness clearer by some rather random comments, running through the manuscript. I apologize in advance for the critical nature of these—I'm concentrating on what seems to me dubious, not what looks right and important, since I suppose this is what you'd prefer hearing about.

1. [PP. 91–92] I'm skeptical about this view, which smacks of Galbraith and Bell. I think, actually, that a more accurate appraisal was that of Anton Pannekoek, many years earlier. Yes, "knowledge workers" are essential, increasingly, to industry and so on, but no, they don't have any real power except the kind of power that derives from willingness to follow orders. Henry Kissinger, a typical example of the species, had it basically right when he defined the "expert" as someone who can elaborate the consensus of those with power, i.e., who can grovel before authority and do his job. But I won't go on with this. My own views are expressed in the first two chapters of *Towards a New Cold War*, inter alia. I think, incidentally, your further remarks on p. 95 reinforce the point. Let's say that WWI was the chemist's war and WWII the physicist's war. Then how much did chemists (respectively physicists) influence the decision-making concerning the war?

2. [P. 94–95] Here there is a very important point: we need to become more aware of the moral values linked to epistemology. Also, it is correct as quoted above that no activity of the human mind (or body) can be free from moral issues, in that the activity may bear consequences. But notice that these valid points imply or suggest nothing concerning the nature of rational inquiry, etc. I think this point should be made much clearer than it is throughout. Yes, science, like other activities, is conducted within a framework of institutions, prejudices, etc., and this is something worth analyzing and understanding, and changing. Yes, science like other activities has consequences, and one surely has a moral responsibility to consider this very carefully. But from this nothing, nothing whatsoever, follows about the nature of rational inquiry. If that is to be "deconstructed" and revised, some other type of argument is needed.

3. [P. 97] Here, and elsewhere, there is a disparagement of "linear" and reductionist form, referred to as "the ruling methodology." I often read such comments; I never understand them. On "linearity," I'm completely baffled. What does it mean to call an argument "linear"? That the conclusions follow from the premises? If so, then we had better keep to linear arguments. That there is a steady march from premises to conclusions with no sidetracks, etc.? Then mathematical reasoning is not linear. Something else? Then what. I'm not trying to say that people who refer critically to "linear" reasoning have nothing in mind. No doubt they do, and maybe it is important. But it is their responsibility to show that it is something other than trendy obscurantism. Maybe you do that elsewhere, but here, at least, I don't understand it. Now consider "reductionist" approaches, which are commonly criticized as "bad." Let's

take a concrete example. Suppose that a study of human perception shows that people interpret successive two-dimensional presentations as a rigid three-dimensional object in motion. Suppose now that someone proceeds to find analyzing mechanisms in the visual system that operate in such a way as to explain these facts. That's reductionism. Is it bad? If so, why? In fact, I have never seen a coherent version of this critique. "Reductionism" is simply a matter of trying to discover connections where they exist. In the only sensible interpretation of the term that I know of, reductionism is "holistic." Unless there is some virtue in ignorance, I can't see how one can object to "reductionism." The actual criticisms of "reductionism" that I'm aware of turn out to be criticisms of bad arguments, not of "reductionism."

### *[The Analysis of Science]*

4. [On P. 100] you introduce the interesting concept of "colonizing knowledge." But I think the discussion is highly misleading, given the context and some unclarities of presentation. It is like the point about technology I mentioned earlier. There's nothing "colonizing" about the knowledge in abstraction from institutional structures, nothing inherently "colonizing" about the method by which it was attained. Like information-processing technology, psychological testing (etc.) is a basically neutral technique, though its usage in a particular institutional setting is far from neutral. In a decent society, I'd like to see psychological testing just like medical testing, to determine how people might be helped, etc. Perhaps the very same techniques would be used. Would there be something wrong, say, with testing to determine whether some kid is having problems learning because he is dyslexic (a physiological problem, it seems, to take a "reductionist" stance), and so ought to have special help to overcome the effects? I can't see why, any more than there is something wrong with a test to determine vitamin deficiency. I think the discussion here is very confused. You move much too quickly from [suggesting] a "form of rationality" to an attempt to assign people their proper places. Yes, that is how rationality (not a form of rationality) is used in its institutional setting; no, this has nothing to do with the "form of rationality," but rather with the institutional setting. Again, the point becomes clear immediately when you refer to the "so-called policy sciences." The "so-called" should be understood, here, as referring to the misuse of the term "science" for what is mere ideology.

5. [P. 102] I'd like to see how Keller has "shown" that the way men approach science results in "skewing of our understanding." I think some examples would be useful here to support the point.

6. [P. 102] Is there "another way to do science and technology"? If so, what is it?

7. [PP. 105–106] I think the discussion of Feyerabend is misleading, though it may be true to him. From the concept of freedom of inquiry (let 1000 flowers bloom) it does not follow that one thing is as good as

another. Commitment to freedom does not entail lack of intellectual or moral standards. This is a real vulgarization of anarchism. I didn't, incidentally, find anything much in the way of traditional anarchist views in Feyerabend (whose book I thought was quite amusing, however).

8. [P. 107] Things move much too fast here. From the fact that in a complex society there will be experts, it doesn't follow that one "invariably defers" to them. That leap assumes some institutional arrangements that neither you nor I accept. In a decent society, there would be experts; there would be democratic methods to evaluate what should be done, given their contributions. I should say that the idea "every person an expert" that you flirt with later on doesn't move me. It is simply impossible to obtain more than superficial understanding apart from very narrow spheres. We can therefore either retreat into a kind of mindless know-nothingism, eliminating the arts and sciences from our lives, or accept specialization, experts, the unique contributions of the talented, etc.

9. [PP. 108–110] I don't understand what the "reconstructive" approach is supposed to be.

### [Relocating and Changed Focus]

10. [P. 111] on [nuclear] deterrence. Even here, questions arise, and they have to be answered by the methods of rational inquiry, not blind faith. Cubans, for example, might not be so quick to dismiss deterrence, since they might argue that it may well have succeeded in deterring the US from aggression that would have restored them to the happy state of Guatemalan peasants.

11. [P. 113] I think the reference to Heisenberg is dubious. This is true only in a narrow and technical sense that has no obvious general lessons (it is a bit like taking relativity theory to show that any moral choices are as good as any others). As for therapy, what does that have to do with science? As for the need for refocusing, sure, but that seems orthogonal to the question of the nature of scientific rationality or possible alternatives to it (which are not sketched, and which I don't see). [On p. 112], the statement that scientific and technological inquiry is leading civilization to its demise seems extremely misleading in this context. It is, again, the institutional framework that is crucial. Eliminate scientific and technological inquiry and, shortly, several billion people will die of starvation, rather more than will die in a nuclear war. Same [, p. 113]. How do our problems result from "the limiting forms of rational discourse"? To me it seems that the problem is quite the opposite: we are excluded from using rational discourse for ideological reasons, and the way to overcome this is by overcoming the conditions of power and authority that exclude rational approaches to the problems we face. As for the logic of programming, I don't see the point. What is "limiting" about Turing machine theory, for example? What could we do with computers if we transcend these limits? As for the counterargu-

ment that computers have limited uses, and in our current institutional setting often anti-human ones, I'd be the first to agree, but that is another point altogether. I see nothing "limiting" about "the logic of programming." Again, it seems to me the same unclarity, or perhaps confusion, noted throughout.

12. [P. 113, line 21.] If I read this correctly, it seems to be saying that physics is concerned only with "the measurement of appearance," which is certainly radically untrue.

## [Values]

13. [P. 115.] I don't see any argument here that our disciplines are mythical or [p. 117.] tautological. You seem to be saying that physics has the status of the Iliad or of "p or not p." Is that what you mean? If so, I don't think it has been shown.

14. [P. 118.] Putting aside what Lakatos may have said, I find the point here confused. It simply isn't true that science is "thought to be more accurate" as it removes itself from humans. Take, say, the phonetics of spoken language, something uniquely about humans as far as we know. That is highly "accurate" (in the sense of this discussion). Same with much of human physiology. The point is that as we move towards spheres of greater human concern (e.g., questions of choice and will, of creativity, of social structure) we find that science has nothing to say. This is not something that is "thought to be" the case; it is the case. One may ask why (I've offered my own speculations). But that is a different matter.

15. [P. 119, note] This seems to imply that there is something in the "knowledge system" that keeps me from thinking about quarks. But that's not true. What keeps me from thinking about quarks is that I don't know enough, and to learn enough is too low a priority for me.

16. [P. 120.] The discussion of geometry seems to me wrong. The question is whether physical space-time is or is not Euclidean, a question on a par with whether atoms are indivisible. With regard to these questions, there has never been a change of "axioms," but rather, of assumptions about the physical world. True, at one time (say, Kant) it was erroneously thought that human understanding "couldn't be otherwise." That was just an error.

## [Method]

17. [P. 123.] Suppose we grant that mathematicians are coming to realize . . ., etc. Have mathematicians changed the concept of "proof," by these alleged new insights? Has the mode of rational inquiry in mathematics changed at all as a consequence? Or have mathematicians come to realize that their choice of topics, etc., is externally constrained (another matter entirely, which has nothing to do with the nature of mathematical inquiry; rather, its social context)?

*[Why Political Philosophy of Knowledge is Possible and Necessary]*

18. [P. 126–127.] Here the point becomes clear. Gould, Green, etc. are saying nothing about the methods of science; rather, about the extrinsic factors that determine what is asked and why. These things shouldn't be confused. Assume Gould-Green to be exactly right: nothing follows about whether science should be linear, holistic, reductive, etc. All of this has nothing to do with reconstruction in your sense, as far as I can see.

*[Limits of Language]*

19. [P. 130F.] I don't agree that outside of physics, scientists assume that the scope of their science is in principle universal (nor do many physicists assume this). The reasoning here is flawed. Psychologists don't assume that physics can be reduced to psychology. They study how humans interact with a real world out there, and what systems they come up with. But from such inquiry one cannot determine whether there are free quarks, nor would any psychologist claim that you could. Sociology of knowledge doesn't assume that it can answer the questions of the special sciences it is investigating. As for the arts, totally different issues arise.

20. [P. 131.] Here, for the first time, you say what the alternative is supposed to be. The problem is that "associational" and "analogic" methods are not only not rigorous but essentially useless in argument (though they may be useful, like taking a walk in the woods, in getting ideas). And as for the "holism," ["type of thought which sees in each event or problem new aspects of the whole"] any physicist would agree that each event has relations with any other. Let's be concrete. Suppose I am interested, say, in the question mentioned before about perception of rigid objects (or take any other question you like). How do I approach this question from a point of view that is associational, analogic and holistic? How would that be different from an approach that is linear and reductionist (or male)? Without an answer to this question, at least a glimmer of an answer, it is difficult to evaluate what you are suggesting.

21. [P. 132.] No doubt education for the uninitiated would be a great thing, for reasons apart from those discussed here. That would create a wider class of specialized experts. It is mystification to believe that it would create "generalists" (another empty term). Take linguistics, a small field, highly improverished by the standards of the natural sciences though in another world from the social sciences, so-called. You simply cannot do serious work in some small area of this field, say the syntax of the Romance languages, unless you devote a good part of your life to thinking about it, reading relevant work, learning about ideas that have been proposed, trying out your own ideas, etc. And if you do that, there are lots of other things you just won't know enough to say anything sensible about, maybe even things that are rather close, like the phonol-

ogy of the Romance languages. Of course, there are others who try to take an overview, and so on, but they are simply experts of another kind. This is the human condition; it can't be changed. In nontrivial areas of inquiry, you simply can't master more than a fragment. The conclusion is, then, that either we move towards trivializing intellectural and artistic pursuits, or we accept a high degree of specialization. I don't see what alternative you are offering here.

22. [P. 133.] All true, and important, but irrelevant to the matter of reconstructive knowledge so far as I can see. Rather, it has to do with the institutional setting of ordinary science.

### [Myth]

23. [P. 137.] Are you suggesting that we only retain in science ("the current myth system") what is "pragmatically useful"? That is, we eliminate what is deep, intellectually exciting, beautiful, explanatory, insightful, etc., unless it can be shown to increase bonding and affection, or whatever? That would seem to me to amount to such an impoverishment of human life and thought that you could be accused of profoundly anti-humanist sentiments, I think. Also, the parts of science that are pragmatically useful in your sense would quickly fade or stagnate, since they cannot be dissociated from the parts that are concerned with deepening understanding. I don't follow this.

24. [P. 138.] You say we should "admit" that there are alternative modes, etc. Why should we admit this? Has it been shown? Has an example been suggested? It seems that you are asking people to accept what you proclaim, essentially without argument. I'm sure, incidentally, that there are ways of improving the methods of rational inquiry. That has been shown over and over since the 17th century scientific revolution, and less strikingly before. But these changes occur when they are shown to lead to deepening understanding, etc., not by exhortation.

### [Four Myths]

25. [P. 138.] I can't believe that the narrowest molecular biologist would be surprised to hear that people are related to groups and nature as a whole. What are some of the "ways of knowing" that violate the assumptions ("dichotomies"?) of modern practice? I don't find these examples at all convincing. Suppose acupuncture, or holistic medicine, seems to work. Any inquring mind will want to know why, and then we're back to the "myth" of science, i.e., to the methods of rational inquiry, honesty about evidence and argument, etc. What are some of the progressive solutions that Art Waskow has derived from the Jewish tradition? Etc.

26. [P. 145.] The question is interesting, but I'd like to see an argument, not just obiter dicta quoted from Keller. I've never seen an intelligible argument. The following comments at the bottom of the page don't inspire confidence. Again, all of this has to do with the

institutional (in the broadest sense) setting of science, cultural factors, etc., but not with the nature of rational inquiry itself. These are quite different things. Your point, throughout, is that they are not different things, but you don't show this, at least to my satisfaction. Thus, to show that something about the very nature of rational inquiry (as currently understood in the sciences) follows from the distorting effects of capitalism, male dominance, or whatever, it is necessary to do far more than to show, what is true, that nuclear weapons research is undertaken for this or that reason, that psychological testing is used to put people in their place, and so on. I'm skeptical as to whether that "more" can be shown.

Maybe this gives some idea of my qualms about the whole enterprise. I think there are important insights here, but to me, they seem to be insights about the setting in which rational inquiry proceeds, not about its nature. So far, at least, I don't perceive what the feminist critique has contributed, beyond the obvious: that there is enormous sexism in the practice of scientists, often. I can't make any sense out of the talk of linearity, reductionism, holism, myth, observer-world interaction, axiom-changing, etc. I also tend to think that the important thrust of what you are doing will be undermined by what seems to me a misinterpretation of it, as concerned with the very nature of rational inquiry, not its setting (again, in the broadest sense). The problems of nuclear war, starvation, exploitation, racism, sexism, etc., are severe. In my view, they don't result from the fact that we approach the problems with the methods of the sciences as currently understood, but quite the contrary, because institutional and ideological constraints, conditions of power ultimately, prevent us from approaching these problems with the rational methods of the sciences. Take, say, foreign policy. I think I understand U.S. foreign policy pretty well, and I think the task is intellectually trivial. What seems to me intellectually trivial, obvious on the face of it, supported by massive evidence, etc., is regarded as so lunatic by mainstream scholarship and intelligentsia that they can't even hear the words. Of course, it may be that I am crazy. I think not; rather, I think, and think I can show (and have shown), that the religious doctrines of mainstream intellectual life prevent minimal understanding. If I'm right, then the answer is not to move to holistic or feminist thinking and attack reductive linear rationality (or whatever), but to overcome the barriers of superstition that prevent rational analysis, one part of this being to show why they are erected (not very difficult, again). I think the same holds across the board.

Evidently, we differ considerably in our judgments about this. It is something I'd like to explore further, if there is ever a chance. Hope that these reactions are of some use to you.

Best,

Noam

December 5, 1983

Dear Noam,

I am alarmed by your conjecture that there might be a fundamental defect of the species. If you are right, we are now in the unenviable and hopeless position of waiting for an inexorable end. I am not quite at one with you about the "finger in the dike" strategy. It seems that every piecemeal effort attempted by the peace movement, even if it is accomplished, merely adds to the arms system.

This being so, I agree that we need a new consciousness and institutional structures that reflect this changed consciousness. Indeed, it is this very need that led me to work on questions of reconstruction and reconstructive knowledge. I do not want to leave such work to the likes of the moonies and their scientific supporters, namely Wigner, or the followers of Teilhard. There is of course a quixotic quality to this undertaking. My political hope is that changing consciousness, working for it and working with others to generate a social system which reflects this consciousness will allow humankind the chance to experiment with systems and relationships that might lead to greater equity, liberation and peaceful resolution of conflict. In a very dark time such hopes sound hollow and unrealistic. Nevertheless, I feel compelled to carry out this project.

In attempting to bring about these changes I thought about the nature of modern knowledge and inquiry. Science of course is presented to us as the hope of the future. This being so, it is mistaken to exempt modern inquiry (including science) from every bit of critical examination of its method, the problems that investigators choose and the ethical issues raised in the context of the experiment. Furthermore, the high value that we place on modern inquiry in the natural and social sciences requires that we examine carefully how certain knowledges are constructed and whether they reflect rather than ameliorate human problems. There is an added dimension which has to do with the meaning of understanding. You seem to hold to the view that understanding comes from "rigorous demonstrations." I argue that "rigorous demonstrations," while useful, may in fact lead us quite off course. I accept William James's definition of truth. "Truth is simply a callous name for verification processes connected with life. Truth is made, just as health, wealth and strength are made, in the course of experience." The question of understanding or proofs in the usual sense is less satisfactory to me than understanding as it may come to us through existential *verstehen* as well as the examination of *why* a particular premise or assumption is taken as the starting point. There are ample examples throughout history of rigorous proofs of utterly mad propositions and dangerous, wrongheaded views about people and the nature of things. Often intellectual rigor and specificity "flourishes at the expense of wisdom." I commend to you the *Hammer of Witches* to see one level of rigorous proofs and "factual evidence" which were used to prove the existence of witches and the cures for them.

I favor an existential reconstructive approach because I am not persuaded by intellectual activity at the expense of aesthetics, ethics and wisdom; characteristics which come from widening—not narrowing—the frame or concern. In Washington I have come to see the extraordinary number of "rational" justifications, empirical studies, whether from universities or from the National Academy of Science, as little more than put-ons, justifications for power, empty-headed. On this you and I can agree. But the question is whether there is a pristine science, a thoroughly rigorous inquiry which is anything more than another myth system. How can the answer to this question be found? It is necessary to study the work of people who were and are not guns for hire, but people who are recognized by scientists as scientific. We must look at their work and ascertain whether their inquiries are not shot through with considerations which prove that our experiments and proofs are limited and self-reinforcing systems. Furthermore, what we see or intuit is no longer separated from what we do. We influence what we do.

When we want to take the "best" in science it is worthwhile to take an important issue, seeking to comprehend it in its fundamental and profound implications. In this regard, I would raise the EPR paradox of Einstein, Podolsky and Rosen. Einstein holds with you that there is an "out there" out there which can be known separate and distinct from the investigator. Bohr's contrary view is that there is no causal relationship between things, that is, two correlated subatomic particles. Rather, they are both part of an indivisible whole. Some argue that this refutes the Cartesian view of the universe. Now there are four ways to look at their disagreement. One is that Einstein, et. al., are correct, the other is that the quantum theorists are correct. The third way is to say that both are wrong and there is an alternative explanation. The fourth way is to say that we cannot know what is an accurate reflection of reality. Our words and symbols, the Heraclitean nature of things, makes it impossible to report accurately on reality. What may be true for two subatomic particles may not be true for all subatomic particles. Induction takes us so far and no further. So where does this leave us, if as I do, we conclude that both Einstein's view and Bohr's view are limited and both are myth systems? That is, they are literary or mathematical shorthands or reflections. If this is accurate, then what matters in a pragmatic sense is the effect that each of these views has on the construction of science and social systems.

You may wonder how the pragmatic test would tie to the EPR question. In part it would be necessary to put the question into a social and historical context; 1935. Einstein sought to pursue strictly scientific inquiry, arguing that rigor demanded a separation of scientific axioms from moral axioms. He believed scientists were giving up the classical definition of science, namely, finding out the rules of the universe, for the less stringent stance that it is enough to know that particular explanations work operationally. According to the quantum mechanicians, it is hopeless to seek fundamental causes. I suspect that Einstein feared the social consequences of scientists who settled for the more comfortable proposition that "it works." Perhaps he did not trust scientists who stopped with such an explanation, because he believed that without the discipline of having to find truth they could be easily manipulated by the powerful, namely, capitalism and the state. No doubt he was concerned about the racial implications of the eugenicists' work, just as he himself had been criticized, as Lauren Graham points out, for his political and philosophical positions. He wanted to protect the scientific kernel. It appears now that Einstein's scientific position was less correct than that of Bohr and the quantum mechanics school.

Bohr's position puts man, or at least his machines, at the center of scientific inquiry. If he is correct, science's style and purpose has to change. The problem has been that the physicists have not wanted to make any critical evaluation of their scientific work, an evaluation which their research cried out for just because of their belief that human beings remain at the center of inquiry, and man cannot know fundamental laws of nature. They rejected Einstein's conception of a Kantian reality and without saying it, his view of scientific purpose. Even though no fundamental laws can be found independent of man's beliefs and machines he constructs, scientists abjure making moral judgements as part of their work, even though they know—and knew—that the very character of science had changed.

Standards for rational inquiry demand that moral judgements should be added as an integral part of any particular experiment. Unless shown otherwise, I do not see how transformations of social systems, or the generation of a new consciousness can occur if we hold on to narrow conceptions of rational inquiry. Inquiry must now focus on relationships. The reason is that rational inquiry is not, cannot, and should not be sealed from everyday life, institutional setting or the struggles which are carried on throughout the world. How rational inquiry is carried on, who we do it for, what we think about and *what we choose to see* is never insulated or antiseptic. Once we communicate it through the medium of language, the symbols of mathematics, the metaphors and cliches of everyday life, we call forth in the minds of readers or fellow analysts, other issues and considerations that may be outside of the four corners of the experiment or inquiry. What they bring to what they see, read, or replicate is related to their purpose or agenda or their unconscious interpretations.

By your formulation of Henry Kissinger's role in international politics [p. 155 above] you seem to be implying that those who engage in rational inquiry and science, knowledge workers (whose production is more information and ideas) do not add, shape, change, or even cause things to be. But this view does not seem to be correct. Knowledge workers do cause events and things to happen. This is not because they know anything fundamental (that is, truths which escape human history). Rather, the scientists have influence because what they do "works" through the technologies that are constructed on the basis of their explanations, or vice versa. These explanations are often surrounded in irrelevant notions of cause and the centrality of particulars I would call reductionism.

You defend reductionism with great vigor. However, I would put you another way of looking at the world. It seems there are two metaphors which describe the difference in the modern point of view with regard to rational inquiry. I am choosing one over the other, not necessarily because it is correct, but because it is no less wrong, and it has, it seems to me, far more positive ethical human implications. The building block theory assumes that there is a determinism and cause of things in which all things are explained according to fundamental or elementary parts; whether they are sentences, genes, cells or subatomic particles. The second view I would describe as the flow or stream view of life. In this view what we know and experience, what we see is a reflection of a reality which invariably remains mysterious. We may explain it, we may develop rules of induction about it, mathematical forms of approximation, but ultimately reality remains mysterious. Each part of the stream is different and each "thing," that wonderful ambiguity, is made up of different things, all of which exist in arrangements we guess about, and describe to one another through words and allusions which themselves have their own meanings and realities.

It is true that I seek to regenerate a pragmatic view. But the pragmatism that I hope for is one which includes bonding and affection. In this I agree with William James who argued that our opinion about the nature of things is integrally tied up with the moral life.

You tax me with being confused about the relationship between "the nature of knowledge and institutional structures." But you assume a split between form and substance as if there is an impenetrable wall between them. You argue that "technology is neither pro-human nor anti-human, etc., and in fact is entirely neutral." Your view is mistaken because technology is a process. Technology does not only refer to the thing itself but to the processes of making the thing. For example, what does it take in terms of resources, of types of work styles, oppressive or liberatory methods and ends to make the particular thing? What materials and machines are used to accomplish a particular end, and why are they used?

Even if one were not to analyze the making of the thing itself but just its result, one would still have to judge such things as computers according to their organization-technological use. Note what William Casey, the Director of the Central Intelligence Agency said when he picked up an honorary doctor of law from Westminster College,

I feel more at home here than you might imagine. I came here from the CIA campus in Virginia, across the Potomac from Washington. Contrary to the spy novels and movies, most of our people in intelligence spend their time sitting at computers or in libraries evaluating and analyzing information. Today's James Bonds have graduate degrees and are more conversant in economics, science, engineering, demography and history than with gambling casinos, fast cars, smokey bars or run-down hotels around the world. They develop and use technical marvels and apply the finest scholarship to gather, analyze and interpret facts and relationships from every corner of the earth and beyond.

I doubt that the computers which are made for the purpose of centralizing behavior and spying, will be the same sort of computers that could be used to generate a decentralized participatory system. The institutional framework is influenced by and dictates as well the type of computer which will be made, and the use to which it will be put. Technology as a process is utterly intertwined with the institutional structure. By saying this I want to be clear that there are technologies which in fact are liberatory both in their result for others and for the workers involved in the process of making the particular technology.

I am puzzled that you cannot "make sense" out of our claim that certain knowledges are "masculine," "elitist." We mean that knowledges are meant to serve a particular class and gender. Certainly the "liberal arts" as they were once taught and concerned favored a particular class. Thus, as John Dewey pointed out long ago, certain forms of liberal education were related directly to the will to govern and to seek the reproduction of a particular type of class society. One sees this in the sorts of notions taught in school, in for example, such "estimable" institutions such as Harvard, where there is clear preparation for elitist activities. Gender definition can be found in Bacon, who compared nature to a woman, requiring certain skills on the part of the obviously masculine scientist. I will have more to say about this later. [The following numbered comments correspond to Chomsky's numbered comments in his letter, above.]

1. My view on the definition of the knowledge worker stems in part from changes in the productive process. You may wonder whether I think everyone in a post-industrial society is a knowledge worker. A knowledge worker does not work primarily with his hands, nor are the tasks he works at repetitive ones. His tasks relate to taking bodies of information, other peoples' insights, information and ideas. It does not matter what the content of the subject matter is. Knowledge workers may find themselves in a bureaucracy, university, scientific laboratory or in a law firm.

To say what knowledge workers do is to recognize that they create the basis of modern life. Whether in the laws we write, the psychological categories we accept or the attitudes and perceptions we believe about others not directly involved with us in face-to-face relations, whether in the inventions of mass destruction we fear, or the information we receive on how the universe and economy appears and works, knowledge workers have spun the web of our consciousness and belief world. Their knowledge web shapes material reality.

Since knowledge workers exist in the context of a power matrix, they are usually responsible to and responsive towards an "employer" or some seemingly autonomous institution that sets the framework in which knowledge workers perform their tasks. In many circumstances knowledge workers, whether they are lowly bureaucrats or Henry Kissinger, clearly articulate or rationalize the desires of the powerful.

The unwritten assumption of modern science was that scientists would be able to escape the framing conditions of their work by their "pure" discoveries which would add to progress and understanding. This situation did not obtain although no one can deny the benefits of certain scientific and technological inventions. The reason that the knowledge workers who are scientists and technologists have not been wholly successful is related to the requirement of capital. The more capital the scientists needed for their work, the more intertwined knowledge worker scientists became in the prevailing power system. They cared not a whit for the implications of what they worked on. As you know, in Vietnam, the Vietnamese people continue to suffer from the work of scientists as it was combined with military power and fury. The land is fallow in the southern part of Vietnam as a result of the American use of Agent Orange, the deadly toxin which was sprayed across Vietnam from 1962 to 1971 in order to render the land fallow. This accomplishment could not have been achieved without American scientists and technologists.

Of course no social system remains a closed loop for very long. The information, ideas and insights gathered, the discoveries and inventions made by knowledge workers which shaped our view of the world and its social organization also have elements within it which transcend the pyramidal distribution of power and the internal crises that society now faces. I am not familiar with the chemist's role in World War I although I am sure we could learn a great deal from a history of du Pont Corporation's involvement with the military establishment and the growth of the university from 1900 to 1918. In any case, there can be little doubt that Oppenheimer and his friends played an important, participatory role in deciding whether the atomic bomb should be used, the character of the design of that bomb, and the view that it should be used on innocent populations. There was a payoff to the physicists. They became part of the permanent apparatus of power. They may not be on top, but throughout this period, they have been on tap. They are now part of the permanent nexus of power between the state and science well described by Feyerabend. It can be seen at Livermore and Draper Labs where our laser, space, and nuclear scientists are involved in technical and scientific schemes to make their mad wishes come true. This brings me to the next point.

2. You appear to be in agreement with me that no activity of the human mind can be free from moral issues. Yet you assume that "rational inquiry" can be exempt from such a claim. As with so much of what we describe in literary statements such phrases as "rational inquiry" are approximate reflections of processes. In other words the phrase rational inquiry is a short hand for a way of doing things which some of the priestly define as acceptable. Nevertheless, once we understand that rational inquiry is a process, a series of procedures, there is no way of not introducing "extrinsic" considerations in them, whether through conscious choice or through unexamined or habitual ways of acting. If inquiry is perceived as a thing or a single act, torn out of life itself, we will be stuck with inadequate and mechanistic ways of looking at the rich and diverse nature of humankind—and inquiry. We will be hiding from ourselves obvious realities. A linear argument is one in which we exclude seemingly unconnected insights, concerns and competing premises for the purpose of working out a supposedly necessary and inexorable conclusion from a premise.

I suppose algorithmic thinking is the quintessential representation of this method. Premises may be chosen which seem to be correct in a particular universe of discourse but in fact when applied in other universes or to social practice are very weak indeed, even though the logic may appear to be faultless. Thus, for example, the only time numbers are "true" is when they deal with numbers non-referentially. Once they apply to things or people, the only way they can be taken as true is if we accept the interchangeability of things or people. The principle of interchangeability overthrows uniqueness. This a profound political and social choice. When this choice is made (and who should make it?) we have to decide what qualities of uniqueness we are prepared to overthrow for the sake of being in a conglomerate known as society. Under what conditions, for example, are we prepared to say that one Noam Chomsky equals one Ronald Reagan? This question is profoundly political and ethical, although we do not know this when we say one equals one. One equals one, for example, is only a true statement when one is not a modifier. Once we talk about one person equalling another person we are in, as I have said, an ethical and political discourse.

This brings me to the meaning of reductionist. I mean by it the taking of things, atoms, entities, and reducing them to their physical parts according to laws of physics and chemistry in the hopes that by understanding the part the whole may be explained. The term is of course used more broadly now. As you suggest, reductionism does not explain connections nor does it explain processes or relationships. On the other hand, there is no denying the success of reductionism in biology as a research program. But its operational success does not mean that it can or should dictate a worldview. Instead, reductionism should be challenged to change just because of the worldview that is embedded in it. The fact that it is silent on consequences and implications does not mean that there are not huge implications and consequences to its method and program. The dangers presented to us by biotechnology, behavior modification or weapons and space research cannot be written off. There is no way to correct or get a handle on these questions if scientists and technologists write off those concerned with value or those concerned with older religious systems as wooly-headed and silly. Furthermore, the dangerous direction that science has taken us by refusing to develop a value based epistemology and research for the basis of science or being willing to undertake a more generous attitude towards that which is not quantifiably explicable is placing humankind in increasing jeopardy.

Now as for another point. Two dimensional objects appear as three dimensional because each eye sees three dimensional objects as only two. Such an experiment as you describe is not the kind I would devise to test perception.

4. You continue to argue the neutrality of technology. You call information processing and psychological testing "basically neutral." I take it that the word "basically" leaves room for a number of unneutral characteristics. At present, technologies and psychological testing are used to re-enforce class power. To see it otherwise is to assert an ahistorical role to technology or to such derivative activities as psychological testing. It is hard to see information processing as anything more than a system of hierarchic control which narrows and "reduces" persons to aspects of themselves. When technologies operate in that way, seeking identification between a word and an attribute of a person, for example, as if the word and the person are the same, we are losing our rationality and our humanity. Where technology is used as the means to prove basic knowledge or to apply it there is no longer a meaningful separation which exists between basic knowledge, its application or technological instrument.

As for the dyslexic problem, the question of reversals is an historic and social one. Thus, spelling changes over years. I point this out to suggest that word shortenings, letter reversals, etc., can be seen as a continuing social process which does not necessarily have a physiological base to it. Rather, what is thought to be correct spelling is related to what we think of as socially correct at a particular moment. Spelling a word one way or another is not physiologically necessary. Do you think Israelis are dyslexic because they read from right to left? I wonder if the Chinese have instances of dyslexia?

Presently, genetic tests are being used to show the actual relationship between institutional and property requirements and physiological reactions. This is a form of colonizing knowledge.

According to Lewontin, DuPont and other corporations are now engaged "in screening workers for sensitivity to the various toxic chemicals they use. If a prospective employee is found to be particularly sensitive that person is not employed." And as one might expect, Harvard's School of Public Health is helping in the devising of such tests to screen individuals for hypersensitivity. As Lewontin points out, "The whole movement seeks now to remove the obligation from the corporations and the government to protect all workers and all persons, and to place the obligation on the individual as the locus of the problem." In other words, the type of tests devised cannot be wrung from their institutional setting.

Suppose you are the head of a laboratory at Harvard or Bell Labs; do you think your experiments, your very mode of knowledge work in the laboratory would not be utterly intertwined with institutional considerations? I fear that your definition of the word science is far too pure, perhaps reflecting your own gentle and noble nature.

5. I. I. Rabi is quoted as having said to Vivian Gornick, "Women just don't have it and that's all there is to it; they haven't got what it takes." Now this attitude is one which surely colors what goes on in the laboratory. As Keller points out, the metaphor of the master molecule, as the cause of what happens in genetic expression, rather than a more "democratic" *method* explanation suggested by some women on the basis of the same evidence, is contrived out of masculine favoritism. Both descriptions were metaphors. Which should be chosen if they are about the same in descriptive validity?

6. I suggest that the present way of doing science and technology is directly related to the management of specific pieces of information, nature and people. This management is to be carried out for the very few. Surely there is another way. Let me give some examples and clues. In the social sciences, there should be subject-to-subject participation. To the extent possible, we do not invade others without their permission, their understanding and their active participation. The information that is learned is for their benefit, not others.

The style of machines built are meant to be for general use and understanding. There should be non-peer discussion about experiments and work. In *Being and Doing* I listed a series of questions which should be asked on issues having to do with technology. I am including that list below and also a list which Bernstein and I have devised for the essays we have done on reconstructive knowledge.

Questions on Technology

• What is the effect on the people who are living in the immediate area of a particular activity if it is undertaken? For example, uprooting people for a highway which would probably result in the early death of older people, concentration camp fences in the cities to keep children away from the inner city highway, probable destruction of the social fabric of those who live in the area. What are the probable benefits to certain groups? Highway contractors and more profits, greater employment in the local area, greater access for traffic and continued existence of the automobile industry.

- What is the effect on men? Will different classes of men be affected differently?
- What is the effect on children? How will they be affected by the action? Which children? Hosts as against users?
- How will women be affected by the action? Will they be helped or hindered? Which women? Hosts against users?
- How many people are affected by the action undertaken? For example, if a modern power plant is built, should those not apparently aware of its effects be protected through government or should they have a direct voice in deciding whether it is to be built?
- How does the action affect the natural habitat of the area? In the foreseeable future; in the next several generations?
- How does the action affect the level of noise and, once it is built, the assault on the eye of the individual? (Are such questions now more than matters of taste?)
- How are animals affected by the action undertaken?
- How does the action taken fit with apparently unrelated other actions in the immediate area, regionally, nationally, internationally?
- What is the effect of the action on a) water, b) land, c) air?
- What is the cumulative effect? Are there long-term effects which differ from short-term effects that compensate for disruption for children, women, men, air, land, water? Are there long-term effects which have bad results for land, water, sea, air, men, women, children so that the apparent action is in fact illusory?
- Does the action cause better distribution of services?
- Does the action result in democratization of power?
- What are the points of intervention if the wrong judgment is made?

A number of questions are tied to the reconstructive discourse. First of all, while we recognize the value of Karl Popper's approach in translating scientific discourse into problems, our view is that the problematic form does not readily allow the analyst to appraise incisively the historical framework, the hidden questions or the consequences of particular modes of research. We believe that certain questions are meta-concerns which transcend any particular problem. Each of them has normative and instrumental implications that can be addressed.

- So far as can be known, what are the effects of a particular research program, or technological enterprise on the humane, liberatory organization of society, the democratization of it and the ought purpose of greater distribution of non-destructive power and wealth in the world? Can a reconstructive research program be generated under present social and economic conditions?
- In any particular discipline, how does reality get constructed? What is the means used to test the validity of that reality and how does it relate to other concerns seemingly unconnected? What are the limitations that knowledge in a particular discipline has run into, such as limitation theorems, (e.g., Godel's proof, the Hawthorne effect)?
- How much into the future must the knowledge worker consider consequences

to the work he or she performs? What is the social organization which will emerge as a result of the knowledge worker's creations? Is the knowledge worker's result determined by "hidden" social invariants?

- What are historical branch points of the particular discipline which either changed the direction of that discipline or the class of questions that are rejected? Why were they rejected?

- With respect to the branch points, what are the alternative routes which could have been taken? Accepting the obvious, that there is no exact foreknowledge, how do we become more aware of implications of a particular course?

- What are the particular "calculative tools" which are brought into a discipline? What values are brought with such "technical aids"? (Obviously, the computer has had a profound effect on the character of economics and social science as well as theoretical physics. Indeed, it has made possible the missile and nuclear arms race.)

7. I agree with you on this point. The more correct version of this statement is that there should be no externally enforced system of standards which are laid on the researcher, or anyone. What do you mean when you say that Feyerabend's views are "amusing"?

8. Several points need to be made about experts. The issue is whether, in what, and how we determine expertise in a particular set of activities? In *Being and Doing* I outlined a way experts could be used on environmental and ecological questions. I do see a need for the expert, or that person who chooses to specialize in a particular area or thing. However, the question may be whether we need that particular field. Thus, the Japanese have very few lawyers compared to the U.S. Would we be able to do without legal expertise or the expertise of accountants, their research and knowledge into laws that should not exist? Legal existence and need is clearly institutionally based. Or, there may be experts in witchcraft. Do we know, need or care about such expertise? Or can their particular knowledge be subsumed under a larger and different category?

By no means am I advocating mindless amateurism. There are some people who can play the Appasionata Sonata and others who cannot, there are others who are masters of language and those who have no ear for it, just as there are surgeons and butchers, both their own specialty. But this does not mean that specialties cannot be judged from the "outside", understood by others not doing it. Nor does it mean that there must be walls between disciplines of knowledge, different experts and the "outsider". There is a great deal of cant in expertise which can be quickly exploded by the non-expert. The "expert" in today's world assumes as given stable and fundamentally correct the world around him. And they believe in their profession or expertise.

9. The answer to this point can begin to be found in number 8. A short definition can be found in my various articles. This is from a working paper by Bernstein and me:

We believe there is a field of knowledge which is begging to be born. Those committed to working in it will expose the social and epistemological assumptions of the natural and social sciences, illuminate the interrelationship of different disciplines, their ethical and political consequences, and the ways these disciplines relate to the human construction of physical and social reality. The knowledge workers of this new field will appreciate the tenuous and changing nature of both facts and truth. This realization will help them crack open facts to make public the values mingled within them. The laborers in this type of thought and practice will recognize that the human condition is such that individually and collectively, we are condemned to limited understanding. They will recognize that our single reality is comprised of many realities which must be shared among us. Needless to say, the concept of shared social reality raises the most profound questions of power, domination and subservience, of social, political and economic organization.

There are further starting assumptions of this field. Workers in it will emphasize connections and relations rather than fixate on individual entities, fundamental causes or the thankless "quarkian" task of reducing one set of things to another set of things. Instead, the newly conscious knowledge workers will seek to make public the nexus of social relations, economic, technological and social determinants, political deals and customary conventions which define our "objective reality". In this process they will deemphasize formalistic distinctions which separate one discipline from another, the creative arts from the other human creations, natural and social sciences, because they accept the notion of freely chosen ideas which frame reality. We choose to call this field of inquiry reconstructive knowledge. It is both normative and pragmatic by which we mean it mingles a concern for practical results in terms of the good end and it recognizes any particular object as part of a series, or better stated, as part of a flow of activities and processes. It begins by assuming that isolating a thing does not give greater understanding or clarity, especially if we seek to understand the consequences of particular actions or pieces of knowledge.

10. The issue of nuclear weapons and deterrence have to be judged in terms of what would happen if nuclear weapons were used. The fact that people are frightened of nuclear war does not mean that deterrence is working. They could just as easily be frightened for psychological reasons having nothing to do with real consequences. The American intervention into Grenada has made very clear to the Cubans that the United States is not deterred by Soviet weapons or the Soviet Union. Whether or not it should be is quite another story.

11. The point about Heisenberg is a statement of interaction which can be found in profoundly disparate physical and social realms. Perhaps this should be thought about in Hegelian terms. The master and the slave change each other. That it applies to physics merely shows its greater applicability and the impossibility of separating the viewer from the object.

I am mystified at your view that the elimination of "scientific and technological inquiry and shortly, several billion people will die of starvation, rather more than will die in a nuclear war." I think the reality is quite otherwise, at least as it applies to the question of food. I would take seriously the work of Susan George, Collins and Lappe, who tell us that the present mode of agricultural science and technology has led to problems of starvation rather than alleviated it. Again to quote Lewontin,

> Even Khrushchev knew that American farmers were productive because they had hybrid corn, and he tried to import hybrid corn production into the Soviet Union. The fact is, however that the production of hybrid corn is based on a scientific error. It can be shown and it is agreed by all breeders and plant geneticists (at least at the present time), that if, in the 1930s the United States had not devoted its entire effort to hybrid corn, but instead had selected varieties of corn as it developed them at that time, we would have at least the yields we now have, if not greater yields.

Lewontin's argument is that hybridization is a direct result of the seed producer's drive for profits. "Hybrids are here, not because they are intrinsically better, not because standard methods of plant breeding couldn't produce varieties that are just as good, but because in order to commoditize the product, hybrids were introduced. . . . The entire apparatus, private corporations, scientists, the land grant colleges make research and publish papers on hybridization. As Lewontin also puts it, "the entire apparatus serves those who are trying to make money. That's part of science too."

Here we may be talking at cross purposes with one another. However, if the definition of rational discourse is given by highly tendentious and ideological institutions parading under free and rational inquiry, then what is one to do?

12. I am eager to get your view of what physicists do. If it is not the measurement of appearance, or the creation of appearance which then can be measured, what is it?

13. Physics does have those mythical qualities, especially if one accepts the arguments of quantum mechanics.

14. The examples you give, namely phonetics and physiology, are correct, although I think it is important to distinguish between the naming of processes and the explanation of what is happening. Much of what we do I suspect is naming and then speculating. If science has nothing to say on "spheres of greater human concern" and does not see the interrelationship between those questions and the processes of science, then we are surely lost.

15. I did not follow your point here.

16. In practice, assumptions about the physical world are axioms that are to be tested. Different aspects of the universe may respond to different assumptions about it and so therefore, as Dyson argues, there may be complementary axioms. The question of whether Euclidean, non-Euclidean or complementary views of space-time apply, are correct, grow out of social realities of the inquirers.

Before I take up the question of whether mathematicians have changed their concept of proof I want to raise a point which seems to run throughout your letter. It is doubt about Freudian psychology or religion. I share these doubts with you. Doubts aside, the insights in both and the problems which both address are utterly intertwined with our most abstract and "rigorous" subjects. I can do no better than quote mathematicians on their belief that they are dealing with the "infinite," the supernatural and all sorts of other platonic entities. One of the dissenters in the Soviet Union, the mathematician Shafarevitch says that mathematical work has an "inner logic" (like musical composition, I suppose) in which a theme passes from one instrument to another. The theme is part of a "symphony composed by someone." He closes his article by saying that "mathematics may serve now as a model for the solution of the main problem of our epoch: to reveal a supreme religious goal and to fathom the spiritual activity of mankind." Hermann Weyl also holds to this view, namely, that mathematics is the science of the infinite. Mathematics "lifts the human mind into closer proximity with the divine than is attainable through any other medium." According to this sentiment, the topics chosen in mathematics are chosen by God. There is an unconscious net which relates what is thought about and "proved" by one person at one place and time and someone else unknown to the other does the same work at another time and place. Together the two mathematicians make a pattern of proof. Now I don't know whether this is true, false, or touching, but surely this notion has been part of mathematics for centuries, just as, may I add, it has played a part in music.

Now to the question of whether rational inquiry in mathematics has changed or, alternatively, whether the concept of "proof" changed in mathematics? You will recall Russell when he set out in the early part of the century to restore the edifice of mathematics "against that kind of skepticism which abandons the pursuit of ideals because the road is arduous and the goal is not certainly attainable. He knocked those who doubted the attainment of absolute Truth, who held to the idea that there was only "opinion and private judgment" and that there are only separate "truths". He once thought that "of such skepticism mathematics is a perpetual reproof; for its edifice of truths stand unshakable and inexpungable to all the weapons of doubting cynicism.

As Lakatos points out this brief Euclidean 'honeymoon' surrendered to "intellectual sorrow." His proofs "degenerated into a sophisticated system, including 'axioms like that of reducibility, infinity, choice, and also ramified type theory'—one of the most complicated labyrinths a human mind ever invented. 'Class' and 'membership-relation' turned out to be anything but 'perfectly well known.' " Lakatos points out that proof had to give way to "explanation, perfectly well known concepts to theoretical concepts, triviality to sophistication, infallibility to fallibility, Euclidean theory to empiricist theory. Now there are smart aleck answers to the meaning of proof. One is that it is what people who call themselves mathematicians say it is; and they have the guild and university in back of them to state that a proof is a proof. In other words, a social system. Or we can say that a proof is a religious exercise in which you use a "formal language with a given list of symbols or alphabet. Then you write down the hypothesis of your theorem in the same symbolism. Then you show that you can transform the hypothesis of our theorem in the same symbolism. Then you show how you can transform the hypothesis step by step, using the rules of logic, till you get the conclusion. That's a proof." Now since no one every really does that, a proof is up to the satisfaction of the jury, that is, the people we are trying to convince.

18. You are right. Green and Gould are trying to be more rigorous. They believe that their opponents are "ideological" or "liars". Their activity is the reconstruction of knowledge, seeking greater "truth" within the confines or limits and assumptions of the presently defined disciplines. Their work is not necessarily reconstructive because it does not recognize the fact that they are tied to a series of very sensible and ethical propositions, attitudes, etc., which define their concern, and the way they look at a question. Now you raise the question of a confusion around the methods of science. I am saying that the word science is part of an historical process as well as a method. Its methods must change. It was once distinguished from conscience which was an existential truth, knowing something with conviction and commitment as against science, which meant knowing something "theoretically" or, I would say, from the outside. My argument now is that the split between these two meanings has done grievous harm. This same split exists in the difference we ascribe between experience and experiment. Experience carries with it a personalized, existential quality and experiment is supposedly replicable. But I challenge whether these linguistic distinctions are valuable. We need the existential-ethical in the laboratory to experience what we are doing with a sense of conscience.

19. I think your point is partly correct. However, psychologists believe they can understand how the real world is interpreted if they understand those who interpret the real world for the rest of us. Clearly, some psychiatrists, enamored of chemical cures believe that molecular and electrical and physical reactions in the brain do define what psychological reactions might be.

Sociologists of knowledge have been timid in questioning the sciences because they believed that there was a door marked complexity and purity which could not be opened. This, as you are painfully aware by this time, I view to be a big mistake.

20. I am eager for your definition of the word "rigorous." Now you say that associational and analogic methods are "essentially useless in argument." I do not agree. For example, the entire method of legal reasoning in the common law is reason by analogy. It proceeds by taking seemingly dissimilar fact situations and placing them under over-arch-

ing principles which themselves are built from particular fact situations. Associational reasoning is that reasoning which connects seemingly unrelated ideas which we have in our head to one another. It is connecting the seemingly unconnected, the unobvious. As William James has said, "What a thought is, and what it may be developed into, or explained to stand for, and be equivalent to are two things, not one." What you describe as rigorous thinking reminds me too much of computer thinking. While I suspect Jacques Barzun to be a foul elitist with the soul of a tortured adding machine, nevertheless, he has an important point when he says that "A computer does not think, it feels nothing, and what it is said to 'know'—bits of information all cast in the digital mode—has no fringe. Nor has it a memory, only storage room. On any point called for, the answer is all or none. Vagueness intelligent confusion, original punning on words or ideas never occur, the internal hookups being unchangeable; they were determined once for all by the true minds that made the machine and the program work." Now as for the question about perception of rigid objects, there is no way for the brain to think about rigid objects except through association and analogue. The process which the brain goes through is one of reinterpreting the two dimensional object into a three dimensional one. This is not reductionism.

Holism has a clear meaning. Processes and complex organic activities cannot be understood in isolation. The whole is always greater than the sum of its parts and knowing a particular part does not mean that we know the whole. Furthermore, processes take place in history which itself should be known.

21. There are certain things worth knowing about and others less so. This obviously is a matter of taste and interest. There is no question that mastery of anything is not a casual activity and knowing one thing well may keep a person from not knowing another discipline or field very well. Nevertheless, are you denying that there are certain things which are more important to know than other things? And is it not the case that in a particular fragment are *you* not seeking fundamental laws which go beyond the particular case? And if not, is it the case that there is no sensible connection which can be made between particular knowledges and other ones?

Surely there are some knowledges you would be very happy to see dry up and others stimulated? This must relate either to some notion of value, either that they explain more than others or reflect how we can deal with the human condition more sensibly. I have no interest in trivializing various areas of intellectual and artistic inquiry. Quite the contrary. I am hopeful that we may expand those who take part in them and that we do not have to assume closed doors of what can and should be known, what should be related to each other and what consequences emerge from that realtionship.

We cannot forget that there are fashions in knowledge which often guide what is to be known and what is to be dropped. These are often determined by the fact that the old guys die out and the new guys bring new styles. Or they are brought by one group invading another field, as, for example, the physicists "invading" biology at the end of the second world war which resulted in all sorts of ideas, skills and work drying up in biology, much in the manner I suppose, that someone might come forward and say that to divide syntax from phonology in understanding any language leads to a button-in-the-buttonhole view of language construction and language use.

22. Reconstructive knowledge includes consideration of the human factors which framed the specific laboratory work which went on.

23. I am saying that what is pragmatically useful must increase bonding and affection. There is no reason, empirical or otherwise, for not emphasizing that form of insight, beauty and explanation which *finds* the bonding and empathic system as it already exists, while it presses forward means and inquiries to generate that view of wholeness and relatedness. Why not? Why is this exactly, without sounding religious, the spirit that is now needed? Do we need any more discrete facts? Or do we need explanations that are bonding ones? These do not have to be truths for all time, merely for now and the next several generations.

I hope this letter elucidates some of our points. The question of various forms of rhetoric is important here. In Aristotle's rhetoric there is a discussion of the Enthymeme which, as I recall, is a method for proving probable statements. All of science is a method for proving probable statements. But exhortation is a method for proving and asserting probable experiential statements to change the way the person being exhorted thinks and acts about work or life. It is a shorthand based on a stated relationship and joint set of unstated experiences between the exhorter and the exhorted.

In virtually every aspect of modern life man attempts to liberate himself from his present situation and from his past. This escape from both a temporal history, whether through films, books, poetry or other means is a way to recenter oneself. It throws the person back on the invention of myth, a system of explanation which centers the person without awareness of temporal history. Non-western rational man knows the need for myth intuitively, for sacred traditions, customs, and taboos match up in a pragmatic and materialistic sense to what is needed in order to survive as a people, even though personal death is ordained. I am not a defender of all non-western myths, only those myths which center people in non-oppressive ways. And if western consciousness allows us to be liberated in the sense of seeing the limits and oppressive nature of certain myths, then perhaps we can choose which ones we want once we are conscious of the role they play within us.

The Judeo-Christian myths of Marx and Waskow, of struggles against good by evil, of this being the dialectic to history are sustaining myths, unprovable but rather nice when they are accompanied by principles of complementarity, yin and yang and the belief that good will win out.

I think you are right about some of the prose in this paragraph. I want to try another case, one from the newspapers. November 6, 1983. Supposedly in the "genetics revolution" geneticists will be able to code three billion characters which comprise the chemicals of the body. The biotechnologists will supposedly uncover the underlying causes of diseases and disorders "thought of as genetic." Then biotechnologists who are in universities, business for themselves, etc., will seek to cure these "disorders" through genetic intervention. Now suppose after mapping there is a .1 percent chance of error in the encoding of characters. Now do you not think this entire system should be subjected to rigorous moral inquiry? Is it not obvious that profit and the will to domination are part of the scientific experiment itself? And is it not clear that the whole enterprise assumes non-interactive relationships between gene molecules which must surely be wrong?

There is no possibility for rational analysis which does not include the observer, that bundle of roles and functions, superstitions and traditions, emotions and institutional framings which are utterly intertwined with rationality. The definition and content of science and its method must now change. Otherwise humanity is quite lost.

I look forward to seeing you and continuing the discussion.

Best,

Marc


January 4, 1984

Dear Marc,

I appreciated your thoughtful response, but frankly, I think it is not to the point. There is no doubt that the institutional structures in which scientific activity is conducted significantly influence the choice of topics and the use that is made of results. There is no doubt that "reason is the slave of the passions," an assumption unquestioned by the most committed scientific naturalists. It is also beyond question that much of our understanding is intuitive and beyond the reach of science, certainly in fact, probably in principle (something that I've argued at length). What is in question is something else, namely, whether science is a "myth system," alongside of religion, literature, etc., and whether there is something inherently ideological about the very use of reason. I don't see that you've presented even a particle of evidence for this view. If I am interested in learning about people, I'll read novels rather than psychology. But if I'm interested in understanding the nature of planetary motion, or the growth of organisms, etc., etc., I'll pursue the only methods that exist—those of scientific rationality, something that we come to understand better as we practice it but that is in no sense a "myth" and in itself has zero ideological content. In your "reconstructive knowledge" you suggest no alternative to abiding by the law of contradiction, to accepting the validity of deductive reasoning, to seeking explanation by construction and empirical testing of hypotheses, etc.—for the simple reason that there is no sane alternative. Your discussion is often, I think, quite correct, but it is about another topic—namely, the nature of the institutional structures in which scientific work is conducted and the historical conditions that effect the choice of premises. The reference to the "rationality" of the policy sciences, etc., is completely irrelevant; these are neither scientific nor rational, and in fact, violate the most elementary conditions of scientific rationality with remarkable thoroughness, something I've written about extensively as you know. As for what you say about the sciences, I simply don't agree at all.

Take Einstein and Bohr. No working physicist (I disregard here physicists in their mode as "great thinkers," in which they are just as absurd often as other people) regards their views as alternative "myth systems." Rather, any scientist (i.e., any reasonable person) will seek to formulate their positions in such a way as to extract empirical consequences that can be tested. I know too little about this topic to offer any judgments, but there is little doubt that this is the way the matter is generally perceived—and from my tenth-hand knowledge, I can only conclude that it has been a reasonably successful approach. There was a review-article in *Science* about the whole matter a few months ago, elaborating on experimental tests that bear on the real issue and that undermine "hidden variable" and deterministic (a la Einstein) approaches, so the author argues (how accurately, I can't judge). If we move to areas of science where I have any understanding, this is the way work always proceeds, and properly, since there is no sane alternative. Your comments about Bohr and Einstein may or may not have something to do with their personalities and the "passions" that their reason was the slave of, but it has nothing at all to do with the nature of their intellectual interchanges or (so far as I can judge) the way in which the issue has since been pursued, and, I understand, pretty well resolved, temporarily at least (as is the nature of inquiry into contingent fact).

As to the matter of "transformation of social systems," I would have the deepest fears about the path you suggest. This is a domain where our rational understanding is very shallow, a domain that may, in fact, be beyond the range of our scientific faculties (for reasons I've discussed elsewhere). As a result, we proceed largely by intuition. The advocate of social change is positing that human needs and values are such-and-such, and then argues that certain institutional changes will lead to better satisfaction of these needs. The fundamental assumptions should be regarded by any rational (=sane) person as highly tentative. If it should turn out, to our despair, that the Grand Inquisitor is right in his assessment of fundamental human nature, then it would be hard to resist his conclusions as to the necessity to found society on miracle, mystery and authority. If Rousseau (i.e., the libertarian Rousseau) is right, then very different conclusions follow. And so on. Again, we have only one method, the method of scientific rationality, though the bounds within which it can be applied in this domain are very narrow, so that any position that will be taken by an honest and sane person will be highly tentative.

You misunderstood my views about Kissinger. He does not "engage in rational inquiry and science." Rather, he is a man of astonishing ignorance about social, political and historical affairs, and one who hasn't the faintest idea what a rational argument might be and couldn't care less. That is why, I presume, he tends to place the word "truth" in scare quotes, when he uses it. In fact, his approach is uncomfortably close to the one you are suggesting, except that his values are different. He expresses himself quite clearly on this score, defining the "expert" as the person who is capable of articulating the interests and desires of those in power. I think you are much misled, quite generally, by the practitioners of the "policy sciences," who haven't the foggiest idea what rational inquiry is in the sciences, or anywhere, though they ape some of the surface features for ideological reasons, or in the case of Kissinger and others, possibly just out of total ignorance. One doesn't become an experimental scientist by putting on a white coat. Again, I've written about this at length ré Kissinger and others with, I think, more than ample documentation and argument to demonstrate.

The approach I suggest does not entail "reductionism" or "determinism." In both respects, we should accept what rational inquiry leads us to. My own work, for example, is based on explicit rejection of what is called "type reductionism" and is agnostic about "token reductionism" (though as a working hypothesis I would accept the latter, seeking to find out to exactly what extent it is true, expecting that this will be 100 percent in the domains in which I work). I don't see why you say that "reductionism does not explain connections nor does it explain processes or relationships." That is exactly what it does do. Reductionism is just the search for connections: as I wrote last time, the only alternative to it is a perverse commitment to ignorance. You seem to regard the dangers posed by biotechnology, etc., as part of "reductionism," or the "reductionist worldview." They have no connection to reductionism that I can perceive. In particular, "reductionism" has nothing to do with "writing off those concerned with value or those concerned with older religious systems as wooly-headed and silly." Personally, I'm committed to "reductionism." That is, I'd like to find what physical mechanisms are responsible for the fact that our cognitive faculties have such and such properties that for now we can only describe in abstract terms. But it does not follow that I am not "concerned with value"; I am, very much. As for the "older religious systems," they are best abandoned in my view, and as for "dangerous directions," I have little interest in seeing a return to religious wars, the Inquisition, persecution, imposed ignorance and the rest of the garbage that the Enlightenment, at its best, sought to get rid of.

As for "determinism," I've written frequently about the strong likelihood that constraints on our science-forming abilities (part of our cognitive faculties) may make it impossible for us to develop a rational understanding of matters of will and choice for which neither deterministic nor random models are appropriate, so I have no idea what you have in mind here. But a "flow or stream of life" approach adds a flat zero to my understanding of these issues, in fact, subtracts (or would, if I could take it seriously, which I can't) since it would provide the illusion of understanding, whereas I would much prefer to confront honestly and with eyes open my own cognitive limitations—in part, I have no doubt, biological. Similarly, "bonding and affection." I'm all for them, but also recognize that they add nothing whatsoever to understanding of these and innumerable other questions where rational approaches are applicable, or which may lie beyond the domains of our particular form of scientific intelligence so that we will therefore wander without hope of understanding, rather like a rat faced with a maze of a structure that lies beyond its cognitive limits.

On psychological testing, etc., you're again, I think, confusing the nature of the technique with the uses to which it is put; separate matters, for reasons I mentioned. As for dyslexia, it appears that it is related to physical changes in the language area of the dominant hemisphere, perhaps related to testosterone imbalance in prenatal development. Thus, there may be a "reductionist" account, i.e., a way of relating behavorial facts to physiology, exactly what we should hope for. This has nothing to do with what we regard as "socially correct."

You say that genetic tests are being used for particular social ends, hence "a form of colonizing knowledge." Here the confusion between the nature of knowledge and the uses to which it is put emerges clearly. The underlying knowledge is completely neutral; it could be used for controlling people or for helping them. What is "colonizing" in your sense is not the knowledge, but the nexus of institutions. Same ré the other comments in this connection. Nothing is suggested here about different ways of acquiring knowledge.

On technology, we're just talking past one another. In fact, as I wrote, technology is entirely neutral. It is also true, as you wrote, that the way in which technology develops and is applied under given social and historical conditions is anything but neutral. There is nothing at all at issue here. Take any example you like, say, computers and information again. Used by McNamara, it will be a technique for the centralization of decision-making and for repression. But that is not inherent in the technology, which is just as adaptable to bringing information in real time to every worker in a plant so as to allow for implementation of meaningful worker's control. It may be, as you suggest, that different computers would be designed for the latter purpose, but that is simply a matter of the use of technology. I am not, after all, suggesting that an MX-missile is "neutral." I think you are simply introducing verbal confusions here.

With regard to Casey and the CIA, again you are, I think, being fooled by people who haven't any idea what science and scholarship are. I am not of course privy to CIA deliberations, but I've been intrigued by what has become public, say in the Pentagon Papers. What it shows is that the CIA analysts are hysterical fanatics, incapable of rational thought. Thus, one of the most startling discoveries in the Pentagon Papers was that in over 20 years, the analysts could find only one staff paper in the whole intelligence record that even raised the question whether Hanoi could be following its own interests instead of loyally serving its masters (Moscow or "Peiping"). This is fanaticism, of the kind illustrated by the work of Douglas Pike, Henry Kissinger, or most of "scholarship" in the social sciences, and has no resemblance to science or scholarship, though it is very familiar from the history of organized religion. Many more examples can be given.

From the fact that certain inquiries (I don't understand, hence won't use, your term "knowledges") are "meant to serve a particular class or gender" it simply does not follow that what is learned is "masculine" or "elitist." Hence I continue not to understand what you are saying in this connection. In fact, the whole idea sounds to me rather sexist. How would we react to the notion that there is a special "black" way of thinking (maybe with rhythm)? We have about half women students in our graduate department. I've never noticed over the years that they have any special incapacity in understanding that conclusions should follow from assumptions, that assumptions should be questioned and compared with others, that theoretical ideas should be formulated in such a way as to meet the test of observation insofar as possible, etc.; nor have they suggested some other approach to our common endeavor. No doubt "certain forms of liberal education were related directly to the will to govern," and other forms of education are designed to instill obedience, patriotism, stupidity, and so on. But again nothing follows from this with regard to the point at issue.

I don't understand at all what you mean by "linear" argument or "algorithmic thinking." Take "linear argument." People who want to determine the consequences of some set of premises will conduct what you disparage as "linear argument," at least if they are not crazy. They will also bear in mind that there are competing premises, and in this regard will not carry out "linear argument." You're just describing here, in odd and confusing terms, what is generally called "rationality." As for "algorithmic thinking," your point seems to be that premises can be misapplied. True, no doubt, but this has nothing to do with any concept of "algorithmic" that I know anything about. As for rational inquiry being "a process," of course I agree, but I don't see what follows from that.

I won't try to comment point by point on the remainder. I agree with much of what you say, but don't see any relevance to what I was saying. For the most part, you are bringing out, uncontroversially, the impact of the institutional and socio-historical nexus in which scientific work is conducted, but this has no bearing on whether there is some alternative to scientific rationality (which, again, evolves, but that is another matter entirely). The fact that some male physicist fool may color what goes on in his laboratory leads to no conclusions about "masculine" and "feminine" science. I know of no reason at all to suppose that women are more given (biologically?) to "democratic" or "wholistic" approaches—there is much nonsense about this topic in some of the margins of feminism, on a par with the idea that warlike behavior is somehow "masculine," and wouldn't be conducted if only we could have people like Jeanne Kirkpatrick, Margaret Thatcher, Golda Meir and Indira Gandhi as our leaders, in which case love and caring would replace violence and repression. A few other comments:

About Feyerabend, his book was amusing, in that it rather wittily constructed a semi-fictional, semi-accurate account of what Galileo was about. I suppose that it is hard to take seriously as real history of science, and his "everything goes" suggestions are, I presume, not really intended seriously. At least, they can't really be taken seriously.

On deterrence, I don't think the Grenada invasion affects the point I was making. The USSR had not offered Grenada the kind of "guarantee" that was offered Cuba, so that there was no deterrence effect in this case. I think the distinction illustrates my point. It can't be proven, of course, but my sense of recent history is that the Kennedy administration moved towards an extensive terrorist war against Cuba (followed up by its successors) instead of direct military attack that surely would have succeeded because it was deterred by the risk of general global war. To the extent that this is plausible, it shows that violent powers can be deterred by nuclear weapons. Similar factors may have been operating in Vietnam.

I think you are wrong about the food matter. By now, much of the world depends in part at least on agricultural surpluses produced by relatively highly capital-intensive agriculture. It is far from clear that the recent population explosion could exist, even at bare subsistence level, without these factors. What George et al. have shown is something quite different. It is no doubt the case that agricultural technology has been heavily influenced by institutional factors, to the detriment of human welfare, but that does not change the fact that current population levels could probably not be maintained—nowhere near it—without it.

You suggest that "the definition of rational discourse is given by highly tendentious and ideological institutions." But that is not the right way to put it. Rational discourse is defined by commitment to the principle that conclusions should follow from premises, that hypotheses should be subjected to the test of experience, etc. This is all quite apart from ideological institutions, and the only alternative to it is mysticism.

Physicists try to discover the way the world works. For this end, "measurement of appearance" (i.e., experiment) is crucial, but it is a serious error to identify physics with measurement in some sort of super-operationalism. As for quantum mechanics, I see no reason to suppose that there are any "mythical qualities"—excluding here the musings that some physicists have been given to in their "great thinker" mode. I would also strongly urge that you disregard the comments of Weyl and others and pay attention to what they and other mathematicians do. As for what a proof is, the standards are quite clear and are unaffected by problems about the foundations of set theory, and so on. I think you've missed the point of Russell, Lakatos, etc. Proof is far from a religious exercise. Proof theory, a product largely of this century, has in fact given much insight into the truth-preserving character of various formal operations, and much of the intuitive practice of mathematicians is by now well understood in these terms.

Incidentally, it is in this context that the term "rigorous" has been quite well defined, as an ideal that is difficult to achieve. The hard sciences only approximate it. Most of human reasoning falls far from it. Legal reasoning is a case in point, with its heavy reliance on intuitive leaps. These are not to be described as "new methods" for attaining knowledge. If legal thinkers can make clear their "overarching principles" and the criteria for selecting "seemingly dissimilar facts" and placing them under these principles, then they will approach rigor. Whether there is any point in this exercise is another matter. Given the nature and function of law, it is far from obvious. As for "associational reasoning," I don't want to quibble about the use of the term "reasoning," but if I am interested in knowing the consequences of certain assumptions, I will hardly be satisfied with the "method" of "connecting seemingly unrelated ideas which we have in our head to one another." As for the way the brain thinks about rigid objects, what is now understood suggests that you are factually in error. It seems that peripheral systems of the visual cortex analyze retinal images in terms of a "rigidity principle" that takes them to be appearances of a rigid object in motion (under a fairly broad set of conditions). Again, these are not matters of decision, but of fact. Shimon Ullman's book on visual motion a few years ago gives some of the relevant background.

About Holism, I'm afraid it seems to me just a term used by people to confuse themselves. It is simply false that processes in general cannot be understood in isolation. Sometimes they can, sometimes they cannot. I've never seen any characterization of "holism" that adds any insight into this question, apart from very general considerations about the nature of knowledge on, say, Duhemian lines.

The question of the epistemic boundedness of human thought is one that belongs to biology, ultimately. It appears to be the case that human science cannot deal with "spheres of greater human concern," as a matter of our biological limitations, I presume. This too is not a matter of decision but a question of fact.

Without proceeding point by point, let me turn to the end. You ask whether "this entire system should be subjected to rigorous moral inquiry," referring to the "genetics revolution." Surely yes. This is not in question. But it seems to me that you are confusing this entirely valid enterprise with another one that I think makes no sense at all: challenging the notion of "rational inquiry" and regarding it, falsely, as a kind of myth system like religion, Freud, etc. Once this distinction is kept clearly in mind, I think we can then sort out intelligently what should be done and what is just a morass of confusions. That is the way it looks to me.

Best,

Noam


March 23, 1984

Dear Noam:

I was very happy to see you a few weeks ago and hope all is well in Cambridge. I have been to Amsterdam and Moscow on two separate trips and have not had the reflective time necessary to answer your letter of January 4. Needless to say, I read your letter several times and am of course challenged by its insight and dangerous rigor. Indeed, I was at first somewhat intimidated by it. For example, you assure me that "there is no sane alternative" to "abiding by the law of contradiction . . . deductive reasoning . . . empirical testing of hypotheses, etc." (what means this "etc.?"), that "A person who wants to determine the consequences of some set of premises will conduct what you "disparage" as "linear argument," "*at least if he is not crazy*," that empirical consequences are extracted from "positions . . . that can be tested," "since there is no sane alternative." I then also learned in this correspondence that you are not a fan of psychology, preferring novels to learn about people, and in the last letter you bumrap Freud.

So here I am stuck in Washington. I am told that sanity can only be related to a *particular* mode of doing rational inquiry, and that if I stray from this path the standard methods of psychology and psychoanalysis will not help me because they themselves are garbage. This leaves me thinking that you believe the answer to my problem is a mind pill, arrived at through reductionist thinking, which would increase my capacity to reason "rationally." Having thought about the question in this way, I decided that you are either mistaken or utterly entrapped in a fatal error of thinking that propositional forms are actual ways we think rather than descriptions of how or what we think, which are arrived at in quite other ways. In Hilary Putnam's recent book there is an instructive quote from a paper by two younger scholars. "A man is climbing a mountain. Halfway up he stops, because he is unsure of how to go on, he himself continuing via one route. In his imagination, he proceeds on up to a certain point, and then he gets into difficulties, which he cannot, in his imagination, see how to get out of. He then imagines himself going up by a different route. This time he is able to imagine himself getting all the way to the top without difficulty, so he takes the second step. This is a rational way to solve a practical problem and yet this sort of reasoning need not at all be reducible to any kind of linear proposition." The fact that it can be reduced to propositional forms is a frill. It is not a description of our thinking process. It is a model of a set of propositions which are representative of how we can communicate to others in some logical form *what to think* even though it tells us nothing of how we think. Now you may conclude that this is Kantianism gone wild, but I do not believe that it is controvertible. By the same token, you seem to overestimate empiricism or its validity as a system of indisputable proof. Einstein pointed out that even in the light of the best empirical analysis of physical phenomena it was often that empiricism was wrong and experiments wrong and the results of such investigation quite off point. The facts that scientists developed were wrong or irrelevant. Indeed, various of Einstein's theories were at first disproved factually. You are no doubt aware of the Nazi Nobelist Lenard who railed against the Jewish physicists and their supporters because they had given up on "facts" and empirical studies. The limits of empirical studies are well known, often related to the lack of equipment or overarching political/intellectual fashions which scientists share with the society as a whole. Lakatos points out that it took 150 years to prove Copernicus correct. The facts of his time and the empirical investigation conducted contradicted his theories. In this sense, theory, that is the willingness to frame questions in new ways is far more important than facts which themselves are shot through with the debris of past understandings and discarded facts (often encrusted theories plus previous emotionalism) soon to be rejected by new vision, insight, or theory. I am sure that you above all appreciate this point. In any case, you will be sure to warm to the text of Francis Crick who is less racy than Jim Watson on the question of what is going on with the scientists when they "do science." Nevertheless, Crick recognizes the imaginative or artistic nature of what is being attempted.

The point is that evidence can be very unreliable, and therefore you should use as little of it as you can. And when we confront problems today, we're in exactly the same situation. We use three or four bits of data, we don't know which one is reliable so we say, now, if we discard that one and assume it's wrong—even though we have no evidence that it's wrong—then we can look at the rest of the data and see if we can make sense of that. And that's what we do all the time. I mean, people don't realize that not only can data be wrong in science, it can be misleading. There isn't such a thing as a hard fact when you're trying to discover something. It's only afterwards that the facts become hard.

And I would add, how hard is hard?

You are rightly skeptical when you question my view of the "transformation of social systems" as that notion relates to rationality or rational understanding. At the moment I can think of three positions that we can hold about knowing and social transformation. One is that all we have is our system of scientific rationality or intelligence. Ultimately, this intelligence is unknowable, *nous,* as Aristotle would have it. It is something almost divine and we should hang onto it for dear life because without it we are nowhere. Rationality is cold and alone, unrelated to love or other passions in its mode of work. Furthermore, we should look to history and what man has been up to until now and we should expect little if anything from him in terms of his attempts at social transformations. Furthermore, if I understand your point, certain social matters should better be left unknown for fear of what we might learn about man since his or her nature may be both knowable and may require the services and analysis of the grand inquisitor. Does this misrepresent you? There is another view. Let us call it Deweyan in nature. Science should be expansive. It was born into a system of institutional conditions which created a dialectical tension between itself and the institutions around it. However, the "scientific method" has not been used systematically in analysing the institutions and institutional consequences from which human beings derive their unaccidental consequences. Thus, once we change institutional structures through scientific inquiry, we will then be able to change human beings whose attitudes change. Their social character will change as a result of deeper understanding of the effects institutions have on the human project and human beings. Pragmatism, which judges in terms of future moral results does not assume fixed natures out of social context. Therefore, intelligent planning can bring about transformation of the social system. I am saving the best for last. My position. The scientific project is inextricably intertwined with institutions. This is even more obvious as science becomes capital dependent requiring huge resources to carry out experiments and scientific programmes. The choice of topic is usually institutionally caused and is at the very least, often described by the recipient in language and terms the patron or grantor will accept. The scientist may think he is fooling the grantor but of course this view is hopelessly naive. The grantors know exactly what they want from the scientific experiment or enterprise. And, I doubt if there are many scientists touched with the flame of Prometheus when it comes to grabbing of funds for their own "real" work.

Now it is also true that before the scientific method was invented, cruelty and barbarism existed and the hope of philosopher-scientists, whether Bacon or Descartes was to find ways of studying nature that would liberate men from crazy authority and even lead to progress. They believed that science was liberationist. Of course, the entire history of Marxist infatuation with science was that it would lead to human progress and liberation. The point about all of this is that the scientific project has turned out to fit rather comfortably with authority, hierarchy and just plain insanity, to use the obverse of your word. The scientific method, through its insistence on exclusion of what it claims to be irrelevant has excised from the scientific project just exactly those ethical questions which are both there and immanent in the work itself. It is as if scientific rationality chooses to remain silent on those very issues which come up in the day-to-day activities of doing scientific work. Such questions range from why certain notions are rejected out of hand, what evidence is thrown away, and why, what routes of experimentation and inquiry are closed because they supposedly take too long, don't fit the current conventions, or are rejected by the wielders of power and money.

When, therefore, can the scientific project really matter in the way that Bacon and Descartes had hoped, that is, as a socially transformative instrument? It seems to me that there are two answers to this question. The first is that the scientific project must be more *self-conscious* and open to having its own programme changed from the outside, but not by those with money and power. As C. D. Darlington pointed out, "It is no accident that bacteria were first introduced by a canal engineer. That oxygen was isolated by a Unitarian minister, that the theory of infection was established by a chemist, the theory of heredity by a monastic school teacher, the theory of evolution by a man who was unfitted to be a university instructor in either botany or zoology." (I point this out—even though his comments are only partly accurate—to suggest the importance of understanding that what may appear to be scientific rationalism within a particular discipline may be overturned rather easily by those who take a fresh look at particular issues or questions which are unencumbered by the weight of the discipline.) This leads me to a double set of considerations of how to analyze the scientific project and determine its ethical and truth value in relation to social transformation. First of all, it is necessary to bring to bear a critical analysis of the institutions in which the scientific project is being performed. Second, it is as important to do the same within the scientific project. That is, to look critically at the activities and the enterprise itself. By critically I mean the type of analysis which forces to the surface *implications of choices* that are made and decisions about the political questions of *power* which lie beneath the seemingly inoffensive "objective data" that are given to explain processes and nature itself.

Now I would like to revert to the question of myth. I am told that you are the leading model builder in the world. Therefore, I am eager to hear your views on the distinction between model building and myth. I do not want you to take that question as an offensive challenge. Rather I want you to consider the question of what man the maker does in his poetic or scientific activities. I think you are too literal-minded in understanding the meaning of myth. It appears that you think because myth is not "real," it therefore is not true. But in affairs of people, certainly in novels that you prize above psychology, good novels continuously illuminate stories which have been told and retold throughout human history. These stories explore the varieties of truth in its many quantitatively uncapturable dimensions. The same is true for the lover of scientific ideas. He builds myths of explanation which may or may not have much to do with reality, that is, that which goes on outside of what he makes. The fundamental point here is another one. It is that man is the maker, whether he is a man of action, a man of poetry or science. Men and women make the ideational constructs which human history lives within. The social construction of physical and social reality includes, demands the structuring of myths. One should be modest about these constructs. They have clear limits, whether they are in mathematics, science, politics or novel writing. And because they are man-made, the process of making them and their implications are inherently human, therefore having a moral and political side.

There are points which you make that strike me as just wrong. First of all, your faith in the law of contradiction and empirical testing, etc., does not deal with the problem of *choice* which is presented to us constantly in all situations outside of mathematical description. Choice is invariably fraught with ambiguity. Ambiguity is only transcended when there is social agreement, that is, human agreement between people, whether it is the agreement to read a meter in a particular way or to have a meter to read, whether it is the agreement to pursue and read the primary characteristics of quantity, measure, etc., as critical, or whether it is to agree that man has fundamental grammatical sentences which generate other sentences that are individually and therefore creatively derived, or man was given his power of generation by God but he then creates his own life. There is another issue which strikes me as one you might reconsider. You have adverted in these exchanges to my tendency to exhort and assert. The distinction between finding truth and asserting it is far less separate than you assert. The basic premises of any science or mathematics show its limits and sogginess partaking of the literary device of the suspension of disbelief.

Let me take up your question concerning Professor Kissinger. I have just read his latest ploy as the Chairman of the Bipartisan Commission on Central America. This astounding exercise in lying and bad faith which makes a joke of analysis, and more important, of the suffering of people, has nothing to do with my views of how reports should be written, how one attends to matters of history, and how the intellectual comes to grips with struggles of the wretched to survive and perhaps find some liberation and dignity in their lives. On the other hand, you have to explain what the propensity is of your Cambridge colleagues—

not friends—to look at Kissinger as the Alpha and Omega of success and capacity to use intellectual skills, reading, writing, and lying in the service of the status quo, or better put, in the service of power. Are you saying that there is something invariant in man which causes him to act like the flatterer and the pimp, is there something in the institutional structures of our finest places that cause such values to be instilled or is there something as well in the course of the way we work, or do things, which creates the impulse to honor the winner who happens to be a killer?

There is, I am afraid, a naiveté which you have about the university enterprise. The university in its social and scientific aspects is given over more and more to policy sciences. Universities are now scientized. By this horrible word I mean that the universities in the social and natural sciences, and in their bastard form of political theory and philosophy, the policy sciences, have accepted and championed very basic notions of scientific thought. As Hans Reichenbach pointed out in his essay on probability which appeared in a Rand, Hoover Institution and Stanford University sponsored book, *The Policy Sciences,*

Probability methods are indispensable for logical reasons; that a concept of causality unrelated to probability is empty or even meaningless; and that the rationalist philosopher, who speaks of necessary laws of the universe, is not aware of his using a term which is meaningful only when it is translatable into a statistical meaning . . . if the causal laws of the physicist are dependent on statistical meanings, the social scientist need not feel embarrassed if his investigations cannot go beyond statistical laws. [p. 121]

Now I point this out to you to show that this formulation by a premier philosopher of science is found in a book on the policy sciences which was the single most important catalyst in getting people at our elite schools to begin thinking in terms of statistical probabilities, operations research serving as the tool for a new class of mandarins who later incorporated cost-benefit analysis into their thinking. These people think they are rigorous rationalists, scientific to the core, they think they are employing modern scientific methods and they think they have learned a form of discourse common to scholarly analysis. Who am I to disagree with the weight of the heavy thinkers of our time that want to characterize themselves as doing rigorous rational work and who are legitimized in their belief by our academies? Now you may say that they are aping the sciences for ideological reasons, and I used to take that view. I am more and more persuaded that what they do *is* the scientific method.

A few more words are in order with regard to reductionism. You are agnostic or reject reductionism just at the point where it becomes interesting. You have turned reductionism inside out and stated that it does explain connections. Obviously, there are connections and there are connections. I would argue that the type of connections which reductionism teaches us lead to greater mystification. For example, do you believe that the present reductionist approach adopted by molecular biologists teaches us anything about the *integration* of the human body within itself, or the interactive relationship, the connections which human beings have with their environment. The adoption of the Cartesian model and the success it has wrought in providing a particular kind of explanation which grows out of an unstated ideology of specialization has left an enormous number of questions unconsidered, unexplained and in my terms unmythicized.

God forbid, I have no interest in returning to the days of "religious wars, the Inquisition, persecution, imposed ignorance, etc." The problem, however, is different. We must ask why science has not been able to transcend these attitudes. Instead, it works rather nicely with the forces that bring these conditions about. Khomeini has fit well with his engineers and technocrats. The Israeli government has learned to ride the Orthodox rabbis and the "hard" scientists so that they work hand in glove in Israeli policy. In the United States the fundamentalist ministers work well with engineers in southwestern states. And comment on MIT is superfluous.

Now as for your point about determinism and choice. You beg the question when you say that we may be constrained from developing a "rational understanding of matters of will and choice." The problem here is that you seem to assume that will and choice are not part and parcel of the activities of the scientist in his work as a scientist. Do will and choice stop when you enter that priesthood? Obviously not. And if not, then it means that we have not escaped *will* even within the context of activities you would conclude are capable of being known.

It is mistaken in the extreme to believe that bonding and affection are unrelated to rational approaches. Do you deny the validity of those innumerable studies which show the interactioin between learning, bonding and affection? Is there no direct consequence of the doctor who assumes a cold chemical model of the body when he approaches a patient?

Several years ago I happened to pick up an old copy of the *Journal of Philosophy and Psychology* which was put out at Columbia University. The issue was published a year or two after the first world war. One article, as I recall, talked about the importance of psychological testing in the first world war. A major point of the tests, the writer said, was to get people to learn how to sit still, how to take commands, and in this way they would be better able to follow instructions on the assembly line. Now the point of this is that tests are constructed with their objective as the starting point. This objective may be stated or implied. But it frames in a direct way the nature of the test. In other words, the use of the test and the technique are intertwined. One may generalize. Uses, as in the case of genetic engineering or any type of capital intensive activity, are built into the scientific technique, which you hold as distinct from the objective. If my point is correct, it is mistaken to hold to the notion that there is an "underlying knowledge" which is "completely neutral; it could be used for controlling people or for helping them." Do you think that the scientific experiments in concentration camps on how much cold people could stand were "neutral," even if they might have been able to save German soldiers on the Russian front?

With respect to technology, I think we agree once we get past the word neutral. It seems to me that certain technologies by their nature can serve one class or group as against another. That is why they are developed. Those which cannot serve a particular class or group are not developed even though the logical or mathematical principles beneath them may be equally valid.

I am not sure I know how to respond to your point about Casey and the CIA. You hold forth a view of scholarship and social science which does not seem to be prevalent in our institutions of higher learning. In your analysis of CIA scholarship, there is nothing which I can quarrel with. However, it is important to recognize that frameworks get established which are then internalized among the scholars, even those who want to approach questions with a skeptical eye or a free gaze. In this sense, the value of science as a set of customs or of the type of disputation which allows for error and encourages finding it, and allows for alternative explanations or myths of how things are and work is very important. Without it, we have a hegemony of one line of bullshit. Our agreement does not relieve you of a heavy tax which is to show what is good or pure scholarship in the light of the overwhelming weight of academic opinion that praises, say, William Langer and Clyde Kluckhohn, two substantial characters who established the government-university links, and Langer, who established what the nature of CIA analysis should be. His ideas come from someplace and I do not think that either his or those of James Bryant Conant, that estimable chemist, fine fella and president of Harvard, came from Cardinal Bellarmine. No. One must look at several intersecting points: Personal need for power and fulfillment of ambition, ways of viewing the world which emphasize power and control either over other people or nature and being part of institutions which accept this way of analysis as a given all packaged together as enlightened progress.

It is foolish in the extreme to deny culture and gender. That is what I think you are doing in your remarks about blacks and women. The stubborn reality is that different cultures do have ways of interpreting the world differently. The oppressed within one culture and then a whole culture in its relationship to other dominant cultures often mediate their beliefs, values and lives through primarily white male structures in which the *social roles* in the public space are dictated to or established by white men. That there are differences in culture and gender is only important when one group stops hearing another group, or refuses to share in power, or disallows the right of one culture, race or gender to share in the forging of a collective vision of what humanity is and wants, and what rationality is. Blind universalism has the effect of reinforcing the power of dominant groups; for the universalists don't often stop and ask whether the universalism they are enamored of is a way to avoid adding to or changing what we think of as universal. Too often they don't take into account the Other, the other culture, the other races, the other sex, etc. Western civilization has had the distinctly unlovely habit of speaking for all civilization, all humankind, through the voices of its dominant institutions with their values as if their version of the West or the West itself is, à la Spengler, the keeper of human civilization itself.

Finally, on this point, it is hardly surprising that the women in your graduate program hold views similar to the faculty and the other men. Is this not the purpose of the university selection system, to assure that what you describe will occur and to reproduce yourselves?

When you talk about scientific rationality it would be much better to use the phrase scientific opportunism, for it connotes the open-ended nature of *doing* science rather than talking about it. As Einstein said, the scientist "must appear to the systematic epistemologist as a type of unscrupulous opportunist: he appears as realist insofar as he seeks to describe a world independent of the acts of perception; as idealist insofar as he looks upon concepts and theories as the free inventions of the human spirit (not logically derivable from what is empirically given); as positivist insofar as he considers his concepts and theories justified only to the extent to which they furnish a logical representation of relations along sensory experiences. He may appear as Platonist or Pythagorean insofar as he considers the viewpoint of logical simplicity as an indispensable and effective tool of his research." This notion can hardly be seen as any different from that of an artist who makes things and frames what he knows into what he creates without concern of what it is named.

Einstein's notions raise deep ethical questions, for they assume that the scientist is free, that he is an independent operator who is a Protean figure without the baggage of the human being. He is a floating mind picking and choosing what he wants to have in order to effect his goal of knowing truth. Is that what your view is? It may be attractive, but out of kilter with work as it is in fact carried out in the sciences.

On Feyerabend. The issue is not Feyerabend. The issue is whether the political chutzpah of Galileo which meant to replace religion with scientific truth rather than science as being just another truth on the basis of the evidence he had at that time. Or whether it is justified even now. Galileo did not want to share power, he wanted it all for science. Now I freely acknowledge that Galileo was the father of modern science. But he was as well the single most important force in breaking down the pluralism of explanation, something which is not usually recognized by scholars.

I don't know if this proves or disproves your point. The United States played down attacks on Cuba after the Cuban missile crisis. I think its covert war with dozens of ongoing operations to bring Castro down were cut back after January of 1963. My guess is that the demarche which came about after the Cuban missile crisis towards overthrowing Castro probably cost Kennedy his life.

I do not know how we can resolve the question around agricultural surpluses and food. The traditional left argument is that the Green Revolution was in fact a subsidy to the petroleum industry, that it caused enormous pain among the poorest peasants who were displaced, that food markets ended up even being more rigged by the largest operators and that production of food in terms of its quality has been generally harmful while the industrialization of the farmer's crops has resulted in the possibility of terrible famines. I am not aware that this view is fatally incorrect.

I hold that proofs are not absolutely true when we use that term less rigorously to describe living things or processes. They are provisionally so. Once the term *provisional* is introduced we should realize that new understandings may be based on other notions which cannot be proved, which are based on partial knowledge or myth; that is, the continuation or repetition of events from which we deduce certain "truths." That we act on them does not make them true for all time. Because skepticism can deny any proof, we still have to believe something. (As Russell puts it, no one demands a proof of the principles of deductive logic.) We introduce a hidden system of common sense which is grounded on what we really believe. What we "really believe" is not determined, so far as I can tell, by genes, but by cultural social interaction. It may from time to time be based on *proofs*, but very seldom.

I am not sure I know what you mean when you refer to Duhem. Are you talking about his belief that individual experiments cannot prove complex scientific theories? If that is so, are you saying that "processes cannot be understood in isolation"? In any case, I wonder if you think Duhem's clerical anti-semitism played a part in attempting to savage Einstein.

Perhaps it is not necessary at this point to name what we do as "rational inquiry" or otherwise, but rather to do what we think seems to fit with a constructed or discovered reality with the understanding that we can call it and what we do by different names. If we can proceed this way, then we should choose some critical concern and see how we would handle it, following it through its various stages from thought to practice.

All the best,

Marcus G. Raskin

April 8, 1984

Dear Marc,

Thanks for the very interesting letter [March 23, 1984]. I'm answering quickly because correspondence piles up very fast and what goes to the bottom of the pile may not be found for months.

Turning to our continuing discussion, it's clear that we are now involved in a serious misunderstanding, namely about what I've been calling "the method of rational inquiry." Your observations on [p. 179A–179B] I not only agree with, but insist upon. In fact, I've been arguing this position forcefully for about 30 years, as part of an effort to get linguists and people interested in cognitive issues generally to depart from the hopeless and pointless taxonomic and data-oriented approaches of the social sciences, and humanities and to turn to the methods of the sciences. I've long felt that one of the major contributions of the so-called "Galilean revolution" has been precisely to make clear that data in themselves are useless, meaningless, uncertain and unimportant, and that the task of the sciences is to develop insight in those particular areas where we are capable of doing so. I've always emphasized, giving examples, the ease of discovering data that appear to falsify any physical theory, even the most advanced, always put aside in the natural sciences on the plausible assumption that we don't understand enough yet to see why this one is irrelevant (a move that may prove to be misguided, but is a central part of the method of rational inquiry.) And so on. My own position has typically been castigated for excessive "idealization" (i.e., pursuing the methods of the natural sciences). One colleague recently remarked, rather bitterly, that I seem to regard "facts" the way devout Christians regard sex: something to be indulged in only for higher purposes. In short, on all of this there is no dispute.

Where we differ is where we go from here. The method of rational inquiry (what is called "the scientific method," though in reality there is no well-defined "method") insists that conclusions should follow from premises and that theories should be subjected to empirical test. In part, the relevant evidence is itself theory-dependent, in that the very concept "relevance" is determined in part by the possibilities of explanation that goes byond the trivial. But that doesn't change the fact that science has to keep to a rational structure and one that admits empirical confirmation. It is here that science is crucially distinct from myth (to respond to another query of yours). It is also here that science is crucially different from psychoanalysis, the "policy sciences," and other forms of religion, which lack either rational structure, or explanatory depth, or significant data (significant, in that they contribute to understanding), a concept of relevant evidence, etc. Reason may be the slave of the passions, as Hume stated and Russell and others insisted. But science is distinct from many other human activities—some worthwhile, some not—in that it does insist upon rational structure and empirical verification, in a form that is, in part, theory-dependent and oriented towards understanding and insight, not butterfly collecting of the sort practiced typically in the humanities and social sciences, or mere fraud as in the "policy sciences." I'm of course overstating the point here; there is fine work in the humanities and occasionally, though rarely, even the "social sciences," but the general features sketched here seem to me of no little validity.

On psychoanalysis and political science (have you noticed that fields tend to call themselves "science" roughly to the extent that they have not the most marginal connection to science, e.g., "political science," "behavorial science," etc., but not "biological science" or "chemical science"?) the point is revealed neatly by some recent events, partly personal. Take, for example, the response to Masson's book on Freud. I read his *Atlantic* article, which I thought was rather amusing and not implausible, and also read the comical series of reviews and letters in the *Times* and elsewhere. The *Times* review, by some Oxford U. analyst (Storrs, I think his name was) was a typical cult phenomenon. He completely avoided the content of Masson's work. Instead, he went into a silly discussion of his personality defects, ending by urging that he and his book be consigned to "oblivion." The only serious question, in his view, was how a reputable psychoanalyst could have been "seduced" (it is interesting that he should have chosen this term) into allowing Masson to become director of the Freud archives, not realizing that he might actually expose some of the hidden secrets in them. A series of follow-up letters by various New York analysts applauded this magnificent performance and went on to add that they hoped that this call to dump the whole matter into "oblivion" would prevent people from buying or reading the book. It was all a curious example of the hysteria of people who fear they might be exposed. It is, in fact, rather intriguing that professional psychoanalysts could not see how they are exposing themselves by this infantilism. Maybe Masson is crazy or dishonest, but I must say that the response to him tended to confirm his credibility.

Turning to "political science," I can recount a recent incident, quite a familiar one to me. I recently gave a series of invited lectures at the U. of Victoria in British Columbia on various political topics. There was a substantial effort to prevent me from speaking, partly coming from the local Jewish community (one talk was on the Middle East), but mainly from academics: the chairman of poli. sci. and a number of his colleagues. Since Victoria is something of a backwater, and they are a bit unsophisticated, they did in public what their colleagues usually only do in private: they published letters in the press, etc., saying that since I'm a linguist, I shouldn't be allowed to talk about "their field." This was an unsubtle example of something I've often seen in the past 30 years. In fact, I'm not a linguist either; I have no professional credentials in anything (which is, incidentally, why I'm teaching at MIT; the work we were doing is still fairly marginal in many Ivy League colleges, and 30 years ago, could be blocked by people in humanities and social sciences, wherever there was an established "tradition"). Over the years, I've worked in areas ranging from mathematics and automata theory to philosophy to intellectual history to the domain of "political science." I've noticed something quite striking: when I'm invited to give a talk to a graduate math colloquium, or a physics or biology colloquium, at some major university, no one asks about my credentials, though it is obvious at once that I'm not a pro. Rather, they ask whether what I'm saying is right, can it be improved, etc. Same in philosophy, where there is a tradition of intellectual honesty. In intellectual history, however, people go bananas and produce the most outrageous falsifications and absurdities to try to send what I am saying to "oblivion." And in "political science," the quite standard response is that I have no right to speak because I lack credentials. (There are, of course, exceptions.) The explanation is obvious: in the sciences, there is no need to worry about credentials since the fields have intellectual substance and integrity. In the humanities, where a substantial number of practitioners are people with tiny minds and limited understanding, it is necessary to keep outsiders from prying in (they might have ideas, which would be terrifying). In political science and other forms of ideology, it is obvious that protection is necessary. So this is all clear enough. In fact, such terms as "Marxist" or "Freudian" give the game away. In mathematics, one is not a "Gaussian," and in physics one is not an "Einsteinian." The interest is in the ideas, not cults and Gods.

Turning to p. 4 [p. 179d], I do not hold that certain social matters should better be left unknown, but rather that it is highly likely—indeed, virtually certain—that human intelligence, like other biological systems, has its specific scope and limits, and there is no reason to suppose that any question we address we are capable of answering. Science, in fact, is a kind of accident; in some areas it turned out that the structure of our intelligence and the structure of aspects of the world happened to more or less conform; contrary to Peirce, who in part argued similarly, we cannot appeal to "evolution" as a deus ex machina; there is no evolutionary argument that human intelligence should have been "selected" to deal with questions of quantum theory. In some domains, we have no answers, even bad answers, to what seem to be simple questions: e.g., the Cartesian question of the difference between being "compelled" and being "incited and inclined," the essential difference between machine and man. Frankly, I think this may be a good thing, but that is another matter.

Science should be as expansive as it can, but we should also understand that the human mind is not, as was once believed, a "universal instrument." The Deweyan arguments add nothing to this. Insofar as it denies "fixed natures," it is simply denying obvious fact. Humans can't become birds by changing institutions, and their intellectual properties are also biologically based, at least, for nonmystics.

Science doesn't "excise" ethical questions; it just doesn't have the means to deal with them. Scientists must deal with them as human beings (not everything we do, not even a small part of it, is science or can become science). The scientists at Los Alamos were, in my view, profoundly unethical, at least by early 1945; that reveals human frailty, of a most remarkable kind, but I don't see what this has to do with science.

About institutional influences in the development of science, there is a question of historical fact. My own view, based on my own experience in the sciences and what I know of the history, is that these factors are powerful in technology and have an indirect effect on science, but that they are not central; to a large extent, science develops out of intrinsic factors. We can't argue that in the abstract, but have to consider real cases.

Back to "myth" again, recall that I do not at all denigrate human attempts to understand the world, and the people in it, outside of the framework of scientific inquiry. Again, I think the Victorian novel tells us more about people than science ever will. But the difference between myth (in the broad sense that you are using) and rational inquiry should be recognized, simply for clarity and understanding. (They are, roughly, as indicated above, in my judgment.)

On p. 9 [p. 179i] you say that I "have to explain" the behavior of my Cambridge colleagues. I realize that the term is used ironically; they are not my "colleagues." We are not engaged in the same enterprise, at any level. The corruption of Cambridge intellectual life was dramatically revealed in the Kennedy years, and since (and before). The Kissinger phenomenon, which you cite in particular, is an interesting one in this regard. Kissinger himself is a fool and an ignoramus, though he has a certain animal cleverness. His self-definition is quite appropriate: you may recall that he defines an "expert" as one who knows how to articulate the consensus of those with power. That is, an "expert" is someone who knows how to fawn and grovel properly. I used to use his academic essays in my undergraduate classes, but had to stop, because MIT undergraduates simply found their absurdities hilarious on close reading. His later writings reveal ignorance and stupidity of such a colossal nature that one wonders how his reputation can survive (I gave many examples in my review, reprinted in *Towards a New Cold War*). The answer to the question is obvious when we consider the academic milieu: his colleagues won't expose him for two good reasons, first, that by doing so they would expose themselves, and second, that they live in utter awe and fear of power, and Kissinger did have power.

About the university, you misunderstand me. I don't respect it as an institution; in fact, it is intellectually corrupt and morally debased. The policy sciences are the worst, merely fraud and silliness, attempting to ape some of the surface features of the real sciences. You ask "who am I to disagree with the weight of the heavy thinkers of our time that want to characterize themselves as doing rigorous rational work and who are legitimated in their belief by our academies?" That's the heart of it. There is no reason for you to accept this cheap fraud.

About reductionism, I simply don't understand your point. To the extent that we can explain, say, why the human body (and, I presume, mind) have the properties they do on the basis of biochemistry, I will only cheer. Many problems remain unresolved, and I do not believe that what is called "type reductionism"—i.e., reducing principles at a higher level of organization to formulations in terms of elements at a lower level—can succeed, though I do presume that "token reductionism" can succeed, to the extent that our minds are capable of carrying out the project. I don't see what is at issue here.

Turning to will and choice, I doubt that we can develop a rational understanding of it, and I agree that it is part and parcel of the activities of the scientist. From this it follows that there is much about this activity, as it is conducted, that we will probably never understand. But this does not bear at all on what I said about the method of rational inquiry: its insistence that conclusions follow logically from premises, that theories meet empirical tests, that evidence must be carefully and judiciously selected, etc.

I also don't understand what you say about bonding and affection. No doubt they are important for human life in all its aspects. What does this have to do with what we are discussing?

About the uses to which science is put, I think you are again missing my point. Given certain institutional structures, knowledge will be used in certain ways, and certain kinds of work will be encouraged. But the scientific knowledge in itself is neutral in that under alternative institutions, it could be used in different ways. This is even largely (though not entirely) true of technology; take the information-processing example I mentioned earlier. I think you are confusing here the knowledge itself, and the institutional nexus in which it is put to use.

I don't find any problem in explaining why the "overwhelming weight of opinion" praises various courtiers and frauds in the academic professions, nor do I see that the question bears on my view of rational inquiry. I simply see no reason to accept the self-image propounded by the mainstream of the social sciences and much of the humanities.

I don't know what you mean by saying "it is foolish in the extreme to deny culture and gender." Certainly they exist. What you have not shown, at least to my satisfaction, is that these factors have any relevant relation (relevant to the topics we are discussing) to the enterprise of rational inquiry. I don't know any reason to believe that women, or Pakistanis, or Japanese, do scientific work any differently from white American males.

I don't see the relevance of the Einstein comments, which seem to me correct but not particularly profound or surprising. I also don't see your point about Galileo. I'm also not sure any more what we are arguing about with regard to the green revolution. Maybe the "traditional left argument" is correct. If so, this would reinforce our joint belief that the institutional nexus has an enormous effect in the way knowledge is put to use, and in areas more remote from the fundamental sciences, even what work is done (and even in the fundamental sciences sometimes, though in my judgment much less than you seem to believe).

I don't recall the context of my mentioning Duhem. I doubt that it bore on the question of why he attacked Einstein (in fact, anti-Semitism apart, Duhem thought that physics had gone crazy by the early years of the 20th century).

I hope we can get to what the real issues are between us. I don't think we've succeeded in doing so yet.

Hope to see you soon. It was great to have a chance to talk in Washington. Hope to do so again soon. We'd better make it soon, given the rate at which the crazies in Washington seem intent on blowing up the world.

Best,

Noam

February 26, 1985

Dear Noam:

This letter is in answer to your April 8th letter. I have been thinking a great deal about your last letter and also about the question of symbols and how symbols might be used in scientific and technological projects which would signify the conclusions and experience of others, or even their fears. Such symbols would signify "danger," like damaging consequences and unknown results beyond the particular scientific operation. The symbols would act as a brake or door opener to other types of thought and research as well as restraining action which might otherwise not be attempted. A symbol could be of value within the scientific project itself, bringing issues directly into the laboratory which are not considered because they are not thought to be "hard."

As I mentioned when we talked in Washington, a set of symbols might be added, possibly integrated, into scientific experiments which would have a distinctly consequential and ethical character to them. Now obviously the argument can be, and should be made, that the introduction of such symbols which supposedly deduce "ought" principles could be dangerous, "unsuitable," and so on. I would argue that certain conclusions can be drawn from history, that they can be used, if not as certainties, then at least as probabilities and therefore as guideposts, to be accepted or rejected although of necessity they must be noted. Indeed, probability translates into subjective judgment. Obviously, scientific experiments are modes of communicating the experience of one group to another with the unstated understanding that no experiment is duplicable but that experiments have a probabilistic character to them which makes it possible to describe them in symbolic terms. This is surely what happens in everyday life although scientists who have laboratories and access to capital have fancier methods. The development of these symbols, almost like a Boolean algebra, could be the link of science to ethics and choice making. This program would be based on the belief that there is no way to factor out "man" from science, recognizing that by so doing the scientific enterprise becomes a sterile one. I do not see how you can object to such a project. If language (not generative sentences) is not a mental mirror but an active participant in how we see, what we can see, and how we transmit it, why then not accept the root of science as man, woman, rather than free floating minds which supposedly discover fundamental laws of nature? In any case I would hope that in time scientific projects, not necessarily a specific experiment, even those mathematics which are seen to be abstract, irrelevant unworldly, would include within them and within the context they are considering a symbolic mode to describe their likely short-term and long-term effects on human life and nature. They would be judged by an expanding set of constantly refined and continually debated axioms which themselves get to be symbolically presented. Through the symbol the project of science would be humanized and demystified.

Science would reenter the realm of moral and political philosophy. I acknowledge that there are potholes on the road of this approach, (you might say caverns). I recognize that moral and political philosophy, including Marxism, has too often been a tool to beat people over the heads with and to get people to accept blindly the authority of a party, church, or political philosophy with humanly devastating effect. But do we think that by averting our eyes from these questions within science and technology these questions disappear? In reality they grow ever larger and more important in our daily lives. By saying all of this I have no intention of suggesting that there is anything more than probabilistic agreement on ethical "axioms." Thus what a system of symbols would do is put on the table values which can then be seen and analyzed, making the public at large and the scientists themselves conscious of their judgments and choices, realizing that what they describe is also what they manipulate and shape through their experimentation. I want to open up scientific and technical questions which have future consequences as part of their present activity, especially in activities which are unbounded in terms of time and are likely to lead to automatic institutionally reproductive results.

I am painfully aware that the attempt to enter the scientific project raises a number of difficult questions. For example, does the introduction of a new symbol system in fact act to stifle or free inquiry? This is a question of deep concern which I hope we could talk about once I put together the definitions of the symbols. Bernstein has suggested that I use the symbols on word processors as the means of creating the framework for this language of "oughts," experience, and warnings. I have not had the chance as yet to work the symbol system through. One reason is that if I use Bernstein's suggestion I would be required to break down and buy a word processor.

Now to your letter. I thought it quite wonderful and very instructive. I want to take up your central point first. I take this to be the definition of rational inquiry which "insists that conclusions should follow premises and that theories should be subjected to empirical test." Later you reintroduce the same point, "that conclusions follow logically from premises, that theories meet empirical test." Then you add what could be carefully and judiciously selected, etc.

The question to ask is whether the definition of rational inquiry continues to change and that the fashion of standards for rational inquiry is open to constant revision, not only in its methods, which often appear rational and schematically clean *only* in the retelling, but in its assumptions and pursuits as well as what is considered "rational," a "premise" and a viable "conclusion."

Unless words are thought to be relatively obvious with a common-sense meaning to them and therefore not a subject for debate, you are stuck with a type of scientific view of rationality which is not inside history, and indeed is hermetically sealed from it. It is not only sealed from what [are] thought to be past developments in the meaning of rational inquiry, it may also end up separating itself from non-obvious but equally rational strands of people's behaviour and thought which are not necessarily blessed with the stamp of acceptance among those who exercise power. I don't have to tell you that in our time, the hegemonic form of culture which comes through the laboratories, universities, banks and governments is profoundly technocratic and linked. Rational inquiry becomes a mode of reenforcing or challenging this hegemonic structure. I don't think it can be independent of that struggle. Thus, within one framework a conclusion may follow a premise, but by shifting the framework or the social class the conclusion may become either false or ambiguous. Obviously any set of true statements which have to be verified has a validity limited to the framework to which that statement is attached. And indeed, one can provisionally accept the notion that scientific investigations are predicated on the assumption of limiting conclusions to specific circumstances, fearing like the plague generalization. But the fact is that this is not the way human beings or institutions operate. They do not circumscribe. It is why a new language must be invented so that the debate can be entered into with other considerations that will count as rational. These symbols will reflect the place that bonding and affection must play in keeping humanity alive. Do you think that if bonding and affection were made a conscious part of the consideration of the scientists at Los Alamos they would have been so quick to lend themselves to the enterprise? What I am saying is that rational inquiry must now include a mode of thought which includes "seeing far" and self critical analysis of what the particular work will yield. Perhaps this could have an inhibiting effect on knowledge creation. I think, however, that there must be inhibition at least at the state which is commonly referred to as institutional and developmental.

I want to say something about the university. Some place in White-head, perhaps the *Adventure of Ideas,* there is a discussion of how at certain times creative thought is inside the university and at other times it is in groupings outside the university. I think the university is going through a very bad time indeed. Just because this is so, I would put to you the question, what should IPS [Institute for Policy Studies] be doing to both confront fascism, come up with alternatives and basic social theory? How can we get help from people within the universities who want to connect up, or who want to rethink their own program or project?

For the time being I want to leave the reductionism question aside. I think we are talking past each other. As for will and choice the issue may be less a rational "understanding of it" than a means, both calculative and qualitative, which tells us the results of certain choices which we make. Obviously one cannot know the future with any certainty, but what we can know is our likelihoods. These tell us the results of certain results of will, intentions and choice. And if this is so why can't such considerations be linked to science?

Now as for the question of scientific knowledge in itself being neutral, I remain unconvinced. Certain knowledges are developed in certain institutions and they would never be developed in other settings. Yet it might appear that that knowledge is neutral. I would appreciate more of an explication of your point with some examples. I am willing to bet you dinner at a Chinese restaurant that without straining I will show you that the particular "science" or "rational inquiry" is not neutral, is of necessity part of a particular institutional structure and within its own terms requires a particular type of institutional structure. (My heart skipped a beat with this dare. Nevertheless, I'll stand by it.)

Let me give you an example of what I mean. Let's take something obvious. Under what circumstances does AB equal BA? The question turns out to be more complicated then one might ordinarily think. At best what we might be able to assert is the principle of approximation: AB approximately equals BA.

Obviously, if A and B represent something other than themselves, as for example, orange and pears on the left side of the equation and pears and apples on the right side of the equation, they are only ideally equal if we agree they are equal by using signs to indicate that we *want* them to be equal, by finding a third element, either hidden or stated, which makes them equal in relation to that third element, such as a social measuring unit, say, money: or if they represent nothing in reality except themselves. Even in that case we must be careful to state that they represent nothing in which case they are equal, if you and I understand the words in the same way. After all, it would not take much to show that the writing or print weights of the letters on one side of the equation are different than the other.

The difference is whether these distinctions or differences are trivial. I contend they are not. First of all, they show the reality of approximation and the hidden judgment of social consensus that is needed to accept even the seemingly most obvious "rigorous" statements. Second, it means that there is an invisible set of agreements which in fact are the ground on which the "truth" of logic and mathematics operate. Third, the attempt to narrow the "circle of unprovable primitive truths as small as possible" (Frege) is a formal and evasive exercise which masks the fact that the "improvable and primitive" infest all of our thought. It is better, therefore, to think about the invention of conventions which become habits, like hand washing before an operation or a question mark.

In policy terms these are important questions, for we now use mathematics as if they represent differences and similarities and equivalences with a great degree of accuracy behind them. In reality the symbols are incommensurable.

Even the notion that every object is identical to itself can only be true if we assume that that object doesn't change or decay. Is a fresh tomato the same tomato when it is rotten? Only in the formal sense, certainly not in the eating sense.

The question about the academic professions and their self image is a little like saying that there is a true socialism and the Soviet Union or Albania, or whoever else, are not socialists. Surely, we have to begin with what people think they are, especially since they've built one helluva rampart to protect themselves. It may be that 75 years later we discover that Cyril Burt is a liar and a racist or we may learn that the Columbia faculty after the Civil War sought ways of making blacks into less than human beings. Yet, what can we say when we are in the middle of things without sounding like keepers of a true faith which never existed?

There is a very interesting book I'll find for you which talks about the difference between the Japanese approach to physics and the western approach, by a Japanese Nobel laureate. I am publishing a book called *The Common Good* with Routlege and Kegan Paul. The editor, Professor Apple of the University of Wisconsin, criticized me for not beginning from the differences that women would approach scientific and social questions from. He gave me a number of citations to read which I will do and then pass on.

Finally, the major issue is this. You and Schrodinger make the point that science (and scientific method?) cannot tell us anything that is of profound human concern. But our problem is that science is causing profound human concern, adding to our problems immeasurably. If this is so, and if we believe in rational thought, surely we can find a means of going beyond the type of science which is so patently destructive, and surely we can find a rational method of pointing the way. For example, is there not a rational method, immanent to science, to stop the Star Wars madness? Is there not a language which will help our actions? This is what the program of reconstructive knowledge is. The question of course, is whether we should use mythic symbols, "punctuation habits," to protect the future.

Best,
Marc

# 5

# Ending the Faustian Bargain
## Toward a Knowledge for Social Reconstruction

MARCUS G. RASKIN

What I have to say is not in the way of giving a definition to reconstructive knowledge.* I see reconstructive knowledge as an epistemological and conversational path that uses all we know and perceive, relating them together in such a way as to help humankind become subject-actors of history conscious of their dignity, liberation, and nondominating purpose toward one another. It rejects Pythagoras and Parmenides in a special way, for we would now question, correctly so, whether anything is true or correct for all time, whether it be a sociology, a philosophy, or a mathematical physics. Obviously, humankind's inventions occur in history. Therefore, axioms and content of disciplines change. Reconstructive knowledge asserts (and notices) that humankind is inside history making things, ideas, and institutions. Accordingly no knowledge or discipline can escape its human purpose and content. And therefore we are called upon to judge institutional arrangements and knowledges to see which and what forms of knowing will tend toward reconstruction. To this end the purpose of knowledge workers must be beyond its particulars, relating what they know in the particular to a universal, and seeing aspects of the universal in the particular.

As Ernst Cassirer has said, "epistemological reflection leads us everywhere to the insight that what the various sciences call the 'object' is nothing in itself, fixed once for all, but that it is first determined by some standpoint of knowledge."[1] As I have said "the standpoint of knowledge"

*After trying out a number of definitions of what reconstructive knowledge is, I found myself responding to my own self-inquiry and those of others with a Zen "quip." If you ask me what Zen is, you surely can't know what it is. And if I give you a definition of it, I don't know. At one stage of my frustrating quest I thought that silence is the best answer to the "what is" question, whether the question is about reconstructive knowledge or anything else. There is an undeniable attraction to the Hasidic rabbis and some of the modern French structuralists, who seem to counsel this course as the way to practical virtue and understanding. But silence is a distinctly inward path in which one has dialogues with oneself. Having too many of them may cause one to wonder about his or her own sanity. Although it is doubtful that there is any greater amount of sanity among us when we are silent, silence is most assuredly not the way of the modern world. Furthermore, it is questionable whether silence leaves us ethically better off than spoken or written language. It may guard us against unnecessary error. But it also denies the possibility of any collective advance in understanding.

also constantly shifts so that we see the viewer shifting and changing, the object shifting and changing and the subject matter of the knowledge shifting and changing. *These shiftings, without moorings, increase rather than decrease critical and ethical responsibility.* It is why beliefs are so important. That everything is in flux does not assume that we are able or want to rid ourselves of certain beliefs. However, the modern Socratic path which knowledge workers must walk exposes beliefs, reified knowledge systems, and empty phrases that inhibit expanded consciousness—those knowledge systems which seek to deny subject-actor status to human beings.

The path is hard to find because there are no fixed boundaries and categories, no authority systems or guideposts except those that are intrinsic to the work of increasing collective dignity.

It is a terrifying realization that even in science all rules are man-made, that "laws" work only under specific and specified conditions, and that it is "man" who specifies those conditions. Because this is so, each activity of knowledge and action is concerned with choice; and choice, whether in the context of the laboratory, the political group, or everyday life, involves judgment, that peculiar amalgam of politics and ethics which steers us away from or toward humane understanding. Our choices, whether in one field or another, of what we see, and how we choose to look at what we see are freely made; by which I mean that there are specific choices made by either ourselves or others, now or in the past which impede or enable thought and practice to move in one direction or another. That a person is not free or conscious either of his or her perception or choice does not mean that he or she is any the less able to choose and steer the patterns of history. When we speak of history we are describing likelihoods but with the possibility of change and human intention. Patterns, therefore, tell us that "things" change. And they act differently in one boundary as against another. They act differently according to the way they are perceived and categorized by our language and ways of organization. The notion of pattern allows us to realize that that which is there is not preordained. A pattern is not a brooding omnipresent, a law that cannot be changed. We decide on the patterns that exist in the search we undertake, and therefore moral questions become critical. We create "order" by our choices. "There is no way of pointing a finger or camera at it [order]; order must be discovered and, in a deeper sense, it must be created. What we see, as we see it, is mere disorder."[2]

These notions become important even for Marxists concerned with the "laws of history" because they allow us to escape the emulation of science which we must come to understand as incapable of finding laws of nature, merely models and metaphors of what is studied. We know that certain things work or have explanations. But we do not know why.

Accepting this conclusion we are then able to see that it is the moral purpose as propounded in politics and in the science itself which needs to be explored. It is not science in its present form that can do much for us. That we can quantify nature and objectify it does not mean that that is what nature is. Without sounding animistic in the analysis, is it not obvious that how one acts towards nonhuman nature defines how nature will act? A monkey in a zoo cage is one kind of animal. A monkey in his natural habitat is another. The present experimental methods used on animals do not see them except as objects to be worked on, "dissected and named."

It is no wonder then that reconstructive knowledge should question the nature of the disciplines of knowledge, their assumptions, methods, and the ethical assumptions behind them. How to begin? Facts can no longer stand as pristine. They are to be "deconstructed," broken into different elements to show their speculative nature or value-hidden spin. (The reader should try this exercise for that set of "facts" in any "discipline" he or she really trusts. How "solid" are those facts? How did they get to be that way? How often are they almost facts or products of measurement, in other words, products of social agreement to objectify the other, moving the "thing" under study from subject to object?)

Like everyone else in America I have been taken with empirical knowledge. We have had a mania for facts, discrete, unconnected, and stored within us for use and "delight." I was taken with Alfred North Whitehead's phrase "irreducible and stubborn" facts. But somewhere along the line I began wondering about "facts" as a basic category of anything.

Were they proved or true? What was it in their nature which got me to accept their validity? A moment's reflection would tell us that any fact is predicated on hidden beliefs, assumptions, and social relations. Even, as Marjorie Grene said, such an innocuous "fact" as "This is red" had behind it enormously complex social relationships. Why and how did I accept certain facts? "In fact" it is a very complex social network of authority, persuasion, coercion, and laziness which gets any of us to believe anything. We accept facts on the basis of a vast and hidden ad hominem system of authority which we do not or can't possibly know first hand, or have any way of cross-examining. Because facts are divorced from our own experience if they occurred in the past, or if they cannot be easily replicated either in laboratories, bureaucracies, or scholar's studies, it is clear that without first-hand participation facts are not necessarily hard, stubborn, or true. I did (and do) believe that there were certain facts which were "hot"—that is, they caused us to shift how we saw the rest of the world. But even here I was not sure whether those were facts or new metaphors. Just by listening to the speech of a politician, scientist, or scholar in which "facts" are cited, we may conclude how infinitely malleable and socially dependent facts really are.[3] This means that we judge what we hear through either a priori categories or feelings of passion that often as not we hide.

Institutions which stem from eighteenth-century assumptions arrange these reifications (facts) according to their needs, institutional bias, and class spin. This generation is beginning to intuit the skewed nature of facts. Nevertheless, we continue to celebrate them and assume their power and immediate value in, for example, social relations. We use them to divide people into categories through a kind of semiotic magic which commits some to riches and others to insane asylums. A Professor Jensen serves as the traffic cop to assert the meaning of the intelligence of one form over another. Throughout the twentieth century in the Anglo-Saxon world it was assumed that the emphasis on orderliness and *factuality* was the way to bring progress, with the assumption being that the scientists was like Sergeant Friday, of the TV drama *Dragnet,* who was interested in "just the facts, ma'am." Thus, for example, the philosopher Whitehead saw science, its facts, and the hoped for consciousness of the immanent order of things as being *the* gift from West to East, I suppose, in exchange for visiting imperialism on the Third World. Science was "transferable from country to country, and from race to race, wherever there is a rational society." But what gifts were we really giving other than our own prejudices and "superior" ways? What did it mean that fundamental questions of ontology, faith, and pragmatic implications of actions no longer had to be asked? And were our disciplines of knowledge liberating?

In a modern state, colonizing knowledge is often grounded in derivative empiricism, where a set of "facts" is formulated through calculation of someone else's view of something defined as an event. Its conclusions are accepted, but the reasoning, context, and proof remain unknown. Without admitting it, colonizing knowledge relates to the elimination of alternate explanations, and the unwillingness to accept the interrelationships between the sort of science we do, how we do it, the questions we ask, and the sorts of "proof" we require. At least since World War II scientists and technologists have integrated themselves with remarkable ease into the research and political programs of the powerful. They were expected to come up with those "facts" that "made things work." As Hitler's Reichsminister, Albert Speer explained in his *Memoirs* about his role and that of the technicians' service to Naziism:

Basically, I exploited the phenomenon of the technician's often blind devotion to his task. Because of what seems to be the moral neutrality of technology, these people were without any scruples about their activities. The more technical the world imposed on us by the war, the more dangerous was this indifference of the technician to the direct consequence of his anonymous activities.[4]

The technician's or scientist's moral blindness is no greater than that of most of us. The only difference is that in the twentieth century his blindness matters because he makes matter and presents us with facts that we come to accept and believe. This can cause great grief. One example is in the "transfer of technology" to the Third World. We are used to hearing that technology is neutral; that it can be used for good or bad, but in fact technology is a social process and tools are its products. To put this another way, technology is the product or end point of a complex social process which is both necessary to the production of the instrument or product and which in turn shapes the nature of the social process. The more complex the technology the more the social system around it will reflect its inertial demands. State socialist leaders are not prepared to admit this, so they assume that nuclear energy, for example, is neutral depending on how it is used. This is mistaken since a particular social system must be created to sustain nuclear energy, one that includes scientists, police guards, hierarchic authority, secrecy, and punishments.

There are some who believe that the "laws of dialectics" will operate to transform social systems and that technology in this process will also be transformed. For the time being, however, in the West we see variant forms of fascism emerging and a type of militant authoritarianism which drops the caring principle from society. Nature is to be conquered and acted upon. What is seen as nature is that which cannot talk or fight back or "must" be controlled. There is no room for the caring principle in either the Cartesian or Baconian model of science or in an international system that takes its cue from those models, perhaps because caring and nurturing are thought to be in the female realm. One need look no further than the emphasis on organized violence against one's own population and against other nations to see the strangulation of the caring principle. So what are the needed attitudes or paths to move beyond our present quandary? What are the elements we have to work with?

The first is the intuition that there are other ways to fashion a path of inquiry so that the knowledge created does not have to be an enemy of either the good or the decent. The second is a surplus of consciousness among knowledge workers and other groups who have been able to cultivate (because of self controlled time and some wealth beyond necessity) an empathic sensibility which emerges from knowing about others and nature, their need and pain. The third is that for most of humanity there is a surplus of pain: people can no longer accept or take on the positions which have been assigned to them through social structures and knowledges they neither understand nor control, whether it is the "knowledge" of the standardized achievement test or the knowledge of how to make and package the atomic bomb. This is now especially true as these social structures begin to crumble like sand castles. It means that knowledge workers must stand with those in pain to lessen that pain.

Political changes come from either a surplus of pain or a surplus of consciousness. Those with a surplus of consciousness feel the pain of others and use their consciousness of other situations and patterns to bring about change in the world beyond interest or class. Marxists have thought that such surplus consciousness was unnecessary in bringing

about substantial change. It is utterly necessary and it is among knowledge workers that that surplus is present and can be focussed. But most
have a surplus of pain. Except where the situation is utterly incendiary,
those with a surplus believe that politics is one profound reason that
their pain exists.

The obvious but wrong conclusion to draw is that humankind will be
liberated if it escapes from politicians. But to run from politics would be
about as sensible as to stop ourselves from breathing. The great psychoanalyst and Marxist Wilhelm Reich mistakenly concluded from his own
experience during the ill-fated days of the Weimar Republic that politics
with its programs and authoritarian structures, studied ignorance, and
demonic concern with power was in fact a harmful and unnecessary
diversion from those elements which he took to be the ground of
civilization, namely, work, knowledge, and love.

In modern times these aspects of life are mediated through politics.
In other words, politics dares us to ask "What kind of knowledge?"
"What kind of work?" "What kind of love?" While reciprocally knowledge, work, and love ask "What kind of politics?" The character of this
mediation will either transform politics or work, knowledge, and love or
on the contrary will be so deformed, one by the other, that life will not be
able to be lived. These are the modern Socratic questions. Reconstructive knowledge therefore is consciously and analytically framed in the
context of politics and concerned with the path of liberation and
responsibility. Consequently, it is not only the study and practice of "this"
or "that" or "is." It is rather the study of the "ought." It forges a set of
ethical axioms which are to be tested and grounded in our feelings,
needs, and practice. These axioms are literally the alpha and the omega,
the beginning and end of where we start from and what we seek to
create or make into shared reality. They are not, however, a procrustean
bed.

Historical forces are often confusing for they are metaphorical statements of continuing and past events that are hard to explain. Nevertheless, it would be a foolish person who did not recognize a spirit of
liberation which is meant to transform the institutional arrangements
that cause domination, colonization, exploitative hierarchies, and dangerous technology. The project of reconstructive knowledge is to bring
together this spirit with spontaneity and systematic discipline. To accomplish this end we are required to experience the world in a new way if we
are to "see" this spirit. In part this is a question of epistemology and in
part it is a question of myth construction. Each thing and event is no
longer discrete or separable. Instead the connection is there between us
who attempt to see within the event or explain the "this" in terms of
energy, liveliness, anything but dead matter. Thus, we skip and jump
categories. Our axioms must reflect this lack of concern for discipline or
category. As in quantum theory between the object being measured and

the thing used as the measure, my thought is related to you the reader. Both of us are related to my pen and the publisher, even my hidden realities (and yours) of sadness (in my case not seeing my beloved children or loving wife today). Therefore, what we learn, what we think, and how we see what is "out there" and relating what is within us to the out there must change. Otherwise, we become overwhelmed with a particular, thinking that that particular is the *this* or *that* which cancels out all other things and events, or understandings—all other *this*'s or *that*'s.

If we take seriously knowledge, love, and work, when we think of how to act on the out there, indeed, how we intend to describe it, or ourselves to it, we are faced with considering the question of virtue, not only in the renaissance sense of skill, but in the Socratic sense of wisdom and "right" ethics. Once we decide to consider this question we are self-consciously seeking the good both in knowledge and politics. It should have as much place in our thoughts, as Rustum Roy has pointed out, as the true and the beautiful. In recent years there is an unstated conclusion that what is true or even beautiful may be found or pointed to, but what is good cannot be of serious concern in an age of atomic bombs, missiles, gratuitous killings, unspeakable poverty, mass starvation, mission-oriented science, imperialism, and other chilling realities that cannot be denied. It is because these conditions exist that we are again looking for the good and hoping that humankind's thoughts—the way we think, what we think we see, and how we categorize what we see—will bring us to some understanding which could move us to the good, by which I mean consciousness and commitment to the Other as subject-actors of history. This point of view should not be terribly shocking. Because the process of knowing plays a central role in the nature of the society itself, it can be integrative or dissociative, depending on what we want from it.

Just as logic depends on ontology and the types of cues we get from our "soul"—which are then mediated through consciousness and specific knowledges that serve as the connecting links between our "souls" and the society. So it is that society, its institutions, and even social relationships revolve around particular forms of knowledge, even unstated ethical concerns. These forms and their content have clear consequences. They have particular methodologies which bring with them the conclusions that are embedded in the methodologies. And they reinforce social institutions and social structures. Of course there is a "feedback" loop in which these institutions then reinforce particular sorts of behavior, experiments, and what is to be "officially" remembered, as well as the standard for what is thought to be true. Where we consciously seek to fool another or set up our institutional structure accordingly, humanity is in very big trouble.

Now not much of this is a surprise and in one form or another these questions have been explored by Marx and Marxists as well as by Karl

Mannheim and his sociology of knowledge and the Frankfurt school of Max Horkheimer and Theodor Adorno. But what is news is that science, technology, and their methods are to be dethroned. They are just another enterprise. They are not the rigorous truths about reality which Marx and Marxists believed would be the core upon which liberated humankind would walk. As an enterprise it is not in any way separate from what, as I have put it, goes on outside the laboratory door and what happens within the laboratory. Truth telling, let alone truth, may not be the object of the enterprise. At worst it is a "gun for hire" activity without concern for implications or method. At best inquiry is its goal. On the other hand, the standards used in a project of whatever kind are integrally wound up with the question of good faith, by which I mean telling the truth much in the manner Jacob Bronowski discusses the issue of truth in science. We should not make too much of a mystery of the truth. I prefer an operational definition in which the phenomenon or event studied is not separated from what we communicate as honestly as we can. Telling the truth is being aware of what you see—what your senses report to you, sharing and reporting that to others, and allowing others to check what they sense against what you sense. (Sartre once said that in a liberated society there would be no secrets.) In all cases the pattern of truth telling operates well only to the extent that everyone understands that this is a pattern which is human, subject to illusion, political, and either ethical or unethical to the core. Truth telling as a process is based on love and centering, by which I mean that we do not paint our mice to suggest that an experiment is something it is not.

Truth telling as an operational minimum for scientific activities (and all other activities) can only operate where the means of production—the laboratores, accelerators, and computers—are *co-owned* with scientific workers and where there is access to anyone either competent or otherwise (a peer or an outsider) to repeat the experiment. If no one wants to repeat the experiment we may conclude that it is trivial, and if it can only be performed in large laboratores under elaborate security conditions our presumption might be that the inquiry is a dangerous and possibly antihuman one. If outsiders cannot learn to work the machine or replicate the experiments we may want to conclude that they should not have been performed originally. Without openness to replication and public but decentralized ownership, the standard of truth telling is limited and institutional; it is not public or replicable by anyone. On the assumption that truth telling is not trivial because it includes a changed definition of property ownership of the equipment, we will find that truth telling has distinct social ingredients: (a) That which is perceived or that which is carried out by the experimenters, and (b) the general (usually unnoticed) conditions of the institutional, political, and economic setting which is the ground that the experiment stands upon. Nothing is thrown away and everything bears on the truth, both the local particular one and the larger general one. The reader will say, isn't this little more than an honest statement of a search for facts? Yes, but in a new way. Once it is seen as a "motion point" it cannot be seen outside of a larger context or judged and used without regard to it. The particular "fact" then is to be understood as a microcosm of a number of other forces and it is also to be placed and linked with other "facts," other *motion points*.

There is no reason to contradict the view that pure mind cannot discover the laws of nature (really patterns) which are supposed to be there. Instead what we constantly create is metaphors and models for what goes on. Because, as I have said, our science is not only immanent, but suffused with cultural realities, and because our sciences are human constructs that are metaphorical and mythical and which use statistical or correlative proofs as their method, we are left with profoundly ethical human questions of what we are doing, just because there is no "out there" that is not part of our personal "there." The myths which are chosen and recreated in each generation order the world. And in this sense we always have a choice. For example, the yin-yang myth tells us about "male-female" complementarity, which can be used as a guiding principle for a better future if we shake out vestiges of dominance-submission from the application of the myth. This myth can help us live in the human world and bring from the culture possibilities of egalitarian interdependence in the public and private space. I find that a restatement of myths can be far more explanatory and useful than the type of rational calculative knowledge which governs most of our social and natural science attempts at comprehending either social relations, economic situations, or "ought" behavior. If properly used such myth will not yield the disastrous consequences that linear knowledge consistently draws from social reality.

Alfred North Whitehead believed that

There can be no living science unless there is a widespread instinctive conviction in the existence of an *order of things,* and, in particular, of an *order of nature.* I have used the word "instinctive" advisedly. It does not matter what men say in words, so long as their activities are controlled by settled instincts.[5]

But an order to nature and things is, as Cassirer has told us, what humankind puts on reality. And therefore it must have an ethical content through its epistemological and mythical systems if we are to survive as a species. Is it too late to formulate an axiomatic path through our present situation which seeks to get us out of a virtually hopeless quagmire? And indeed, who is the "us"? Is this a question which now must be shared by all subject-actors and not just intellectuals? Is this not the dual challenge of a democracy and socialism that seek to recreate and hold humankind as their root and of a sociology which shows a way of acting and analyzing that does not assert either continuity or revolution, but instead asserts a path of enabling?

## Notes

1. Ernst Cassirer, *Substance and Function and Einstein's Theory of Relativity* [1923] (New York: Dover Publications, 1953), 356.

2. Jacob Bronowski, *Science and Human Values* (New York: Harper & Row, 1965), 14.

3. This is why the method of sensory data is a limiting and particularistic enterprise which assumes without knowing it the same methods as Sherlock Holmes.

4. Albert Speer's memoirs, quoted by Bob Broedel in *Science and Liberation,* ed. Rita Arditti, Pat Brennan, and Steve Cavrak (Boston: Southend Press, 1980), 245.

5. Alfred North Whitehead, *Science and the Modern World* (New York: Macmillan, 1925), 6.

# 6

# The Human Meaning of the Information Revolution

MICHAEL GOLDHABER

The philosopher Ernst Cassirer suggests a definition of knowledge that may be briefly summarized as follows: knowledge amounts to a structure of relationships that exist between a person's experiences. I adopt that view. Further, I shall define information as transmissible knowledge. Thus in taking in and understanding information one is adding to and reorganizing the structure of relationships between experiences that one already has. It follows that in taking in information, one is in effect creating a new structure in one's mind, a structure that most likely never existed in full in any other mind (since based on one's unique set of experiences), and a structure that one subsequently may be able to transmit (in part) as further information.

Another crucial consequence of these definitions is that information is itself a set of relations, of form and not matter, since otherwise it would have nothing to do with knowledge. To clarify this, think of the set of processes involved in getting a public lecture from one mind to another. Somehow I get my lips, tongue, and vocal cords to shape vibrations of the air called sound. These then pass to a microphone which converts the sound to electrical impulses in a wire. These impulses then enter a complex electronic circuit, in which the signals get amplified and sent on to a loudspeaker. The electrical impulses are converted into mechanical motions of the loudspeaker, and then into air vibrations again. Finally, these are reconverted into mechanical vibrations of your ear, and finally into impulses passing along your auditory nerve. Nothing material has gone from me to you, even though at each stage, the information was embodied in some material or another (air, electrons, paper—in the loudspeaker—air again, and so on). What has to be preserved in all this is some set of relationships, some form that remains the same despite its different material embodiments.

Information is form and not matter, and this is not just a point of interest for metaphysics. It is for this reason that any technology from brick making to electronics may be used as an information technology. That means that whatever technology permits the fastest movement, deals with the smallest units, is cheapest, or is most versatile may always be adapted as an information technology. The preceding sentence would simply not be true if we substituted words like "agriculture," "shelter," or "transportation" for information. Thus it is no accident that as twentieth-century science developed new understandings of matter on the smallest—the most microscopic—scale that we have experienced a vast flowering of new information technologies.

The emergence of these new technologies means that my definition of information as transmissible knowledge has an intrinsically historical dimension. What is transmissible has changed, and presumably will continue to change over time, meaning, loosely speaking, that an ever larger fraction of knowledge can be information. It seems probable too that the fraction of our knowledge that comes to us as information, rather than being learned through experience, also continues to grow.

The need for information appears insatiable. It is not merely a commonplace that the more one knows, the more one knows how to ask and therefore can be aware of not knowing. A fundamental economic consequence is visible in our society at present. In the few centuries of the dominance of the market, we have gone through many sorts of technologies, industries, and businesses. Each spurt of innovation has ended in a period of stagnation in which any considerable growth of the industries dominant at the time no longer seemed possible. Because of the apparent insatiability of the need for information, once it is developed, there is some reason to believe that information offers a way out of this process—that when all other industries have failed us for lack of space or their stress on resources, or because demand (at least among those with money) has stagnated, information is the one hope for future growth. I am simplifying here, but sentiments not too different from this have in fact surfaced in the corporate community. One index is the serious commitment to information technologies on the part of major corporations of whatever sector—automobile, oil, or banking.

By some measures information-related activities account for roughly 50 percent of all employment in this country already. Adding the time we spend in absorbing information in classrooms or through television, information-related activity actually occupies a larger fraction of society's total time than those activities associated with more traditional material goods production and with services that have mainly material effect (such as haircuts). Information industries such as publishing, entertainment, news, data banks, education and training, conferences, consulting, managing, and perhaps also the financial sector share in common the characteristics that they can be started with relatively little capital, can easily grow, and seem unending in range. Therefore they appear to be the economic phenomenon with just the character needed to save our system of quasi-free enterprise. While this is the appearance, it may turn out not to be the reality.

The difficulty is precisely the fact that information has become a major new category of wealth. For the information industries to become the backbone of a market-based economy, as ours supposedly is, it is utterly crucial that information be capable of being bought and sold. But is it? I shall argue that information may be regarded as property only if we accept some restraints so severe that they pose an impediment to the continued operation of anything resembling a free market. The reason is that information, as form rather than matter, differs fundamentally from things more typically bought and sold in the past. A form, as opposed to a specific embodiment of it, is neither localizable in space nor in any particular extension.

If I eat your hamburger, I am depriving you of its use completely. On the other hand if I use your information, I do not prevent you from having it. This is a striking and basic difference between information and ordinary goods and services: there is no reason for me to own information if I simply want to hold onto it.

I can possess information (without legal ownership) and still present it to you. In fact, in doing so, I may come to understand it even better, thus improving my own possession of it. This runs entirely counter to the justification for owning property of other kinds.

Furthermore, there is no reason to assume that information I present to you was mine to begin with. It is only possible for me to transmit knowledge to you if prior to that we shared in common the words, grammar, concepts, and experiences out of which the specific information was structured. That is totally different from the hamburger that can be traced back to a specific cow that someone could have owned, or even further back to grass or other feed crops that could equally well have been privately held—in our society at least. In the case of the hamburger, it is possible to trace a series of economic exchanges—of buying and selling at every step of the way from earth, water, and sunlight to the final product you obtain at the fast food restaurant—that is, to the point at which you eat it and it disappears.

An ordinary good then assumes no prior sharing in common, and is normally used up in the process of being consumed. Information must rest on a common shared basis, since otherwise it would be unintelligible and therefore useless. Rather than being used up in being consumed, it becomes incorporated with prior knowledge in your mind to form a new structure that permits you to express new information, so that information consumption, rather than being the opposite of production, is the same process.

As information-based industries multiply, the effort to maintain their profitability leads to pressure to protect information as property regardless of the unsuitability or difficulty of doing so. This requires going against the fundamental nature of information and also against the obvious trends of information technology.

Within a decade, home copying machines could be quite common (current models are in the price range of a stereo or a refrigerator.) Copying books to sell to or give to friends and neighbors constitutes theft—that is, a violation of the copyright laws. At first glance this may not seem to be a new problem. Yet in practice it is.

In fact, copyright, as a form of intellectual property law, is much newer than laws protecting other forms of property. The earliest beginnings of intellectual property laws—in the form of design patents—cannot be traced beyond the twelfth century in Italy. Copyright itself is considerably more recent. It is true that copyright and patent are enshrined in the U.S. Constitution as protection of ownership of invention or expression for limited periods of time. However the difficulties that these laws create are enormously magnified by the very spread of information technologies that enhances their economic importance.

Despite having been outlawed in principle for some time, theft of intellectual property in the comfort of one's own living room has only recently become a practical possibility. Thus the intellectual property laws imply a new kind of police power to investigate activities conducted in privacy. For the foreseeable future, new information technology will continue to make easier both violating such laws and justifying intrusive enforcement. The result is a heightened conflict between our long-held notions of liberty and of property. The myth of the free market will ultimately become untenable if either restrictions on the buyer reach the level they must, in order to promote information as property, or conversely, if information is permitted to be freely transmitted.

Because of the enormous importance of property rights in human affairs, conflicts over changing definitions of property have been a feature of substantial transformations of the social order. In medieval Europe land that was held in common in a village was often under the jurisdiction of the local noble family, but this gave them no rights to sell it or to use it for their own purposes. But in the transition to modernity, this jurisdiction was redefined as property in the modern sense, depriving the peasantry of a substantial source of sustenance and altering the social order. During the pre-Civil War period in the United States the Supreme Court held that if slaves were property in the South, they still had to be regarded as property if they escaped to free states in the North, thus helping set the stage for a violent confrontation over the issue of whether people could be property. Currently the intensification of importance of existing intellectual property laws, as well as their extension to new areas, is altering social relations nearly as profoundly. We shall have to choose between the right to know and freedom of expression on the one hand, and the right to hold information as property on the other, and the choice we make will inevitably have momentous consequences for the future direction of our society. We may already read, in the actions of the executive branch and in various judicial and legislative initiatives, signs of the potential conflict. Unfortunately, until now, the interests of the vast public have been ignored in these struggles. It is one of my purposes here to raise the alarm.

In recent years, patent and copyright laws have been extended to life forms, to computer architecture, to software. There was a recent widely publicized effort to prevent home videotaping. There have been crackdowns on video and audiotape "pirates" in the Caribbean area. The current form of the Caribbean Basin Initiative extends help only to those countries who agree to prevent their citizens from "stealing" U.S. movies from satellite broadcasts.

Recent conservative administrations have also been active in extending export controls to information, restricting visas to Eastern bloc scientists, and even attempting to restrict access from friendly nations. In the area of trade secrecy, the main villain for the administration has become Japan, with large Japanese corporations subject to prosecution for buying IBM secrets. At the same time, firms in Silicon Valley that previously allowed the relatively free exchange of ideas between their engineering employees have received official encouragement to impose much tighter restrictions. Meanwhile, administrations have sought to prevent leaks of information by imposing mandatory lie detector tests on public servants; this effort fits nicely with the notion of information as property.

Further, the vast stores of information of all sorts held by the government have been turned into commodities for private benefit wherever possible. For example, 1980 census information is available on a computer tape for around forty thousand dollars. Not only is this exorbitant, but most of us would have no way of utilizing the information in this form. However, an enterprising publisher bought the tape, developed a small amount of computer software necessary to print it out, and is selling the information collected at public expense for five hundred dollars the five-volume set. By dint of the precise format in which the data are printed, the company has been able to claim the protection of copyright for this unfairly expensive publication.

The sum total of efforts of the sort just discussed threaten to create two highly unequal classes. There will be the extremely rich—mostly the heads of large corporations, with access to whatever information they want—and a much larger class of those who can afford little information compared with what is needed to have any power in society, to enjoy equality, or to be able to exercise democratic rights. The very humanity of this large class will be seriously impoverished.

Many of the wealthy will constitute the new group of what I call "information millionaires." Those, such as television personalities, sports stars, or software publishers who will owe their wealth to the fact that information technology permits them to reach audiences of hundreds of millions. (It is the existence of this necessarily small group that tempts many more of us to accept and even support the idea of information as property. Every author hoping to live from writing now has to rely on the existence of copyright, but most authors don't really benefit from this restrictive legislation.)

In failing to oppose the restrictive and repressive practices that will be necessary to maintain information as property, we are giving up what we could have instead—a world of abundance. In allowing each of us to have access to any information we desire, we would also allow an unprecedented ability to share and take advantage of material wealth of all sorts. In addition, information is not simply functional for external ends. The sharing of information is a perfectly valid end in itself. Indeed, it is impossible to understand why half the economic activity of our society is related to information, if we see information as purely functional. The enormous number of government and corporate bureaucrats that we have are really engaged in the same activity we are carrying on here: human discourse, conversation, gab, expression—a fundamental human activity.

Were the fact that our society is no longer really based on the production and consumption of goods and services clearly recognized, were it clearly seen that we have become truly an information society, we would search not for ways to regard information as property, restricting our audience and our range of respondents, but rather for ways to open up discourse further. We would also not make the sort of mischief we often do under the mistaken assumption that we have to turn our words into action.

But to go that different road, to be able to absorb these new awarenesses, we do need to struggle against the efforts now underway to restrict and commodify information. In conclusion, that is a task I would commend to you as both neglected and vitally important. In that struggle, we will also have to come to grips with the legitimate social and personal benefits people—such as authors—now feel obligate them to uphold the notion of intellectual property. We shall have to find alternative ways to support the creative activities we conclude are important, but we must avoid the trap of assuming that only through laws of property can we do that.

# 7
# The Selling of Market Economics

EDWARD S. HERMAN

## Introduction

The question of whether economics has been able to free itself from the ideological influence of class and marketplace and constitute itself as an objective science has long been a subject of professional controversy. In a Marxian perspective, economics is inescapably class-bound, whereas many orthodox analysts have claimed that economics, while affected in various ways by ideology, nevertheless has gradually sloughed off ideological impedimenta and reached ever higher refinements of cognitive truth.[1] The scientific reputation of economics in the United States[2] attained a high plateau in the years 1936–1965, a period spanning the Great Depression, World War II, and postwar expansion and recovery, approximately up to the time of the large-scale United States move into Vietnam (1965). These years were marked by the rise of the theory of imperfect competition and, more significantly, Keynesian theory and "model building" often designed for forecasting. It was also a period of expanding government intervention, including both macro actions to stabilize the overall economy and provide jobs and income security, and micro effort to regulate prices, product markets, and conditions of work. Economics became "relevant," and its new tools, with their mathematical appurtenances, provided the presumptive basis for forecasting and evaluating policy decisions.

In a curious reversal, however, the prestige of economics suffered a sharp eclipse beginning in the late 1960s and early 1970s. This was a result, in part, of the fact that the macro forecasts were proving unreliable.[3] It was also a consequence of the general dissatisfaction with economic-societal developments and supportive institutions, and economic scholarship was showing itself to be one of the supportive institutions. More and more it seemed to be serving very specific political and economic interests in both questions addressed and answers provided. In fact, a number of paradoxes were becoming apparent that called into question the scientific pretensions of the profession. One was that economists seemed to be becoming increasingly relevant and the economic model on which they relied—a model of a system of private, highly competitive markets—receded into the background. The more important the role of the large firm with monopoly power, trade unions and collective bargaining, and the scale of government intervention, the greater the role of the practitioners of a discipline whose central paradigm assumed small, competitive firms, atomized labor markets, and a small government.

The second element of paradox which raised questions about the quality of the discipline was the sharp increase in the openly ideological role of economists. Economists have always been involved in attacking and defending policies. With the greater importance of macro and regulatory policy, however, increasing numbers of economists have been sought out and have attached themselves to specific economic interests, political factions, and parties, becoming spokesmen for these groupings. This has constrained their freedom of action, but at the same time the views they favor are given publicity not accorded to isolated individual economists. The economists for the dominant factions (and even those of the loyal opposition) have become media stars, and their views have been pressed on the public by the force of the interests represented. This has allowed economic doctrines that are hastily concocted expressions of the preferences of powerful interests (such as "supply side economics") virtually to dominate public discussion, whatever the judgments of the less mobilized segment of the profession.

Another manifestation of the ideological mobilization of economists is the increasing numbers (and steadily larger proportion) serving as paid consultants to and witnesses for parties with a position to maintain. A well-known book on regulation refers to one rational response of profit-oriented but regulated firms as "coopting the experts";[4] and there is evidence that this has been deliberate policy, although a de facto cooptation exists by the mere fact of employment, whatever the corporate intent. The extensive growth of the marketing of technical skills and brand names[5] by economists to private buyers with an axe to grind weakens both the image and the reality of economists as professionals and scholars engaged in the untrammeled pursuit of "truth."

A curious aspect of this enlarged market role of the economists is that the economists themselves have built an analytical framework that could be interpreted as a coffin in which to bury the "science," although they have not yet made the interment. Gary Becker, of the University of Chicago, has led a new trend in which the satisfaction-maximizing premise of economic science is applied in previously sacrosanct areas on the supposition that economic calculations in human decision processes are well nigh universal. Cost benefit calculations have been extended, for example, to choices as to number of children, marriage and divorce, the selection of spouses, sexual behavior, cheating and lying, crime, and drug addiction.[6] But Becker and his associates have not applied this new search for plausible applications of the economic calculus to themselves.[7] The point is suggestive, however, with a potential relevance to economics that flows not only from the logic of Lord Halifax's famous cynicism—"They who are of opinion that Money will do everything, may very well be suspected to do everything for Money"—but more particularly to the institutional environment in which the services of the economist have become more marketable.

In this paper I will review briefly some of the traditional controversies over the role of ideology in economics, examine the recent forces that have tended to enlarge its relevance, and then look at some of the manifestations of the new and more powerful market impact on the content of the discipline.

## The Role of Ideology in Economics

Ideological influence has made its way into economics at three levels: in choice of problem, in the predetermination of the correct answer, and in the processes of mustering support for a priori truth. The first form of influence involves value judgments as to what is important, and is not amenable to scientific debate. It is of enormous importance, however, that up to the 1930s the core of economic theory in the west, the central paradigm, assumed full employment as one of its "givens," with unemployment therefore not constituting a policy problem to be addressed by the profession. This is clearly a reflection of class bias, as the working class and small farmer majorities of Great Britain and the United States during the heyday of classical and neoclassical economics, say 1830–1914, would have given a high weight to instability and unemployment as economic problems to be addressed directly and forthrightly.[8] Yet aggregate employment and income did not become a central theme of economic analysis till the depression of the 1930s and the emergence of Keynesian economics.

In his outstanding history of economic thought, the economist Leo Rogin made a persuasive case that virtually all of the great theoretical advances in economics, from the Physiocrats in eighteenth-century France to J. M. Keynes in the 1930s, were intimately tied in with very specific policy arguments.[9] The theorists were motivated by what they regarded as a flawed institutional condition or a seriously erroneous policy choice, and they put forward analyses to demonstrate formally that the offending instrument disturbed a "natural order."[10] The removal of the disturbance would allow a return to conformity with nature and hence produce long-run social benefits. A telling illustration of this thesis is David Ricardo's writings, in which a distinctly propagandistic pamphlet of 1816 ("On the Effects of the High Price of Corn on the Profits of Stock") was followed shortly thereafter by a "general theory," his *Principles of Political Economy,* that simply offered a more formal and extended proof of the pamphlet claim that tariffs on the import of corn ("the Corn Laws") would raise money wages, lower profits, and ultimately produce a stationary state. Strong policy positions can also be shown to underlie the general principles enunciated by François Quesnay (dean of the French Physiocrats), Adam Smith, Malthus, John Stuart Mill, Marx, and Keynes (among others). For Smith, mercantilist restrictions encumbered the natural system of economic libery; for Malthus in 1798, it was generous poor laws and revolutionary redistributive schemes that were rendered futile by the workings of the "law of population"; for Keynes in 1936 it was the volatility of private investment that made for overall instability and underemployment, curable by a new government fiscal, investment, and planning role.

As noted, a number of the models developed by these economists were explicitly "normative," spelling out ideal economies that would yield beneficent social results if some perversion in the policy realm were removed. These ideal systems were proposed as "natural"—not merely the preferences of the theorists—in the sense that the deviations from the norms were in conflict with inescapable facts of nature—the force of the acquisitive instinct, the natural facts of human fertility, the law of diminishing returns. This form of linkage of the ideal to the inescapably natural persists up to the present day—the contemporary U.S. competitive market/deregulation school puts great weight on the force of the acquisitive and competitive drives, which will cause a circumvention of controls and regulations and render them inefficient and without positive effect.[11]

In the later nineteenth and early twentieth centuries more abstract models of economic life were developed that derived general economic principles from simple assumptions about utility-maximizing consumers and profit-maximizing producers operating under fully competitive conditions and certain technical constraints. These models described stable systems, devoid of classes and class conflict, with societal changes invariably incremental and demanding only marginal adjustments to small disturbances. For Joseph Schumpeter, in his monumental *History of Economic Analysis,* these were refinements that manifested a growing sophistication of technique and logic in a progressive science.[12] But Rogin was able to show that the theorists explicating these systems, such as Carl Menger, Léon Walras, and Alfred Marshall, were knowingly assuming away formulations that raised disturbing questions (income distribution, class and market power, instability, and unemployment) and creating theoretical models compatible with their own policy biases of status quo or modest reformism.[13]

Given the choice of "problem," ideology and other sources of bias may still enter economic analysis if the answer is predetermined by the structure of the theory or premises, or if the facts are selected or bent to prove the desired answer. At these levels of potential bias, traditional scientific criteria of verification become relevant—predetermined answers can be invalidated by showing the faulty structure of the model and the biased use of fact. It was because of these considerations that Rogin himself viewed the scientific element in economics as quite important. The great theorists, he asserted, "have pursued the scientific method, in the large sense of the term, as distinguished from the purely speculative. There has been a reasoned and disciplined appeal to facts."[14]

Difficulties still arise, however, as a result of long-standing and well-understood methodological problems inherent in the discipline and not clearly resolved over time. The economic world is not only complex but it changes continuously and, in recent decades, possibly at an accelerating pace, so that economists "never step twice into the same stream," as fresh economic facts confront them each day and week. Experimental verification, difficult for simple chains of analysis, is even more problematical for entire models or systems of thought.[15] Elaborate contemporary forecasting models are built on past structural relationships, but as these relationships change continually the model builders have been refining the models by increasingly rapid incorporation of the latest structural linkages. They also rely heavily on ad hoc and more or less intuitively based adjustments; the professional forecasters now "attributing from 20 to 50 percent of the final forecast to the process of judgmental adjustments."[16] When external shocks occur, such as the bombing of North Vietnam in 1965, Nixon's sudden devaluation and imposition of price controls in 1971, or the Arab oil embargo of 1973, the structural relationships are more profoundly disturbed. The models, of course, cannot predict the shocks, but if the shocks are severe the structural relationships may change markedly and require new models—so that their capacity to predict changes is contingent on there being very little change.

For evaluation of larger policy issues, such as the effects of free trade versus protectionism or the effects of drastic tax cuts and expenditure shifts under "supply side economics," economics depends on broad theoretical models that are highly contingent. As all their premises are not usually realized in actual structures or policy, they cannot easily be "disproved." As Mrs. Robinson has pointed out, there is always "a loophole to escape through—'the consequences that have followed from the causes that I analysed are, I agree, the opposite of what I predicted, but they would have been greater still if those causes had not operated.' "[17] This means that the models accepted in a society, especially the broader normative systems from which policies on free trade/tariffs or stabilization and growth are derived, can rest simply on the preferences of the theorists and the institutional nexus that determines their values, as well as the publicity given their opinions. That the most distinguished and popular British economists in the age of British industrial supremacy were free traders, while protectionist economics took a strong hold on the Continent and in the United States, is well known. In the twentieth century, the turnabout in industrial position revealed free trade triumphant among U.S. economists at mid-century, with protectionism making strong inroads in British economic thought in the 1930s and thereafter.[18]

It should be noted that there have always been differences among economists within national economies on the desirability of protection and free trade, and the various business communities themselves have never been completely unified on the subject. They have been close to a consensus, however, on the desirability of private enterprise, a free labor market, and a limited and complementary role assignment to government. The gradual evolution of the competitive market model as the paradigm of economic theory in Western Europe and the United States is the main expression of the enduring ideological underpinning of economics.

As a ruling class paradigm, the competitive model has two substantial merits. First, as a positive description of the real world it retains a certain vitality; price competition, while badly eroded in many sectors of the economy, nevertheless has a continuing impact even on the monopolized sectors and a still more powerful presence in others (especially in financial and raw materials markets).[19] Second, and more important, as a normative model, it can be used to rule off the agenda any proposals for substantial reform or intervention detrimental to large economic interests (for example, government ownership, wage-price interventions, or income equalizing tax-expenditure policy), as the model allows (on its assumptions) a formal demonstration that these would reduce efficiency, savings and investment, or both. In the presumed interest of protecting and subsidizing tenants, for example, rent controls are frequently alleged by economists to disturb proper incentives for producing and using living space and thus to result in misallocation of resources. The economist's argument is that if it is desired to help renters in the interest of equity, this should be done by income subsidies, not by a price-quantity intervention with its consequent detrimental effects on the efficient use of resources. The economist does not normally address the case where a direct income subsidy is not politically or technically feasible and the equity effect might have to be balanced against an inefficiency cost.[20] As another example, in the 1970s a doctrine came to prevail in U.S. courts, based on the alleged "efficiency" of marginal cost pricing, that makes it exceedingly difficult to demonstrate predatory price-cutting behavior on the part of large and aggressive firms.[21] Although the competitive and static assumptions on which the doctrine is based do not ordinarily prevail, it establishes a presumption or plausible rationalization in terms of a social optimum that is hard to refute given the ambiguities of cost data and the fact that "industrial economics does not have available a technique for weighing, much less predicting, the welfare consequences of the exercise of market power."[22]

Along with theoretical demonstrations of the demerits of government regulation, there has been a sharp growth in the United States in the use of formal modelling proofs of the inefficiency of government intervention. In the view of the believers in economics as a progressive science—for instance, Schumpeter in his *History*—refinements in techniques, models, and improved methods of measurement would lead to a greater ability to test, accept, and reject hypotheses, and to arrive at the truth. Things have not worked out that way. Models are established in great number for the relevant occasions, highly contingent, with very modest results in terms of explanatory value, but which allow citation to a scientific source. In the construction of the model, many independent variables may be tested and rejected, and the decline in price of computer runs makes possible feedback alterations of the model according to ex post fit. Instead of a theoretical model being tested, accepted or rejected, the model becomes an adjusted product of a trial and error fitting of a set of more or less arbitrary variables to a particular body of data.[23]

The possibilities of even more serious abuse are also present. It is possible to search out data or combinations of variables that will allow a preconceived result, selecting those that yield the preferred conclusion;[24] or "errors" in the data[25] or program[26] may significantly push the results in the favored direction. In the "standard model" of the Chicago School antiregulation specialists, the effect of government control is incorporated as a residual factor, with the result that the worse the specification of independent variables the "better" may be the outcome (that is, the more causal significance can be attributed to the factor equated with the "residual").[27] These blatantly ideological models may escape refutation because disproof is far more arduous than initial construction, where simple-mindedness and confusion yield positive payoffs. Most critics also like to offer something better in the way of an explanation, which may be difficult on strictly scientific criteria. When such models are being spewed forth on a large scale, approved and often funded by large vested interests, modern technique may help shift the balance between ideology and science even more firmly toward the former.

## The Traditional Institutional Nexus

Before the Great Depression of the 1930s, economics was in the hands of a body of relatively independent professionals. It had evolved from a more heterogeneous mix in the eighteenth and nineteenth centuries to which pamphleteers, businessmen, philosophers, and parsons contributed, to a familiar concentration by specialists affiliated with the academy.[28] The class links of these professionals to the business community were strong and the ideological element was realized in the neoclassical competitive model, accepted by the leaders of the profession (as exemplified by Marshall and Pigou in England and Frank Knight and Frank Taussig in the United States). The problems addressed were often important ones, but they were not the only important ones, and the answers provided were implicit in the competitive model. Spinoff negative effects on the lower classes were part of the "price of progress." It was the elite orientation of these questions, premises, and the central paradigm that caused matters like unemployment, mass poverty, and work hazards to escape the net of mainstream economist interest until well into the twentieth century.

The academic locus of the economists resulted in several other noteworthy phenomena. One was the tendency toward a web-spinning elaboration of preexisting ideas and models into new, irrelevant, and increasingly gothic intellectual structures. This tendency reached even greater heights with the mathematicization of economics in the post-World War II era and the consequent greatly enlarged potential for model construction on the basis of simple premises. (The distinguished economist Wassily Leontiev even cries out in despair in 1982 to the other sciences urging that they express concern over the deterioration and "splendid isolation" of academic economics, whose "irresistible predilection for deductive reasoning" has led to a triumph of theoretical irrelevancy.[29]) Another subtrend was the spinoff of eccentrics who believed the verities of the traditional perfectly competitive models with a certain fanaticism,[30] and who argued for free markets and free trade when realistic men in power thought qualifications in order on matters such as tariffs, railroad subsidies, and the need for commission regulation under conditions of excessive competition. Academia also witnessed minor outbreaks of radicalism, with social critics urging more serious attention to unemployment, poverty, concentrated power, externalities, a greater role for government, and sometimes even nationalization and planning. These pathological excrescences were not common and were dealt with primarily by nonrecognition, ostracism, and ouster (Scott Nearing was dismissed from the faculty of the University of Pennsylvania in 1915 for a too aggressive defense of the coal miners; Thorstein Veblen was never able to obtain permanent academic employment).

Despite these anomalies, the economics profession in the years 1880–1930 was by and large strongly conservative, reflecting in its core paradigm its class links and sympathy with the dominant business community, fundamentally antiunion and suspicious of government, and tending to view competition as the true and durable state of nature. The 1930s brought a wave of change, with an enlarged role of government and theories raising questions about business beneficence and justifying the large government role. Business was in a state of disarray and its traditional solutions to problems were in disrepute. The rise of government interventionism, based in large part on private market failures and public demands for new services and stabilization efforts, also contributed to a spurt of responsiveness to issues formerly relegated to sociology or to the world of "transitions between equilibria." The major result was the Keynesian "revolution" and related theories and rules of fiscal stabilization, with the government as mediating actor. This was a high point in substantive innovation and independence of the profession. World War II and the subsequent Cold War and rapid market growth led to renewed and fuller integration of economics into the market system, as described below.

## The Market-Government Nexus

The 1930s depression and World War II, leading to the rise of government as an economic force in both macro planning and regulation, brought a corresponding increase in the demand for the services of economists. Government employment of economists soared in the period 1930–1945, and it kept growing thereafter. The demand of private business firms, both financial and nonfinancial, also enlarged steadily. While many economists were hired by government and business to work "in-house," the private market for independently contracted economic services has also boomed. In 1977, *Business Week* magazine referred to the economic consulting business as "the capital's fastest growing industry," with "scores of economists . . . turned entrepreneur and selling their professional skills, their contacts, their expertise—and, some claim, their souls—in the murky world of Washington policymaking."[31] Consultants were to be found in every major city, with more than 100 located in Washington, D.C.

Much of the government and private demand was for forecasts: of probable changes in aggregative variables like GNP and employment, of interest rates, and of shifts in the demand for particular goods. New macro models built on Keynesian principles, and quantified by improved mathematical and statistical techniques, brought a new sophistication into forecasting that held forth great promise (only partly realized in forecasting performance). In a world of continued instability, more marked in the late 1960s and 1970s, business firms were keenly interested in buying or renting expertise and models that would make a difference. As with the consultants, forecasting firms proliferated in the post-1950 years, manned by economists who looked upon themselves as marketers of a salable service. *Business Week* described them as participants in "a thriving little growth industry . . . with pretax profits running to 20% of sales, . . . competing for a share of what looks like an expanding pie."[32] Other forecasters did not form companies but were hired as employees of banks, brokerage houses, or consulting firms, or remained in academia while offering their services through nonprofit affiliates or as independent consultants.

The growth of regulation was another basis of market linkage that grew rapidly in the post-World War II years. Commission regulation of the prices of "natural monopolies" was not greatly extended in the United States, but under the unstable and eventually inflationary conditions of the postwar era regulatory "relief" became more urgent, the number of decisions increased sharply, and the mobilization of expertise and influence rose markedly. The so-called "new regulation" encompassing matters like consumer safety, discrimination, work hazards, and environmental damage did grow extensively in the 1960s and 1970s. The employment of economic consultants to advise and serve as expert witnesses increased rapidly to meet this demand. It may also have been further enlarged by the desire to "coopt the experts." Owen and Braeutigam point out that in the case of American Telephone and Telegraph Company (AT&T), the company "has made a major investment, for instance, in very high grade economic talent over the past decade."[33]

An inkling of the extent of this cooptation is provided by the list of consultants to AT&T, and the payments made to them, shown in the Annual Report Form M of AT&T to the Federal Communications Commission. The Report for December 31, 1978, lists direct corporate payments to 104 named social scientists and 215 small consulting firms, many organized by academicians. For the years 1978–1980, this same Form M shows the following numbers of economists, by institution named, as recipients of payments from AT&T: University of Chicago, 5; Harvard University, 6; MIT, 7; Princeton, 4; Stanford, 5; and Yale, 7. Beyond this, AT&T began the sponsorship and underwriting of a scholarly journal in the field of economics in 1970, which has dealt heavily with economic regulatory issues. The *Bell Journal* was provided without charge to interested readers from 1970–1982. The journal had two coeditors who received $24,600 each for this part-time role in 1981; five associate editors receiving $11,000 each; and numerous referees who looked over the incoming manuscripts and received $75 per look. This large fraction of the "very high grade economic talent" mentioned by Owen and Braeutigam appears not to have been bothered unduly by any potential conflict of interest in accepting largess from a very large company with a definite stake in economic opinion.

Other regulated companies besides AT&T have invested in economic talent.[34] Many U.S. firms also have increased their sponsorship of academic research and organization and funding of think tanks that encourage sound views. The business community of the United States was deeply concerned over the excesses of democracy in the United States in the 1960s,[35] and it has tried hard to rectify this problem by means of investments in both politicians and informing public opinion. The latter effort has included massive institutional advertising and other direct and indirect propaganda campaigns,[36] but it has extended also to attempts to influence the content of academic ideas. There had already been a significant portion of academic research money coming from foundations based on business fortunes, but many of these had obtained a substantial degree of autonomy and were not strongly ideological and serving as intellectual enforcers. Much of the new money of the 1970s was ideological money, intended to allow people with preferred viewpoints to be aided financially in obtaining academic status and influence and in producing and disseminating books.

The private funding of university chairs, for example, had long been a feature of U.S. higher education, but a sharp ideological turn is observable in the 1960s and 1970s with the emergence of the "free enterprise" chair (along with businessmen "in residence")—some 20 such chairs were in place in 1978 with many more in the discussion phase.[37] These chairs were established with an explicitly ideological function—to sell a point of view thought to be either uniquely true or needed because of prevailing "antibusiness" bias. The increasing prominence of the business school itself, the locus of much of the funding of chairs and development of structural relationships with the business community, was an important factor in the overall enhanced responsiveness of academia to the opportunities for a closer relationship with business.

According to the director of the John M. Olin Foundation, its new president William Simon "is determined to get results out of our grantees . . ."[38] H. Monroe Browne, president of another rightwing think tank, the Institute for Contemporary Affairs, observed that "It's well and good to say ideas are important but even good ideas need marketing," and Browne's operation presses hard to sell its sponsored studies.[39] An institution called the Institute for Educational Affairs was organized in the mid-1970s as a wholesaler of money raised from corporations to be distributed to rightwing organizations. One of its founders, Irving Kristol, noted that corporations "have seen that ideas are important and they want to get involved."[40] One of their main intellectual vehicless, the American Institute for Public Policy Research (usually called the American Enterprise Institute, or AEI) has more than 300 corporate sponsors, which has allowed it a regular staff of over 100 and has sustained

a vast outpouring of materials and activities, which last year [1977] included 54 studies, 22 forums and conferences, 15 analyses of important legislative proposals, 7 journals and newsletters, a ready-made set of editorials sent regularly to 105 newspapers, public affairs programs carried on more than 300 television stations and centers for the display of A.E.I. materials in some 300 college libraries.[41]

At the AEI and elsewhere, the rightwing education campaign has breadth and scope as well as substantial funding. They cover not merely the sponsorship of policy research but extend to the creation of centers to educate court judges on the merits of the free market,[42] the preparation and dissemination of educational materials for all levels of schools,[43] the sponsorship of local and national TV programs, and the detailed servicing and policing of the media.[44] The resources involved in these efforts have not been compiled in satisfactory detail, but they ran to tens of millions of dollars per annum in the late 1970s and early 1980s.[45]

The industries worried about regulatory trends have also pumped resources into university-affiliated think tanks and university programs sponsored jointly with academia to clarify the cost-benefit and risk assessment complexities of regulation.[46] The Kennedy School of Government at Harvard has an Energy and Environmental Policy Center and a Faculty Project on Regulation, both with heavy funding from interested industries. MIT and Harvard have a Joint Program on the Impact of Chemicals on Human Health and the Environment, also heavily subsidized by the chemical and petroleum industries. In fact, throughout U.S. academia, corporate funding of research institutes and projects, sometimes with corporate liaison or advisory committees, has been eagerly sought and is seen to present no problems of academic objectivity.

The enlarged private demand for the services of economists by the business community in the United States met a warm supply response in the 1970s. The academy had grown rapidly under the stimuli of rapid economic expansion, enrollment growth based on demographic factors, and government funding. These all weakened in the 1970s, and inflationary pressures added to academic woes. The real value of academic salaries fell steadily throughout the decade. The combination of economic pressures and an increasingly conservative environment contributed to a new and far-reaching process of accommodation and adaptation to new market conditions. A hungry profession sloughed off its traditional principles as a snake removes itself from an obsolete skin. And the new ideological response to a pressing economic demand was reinforced in the public arena by the sheer volume of supportive resources and the workings of the U.S. mass media.

## The Theory and Practice of Selling Economic Expertise

As noted earlier, in terms of recent Chicago School economic analyses (Becker), "the economic approach is a comprehensive one that is applicable to all human behavior, be it . . . emotional or mechanical,"[47] affecting choices in all spheres of life. As these potent forces impinge on the market for economists, it should affect the responses of the actors in that market. On traditional economic logic, entry into economics as a profession will be affected by the price of the services paid to economists. If there is a spurt in the willingness of business firms to pay for proofs that proposed regulations of cotton dust in textile factories are "cost inefficient," this makes economics a more attractive occupation. An important aspect of the enhanced demand of the past decade, however, is that it is a "conclusion- or ideology-specific demand," not merely a demand for economic expertise. This applies to the funding for "free enterprise" chairs, visits to the relatively lavish and well-paying free enterprise think tanks, and also to funds available for research or testimony on subjects of interest to the demanders of economic services. The inducement to enter the industry to reap these potential rewards will only be attractive to those prepared to support the special conclusions or premises demanded, either out of prior ideological agreement or disinterest in other than money returns. The entry should therefore be ideologically biased and should result in a skewed ideological distribution within the profession.

More problematic, but surely suggested by Beckerian logic, is the possibility that a further segment of the profession will shift views to satisfy the market demand. This could happen through subtle processes, whereby those receiving grants and serving as consultants and witnesses gradually come to accept the premises of those funding them or whose views and interests they are paid to represent. Even if "coopted experts" retained their intellectual autonomy, cooptation means immobilization.

On Beckerian logic, the choice of conclusions to be pursued could well be explicit: if by taking position A rather than B the present value of my future earnings stream would be enhanced, as a maximizer I will choose position A. Of course, choosing A may merely mean that I am prepared to argue for A in a particular case. But an across-the-board ideological position and known reliability could increase my market rewards even further than quiet ad hoc service. There is the lecture circuit, fellowships at the American Enterprise Institute or the Hoover Institution, and a growing number of other options that make full ideological adaptation the maximizing path.

On the logic of the primacy of self-interested choice, therefore, it is clear that if the demand in the market is for specific policy conclusions and particular viewpoints that will serve such conclusions, the market will accommodate this demand. This writer does not believe "the market" to be as all-encompassing in its impact as Becker would have it, but it is certainly a powerful force, especially in a country like the United States, where communal-traditional factors are relatively weak and geographical and class mobility are relatively high. And if a leading economist of a highly influential school assures us that the cash nexus is overpoweringly important in virtually every cranny of human existence, we must give his testimony some weight. Clearly the questions addressed by the profession will be influenced by a massive conclusion-specific demand, but the potential for a skewed structure of premises, special interest models, and preordained conclusions is also large. This mobilization of bias suggests the possibility that the entire drift of the science— its principles and their refinements appropriate to special applications— may be decisively shaped by market forces. Corrective mechanisms, as we have seen, work slowly and incompletely in a discipline with analyses so contingent and difficult to subject to anything like definitive tests. Ideologies reflecting dominant interests may prevail by overwhelming the market place in the short run. Whether from the standpoint of economic science the long run is more than a series of short runs is still a moot question.

## The Ideological Resurgence

The recent ideological resurgence in economics in the United States constitutes a major setback to the "progressive science" view of economics and to more general beliefs of an evolving rationality of thought in application to social affairs. To some extent the resurgence has been in media attention and public perceptions of economic truths, rather than in the views of the leading professionals. "Supply side economics" has been important in the United States because powerful business interests wanted certain lines of policy and were able to shape public beliefs along those lines. The rather disreputable group of "supply-siders" dispensing the requisite doctrine was catapulted into prominence by the sheer power of their institutional support base. It is an important fact, however, that an intellectual doctrine could be espoused and put into practice, with only relatively muted criticism, even though close to charlatanry from a professional view.[48]

In a sense, however, "supply side economics" and the Reagan program viewed more broadly may be said to constitute a popularization and vulgarization of a number of important ideological strands of thought and doctrines that have come into prominence in recent decades and which *do* have reputable professional support. Many of these conform remarkably well to the conservative free-market agenda of reforms sought by the business community.

As one ideological premise, we may note the institutionalization of the apologetic for militarization, which was a crucial aspect of the liberal Keynesianism of the Kennedy-Johnson era. In their celebrations of the boom conditions of the 1960s as a triumph of modern fiscal theory, it was a part of Keynesian dogma that any tie-in with the surge of military spending was fortuitous. The idea that the system was in any sense dependent on military spending was derided as "Marxian dogma"; military outlays were "givens," fixed by our leaders according to the unyielding needs of "defense."[49] There was a careful avoidance of any analysis of the secondary effects of military outlays on inflation and productivity or other longer-term system trends.[50] The vast enlargement of the Reagan military budget has been treated in the same deferential fashion by the leading liberal Keynesian economists.[51] In accord with the Rogin analysis of the evolution of economic thought, described earlier, an arms race being acceptable/desirable to dominant forces in the United States, the expanding military budget will not be an "endogenous" factor to be explained by, or that generates problems for, the political economy; it will be "exogenous."

A second ideological element common to supply-side and neo-Keynesian economics is the emphasis on "growth" as the proximate end of policy and the solution to socioeconomic problems. The earlier, Depression-era Keynesian stress on income redistribution and socialization of investment as the route to stabilization was gradually watered down in a process of accommodation to the realities of private power and political feasibility.[52] In the words of neo–Keynesian economist Walter Heller, "When the cost of fulfilling a people's aspirations can be met out of a growing horn of plenty—instead of robbing Peter to pay Paul—ideological roadblocks melt away, and consensus replaces conflict."[53] Thus, tax reform, income redistribution, and a greater role for public investment were displaced in the Kennedy-Johnson era by tax cuts to stimulate demand and "bribe" business to invest capital,[54] in order to assure economic growth. This would yield a "growth dividend," from which allocations to social reform could flow—at some future date. Reaganomics operates within the same ideological frame, only the "bribe to capital formation" is to a greater degree a pure class income transfer and the trickling down process does not include any proposed future enlargement of public service outlays.

Another strongly ideological tendency in U.S. economics that continues a trend from the Keynesian era is the building of the case for ever higher "normal" rates of unemployment. In the 1950s and 1960s there was a gradual redefinition upward of the "full employment" unemployment rate, with accompanying discussions of a weakening Phillips curve trade-off between unemployment and inflation. The Keynesians accepted this with some discomfort—and were willing to contemplate limited incomes policies and other devices to improve the trade-off. By the 1970s, however, the problem had become more severe, and the Keynesian solutions became more clearly unworkable. The choices thus involved more radical breaks with traditional policies than Jimmy Carter and the U.S. liberal Keynesians were prepared to support. The conservatives had no real *answers* to the Keynesian dilemmas, but they were prepared to rationalize a ruthless return to long defunct medicine à la Margaret Thatcher.

Part of the intellectual apparatus mobilized for this purpose in the United States has been the "new economics of unemployment." Here, attention is deflected away from the macroeconomic determinants of the overall number of jobs available (namely, the level of aggregate demand in the economy) toward alleged job market "behavior" of individual workers. Great emphasis is placed on forces making for mismatch between different quantities and skills of labor and the "unwillingness" of people to supply labor effort in complementary proportions. Furthermore, the worker himself, as a rational economic decision maker, chooses exactly how much work and how much leisure he desires at any given real wage rate. Unemployment is, therefore, "voluntary." In fact, at some wage levels, workers will choose less employment and more "search time," since this form of nonwork can be considered equivalent to "investment" in labor market information. Unemployment is thus attributed to the desires and motivations of individuals clashing with available work opportunities. Personal "preferences" become causation; and the larger social parameters drop out of sight.[55]

In the Friedman model, government fiscal-monetary policy efforts to reduce unemployment below the "natural rate" of unemployment, which corresponds to a structure of individual preferences, will be at best temporarily effective, and will gradually lead to escalating inflation.[56] Given our inability to know what the "natural rate" is, as it reflects individual preferences at any moment of time, this metaphysical concept affords a plausible arguing point for high natural rates whenever high unemployment occurs together with inflation. In one "rational expectations" model, whatever level of unemployment exists must *be* the natural rate.[57] In a world economy displaying greater instability, with technological change widely recognized as an increasingly important economic force, the new economics of unemployment essentially disregards both the Keynesian focus on the instability of private spending, and the Marxian emphasis on technological change as part of an unemployment-generating mechanism.[58] These abstract, static, deinstitutionalized models—with strong ideological overtones—represent a major scientific regression.

Monetarism is another important strand of contemporary economics that bears a heavy burden of ideology. An attempt by monetarist Thomas Mayer to outline the dozen distinctive features of the doctrine includes two entries that are pure expressions of ideological preference (greater concern over inflation than unemployment and a dislike of government intervention) and a third that is largely an assertion of ideological faith (that private capitalism is "inherently stable").[59] Equally important, as pointed out by Benjamin Friedman, none of the twelve Mayer propositions is of a theoretical nature—they are either expressions of personal preference or assertions of differences concerning the size or stability of parameters included in a common body of thought.[60] Thus, one of Mayer's propositions is that monetarists believe that the size of the money stock—as opposed to fluctuations in the demand for money—is the crucial determinant of money income. That a profession could be seriously divided because of varying estimates of the value and stability of its most important parameters, and their cause and effect relationships, clearly does not speak well for the solidity of its scientific base.

Monetarism has taken on renewed life *pari passu* with the rise of conservative, free-market-oriented economics and politics, and it fits well into a system of conservative political, social, and economic policy preferences—the desirability for a small, nonactivist government; a preference for monetary over fiscal policy; and the bias of capital and financial speculators toward high and volatile interest rates, lower inflation rates, and higher average levels of unemployment. The intellectual credibility of monetarism rests heavily on the difficulties in sorting out cause and effect in a world using money, a situation which allows quasiscientific proofs that money is "the cause" in an interactive system. If the demand for money shifts, consequences only follow if the quantity of money is "allowed" to change—thus the "cause" of any further development is policy "ratification" of the shift in demand. Cause is not identified with the initiating factor but with the shape of the response mechanism, theoretically (but not in actual fact)[61] under policy control. The implicit "natural order," in which demand changes would be offset, not ratified, is one in which a collective of monetarist-philosophers manage a world restructured and behaving in accord with monetarist premises! This is one form of legerdemain employed to salvage the primacy and causal role of money. Another is a shift to money as cause "in the long run," which obscures the real causality issue and short-run policy-relevant relationships under a crude and imprecise ex post facto statistical correlation.

Theoretical refinement and scientific progress normally involve the elaboration of structural relationships that explain processes and causal linkages. James Tobin points out that this form of progress has been lacking in the monetarist counterrevolution; that the monetarists continue to "appeal to simple reduced-form statistical correlations that do not contradict the theory, without specifications of the structural mechanisms that could have produced them."[62] Instead of structural analyses the monetarists of the 1970s retreated into ever more classical and contrary-to-fact assumptions—that product and labor markets are continuously in competitive equilibrium; that participants in these markets make decisions on the basis of "rational expectations"[63] of future values (including those of government-controlled variables), thus nullifying any effects of those actions in the future and leaving "real" activity affected only by real variables and policy surprises.[64] They have even evolved their own concept of efficiency based on speed and effectiveness in the use of "information"[65]—generally unmeasurable and of tenuous relationship to the traditional and basic concepts of operational and allocational efficiency. The twists and turns of the analyses, with massive shifts in conclusions flowing from alterations in invariably implausible premises, describes not scientific endeavor but metaphysics in F. H. Bradley's satirical phrase—the finding of bad reasons for that which we know by instinct.

Even money itself has been treated cavalierly by the monetarists. Tobin notes that[66]

Friedman and other monetarists were impatient with requests to define conceptually the "money" whose quantity was the alleged fulcrum of the economy. What properties of liabilities payable in the unit of account are essentially monetary? What characteristics matter? . . . Monetarists have preferred not to hear these questions but to reason in theoretical models "as if" there were an unambiguous unique monetary store of value, and to identify as its real world counterpart whatever aggregate correlated best with nominal GNP.

There is a marvelous irony in the fact that monetarism has established itself as a serious doctrine in an age when financial innovation, stimulated by high interest rates (partly a function of the political successes of monetarism), has made "money" of increasingly uncertain meaning and has entirely undermined the crucial monetarist premise that the velocity of circulation of something called money is a stable and independent value. (An econometric analysis by Almarin Phillips finds that not only does a reduction in money tend to be offset by an induced increase in velocity, but that "The full velocity response over two subsequent quarters is more than proportional to a downward change in the supply of money in a given quarter!")[67] The traditional, conservative monetarist position was that while velocity could change, it had a rather firm ceiling based on the demand for cash for transactions purposes. This ceiling has been breached seriously, steadily, and unpredictably over the past decade with the growing sophistication of automated cash management techniques.

The monetarist penchant for finding changes in the money stock to be the causal factor, given the a priori symmetry of possibilities of cause flowing from either the demand or supply side, and the fact that the money demand function of the monetarists themselves contains more than one endogenous factor, has a strictly ideological root. Monetarism cannot be refuted, however, in part for reasons of complexity and rapidity of change, in part because of the elusiveness of monetarist criteria—and the always available grounds of retreat to "all my conditions were not met"—but most fundamentally because an *ideology* is beyond the orbit of scientific proof or disproof.

A final set of issues pointing up the great and increasing ideological role of economics in the United States concerns environmental controls and other forms of social regulation, which became critical matters for the business community in the 1970s. In the business view, the control costs imposed by the Environmental Protection Agency (EPA) were excessive, and these and other social regulatory policies were contributing heavily to the productivity slowdown in the United States. The extent to which the new microeconomics and important economic professionals came to express and defend this business viewpoint has been impressive. A background factor has been the previously mentioned "growth" emphasis of the liberals, which has tended to neutralize their traditional frequent inclination to side with the victims of business power and to attach serious weight to negative externalities. An important manifestation of this reorientation was the warm reception by the neo-Keynesians given to Peter Passell and Leonard Ross' 1973 volume *The Retreat From Riches: Affluence and Its Enemies,* which not only laid exclusive stress on growth as *the* policy end, but also leveled its most severe criticism at the environmental movement and antigrowth analysts, who were designated the "enemies." This book had a laudatory foreward by Paul Samuelson and was also warmly received by the Mobil Oil Company.[68] As with business, the economists tended to ignore or substantially downgrade the *benefits* of social regulation. In principle, it is always acknowledged that we must weigh costs against benefits. Data on industry costs are difficult to obtain except by asking the industry. Benefits of regulation are usually even more speculative—they will occur mainly in the future; they may have multiple, interactive, sometimes unknown, and largely unmeasurable effects (aesthetic, for example, or a diminished fear of adverse physical effects). The information usually does not exist that would allow definitive scientific judgments, although sometimes rough order-of-magnitude estimates may be possible for some of the relevant variables. The possibilities for intellectual abuse in putting together cost-benefit estimates are therefore great.

I mentioned earlier the Chicago School standard model of allowing a residual factor called government to account for negative happenings. A Peltzman specialty, the model is applied to show that government intervention has seriously reduced the number of entrants into banking,[69] that more rigorous controls over the introduction of new drugs have reduced drug invention and innovation,[70] and that automobile safety legislation has failed to reduce auto-caused fatalities.[71] In each of these cases, poor specification of explanatory variables produced the desired results. And even though refuted,[72] a scholarly source survives to be cited, quite selectively, as authority for a line of policy.

The underrating of the benefits of regulation was dramatically illustrated during the Carter years in the fight over the limitation of workers' exposures to cotton dust in the textile industry. Based on years of study and review, the Occupational Safety and Health Agency (OSHA) imposed a cotton dust standard to be phased in over a seven-year period. The standard was based on a comparison of prospective industry costs and benefits that were confined to and identified with the average expense per expected disability from byssinosis, a long-standing cotton dust-induced serious disorder. This new standard was objected to and energetically fought by the liberal Brookings-affiliated economists within the Carter administration—Charles Schultze, Barry Bosworth, and others in the Regulatory Analysis Review Group—on the ground of the allegedly nonproductive and thus inflationary effect of a new standard that would only impose additional costs on the industry.[73] The same group also sharply criticized OSHA on a coke oven emission standard, which allegedly would have increased costs and prices of steel by $2.50 per ton. It was noted at the time that a $6 per ton price increase by the steel industry was hardly noticed by the same group.[74] Somehow or other, mere health benefits to ordinary workers were not a sufficient benefit or imperative to justify a cost increase, and even seemed to attract the active hostility of the economists. Class bias and responsiveness to the imperatives of power could hardly be more conspicuous.

Similarly, Brookings economist Edward Denison, in estimating the effects of environmental health and safety regulation on rates of productivity growth found it to have reduced the rate by 1.4 percent by 1975 (on a 1967 base). But Denison not only assumed that the investment in pollution and safety control devices displaced "productive investment" dollar for dollar, he also gave no productivity value to improved health and reduced injury and death.[75] Another Brookings economist, Robert Crandall, also blithely discusses the cost effects or regulation on output while totally disregarding "benefits."[76] These procedures violate the most elementary rules of macroeconomic theory, which recognize in principle that a true GNP is a sum of positive and *negative* outputs. Policy can increase true GNP by increasing the positive outputs (bread) or by reducing the negative outputs (injurious smoke and chemical wastes to which workers and the public are exposed).

The most widely quoted authority on the costs and benefits of government regulation in the United States during the 1970s was Murray Weidenbaum, former chairman of Reagan's Council of Economic Advisers, head of a corporate-funded university-affiliated think tank during the mid and late 1970s. Weidenbaum made regular verbal obeisance to the importance of balancing costs against benefits, but in his studies of 1976 and later, he confined himself to costs while ignoring benefits and applied inconsistent definitions of costs.[77] Other methodological flaws abound: he combined the costs of cartel regulation (commission regulation of utility rates and services), the costs of social regulation, and a category "paper work" costs, which overlaps the preceding and whose most important component is meeting tax reporting and payment requirements of all levels of government. Weidenbaum derived a "multiplier" that related government administrative costs of regulation to compliance costs incurred by the regulated firms, based on a weighted average of this ratio for those regulated sectors for which such information was available from the past, updated by the inflation rate. The multiplier ($=20$) was assumed applicable to all sectors for which the ratio was unobtainable and was then applied to administrative costs in any year to obtain overall compliance and total costs of regulation.

Weidenbaum's message, with precise numbers, that the costs of regulation are huge, although shown in various places to be devoid of scientific value,[78] was given enormous publicity in the United States. As with supply side economics, economics available to the masses and disseminated in the arena of practical politics was determined by institutional support, not scientific quality of argument or conformity with anything that could remotely be called the truth.

There are many other fields of economics and economic policy where the responses of important economic professionals and the publicity given economic findings are correlated with the increased market demand for specific conclusions and a particular ideology. It is even possible to find occasional cases where detailed theoretical argumentation seems to have adapted to the force of market demand,[79] but despite the temptations of Beckerian logic one can hardly draw simple cause and effect relations between, say, the decline in Chicago School recommendations for nationalization of natural monopolies (put forward in the 1930s) and acquiescence in inefficient and corruptible commission regulation in recent decades, on the one hand, and the growth of largess obtained by Chicago School members for service rendered in regulatory cases on the other. There is too much "noise" and intercorrelation between the shift in viewpoint, general drift of the School and larger community toward the ideological right, and willingness to serve the regulated firms for money.

There can be little doubt, however, that the enlarged stake of the business community in specific and general economic policy and viewpoints in the United States has worked through the market to influence both professional and lay perceptions of economic issues. Those expressing opinions favored by "the market" (that is, the business elite) have been provided with disproportionate resources and access to influence and power through the support of their sponsors in grants, access to the mass media, and influence in the political arena. Money and a voice that can be heard have depended, more than ever, on adherence to specific conclusions and ideological service. If the market works at all, and it does, then there should have been a supply response by economists. There has been, as Becker hints at but fails to explore. The market also exercises influence indirectly by its power to render certain kinds of strongly disfavored changes utopian. Business perspectives and demands thus tend to shape the problems that are "relevant" in the sense of being amenable to a politically practical solution.

While the market's influence on professional opinion is clear, its impact on public discussion of economic issues, and the political outcome of such debates, represents a cruder exercise of economic power. With its late 1970s campaign to instill in the U.S. public the view that domestic problems were based on a "government on our backs," and with the installation in power of Reagan and the "supply-siders," the market demonstrated a capacity to force into the public domain and gain wide acceptance an explanation of reality and a basis for policy that was a translation into economics of the preferred business ideology. "Dollar ballots" were effective not only in the market for goods but in the market for ideas as well.

## Notes

1. For the Marxian view, apart from Marx's own *Theories of Surplus Value* (trans. G. Bonner and E. Burns; London: Lawrence & Wishart, 1951), and other scattered writings, see Maurice Dobb's *Political Economy and Capitalism* (London: Routledge, 1937). For other skeptical views see Leo Rogin, *The Meaning and Validity of Economic Theory* (New York: Harper, 1956); T. W. Hutchison, *The Significance and Basic Postulates of Economic Theory* (New York: Augustus Kelley, 1960); Hutchison, *Knowledge and Ignorance in Economics* (Chicago: University of Chicago Press, 1977); Ronald Meek, *Economics and Ideology and Other Essays* (London: Chapman & Hall, 1967); Gunnar Myrdal, *The Political Element in the Development of Economic Theory* (Cambridge: Harvard University Press, 1954). On the optimistic side, describing economics as at core a progressive science, see Lionel Robbins, *An Essay on the Nature and Significance of Economic Science* (London: Macmillan, 1935); and Joseph Schumpeter, *History of Economic Analysis* (London: Allen & Unwin, 1954).

2. Given the shared heritage and substitution relations there is some

commonality of experience between Great Britain and the United States, but this essay confines itself specifically to recent trends in economic thought in the latter country.

3. Richard W. Kopcke, "The Behavior of Investment Spending During the Recession and Recovery, 1973–76," *New England Economic Review*, Federal Reserve Bank of Boston, November–December 1977; Peter Clark, "Investment in the 1970s: Theory, Performance and Prediction," *Brookings Papers on Economic Activity*, vol. 1, (Washington, D.C.: Brookings Institution, 1979); "Theory Deserts the Forecasters," *Business Week*, June 29, 1974, 50ff; "Right or Wrong, Forecasts Pay," *Business Week*, May 28, 1979, 134.

4. Bruce M. Owen and Ronald Braeutigam, *The Regulation Game* (Cambridge, Mass.: Ballinger, 1978), 7.

5. In 1982 economists in the United States for the first time began to sell their own brand names to help move commercial goods. Andrew F. Brimmer, formerly a governor of the Federal Reserve Board, was touting Smirnoff Vodka; Paul Samuelson was coyly linking his Nobel Prize in economics to the merits of moving one's goods via Allied Van Lines.

6. See especially Gary S. Becker, *The Economic Approach to Human Behavior* (Chicago: University of Chicago Press, 1976), ch. 1 and passim. Also Richard McKenzie and Gordon Tullock, *The New World of Economics: Explorations into the Human Experience* (Homewood, Ill.: Irwin, 1975).

7. Chicago School economist R. H. Coase, writing on "The Market for Goods and the Market for Ideas" (*American Economic Review*, May 1974), discusses only the unreasonable bias in the West that makes the arena of ideas less subject than the goods market to intrusion by the government. The implications of private buying and managing of ideas is never raised by Coase. It is mentioned by Becker (11), but quickly dropped without serious exploration.

8. Outside the mainstream and theoretically dominant groups of economists there were distinguished exceptions. Among the more notable were the institutionalists and labor economists associated with John R. Commons at the University of Wisconsin. See John R. Commons, *A Documentary History of Industrial Society* (11 volumes, 1910–1911) and *History of Labor in the United States* (2 volumes, 1918). See also, "The Saga of John Rogers Commons," in Joseph Dorfman, *The Economic Mind in American Civilization*, vol. 3 (New York: Viking, 1949), 276–94.

9. Rogin, *Economic Theory*, 2–13 and passim.

10. There are exceptions. With Keynes, the natural order of private capitalism yields intolerable instability, thus calling for significant government intervention. For Marx, the existing natural order sows the seeds of its own destruction, and endogenous processes generate a radically new, more viable mode of production.

11. On the ineffectiveness of regulation, see George Stigler, "Public Regulation of the Securities Markets," *Journal of Business*, April 1964, 117–42; on the perverseness of effects, ibid.; and Harvey Averch and Leland I. Johnson, "Behavior of the Firm Under Regulatory Constraint," *American Economic Review*, December 1964, 1058ff.

12. Schumpeter, *Economic Analysis*, 6–11, 14–22, 33–47, and passim.

13. Rogin, *Economic Theory*, chs. 10, 12, and 15.

14. Ibid., xiv.

15. For good discussions of the problems of validation, see T. W. Hutchison, *The Significance and Basic Postulates of Economic Theory* (London: Macmillan, 1938), and his *On Revolutions and Progress in Economic Knowledge* (London and

New York: Cambridge University Press, 1978); Rogin, *Economic Theory*; Benjamin Ward, *What's Wrong with Economics?* (New York: Basic Books, 1972).

16. Stephen K. McLees, "The Recent Record of Thirteen Forecasters," *New England Economic Review*, Federal Reserve Bank of Boston, September–October 1981, 7.

17. Joan Robinson, *Economic Philosophy* (London: Watts, 1962), 23.

18. See especially William Beveridge, ed., *Tariffs, The Case Examined* (London: Longmans, Green, 1931).

19. William G. Shepherd contends that competition has increased across the board in the United States since 1939 (or since 1958), based on antitrust constraints, increased import competition, and deregulatory actions. See his "Causes of Increased Competition in the U.S. Economy, 1939–1980," *Review of Economics and Statistics, 64,* #4 (1982):613–26.

20. Arthur Okun noted that "People want to prevent rich landlords from gouging poor tenants. But rent controls destroy incentives to maintain or rehabilitate property, and are thus an assured way to preserve slums. (When I read that some Harvard students were actively campaigning for rent ceilings in Cambridge and Boston, I wondered how many of that group were economics majors.)" Arthur Okun, *The Political Economy of Prosperity* (New York: Norton, 1970), 11.

21. The so-called Areeda-Turner doctrine. See Phillip Areeda and Donald F. Turner, "Predatory Pricing and Related Practices Under Section 2 of the Sherman Act," *Harvard Law Review*, June 1975; see also H. H. Liebhafsky, "Price Theory as Jurisprudence: Law and Economics, Chicago Style," *Journal of Economic Issues*, 1976; F. M. Scherer, "The Posnerian Harvest: Separating Wheat from Chaff," *Yale Law Journal*, 1977.

22. Joel Dirlam, "Marginal Cost Pricing Tests for Predation: Naive Welfare Economics and Public Policy," *The Antitrust Bulletin*, Winter 1981.

23. Ward, *What's Wrong*, 148.

24. Louis Esposito showed convincingly that, after discussing four separate ways of measuring the impact of social security on saving, Martin Feldstein embraced the only one yielding a significant negative effect, on no intellectually defensible ground whatsoever ("On balance then, the empirical results of the Feldstein study do not support the hypothesis [claimed to be proved by Feldstein]"). Louis Esposito, "Effect of Social Security on Saving: Review of Studies Using U.S. Time Series Data," *Social Security Bulletin*, May 1978, 11.

25. For numerous favored-direction errors in data, and failure to make simple and correct inferences from observed fact, see the analysis of the Stigler paper cited above (n. 11) in Irwin Friend and Edward S. Herman, "The S.E.C. Through A Glass Darkly," *Journal of Business*, October 1964, 382–445.

26. A spectacular case of a major programming error involved, once again, Martin Feldstein, president of the National Bureau of Economic Research, whose econometric model of 1974 was long cited as proving a negative effect of social security on saving. Social Security Administration researchers Dean Leimer and Seling Lesnoy, who could not reproduce Feldstein's results—and who spent three years trying to get testable materials from Feldstein in their effort to uncover the source of the inconsistency—finally found that a "programming error" was present in Feldstein's model which, when corrected, showed effects on saving in the opposite direction from that preferred by Feldstein. (See "A Spectacular Debunking of Social Security Critics," *Business Week*, September 22, 1980, 25; " 'Superstar' Feldstein and His Little Mistake," *Dollars & Sense*, December 1980.) This approach to a Sir Cyril Burt level of scientific perform-

ance has had no noticeable effect on Feldstein's status in the profession. In 1982 he replaced Weidenbaum as Chairman of the CEA.

27. Sam Peltzman's Chicago School model explaining the decline in entry of new banks in the United States attributes about half the decline to the effects of "government." Among the methodological beauties in this model, although he examines a period during which new branches largely displaced new banks in the office creation process, he fails to include branches anywhere in the model. See "Entry into Banking," *Journal of Law and Economics* 8 (1965): 11–50. See also Richard Hofstadter, *Social Darwinism in American Thought*, rev. ed. (Boston: Beacon, 1955); Robert C. Bannister, *Social Darwinism, Science and Myth in Anglo-American Social Thought* (Philadelphia: Temple University Press, 1979), ch. 6.

28. Mary Furner, *Advocacy and Objectivity: A Crisis in the Professionalization of American Social Science, 1865–1905* (Lexington: University of Kentucky Press, 1975).

29. "Academic Economics," *Science*, July 9, 1982, 106–7.

30. Darwinian and Spencerian ideas took a strong hold in at least a segment of U.S. sociology and economics in the pre-World War I period, as described in V. L. Parrington's "Main Currents in American Thought," J. H. Dorfman's "The Economic Mind in American Civilization."

31. "A big business in credibility," *Business Week*, March 7, 1977, 84.

32. "Right or wrong, forecasts pay," *Business Week*, May 28, 1979, 134.

33. Owen and Braeutigam, *The Regulation Game*, 7.

34. Amax Corporation pays Yale economist Paul McAvoy $75,000 per year as a "consultant"; former President Gerald Ford's advice is worth a little more at $100,000 per year. See N R. Kleinfeld, "Dual Role of Outside Directors," *New York Times*, May 10, 1982, D-1.

35. On business's great concern over its alleged "loss of control," see the evidence provided in Leonard Silk and David Vogel, *Ethics and Profits* (New York: Simon & Schuster, 1976), 44–61.

36. According to S. Prakash Sethi, business advocacy advertising and grassroots lobbying efforts in the late 1970s was running at about a billion dollars per year. See "Grassroots Lobbying and the Corporation, *Business and Society Review*, November–December 1979, 8.

37. See Ronald Alsop, "Capitalism 101, Programs to Teach Free Enterprise Sprout on College Campuses," *Wall Street Journal*, May 10, 1978, 1.

38. Dan Morgan, "Conservatives: A Well-Financed Network," *Washington Post*, January 4, 1981.

39. Ibid.

40. Ibid.

41. Ann Crittenden, "The Economic Wind's Blowing Toward the Right—For Now," *New York Times*, July 16, 1978.

42. David Dickson and David Noble, "By Force of Reason: The Politics of Science and Technology Policy," in *The Hidden Election*, ed. Thomas Ferguson and Joel Rogers (New York: Pantheon, 1981, 270.

43. See Morgan and Crittenden, notes 38 and 41, for many details.

44. Ibid.

45. Ibid. Also Karen Rothmyer, "The Mystery Angel of the New Right," *Washington Post*, July 12, 1981 (about Richard Mellon Scaife).

46. Dickson and Noble, "By Force of Reason," 281–92.

47. Becker, *Human Behavior*, 11.

48. Professor Sidney Weintraub comments: "Rarely has any set of doctrines with so little substantive content ever enjoyed so rapt a hearing as supply-side theory. . . . No other 'revolution' in economics has ever been built on such

platitudes or has been promoted so spectacularly as profound gospel through the eager uncritical media and receptive ideologues in economics." See "Keynesian Demand Serendipity in Supply-Side Economics," *Journal of Post-Keynesian Economics*, Winter 1981–1982, 191.

49. See Richard B. DuBoff and Edward S. Herman, "The New Economics: Handmaiden of Inspired Truth," *Review of Radical Political Economics*, August 1972.

50. This is a characteristic of the Denison analyses of productivity changes under Brookings auspices; see Edward F. Denison, "Explanations of Declining Productivity Growth," *Survey of Current Business*, August 1979, 1–22. Lester Thurow also hardly mentions this factor in *The Zero-Sum Society* (New York: Basic Books, 1980). This factor is explored almost exclusively by outsiders like Seymour Melman.

51. From at least the Eisenhower years, the leading Keynesians were energetic supporters of an increased military budget, when (in the words of James Tobin) "the world situation cried out for accelerating and enlarging our defense effort" (*National Economic Policy*, 59). In response to the Reagan defense budget they have been cautiously acquiescent, Nordhaus assuming it represents an estimate of our defense needs (although there is much evidence that money allotments preceded any rational plan of use of such moneys) and going to pains to discount its macro impact (ignoring expectations and R & D effects). Tobin takes it as a given in his critique of Reaganomics. His "Reaganomics and Economics," in the *New York Review of Books*, December 3, 1981, makes no mention of military spending.

52. The establishment of "growth" as the vehicle temporarily cementing an alliance of business, organized labor, and the political elite is the theme of Alan Wolfe, *America's Impasse, The Rise and Fall of the Politics of Growth* (New York: Pantheon, 1981).

53. Walter Heller, *New Dimensions of Political Economy* (Cambridge: Harvard University Press, 1967), 12.

54. Samuelson himself refers to the innovative Kennedy investment tax credit as "a bribe to capital formation." *Economics*, 7th ed. (New York: McGraw-Hill, 1967), 769.

55. See E. S. Phelps, ed., *Microeconomic Foundations in Employment and Inflation Theory* (New York: Norton, 1970); E. S. Phelps, "Phillips Curves, Expectations of Inflation, and Optimal Unemployment over Time," *Economica*, August 1967; Martin Feldstein, "The Economics of the New Unemployment," *Public Interest*, Fall 1973.

56. M. Friedman, "The Role of Monetary Policy," *American Economic Review*, March 1968, 475.

57. See Gardner Ackley, *Macroeconomics: Theory and Policy* (New York: Macmillan, 1978), 475.

58. See William Darity, Jr., "Beveridge and the New Search Unemployment," *Journal of Post-Keynesian Economics*, Winter 1981–1982, 171–80. In a sense, the liberals do not entirely ignore technical change; they simply bypass its unemployment-generating role by assuming a degree of knowledge and factor mobility and transformability that does not exist.

59. Thomas Mayer, ed., *The Structure of Monetarism* (New York: Norton, 1978), 14.

60. "The Theoretical Nondebate about Monetarism," in ibid., 95.

61. On the limits of control, based on the elusiveness of the concept of money (M), lags in knowledge of changes in M, problems in identifying the sources of those changes, difficulties in effecting desired changes in M, and the

huge potential of unwanted "side effects" of control actions, see C. A. Goodhart and A. D. Crockett, "The Importance of Money," *Bank of England Quarterly Review*, June 1980; "Defining Money for a Changing Financial System," *Quarterly Review*, Federal Reserve Bank of New York, Spring 1979; Nicholas Kaldor and James Trevithick, "A Keynesian Perspective on Money," *Lloyds Bank Review*, January 1981; D. C. Rowan, "Implementing Monetarism: Some Reflections on the U.K. Experience," *Banca Nationale Del Lavoro Quarterly Review*, June 1981; Ervin Miller, *Micro-Economic Effects of Monetary Policy* (London: Martin Robertson, 1978).

62. James Tobin, "The Monetarist Counter-Revolution Today—An Appraisal," *Economic Journal*, March 1981, 30.

63. On the dubious "rationality" of rational expectations, see J. J. Sijben, *Rational Expectations and Monetary Policy* (Alphen aan den Rijn, The Netherlands: Sijtoff and Noordhoff, 1980), chs. 5–6; Neil G. Berkman, "A Rational View of Rational Expectations," *New England Economic Review*, January–February 1980.

64. Tobin, "Monetarist Counter-Revolution," 36–41, for discussion and citations.

65. "An efficient market is one that quickly processes all relevant information." Lawrence S. Davidson and Richard T. Proyen, "Monetary Policy and Stock Returns: Are Stock Markets Efficient?" *Review*, Federal Reserve Bank of St. Louis, March 1982, 3.

66. Tobin, "Monetarist Counter-Revolution," 40.

67. Phillips, "Empirical Evidence of the Endogeneity of the Velocity of Money" (in manuscript). Phillips points out that no one should really *believe* such elasticity estimates, but they surely call into question monetarist fundamentals of theory and policy. On the nature and impact of financial innovation, see also, Ralph C. Kimball, "Wire Transfer and the Demand for Money," *New England Economic Review*, Federal Reserve Bank of Boston, March/April, 1980; Donald D. Hester, "Monetary Statistics Show Fed Correct on Control Moves," *American Banker*, April 20, 1982 (testimony of Hester before the Subcommittee on Domestic Monetary Policy, House Banking Committee, March 4, 1982).

68. Two of Mobil's institutional ads featured the findings of Passell and Ross.

69. See the article by Peltzman cited in note 27 above.

70. Sam Peltzman, "An Evaluation of Consumer Protective Legislation: The 1962 Drug Amendments," *Journal of Political Economy*, September–October 1973.

71. Sam Peltzman, "The Effects of Automobile Safety Regulation," *Journal of Political Economy*, August 1975.

72. Leon Robertson, "A Critical Analysis of Peltzman's 'The Effects of Automobile Safety Regulation,' " *Journal of Economic Issues*, September 1977; Thomas McGuire, Richard Nelson, and Thomas Spavins, "Peltzman on Drugs," *Journal of Political Economy*, June 1975, 655–60; Mark Green and Norman Waitzman, *Business War on the Law: An Analysis of the Benefits of Federal Health Safety Enforcement*, The Corporate Accountability Research Group, 1969, 96–122.

73. Philip Shabecoff, "Carter Acts to Soften Dust Law," *New York Times*, June 7, 1978.

74. Steven Kelman, "OSHA Under Fire," *New Republic*, May 21, 1977, 22.

75. Edward F. Denison, "Effects of Selected Changes in Institutional and Human Environment Upon Output Per Unit of Input," Reprint no. 335, Brookings Institution, May 1978. Data Resources Inc. (DRI) assumes only a 33–40 percent displacement; see Green and Waitzman, 52–53.

76. See his letter to the *New York Times* on "The Price of E.P.A. Industrial Standards," July 3, 1978.

77. See especially his *The Costs of Government Regulation of Business*, Study prepared for the Subcommittee on Economic Growth, Joint Economic Committee, 95th Cong., 2d sess. (Washington, D.C.: GPO, 1978), 1, 22–23.

78. See Julius Allen, "Estimating the Costs of Federal Regulation: Review of Problems and Accomplishments to Date," Congressional Research Service, Library of Congress, September 26, 1978; Green and Waitzman, op. cit., 22–32; William Tabb, "Government Regulations: Two Sides to the Story, *Challenge*, November–December 1980.

79. According to Owen and Braeutigam, "It is not entirely accidental that this group of economists [AT&T's consultants] has produced a formidable new theory of multiproduct natural monopoly that may serve as a powerful argument in favor of barriers to entry and the exclusion of competitors in AT&T markets. The only other apparent beneficiary of the normative multiplication of this theory is the postal service." ("The Regulation Game," 7).

# 8

## Semiotic Boundaries
## and the Politics of Meaning:
### Modernity on Tour—A Village in Transition

SUSAN BUCK-MORSS

The focus of this essay is Mirtos, a small village in southeastern Crete. In little more than a decade, it has been transformed from an isolated agricultural hamlet, without electricity or paved roads, into a tourist mecca complete with a luxury hotel and swimming pool, television in the cafes, a whiskey bar, and a discotheque. As a social space in which meaning is produced, the village is overdetermined, a tangle of semiotic systems produced through the superimposition of old and new, foreign and indigenous, during the rapid transition to "modernity." This essay draws on material from a book-length study which I call a *Tourguide to Modern Experience.**

In the five years I have studied Mirtos, I have been interested in political questions of power that emerge at the boundaries between semiotic systems when they confront each other, clash, appropriate each other, or resist appropriation. The project is located within this semiotic space: between state boundaries, between discipline boundaries, as well as between those of culture, sex, and class. Material relevant to the general issue of modernity is presented in the text in an unconventional fashion so that the content reflects critically on investigative method as well as vice versa. Specifically for reasons that are both philosophical and political, I rely heavily on images which, as concrete representations of material reality, have the power to challenge conventional theory, not merely to illustrate it.

The essay is organized by themes as a series of monadological studies which without adding up to a theoretical system will, it is hoped, enrich each other through their juxtaposition. Within them, the material elements are not allowed to disappear under abstract theoretical concepts. If they cohere, if they produce coherence, it is due to an objective affinity within the material itself. Eight themes are presented here in an

*A short version of this chapter was delivered at the First International Conference of Cretan Ethnology, Iraklion, Crete, 10 July 1982. My theoretical orientation is indebted particularly to the work of Theodor W. Adorno, Walter Benjamin, and John Berger.

abbreviated fashion. As they are highly condensed, they appear even more monadic and epigrammatic than in the longer text. In regard to questions of method raised generally in this volume, however, I hope they illustrate how, when cognitive methods are used to subvert authoritarian conventions of research and arbitrary boundaries of discourse, a different kind of knowledge is produced, with very different political and theoretical implications.

## 1. Class Movements

The international migrations of workers and tourists are class movements geographically understood, and they are complementary. Tourists come from the upper classes of industrial societies.[1] They move from the center of the capitalist economy to its underdeveloped periphery. Corresponding to tourism is a countermovement, the flow of workers from the periphery to the "center." Since the nineteenth century, capitalist countries have depended on an international migrant labor force in order to industrialize. In the United States, for example, Mexicans were imported to work the copper mines; Chinese migrants built the railroads.[2] The same historical conditions made possible the birth of the international tourist business—Cook's Tours, begun in the 1840s, are the earliest example.[3] Today, despite recent restrictions on labor migrations, the countries of industrialized, continental Europe depend on "guestworkers" who come from Spain, Italy, Greece, Yugoslavia, and Turkey, precisely those Mediterranean countries that compose the most easily accessible "pleasure periphery" for north European tourists.[4]

Both tourism and labor movements are intended as temporary migrations. Both are motivated by the same objective factor, the relatively higher wages at the center which have relatively greater buying power at the periphery. Both, due to the unequal relationship between center and periphery, distribute the benefits of this discrepancy unequally. The guestworkers' wages in north European industries do not represent the value of their production, which, contributing to the creation of wealth in the host countries, reproduces the economic inequality between these countries and their own. If "tourism is the geographical dispersal of the rich of the world,"[5] (expending a surplus of income), migrant labor is the geographical dispersal of the laboring poor (producing a surplus of value). And although tourism generates economic "development" within host countries, it is development adapted to the needs of the tourists rather than those of indigenous populations. Circulation flows of tourists and workers in the "free world" are thus a consequence of what is in fact underdevelopment and serve to perpetuate underdevelopment at the periphery.

The interconnections between these two movements are largely invisible, because the class boundary of migrations has been reflected in a knowledge boundary. From its inception, "tourism" as an object of scientific inquiry has explicitly excluded workers from the category of international travelers to be investigated.[6]

What has been made invisible at the level of discourse becomes immediately visible in a concrete image. Figure 8.1 shows a working-class man in a factory barrack. "Tourism" is present in a poster over the bed: the head of a statue, a classical Greek god, the German work *Griechenland* (Greece) across the top. The context of this room transforms the meaning of the travel poster. Greece is clearly not a vacation dream for this man, but his place of origin. The poster functions as a sign of his homeland alongside family photographs of a wedding, perhaps his own, and the three duplicate photographs of Papadopoulos, leader of the Greek military junta, who was in power when this photograph was taken. The Greek worker sits reading by his bed, upon which is another book. It is clear that he is proud to be recorded visually in a literary act, which belies the lowest-class status of his position as migrant worker.

His bed, an army cot, is neatly made. The guestworker would have learned to do this during his obligatory Greek military service. What is new for him is the carrying over of military discipline—characteristic of an industrialized workforce—into civilian life. When guestworkers live

Photo by John Mohr, in John Berger and John Mohr, *A Seventh Man: A Book of Images and Words about the Experience of Migrant Workers in Europe* (London: Penguin Books, 1975).

Figure 8.1

in factory-owned barracks, their entire existence is regulated. The following are excerpts from a German factory owner's handbook of housing regulations:

Highest rule: In the lodging extreme cleanliness and order must be maintained.
 . . . spitting cannot be tolerated on the stairway, elevator, entryway or yard, nor can these places be dirtied with cigarette butts and similar refuse. Order and cleanliness are expected above all in the clothing cabinets.
 . . . the beds are to be made up methodically after every use. Mounting pictures and the like is permitted only with the consent of the house manager.[7]

It has been argued by more than one social theorist that individual autonomy is valued by industrial society,[8] not as an end in itself, not with the goal of freedom, but as a means of social control. The internalization of social constraints, maintained by anxiety and insecurity, produces cultural traits of obsessive cleanliness, submission to regimentation, asceticism, and the felt need for "rational" domination of both inner and outer nature—traits that have in fact become synonymous with Western "civilization" and historical "progress." They are rationalized as necessary for industrial efficiency, but they are inherently authoritarian and their political implications need to be made explicit: In the semiotic system of which a "methodically made bed" is a sign, the discipline of the workplace has become the social discipline of the worker. These cultural values permeate "modern" societies. They do not stop at the boundary between work and leisure. The industrial values of cleanliness, regimentation, and the control of nature can be read within a place of bourgeois "relaxation" no less clearly than in the workplace (note the strict formal order of the Palmengarten Cafe at Frankfurt-am-Main, shown in Fig. 8.2).

It is from such nonindustrial villages as Mirtos (Fig. 8.3) that guestworkers come. Ironically, if they return to their country, it is not their factory skills that will be useful, but precisely the cultural traits of industrialism which, along with some knowledge of the language, make former guestworkers valuable as mediators between the local population and foreign tourists—as employees in hotels and restaurants. In the case of Crete, beginning in the late 1960s, returning guestworkers found employment not back in their villages, but in the numerous modern hotels newly constructed along the north shore. As the sociologist Vassilos Vuidaskis has written: "They know more and better than their compatriots who have never been in a foreign country what a value tourists place on concepts such as 'performance, punctuality, hygiene and service.' "[9] For while organized tourism presents an adventurous experience of the "other" during the day, it returns people to their cultural womb of cleanliness and order to eat and to sleep.

In brief, tourism, which appears as an escape from the dominant culture, turns out to be an extension of cultural domination,[10] and returning guestworkers function as its agents.

Photo by Buck-Morss.

Figure 8.2

## 2. The Peaceful Invasion

International tourism not only spreads the values of industrial culture. In blatant contradiction to the ideology of a work/leisure distinction, it is itself an industry, one of the largest in the world. Turner and Ashe estimate that it is "roughly as big as world trade in textiles; only trade in motor vehicles, chemicals and fuel surpass it in size."[11] Between 1955 and 1973, approximately 1,150,000 Greeks emigrated; of these, 600,000 went as guestworkers to Germany.[12] But in 1973 alone, 1.4 million Germans took foreign vacations, and 2.6 million tourists came to Greece.[13] If tourism is not considered a legitimate object of study by most social scientists, it is recognized by hotel schools as serious business, too serious, in fact, to allow people to control their vacations themselves. Behind the back of the adventurous tourist, most of his experiences are prepared in advance. As an extreme example: if tourists list as something they like, the surprise of seeing trout jump in a lake, a proposal might be made, and taken seriously, to send electric shocks at intervals through the water to make sure that such "surprises" will occur.[14]

Mass tourism has been called the "peaceful invasion," and the military allusions which the term evokes are apt. Thomas Cook and Son, founders of the industry, were fully conscious of its parallels to a military organization. The official historian of the firm noted that, like an army expedition, "nothing was left to chance"; a tour leader was "one who possessed the qualities which distinguished a successful general."[15]

Photo by Buck-Morss.

Figure 8.3

Indeed, it may be doubted whether the feat which Wellington regarded as a most difficult one, that of marshalling a given number of soldiers in Hyde Park and getting them out of it in good order, was really more confirmatory of great capacity than was the successful direction of a body of tourists from the beginning to the end of their journey.[16]

Moreover, it was Cook's tour industry which, in utilizing an industrial infrastructure to transport, provision, and deploy people in large numbers, first developed skills of movement control which became vital to late-nineteenth-century mass armies.[17]

Today these skills, called Operations Research (or simply O.R.), are characterized by a systems orientation, that is, the quantification of relevant aspects into a model and the manipulation of this model through the use of mathematical, statistical, and most particularly, computer methodologies. Now a standard tourist business procedure, O.R. dates back to World War II, when scientists of different disciplines using the most modern technologies pooled their knowledge to assist the military in solving operational problems. The distinguishing characteristic of the method, its *value*, is that it can be applied within *any* value system, as it turns all problems into procedural ones. Whatever the task—mass movement of soldiers, migrant workers, concentration camp inmates, or tourists—O.R. techniques of movement control can be, and have been, effectively applied.

In short, the knowledge procedure used by the tourist industry is applicable to wartime and "peaceful" invasions alike. For Germans on charter tour flights to Greece, and particularly to Crete, this fact has a special irony. In May, 1940, the first airborne invasion in history took place when Hitler ordered the invasion by German paratroopers of the northwest coast of Crete (Figure 8.4). It was successful, but with a devastating loss of lives, and the ensuing occupation by German troops was long, brutal, and bitter. Yet the magnitude of historical events shrinks with hindsight.

The floating paratrooper in Figure 8.5 is actually a rubber sunshade pull (Fig. 8.6) in a bus that takes tourists along the same north Cretan coast road the German armies followed in 1941. In this bus, a transport vehicle of the peaceful invasion, the image provides a visible trace of the not-so-peaceful invasions which have been the *Ur*-form of tourism: World War *was* a world tour, and for the first time available to Everyman.

## 3. Historical Amnesia.

If you take the bus from the north coast tourist center of Agios Nikolaos south to Ierapetra, and then another bus fourteen kilometers west along the south coast road, you will reach the small, seaside village of Mirtos. The accompanying photograph (Fig. 8.7) was taken in 1977, when the village was still "unspoiled" (to use the tourists' term for their contradictory claim of having discovered the as-yet-undiscovered). There were no tour buses, no neon signs, and the new luxury hotel was not yet even a

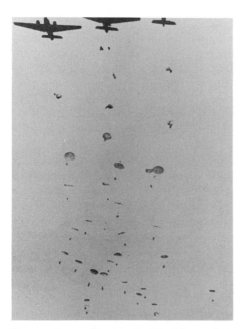

Photo from Vasos P. Mathiopoulos, *Eakones Katochis* (Athens: Metopi, 1980), p. 117

Figure 8.4

Photo by Buck-Morss.

Figure 8.5

Photo by Buck-Morss.

Figure 8.6

cleared space on the road outside of town. Three times a day the bus from Ierapetra swung around the corner of the village crossroads and, spanning the entire street, stopped between two cafes to dump out a handful of foreigners who had managed to escape from the mass-tourist infrastructure.

Figure 8.8 shows the view from those cafes to the crossroads and a third cafe still dominated by villagers. Below a sign in English, "Rooms for Rent," and half covered by a new electrification installation, is the street name: "15 September 1943." The man in Figure 8.9 has just told me the story of that day, when the Germans came to the village, rounded up the men, and shot them in revenge for an act by Cretan resistance fighters. He was among those shot, but the body of his father fell on top of him and hid the fact that he was still alive. His right arm was shattered by a bullet. He has farmed ever since with his one good hand. But tourists who come here have not learned the man's story, and they leave without noticing that the street has a name. They do not know Greek, at least not modern Greek. The young man (Fig. 8.10) with his head bent over a translation of *Zen and the Art of Motorcycle Maintenance*, the traveling hero of which is an existentialist loner, did not come to Mirtos to experience its history.

In the village square is a small war monument (Fig. 8.11); on it, a long list of names. But it is not an ancient monument, and few tourists express interest in it. To them, village life appears as tradition suspended in time. The old women dressed in black for mourning are merely quaint; the ruins from the German occupation, with green trees growing where rooftops once were, seem picturesque. They are part of the "authenticity" of a Cretan village: they make it photogenic.

Photo by Knüppel.

Figure 8.7

Photo by Buck-Morss.

Figure 8.8

Photo by Buck-Morss.

Figure 8.9

Photo by Buck-Morss.

Figure 8.10

Photo by Buck-Morss.

Figure 8.11

## 4. The Meaning of Greece: The Diachronic Development of a Sign

The data of social scientists, like tourist snapshots, record given reality abstracted from the past and hence cut off from any understanding of its historical coming to be. The result of such historical amnesia may be a serious misrepresentation of reality: Relationships between things are understood only synchronically, and the patterns of presently existing objects immediately perceived are granted a systemic coherence which may well be illusory.

But a mere sense of history is not enough to safeguard against illusion. Granted, the construction of intelligibility in the present involves a reconstruction of the past, the reading one gives to the past is a highly political act. In Mirtos there are three factions involved in historical reconstruction: the local school teacher, who is writing a patriotic history of the village; an American feminist, who is writing a critique of Mycenean scholarship; and a British archeologist schooled in the classics, who has unearthed a Minoan "villa" on the hill above the village. Clearly the work of the school teacher and the feminist is partisan. (The very passion of their commitment is translated into thoroughness and care in their writing.) But the classicist belongs to a tradition of Western scholarship which claims with pride to be "objective." This claim is bogus. The study of early and particularly classical Greece is the example par excellence of the reconstruction of history as a political act—an act of racism,[18] sexism,[19] and cultural imperialism in which Western Europe robbed Greece of its own historical heritage, claiming itself to be the legitimate heir.

Figure 8.12 shows fragments of the east pediment of the Parthenon. One might well ask what these priceless Greek relics are doing in the British Museum. Lord Elgin, British ambassador to Turkey, brought them there in the early nineteenth century. He had the permission of the Turkish authorities occupying Greece, but not of the Greeks themselves. One reason the statues are in such fragments is that Lord Elgin's men did a fairly barbaric job removing them from the Akropolis (which, incidentally, was already in ruins, due to an attack on it by the Italians in the seventeenth century.)

In the nineteenth century, the Elgin Marbles, as they are called, became the inspiration for generations of upper-class Englishmen, who developed the myth that Greece was the origin of *their* civilization. They studied the ancient form of the language; contemporary Greek was in their eyes degenerate (as were the Greek people, due to racial crossbreeding). The poet Shelley might write: "We are all Greeks," but the Greeks seemed somehow less Greek than the British.[20] In the Victorian domestication of Greek life, *their* parliamentary system was the inheritor of the democratic tradition of Pericles' Athens. The latter was described as "Prime Minister," the Athenian assembly of the fifth century was described as divided into "reformers" and "conservatives," and Odysseus' Penelope appeared as the epitome of a virtuous Victorian wife. In World War I a recruitment poster on a London bus evoked patriotism with images of classical Greece, and not a few British officers went into battle clutching copies of Homer.

From East Pediment, Parthenon,
in the British Museum, London.

Figure 8.12

The British had no monopoly of this myth of the classics. Across the Channel the Germans had a tradition going back to Hölderlin, Lessing, and Goethe of their own classical Greek origins. Fig. 8.13 shows Nazi officers of the army of occupation proudly viewing "their" Akropolis.

With the onset of mass tourism and the advertising used to promote it, the meaning of "classic" Greece is undergoing quite a modification: Greece. The Classic European Vacation. Admittedly, Greece sounds expensive. You've got beautiful Athens to romp around in. Spine-tingling sites like Delphi, Corinth, and Olympia. Legendary isles like Crete, Rhodess, Corfu, and Santorini. . . . And the dollar is worth 35% more than last year. . . . Call your travel agent. Greece awaits you. At a classic price. [Fig. 8.14]

What this "sign" teaches tourists as to the meaning of Greece is that its historical relics are a stage set for *them* and for their vacation fantasies.

Small wonder, then, that increasingly, as Mirtos has become more accessible to tourists, those who come there treat the village like their own private club. They use the church as a bathhouse, come to the cafes braless and barefoot, walk the streets in bikinis, stroll in "classic" nudity on the beachfront, pluck oranges off the villagers' trees for breakfast, light campfires in the Minoan ruins, and rush to photograph a village funeral or an old woman pounding her laundry at the seaside—all with good conscience.

## 5. Culture at the Crossroads

Figure 8.15 shows a group of village men at the crossroad cafe. Mirtos, of course, has meant something quite different to them. They have

Photo in Mathiopoulos, p. 75.

Figure 8.13

The *New York Times* Sunday Travel Section,
Winter and Spring, 1982, by permission of
The Greek National Tourist Organization.

Figure 8.14

grown up here and they will die here without ever traveling as foreign
tourists. The church is not a bathhouse, but the place where they
married and baptized their children. The oranges represent the product
of their labor in the fields they own and are not (at least not yet) willing
to sell even at a high cash price for the construction of tourist villas.
Traditionally, wealth has been measured in terms of ownership of the
means of production—fields and homes rather than cash—which are
kept within the family and passed down by marriage.

Women are absent from the cafe. In the village's dowry system, where
daughters are the bearers of wealth-transfer, their circulation through
marriage is central to the socioeconomic system; their free circulation
through village space is correspondingly constrained. In contrast, the
young tourist women in Figure 8.16 are unreservedly present in public

Photo by Buck-Morss.

Figure 8.15

Photo by Buck-Morss.

Figure 8.16

village space, sitting together in the cafe and traveling alone without supervision or the company of men. They are wearing casual clothes that reveal their bodies not as sex objects for some male, but as a sign of their sexual self-sufficiency. They are smoking; they are drinking beer (*sketo*) without a meal. Their behavior would be unacceptable not only for village women, but for more cosmopolitan relatives visiting from Athens. These women who enter onto the village scene without the protective shield of class or marriage, the most vulnerable of tourist invaders, are in fact the most threatening. Their very existence here in absolute violation of village custom is a form of cultural penetration. Although in the past decade television may have brought images of such women into the village, this is a confrontation with reality. It is not surprising that in this case cultural difference leads to cultural contact in the form of a power struggle with political implications.

Since the tourist invasion is peaceful, the struggle is not with arms. Since the opposing sides speak different languages, it cannot be a verbal struggle. The form which the confrontation takes is sexual, beginning with eye contact and proceeding to body contact. On one side are tourist women; on the other are village men and (Fig. 8.17) also another, culturally anomalous group, whom the villagers call "Greek tourists" (the term is not a compliment). They are unemployed youth from Athens or Thessaloniki, the urban centers of mainland Greece. Germany has put a temporary stop to the flow of migrant workers, or they might have gone there. As it is, they come south to Crete, work irregularly as day laborers, mimic "hippie" attire, more out of real poverty than fashion, and spend their leisure time "hunting tourist women." Whereas village men join this hunt with a certain discretion (among married men discretion becomes secrecy, reaching an intensity in itself erotic), the Greek "tourists," who have no families in the village to answer to, indulge in free and open pursuit in a show that provides no little entertainment for the villagers.

The men and women, opponents in this sexual combat, might appear to be evenly matched in terms of power, as the tourists' disadvantage in

Photo by Buck-Morss.

Figure 8.17

regard to sex is compensated by their advantage in regard to national origin. Or, the women put up so little resistance that it hardly seems a fight. Or, no matter: since the result of the confrontation is identical for both sides, sexual pleasure, it might appear that whatever the politics and power balance, this is one of those utopian situations where everybody wins. But the sides are playing different games, and their goals are incompatible. Separated by a cultural divide despite the physical intimacy, there is no mutuality in regard to the meaning of the sex act.

For the tourist women it is a sign of emancipation, not only from sexual constraint, but from the constraints of class, which mark such men off limits in their own countries, channelling their desire and keeping both sex and race in their place. Historically in bourgeois culture, women's free erotic expression has been synonymous with a loss of class status: to become a "fallen" woman had simultaneous sexual and social implications.[21] The so-called sexual revolution in industrial societies has done little more than camouflage the class nature of sexual constraint. Now mass culture and advertising channel desire, bestowing erotic power on what is expensive, and propagating values, which the single woman, despite the prevailing ideology of individual liberation, has been forced to make her own. To be accepted socially, she must be accepted sexually. She herself must become the expensive object of desire. She is terrorized into conforming without hope of security, because the terms of a "desirable" commodity are continually changing (the only constant is the impossible demand that she remain young). When such a woman, old or young, thin or fat, chic or not, treats herself to a vacation at the boundaries of commodity culture, the step beyond through a sexual adventure with the "other," whose way of staring at her shows that he is oblivious to the codes of acceptability which terrorize her at home, becomes a uniquely exciting moment in her life. It is literally an experience of utopia, a "no-man's-land," beyond the cultural coding of desire. She feels a surge of eroticism coupled with an intensity of emotion for which the only possible term in her language is "falling in love."

Yet she can maintain this purity of feeling only through blindness to the concrete reality lived by those men who function as the romantic "other" in her own cultural struggle. Behind the utopian appearance, her love is narcissism, and as a form of ethnocentrism, it is made possible by the dominance of her culture over that of the village. (The ease with which her illusions can be sustained is a good measure of the degree of hegemony which her culture has achieved.)

For the men, however, the village space is not free of coding, but culturally overdetermined. Superimposed upon a traditional way of life already fragile is the invading structure of "modernity," controlled by a class and a national culture not their own. The unattached, "free" tourist women, whose sexual presence in the village holds out no promise of dowries, appear less as rebels from modernity than as its farthest outpost.

The bus brings a new batch of women each day. What for each of them is a unique vacation is for the village an endlessly repeated cliché, and as with other historical repetitions, the drama tends toward farce. The man who struts through the village with a love-struck German tourist at his side is walking proudly not because of her, but because last week the village saw him with a love-struck Swede. In the competition among young, unmarried men his own stature rises, whereas the un-aware woman is made to look quite foolish.

Clearly, the man's desire has no purity of feeling similar to her own. Yet he has a right to be defensive and a reason to be cynical. The woman "in love" for two days, or two weeks or even two months, will leave, returning to her assigned place in a culture where he cannot follow without losing the conditions of this love, because her culture codes him as ethnically, hence economically inferior, as well as sexually, hence socially dangerous. (It can, of course, be no other way, so long as hypergamy has no reciprocity of terms—that is, so long as the man's position determines the woman's status and not vice versa.)

Modern Greek has two words for love: *agape* (long-term feeling toward one's family, spouse, and children) and *erotas* (signifying purely sexual desire). Cretan dialect has a further term, *kapzuri* ("hot" or "burning"), but this word also lacks the connotations of romantic senti-mentality characteristic of "falling in love." The latter may well be an emotional luxury in a society where structured family relations are vital to the individual's social and economic security. It is doubtful whether the men experience a feeling which in their language they cannot express. It is even more doubtful that if they do, tourists, of all women, would be able to evoke it. If these women represent the "other" to them, it is as members of an invading culture which threatens to dominate them economically and symbolically. Sex becomes a form of combat against that culture, and against the powerful men to whom these women appear ultimately to belong. In this struggle, rather than ac-knowledging the invaders as the "other," the more successful strategy is to bring the women inside their own semiotic boundary and appropriate their power by appropriating their meaning, thereby robbing them of their potential threat. There may be aggression in the form of competi-tion among village men and Greek "tourists" in pursuing foreign women, but it is an intracultural, fraternal rivalry, whereas in all cases, their sexual exploits effectively neutralize the category of "liberated woman" (the tourist woman's self-positioning), transforming it into the category of *poutana,* or "whore" (the position alloted to them within the indigenous meaning system.)

Single women are *seen* as whores by the village because there is no other cultural term for them. Tourist women are tolerated, accepted, even incorporated into village life, but only as members of this devalued category. It is important that the distinguishing characteristic of the term *poutana* in this case is not the exchange of sexual favors for money—the women give their love freely, and it is they who bring money into the village. Instead, it is the women's singleness which causes loss of status. In the village conception of sexuality there is little prudery. Unattached females, no longer virgins but sexually experienced, are expected to have an active sex life. "Whores" provide a useful social function as a source of sexual initiation for the young men and a physical outlet for discontented husbands (widows, for example, may fall traditionally into this category.[22])

The strange result of this is that the tourist women rightly sense acceptance by the villagers (including the women with whom they may have commercial contact in stores or hotels) and yet only within a category which (if they realize what is happening) is not acceptable to *them*. The single women's attempt to achieve sexual autonomy thus fails in both cultures, because in neither do they have the power as subjects to name their reality, defining the terms of their erotic life. Single women free themselves from being sex objects as commodities in their own culture only to fall behind even bourgeois liberation into the category of sex object as village whores in another.

The situation has a further irony, however, and the women's role in this cultural combat is not innocent, whatever their intent. In pursuit of romantic illusions, they contribute as tourists in bringing to the village precisely that commodification which they themselves are trying to escape. Tourism prostitutes a culture, in the very bourgeois sense of money exchange. As the anthropologist Davyyd Greenwood has written: "Tourism simply packages the cultural realities of a people for sale along with their other resources."[23] In fact a love affair with a fisherman or a mule driver on a vacation to Greece has come to be expected as part of the package deal. The process of the commodification of culture "in effect robs people of the very meanings by which they organize their lives,"[24] and in this case the men are the victims. Flourishing in the present Greek tourist boom is a neurotic syndrome among young Greek men (they are called *kamakia*) of sexual anomie: compulsive sexual activity with foreign women coupled with extreme personal detachment and emotional indifference. Here aggressiveness, originally a form of cultural resistance, has become alarmingly self-destructive.[25]

## 6. Symbolic Violence

Behind the playful appearance of sexual pursuit as well as the peaceful appearance of the tourist invasion, there is symbolic violence. Both are struggles to establish hegemony in the semiotic field created by the tensions of cultural confrontation. What is at stake in the power to name reality is power over the production of meanings rather than over the means of production (although the two are directly related). The appropriation of "the very meanings by which [people] organize their lives" is an act of violence even though it occurs at the symbolic level. In fact, such violence, which may be directed against individuals or groups, is a form of collective brutality with a quality and intensity as politically concerning as the physical violence it often legitimates as its consequence.

The concept of symbolic violence is expressed in the following series of images, the connections between which demand certain cognitive leaps. The leaps exist because each image is related to the previous one in a different register than to the one following. This is possible due to the plurality of meanings which emanate from the objects depicted, and allows extreme condensation of the intellectual point.

The first (Fig. 8.18) is a sign put up next to the mayor's office in Mirtos. It reads: "Tenting and staying overnight on the beach and in the cultivated fields is forbidden. Naked bathing will be punished." It is a sign of resistance against the cultural penetration of tourism. As a gesture of cultural dominance, the message is written first in Greek and below in German.

The sign shown in Figure 8.19 appeared forty years ago during the war, in German first, with Greek below. It reads: "In retaliation for the bestial murder of German paratroopers and soldiers by armed men and women in ambush, the village of Kandanòs was destroyed." In both cases the sign is a message posted at a cultural and semiotic boundary as a warning to outsiders. Compare this with Figure 8.20. It is the body of a man hung by the Germans during the occupation. As a sign it serves a

Photo by Buck-Morss.

Figure 8.18

Mathiopoulos, p. 165.

Figure 8.19

Mathiopoulos, p. 248-49.

Figure 8.20

semantic function identical to the last one. It is a warning that life was taken as retribution. In both cases persons have been killed, yet this sign is so much more shocking. Why? The additional brutality here is that a human being caught within the boundaries of the German occupation, of ultimate worth and ultimate meaning in his own culture, has been reduced to nothing but a sign. A speaker, a producer of meanings, has been silenced, totally subsumed under the meaning system of the occupying forces which make use of this gesture as a demonstration of their power. We identify with this human signified out of fear—not of death, mere absence, but of being present under an authoritarian regime that demands total submission to its order. In the extreme, that is the nature of the symbolic violence I have been discussing. In a more common form, it is true of the next image as well.

Figure 8.21 is the center spread of a Greek pornographic magazine, the title of which appears in the upper-left corner: *Diavase Me,* "Read Me," and let us do just that. It is an image of a woman with Greek features but dyed, Nordic-blond hair. She wears a gold watch, an important commodity status symbol in Greece, and around her neck a gold trinket instead of the traditional Greek Orthodox cross. She is tipping a straw hat, symbol of American party politics (it was Reagan's

Centerspread, *Diavase Me*, Spring, 1980.
Figure 8.21

election year), and is perched for support on a large American flag, ready to wave a small one as if cheering a military parade. She wears a man's shirt out of American flag pieces.

The image is overdetermined. The manifest content is, of course, the sexual eroticism of a nude woman's torso. But there are at least two other levels of meaning. She symbolizes Greece, dependent monetarily on the American dollar since the war (despite the more recent influx of north European currencies through tourism and guestworker remittances), and militarily on U.S. aid through the country's controversial connection with NATO. The image can be read as a sign that Greece has prostituted itself because of this political attachment.

But on another level, she represents the antithesis of traditional Greek values for women. She is isolated from kin, as "liberated" as any tourist sunbathing naked on the beach, free to be desired without the binds of marriage or commitment. She is a woman whose face, figure, and hair are fashionable—in short, a modern woman, a sexual commodity. She symbolizes the dialectic of bourgeois freedom. This Greek woman is not appropriating Western modernity. Instead the magazine's pornographic depiction of her is appropriating the Western way of transforming sexual liberation for women into commodification as a new form of bondage. The image thus has a third meaning. It is a warning that violence will be done to any liberation women may achieve so long as they exist culturally as a sign made by men, for men. (The connection with physical violence lies outside the picture frame, in the higher statistics on rape that as a rule accompany social transitions to the Western model of modernity.)

## 7. Development

Romanticizing tradition does violence to past suffering. I do not wish to deny that in societies based on family relations, women's roles may be intensely meaningful even as they are strongly oppressive. Yet the woman who gives up tradition for bourgeois freedom risks losing something we in the West may be so far from experiencing that we can only sense it in the gestures and touches of a group of Cretan women from a turn-of-the-century photograph (Fig. 8.22), women who, within their space and with each other, had a world of meaning independent of their relationships with men.

The subject of Figure 8.23 is Jana, a young girl of Mirtos, making flower garlands at the church for the Easter celebration. Four years later (Fig. 8.24) she is just at puberty, walking through her village between the tourist cafes. She has seen hundreds of "liberated" women come through Mirtos. There have been a few who stayed longer, independent in a creative sense as dancers, artists, or writers. They were quite remarkable women who, for a period of several years before the onslaught of mass

A. Nenedakis, *Rethimnon: Palies Photographies* (Athens: Gramak E.P.E., n.d.), p. 81.

Figure 8.22

Photo by Helen Hall.

Figure 8.23

Photo by Buck-Morss.

Figure 8.24

tourism, lived in the shelter of the village enjoying simultaneously aspects of both traditional protection and modern freedom. In return, they exposed the village to an alternative definition of modernity, one based on fantasy and innovation rather than commodification and conformism.

In the original stages of transformation, before the villagers were so threatened as to be defensive, and before the tourists were so numerous as to be presumptuous, there was a porosity in the boundaries between cultures, an openness and tolerance despite sexual combat games (to which these women were wise), which allowed for extraordinarily humane, hopeful configurations of culture, composed of a delicate balance of old and new. It was during this very utopian period that I first came to Mirtos. I confess I was tempted to stay there. But like all utopian moments in an international order which is anything but utopian, this one was highly unstable, with no more material base of support than I had, and it did not last.

Within a few years the influx of mass tourism made rooms scarce, inflated prices, and forced local families into combative, competitive postures. The climate of cultural experimentation quickly dissolved as the boundaries between cultures hardened. The artistic women left, lacking the money to live in the changed environment. Creative freedom without economic autonomy is impossible.

But economic autonomy without creative freedom is inadequate. In Figure 8.26 we see women at work just outside Mirtos in a cucumber factory. They are on an assembly line, recently installed to process cucumbers for export to Athens and northern Europe. Previously

Photo by Helen Hall.

Figure 8.25

Greek and other "tourists" worked as day laborers to pack the cucumbers by hand. But since mechanization, the factory employs village women—just as in northern Europe in the nineteenth century, machines initially created a proletariat of woman laborers. Such mechanization represents lighter physical work than in the field. It is also a more sheltered place of employment compared to tourist businesses, although here too women's participation has increased. Wives, daughters, and even grandmothers who stayed at home for most of their lives now spend their entire day working in cafes and hotels run as family concerns. Central to the change in women's work patterns is the fact that cash has become crucial to the villagers in a way unknown a decade ago. Families now "need" consumer items—cassettes, imported cigarettes, skin cream, blue jeans, cameras, beach equipment—that they never then thought of owning, and this is the result of mass tourism.

In the cafes talk of money is incessant. The most frequently asked question to foreigners is *posso kostizi?* ("how much"?) How much was your plane fare? your camera? your watch? The question is the means by which the villagers attempt to position themselves within a world system of abstract exchange. In the process of evaluation, as villagers and as Greeks, they sense their relative powerlessness. In this world system money has taken on an ontological value. As John Berger has written: "Money is life. Not in the sense that without money you starve. Not in the sense that capital gives one class power over the entire lives of another class. But in the sense that money is the token of, and the key to, every human capacity."[26] Increasingly cash is desired as part of dowries

Photo by Buck-Morss.

Figure 8.26

as well as for the purchase of imported commodities which the new breed of tourists has made to seem desirable. Whereas the first wave of tourists were most often in rebellion against the materialism of their culture, the new ones are walking advertisements for commodity culture. Their very presence promotes Minolta cameras, Levi jeans, Nivea cream, Coca Cola, as agents of what might be called "trademark imperialism." The images they provide the villagers, reinforced by television advertisements, appear to be compelling the village into "modernity" less by force than by seduction.

Participation in an international culture as an alternative to ethnic particularism is not itself undesirable. But under the terms of the mass-culture industry such "culture" threatens to be a façade for international control of populations through the power to name the objects of desire. This leads me to my last thematic point.

## 8. Cucumbers

The other side of the village economy and in fact its productive base is the cucumber. This green, phallus-shaped vegetable is a symbol of economic power as an alternative to development through tourism. A decade ago, thanks to small-scale technological innovations introduced into southeast Crete by a Dutch agriculturalist, village families were able to build plastic greenhouses on their fields and produce enough cucumbers by their own labor in a nine-month growing season for a gross return of $10,000. But net profits have been squeezed by the higher costs of fertilizer, plastic, and wood frames; and if winter storms rip out

Photo by Buck-Morss.

Figure 8.27

the plastic, as happens to some each year, families may be left owing the bank for a crop already failed. Moreover, rationalization of the cucumber industry puts pressure on family farming in favor of larger greenhouse complexes worked by wage laborers—the largest, which experiments with plant breeding, is foreign owned.

But industrial rationalization comes up against significant counterpressure. Peculiar to Greece has been a governmental policy of land reform between the wars that strengthened rather than weakened family land ownership, and hence the persistence of small-scale productive units.[27] Contrary to the dominant experience of capitalist countries, Greek capitalism remains largely family-based, "petty-bourgeois." This holds back the process of capital accumulation and prevents economies of scale, tending to make Greek products noncompetitive within a world market. More crucial from a social point of view, family possession of the means of production has hindered the process of proletarianization—that is, the development of a large-scale labor force divorced from the land and without ownership of an alternative productive means.

History demonstrates that a landless peasantry which can swell the ranks of the proletariat does not develop except by force. In the classic example of England in the sixteenth and seventeenth centuries, whole villages were destroyed by a land enclosure movement which forced peasants off their land and produced the "free" laborers necessary for the dynamic growth of capitalism. Much later, a foreign migrant labor force increased their ranks, and Greeks were heavily represented among their number. But even today, when Greeks participate in the proletarian workforce of Western capitalism temporarily as guestworkers, their pattern is to accumulate enough capital outside Greece to make a family business viable at home. Temporary proletarianization in foreign countries has thus strengthened Greek family capitalism domestically. Unlike north European workers, Greek workers have experienced "modernity" without a loss of ownership of the means of production. Mass tourism may change that, however. Since the war, not only have members of Greek peasant families gone to north Europe as guestworkers; in even greater numbers they have migrated permanently to Athens (which now holds almost half of the Greek population). But families maintained their village base with land and houses owned outright, to which they returned to vote, marry, spend the holidays, and retire. For better or worse, tourism now appears to threaten precisely this home base, changing not just the face but the fabric of village society, including its pattern of family ownership, and the implications for Greek social transformation are enormous.

It is ironic that within industrialized societies a "pro-family" ideology is espoused by the New Right, which simultaneously rejects anything but a capitalist economic organization. For as the case of Greece shows clearly, although capitalism and family may originally be compatible social forms, capitalist *development* finds the socioeconomic organization of the family (not to be confused with simple male domination) everywhere its greatest obstacle.[28] In the case of migrant workers, it is cheaper for capitalism if workers are imported singly while families stay at home, and government policies tend to reflect this reality.[29] Within Greece, the mentality of self-sufficiency, quite content with stopping after nine months of labor for a profitable cucumber crop, is no match for agribusiness, where productivity is an end in itself and expansion the condition for survival. At the point of consumption, capitalism divests desire from the social relationships of family and permanent structures of kinship, and reinvests it in an endless series of fungible commodities.[30]

The strength of the Greek family and the economic weakness of Greek capitalism are thus two sides of the same coin, and not only procapitalist scholars lament the situation. From a neo-Marxist position, Mouzelis sums up the consequences: "Greece still lags far behind Western Europe in all aspects of agricultural production and, worse, its agricultural rate of per-capita output is growing more slowly than that of all other sectors of the economy [whereas in Western countries it is rising more quickly]."[31] Vergopoulos argues that despite titular ownership of the means of production, the Greek peasants are in a weak, peripheral power position, dependent on Athens as the market center which fixes prices, and as the state center which controls banking and agricultural credits.[32] From this center-periphery viewpoint, Greek family production would seem to foster the worst of both worlds, the persistence of (family) capitalism within Greece, and the persistence of Greek dependency within world capitalism. Vergopoulos does not see a dynamics for change in this pattern of underdevelopment and the "distortions" of capitalist growth which it sustains in Greece. Mouzelis speaks of a "state of permanent stagnation."[33] Both are writing within a discourse the terms of which relegate tourism to the service sector of the economy, whereas agriculture and industry are privileged as the productive base. This conceptual prejudice is itself a distortion. It leads them to ignore almost completely in their accounts of Greek development the fact of mass tourism, which is so visibly transforming the Greek landscape. They cannot see, for example, the possibility that mass tourism's appropriation of "the very meanings by which people organize their lives" may have the same socioeconomic effect ultimately that the direct appropriation of the means of production did in England at the time of the enclosure movement.

If this does occur, then the situation in Greece is far from stagnant. Whether the changes are progressive or reactionary will depend on whether, how, and by whom cultural meanings are *re*appropriated.

In Mirtos only a few village families actually make their living off the tourists, and the number has risen by just six or seven in the last five years (two new restaurants, one new cafe, and the only discotheque are run by outsiders). But as a symbolically powerful agent in the appropriation of tradition, the new tourism's presence is monumental.

Completed in 1981, the new hotel on the edge of Mirtos (Fig. 8.28) is owned by a village family's son who has already built a large hotel in Iraklion. It has 250 beds and caters to one-night stopovers of European group tours. The villagers themselves number only 350 persons. The sheer volume of tourists and their rapid turnover means that contact between them and the villagers will be reduced to little more than

Photo by Buck-Morss.

Figure 8.28

commercial transactions. Yet their presence cannot help but have a tremendous impact on the way the villagers see themselves.

The construction of this hotel marks a point where quantitative increase results in qualitative transformation. Before, the village appeared as an allegorical stage for the presentation of tradition viewed by a few tourists who responded in romanticized imitation. Now the tourists, as traveling players, enact an allegory of consumer modernity for a village audience, whose response is also mimetic.

The villagers, lacking language and business skills, are not part of the production process of mass tourism, and they are ignorant of what goes on behind the scenes. For factory workers, self-discipline through internalized constraint is the dominant mode of social control. But for the culture industry, of which tourism is a major part, social control is exerted on consumers rather than producers (and this is what the villagers are mimicking), channeling their desire into commodities, including people-as-objects rather than people-as-kin, with an illusory promise of happiness constantly deferred.[34] Both, considered politically, are strategies of manipulating mass populations, but the latter functions by seduction rather than force and is more elusive to perception and more difficult to combat.

The plastic greenhouses (Fig. 8.29) lie in the shadow of the new hotel in more than one sense. It is difficult to convince the younger generation in Mirtos that family farming in a humid hothouse, with fertilizers that turn your hands green and pesticides that make your head ache, is desirable work. (As for the old method of farming in the open air, it is simply not profitable enough to pay for newly desired commodities; among the young, only a foreign family, a Dutch couple with three

Photo by Buck-Morss.

Figure 8.29

children, are enthusiastically choosing it as their life work.) There is talk in the village of making a cement road along the beach, a tourist strip which will inflate property values, as the front row of houses are transformed into tourist shops, night clubs, and the like, and the inhabitants are pushed literally to the "periphery" of their own village space. If and when that happens, it is difficult to see how Mirtos can avoid entering fully into the dynamics of tourist "development."

By opting into this process, they will get a great deal more than they bargained for. Look again at figures 8.28 and 8.29. In the first one, two village women stand next to plastic that will be used to construct greenhouses. They look after a car with the sign "student driver," in which the wife of the village baker (the age of their own daughters) is taking a lesson. They pass around the new hotel every day to reach the village's family plots directly behind it, and they have watched the hotel grow daily. Imagine yourself as these women. Perhaps you are nostalgic for the past; perhaps you are envious of the new possibilities open to the younger generation. But whatever your response, it is clear that you are living through an extraordinary transformation, when ten years ago the road was dirt and when, on the rare occasions when you went to town, it was by donkey. Now look at figure 8.29. Imagine that you are a tourist who, sight unseen, has booked a room here with a group tour. You have asked for a back room, away from the road that brings traffic annoyingly close to your vacationing eyes and ears. Now think of your disappointment, perhaps outrage, when, instead of an uninterrupted mountain panorama, the vista is clogged by hot-houses of torn plastic, reached by trucks and tractors that churn up red dust with each passing. The red dust settles on your balcony. The water for irrigation attracts mosquitoes. Plastic blown out from last year's storm clutters the beach which you reach by crossing the road and walking along the village dump, now full of a wide variety of newly imported, non-biodegradable containers. The advertising brochure didn't show you this. You wanted an "unspoiled" Cretan village, and you got an awkward mutant, half dying-traditional, and half tacky-modern.

You are experiencing a paradox fundamental to the very structure of the tourist industry as a form of development. It is this: mass tourism cannot succeed as a long-term development strategy for a country, because it is precisely the *lack* of development which makes an area attractive as a tourist goal.

The scenario of failed development, destroying the life of the village without providing a viable and lasting economic alternative, is not cause for optimism. Tourists are striving for the illusion of difference and bring the same real world they are attempting to escape. The villagers are striving for equality with the tourists, whose presence in this case is a marker of the village's *in*equality within the world capitalist system. (The capitalists themselves could not care less: they count on a rapid return on their investment so that suitable profits are extracted before the "saturation point" of tourism is reached.) Behind the backs of villagers and tourists there is no cunning of historical reason which works through their desires to set the picture straight. Instead, the needs of the international system manipulate the desires of both as a modern form of social control. Freedom from this manipulation would appear to be of common political interest to villagers and tourists. Indeed, within the context of culture's commodification on both sides, cultural struggle for the reappropriation of meaning would need to become central to politics, guided by an awareness of the problems of symbolic violence which up to now have been most articulately expressed within the discourse of feminist theory.

## Conclusion

In November 1979, the bottom fell out of the price of cucumbers on the Athens market, an economic crisis quite predictable in terms of center-periphery theory. Farmers of Mirtos and the surrounding region launched a political offensive. They refused to sell at the low price, dumping truckloads of cucumbers on the road north to the port and bulldozing them into barricades (Fig. 8.30). The mayor of Mirtos brought food to the cucumber warriors, who continued their resistance into the night. Figure 8.31 is a photograph of the men of Mirtos which appeared in the Athens daily newspaper *Ta Nea* along with an article evoking the legendary tradition of Cretan resistance fighters.

The traditional warriors (Fig. 8.32) fought with rifles instead of

Photo compliments of *Ta Nea*, Iraklion Office.

Figure 8.30

Photo compliments of *Ta Nea*, Athens Office.
### Figure 8.31

cucumbers. The history of Crete is the story of continuous invasions—by Venetians, Arabs, pirates, and Turks, all prior to the Germans—but also the story of continuous resistance. Cretan pride is strong, and the island has been capable of withstanding every prior invasion. The practice and ritual of war strengthened the people's sense of cultural differentiation—the Cretan moustache, the Cretan posture, the Cretan national dress.

Wars destroy people and buildings, but cultural disintegration is more fatal to a social collective. And yet to return to warfare as a method of cultural invigoration is a Nietzschean solution that falls behind the present level of internationalism to which both tourism and migrant labor bear witness, albeit in a distorted form.

The critical question of "modernity" is not if change should occur, but change under whose terms?

Giorgos Dimitrianakis, schoolteacher in Mirtos, deploring the impact of tourism on his village, speaks of the tradition of Cretan hospitality in contrast to the present reality of mass tourism: The village has been stuffed with tourists until, like an animal force-fed, it becomes sick to the point of bursting. He would not reject the benefits of modernity—medical care, electricity, transportation, or even women's equality—but he protests against the speed of the transformation, requiring the villagers to leap a gap so wide that they fall within it. When he argues, "Change must come, but let it be our way," he is speaking to the need for culture to digest change so that, still naming the terms of its transformation, it does not lose control.

Compare the old photograph to that of the cucumber warrior provided in Figure 8.31. The fact that these villagers are still able to evoke a

Palies Photographies, p. 79.

**Figure 8.32**

tradition of resistance in a modern context of tractors and news photography is a sign that they have not lost their capacity for action as political subjects. The fact that their resurrection of tradition is not pure should worry only those who consider culture to belong in a museum display case instead of in the street (in the display case it is not far from becoming a commodity). Village resistance must be integrated with the realities of an international context if it is to be more than romantic nostalgia: Guns set territorial limits to culture; market crops of cucumbers are grown to cross them.

Among the cucumber warriors, Cretan moustaches still abound, but the clothes, the casual postures, and the absence of ritual insignias lack the distinctiveness of tradition. The sign of the raised cucumbers in a "V" evokes an international culture, not of commodities this time, but of political struggles—the end of war, striking workers, the peace movement, student demonstrators—indicating that even in the village's local protest, they are caught up in a far from local system of resistance as well as economic exchange.

I am tempted to close with the image of cucumber warriors, and with a caption from the literature of center-periphery theory which implies that such villages on the periphery of a transnational capitalist system will have their development determined by the developed "center"—urban areas within their own countries and industrialized countries within the Western world generally—no matter what is done at the local level. The photograph would be repeated, this time with the text moving up into the photograph, so that it begins to block out the image. On the next page the text would cover almost everything—only hands clenching cucumbers would remain visible. Finally the photograph would be completely obliterated, simply a white page covered with black type stating a general and abstract theory.

In short, I might end in a very traditional theoretical manner with a very general and global conclusion. But I would not start there. For is such theory merely an explanation of how the reality of the villagers' lived experience is subsumed under the "objective" reality of a world system, or is the theory itself, which subsumes concrete lived experience into general categories, an example of symbolic violence—and does it risk repeating on the level of the superstructure that form of domination which, on the level of the substructure, it presumes to describe?

In fact, it was this kind of concern which first prompted my study of Mirtos. In the years just preceeding, I had had the opportunity to accompany teams of World Bank and AID consultants to what were euphemistically termed "lesser" developed countries: Jamaica, Peru, Nigeria, Ghana, and Kenya. I marveled at these "fact-finding" missions. In the space of several weeks, a team of "experts" (economists mainly) would be led about by some officials and "shown" the country's development problems. The experts had no language knowledge, engaged in no social interaction with the "lesser developed" part of the population, and had no time to do more than gather data that would be fed to computers at home. In fact they had no more knowledge than tourists of the culture or of how the people themselves gave meaning to what they were living through.[35] These missions produced knowledge that was used to legitimate international development programs which would have a tremendous impact on the people, for better or worse. There was a lot of talk about active participation, and even mention of Paulo Freire's work; but there was no real questioning of their own right to be there, or of their monopoly of significant "knowledge."

As I sped through these countries, I caught the mute gaze of a woman or man or child which told me that we clearly did not have that monopoly. It was my first exposure to the powerful and often politically irresponsible uses of academic authority. It was not my last.

The approach which I have used here in studying Mirtos, while indebted to certain "academic" methods and theories (and while not free of an outsider's bias, and certainly not free of subjective involvement) attempts, by focusing on the people of a small, "marginal" village which I knew as a visitor over time, to contribute to redressing the power balance by making visible those who are most often overlooked in the very politically charged discourse of "development."

## Notes

1. Cf. OECD statistics, cited in Donald E. Lundberg, *The Tourist Business* (Chicago: Institutions/Volume, Feeding Management Magazine, 1972), 27.

2. For a critical history of such migrations, see Ronald Takaki, *Iron Cages: Race and Culture in Nineteenth-Century America* (New York: Knopf, 1979).

3. The connection between the development of this business and British industrialization and imperialism is clearly documented in the official history of Thomas Cook, Ltd. See John Pudney, *The Thomas Cook Story* (London: Michael Joseph, 1953).

4. Louis Turner and John Ashe, *The Golden Hordes: International Tourism and the Pleasure Periphery* (London: Constable, 1975).

5. Ibid., 245.

6. Tourism as an "object" (in Michel Foucault's sense) of knowledge was codified by the Committee of Statistical Experts of the League of Nations in 1937; its definition was later the one accepted by the UN and OECD. See *Tourism in OECD Member Countries* (Paris: OECD, 1959), 7.

7. Cited in Maria Borris, *Ausländische Arbeiter in einer Grossstadt: Eine empirische Untersuchung am Beispiel Frankfurt* (Frankfurt-am-Main: Europäische Verlagsanstalt, 1974), 140–41.

8. See, for example, the works of Theodor W. Adorno, Michel Foucault, Max Horkheimer, and Wilhelm Reich.

9. Vassilios Vuidaskis, *Tradition und sozialer Wandel auf der Insel Kreta*, vol. 9 of *Studia Ethnologica* (Meisenheim am Glan: Verlag Anton Hain, 1977), 462.

10. "The tourist demands uniform standards of accommodation, food, and so on, and thus requires the installation of high technology infrastructure. Although he may have been motivated by the desire to escape from his home society, the tourist soon imposes its values on the society he is visiting." (Turner and Ashe, 130).

11. Ibid., 113.

12. Giorgos Matzouranis, *Ellines Ergates sti Germania* (Athens: Ekdoseis Gutenberg, 1974).

13. *Economic Review of World Tourism*, 1974. By 1976 the number of arrivals of tourists in Greece had reached 4.25 million.

14. Cf. Schafer and Mietz, "Aesthetic and Emotional Experiences Rate High with Wilderness Hikers," *Environment and Behavior* 1 (1969): 195.

15. Pudney, 111.

16. Ibid., 101.

17. Ibid., 180.

18. Cf. Martin Bernal, "Black Athena: The Afroasiatic Roots of European Civilization, Volume I: The Fabrication of Ancient Greece 1785–1985" (London: Free Association, 1987).

19. Cf. Marjorie Peyton, *Women vis-à-vis Men in the Bronze Age*, unpublished ms.

20. Two recent books on the subject document the situation clearly: Richard Jenkyns, *The Victorians and Ancient Greece* (Cambridge: Harvard University Press, 1980); Frank M. Turner, *The Greek Heritage in Victorian Britain* (New Haven: Yale University Press, 1981).

21. This was documented repeatedly by the dreams of Freud's female patients. See Sigmund Freud, *The Interpretation of Dreams*, trans. and ed. James Strachey (New York: Avon/Basic Books, 1965), 235–36, 320, and passim.

22. Cf. Adamantia Pollis, "Greek Women: The Struggle for Individuality," unpublished paper, 11.

23. Davyyd J. Greenwood, "Culture by the Pound," in *Hosts and Guests: The Anthropology of Tourism*, ed. Valene L. Smith (Philadelphia: University of Pennsylvania Press, 1977), 137.

24. Ibid.

25. Cf. the fictional account by the author of *Z*, Vasili Vasilikou, *Ta Kamakia* (Athens: Kaktos, 1970).

26. John Berger, *Ways of Seeing* (New York: Viking, 1972), 143.

27. Cf. Kostas Vergopoulos, *Ethnismos kai oikonomiki Anaptizi* (Athens: Exantas, 1978).

28. As early as 1848 Marx wrote that the bourgeoisie had "torn asunder" traditional family relations, leaving "no other nexus" between people "than naked self-interest, than callous 'cash payment.'" (Karl Marx and Frederick Engels, "Manifesto of the Communist Party," *Selected Works* (New York: International Publishers, 1972), 38.

29. "While statements are made by the government favoring the reuniting of families and the integration of these families into German society, the tax structure provides a tangible disincentive for this to happen. The foreign worker essentially must pay a surcharge to be with his family while the native worker does not." Ray C. Rist, *Guestworkers in Germany: the Prospects for Pluralism* (New York: Praeger, 1978), 88.

30. This argument is made by Gilles Deleuze and Felix Guattari in *Anti-Oedipus: Capitalism and Schizophrenia*, trans. Robert Hurley et al. (New York: Viking, 1972).

31. Nicos P. Mouzelis, *Modern Greece: Facets of Underdevelopment* (London: Macmillan, 1979), 39.

32. Kostas Vergopoulos, in idem, and Samir Amin, *Dismorphos Kapitalismos* (Athens: Ekdoseis Papazisi, 1975).

33. Mouzelis, *Modern Greece*, 39.

34. Adorno argued in 1942 that the culture industry's mode of social control had created a new anthropological type, characterized, not by repression and control (the Protestant work ethic), but by consumer readiness for immediate (substitute) gratification and a readiness to treat all objects as fungible and disposable. Theodor W. Adorno, "Notizen zur neuen Anthropologie" (Frankfurt-am-Main, Adorno estate).

35. This point is made well in the extremely interesting study by Dean MacCannell, *The Tourist: A New Theory of the Leisure Class* (New York: Schocken, 1976).

# 9
## Seizing Power / Grasping Truth

JOSEPH TURNER

## 1. Prometheus' Warning

In the 1930s, in the Daily News Building on East 42nd Street in New York City, was one of those museums where visitors watch things in motion and turn knobs—the old Museum of Science and Industry. At the entrance was a particularly striking exhibit. From a spout in the wall, a steady stream of ball bearings shot out, arched down, bounced off a small, polished steel surface—click, click, click, click, arched back up almost to their original height, and landed unerringly in another small hole. What precisely was the exhibit supposed to show? Perhaps it was the wonderful uniformity of the ball bearings always bouncing the same way; perhaps it was the wonderful universality of Galileo's parabolas or the fact that steel could bounce as readily as rubber, and even higher. The museum is long since gone, so we cannot go read the legend. Today, one might take the clicking bearings to represent, as the very name of the museum suggests, both science and industry, and more than that, the human power necessary to build this little scientific-industrial complex. Required was the modest power of the exhibitors who, like Newton's God, kept the ball bearings running on time, and the more pervasive power of the city that enabled visitors to arrive so easily at the museum's doors.

The hand of science needs something to grasp, something on which to work, and that something consists of repeated patterns. Underneath the rarity of a day in June, science discerns periodicity—the succession of days. "The whole life of Nature is dominated by the existence of periodic events, that is, by the existence of successive events so analogous to each other that, without any straining of language, they may be termed recurrences of the same event." So Alfred North Whitehead instructed young people in 1911 in *An Introduction to Mathematics*. Yet, we should also know that events do not come tagged for us, this one "recurrent," that one "never again." Events do not even come tagged as events. Someone has to elicit them, frame them, fashion them. Fashioning and framing of events in science runs extraordinarily parallel to a certain fashioning and framing in industry. Recurrence of the same event in nature is like the standardization of parts in manufacture, parts

237

so analogous one to the next that in any given assembly, or repair, one part may be used as readily as another. Various someones have also taken to standardizing the actions of people, from Maurice of Orange's forty-three positions for the mass loading and firing of muskets to Henry Ford's work stations on his assembly line.

Jean-Jacques Rousseau chose as a frontispiece for his celebrated discourse on science and the arts, of 1750, an illustration showing a graceful young man, seemingly just springing to life, interposed between a muscular Prometheus, torch in hand, and a grinning satyr, preparing to grab the flame (Fig. 9.1). Later, to a puzzled critic, Rousseau explained, "The torch of Prometheus is that of the sciences made to animate the great geniuses [the graceful young man] . . . the Satyr, who seeing the fire for the first time, runs to it and wants to embrace it, represents . . . vulgar men . . . the Prometheus who cries and warns them of the danger is the Citizen of Geneva [Rousseau himself]" (quoted by Roger Masters in his study of Rousseau).[1] The caption reads, "Satyr, knowledge is not for you." And that precisely was the message of the discourse. Progress in science, and in the arts as well, does not serve to purify morals. Were all men great geniuses, it would, but men for the most part are vulgar, half-brute.

Rousseau's warning went unheeded. The great geniuses thought they could safely handle the torch and the satyrs did not think of themselves as satyrs. And so animated geniuses have provided us with beautiful particle theories of the universe, diminished the sweat of labor, eased the pain of childbirth, increased longevity. Yet the flame burns as it illluminates, and more than the satyr's beard has been scorched. Today the flame is just about out of control, bidding in some cataclysmic, nonrecurrent event to set fire to the planet itself. It is not that our new discoveries exceed the bounds of science—exceed the grasping and shaping of recurrences. Quite the contrary, discoveries are growing ever more precise in the exactness of the requisite analogies. Indeed, if we do not burn up, we may well suffocate from new precisions—new knowledge systems—instead. We may not be too far from that day when science will be called upon to determine the precise age of arrival of that rite of passage when children are able to tell the difference between a TV commercial and a TV program. This could be important information. The Federal Trade Commission may need it so as to protect from undue influence children watching Saturday morning TV programs that feature story characters based on toys currently for sale. What society seeks is not parents sharing thoughts at the playground on good ways for children to grow up but cognitive science developing curves of child development for industry and government.

## 2. The Panopticon

In 1791 Jeremy Bentham offered a striking architectural image of recurrences and standardizations in his "Panopticon," which he com-

Figure 9.1. Frontispiece to the original edition of Rousseau's discourse on science and the arts. Reproduced from the edition with commentary by George R. Havens (Modern Language Association, 1946).

piled from his earlier letters. The model brings diverse elements into standardized surroundings and extracts standardized meanings. It can be used to foster production in workshops, inquiry in laboratories, learning in schools, healing in hospitals, and correction in prisons. Bentham's interest began with prisons. The penitentiary Panopticon is a doughnut-shaped building with a tower set in the center of the hole (Fig. 9.2). The doughnut consists of a ring, one cell deep, of identical cells partitioned off from each other and housing one inmate per cell. There are several stories of rings. Through a special placement of lighting and windows, the director in the tower can look at the inmates, but the cats in the cells cannot look at the king, nor at each other. The building is like those state penitentiaries—"big houses"—with tiers of cells and central inspection stations, which were built in America early in this century. It also resembles a modern business office devoted to processing such matters as insurance forms. Workers sitting at computer terminals produce not only the processed forms, which go to customers, but also printouts of their own rates of work, numbers of mistakes, and the like, which go to the manager. With this information, the manager can calculate (also by computer) norms for the group and compare an individual worker's performance with that norm.

In building such a prison, for which he gave detailed instructions, Bentham's purpose was humanitarian. He sought to substitute well-lit cells and frank surveillance for dark dungeons and secret spying. The director and his staff were to institute a regime of corrective procedures, monitor the performance of the prisoners, and administer whatever punishment was deemed necessary. For Bentham, punishment was to be by analogy (it was not yet standardized): punish violence by strait waistcoat, shouting by gagging, refusal to work by refusal of food. Through a little tunnel running under the doughnut, public authorities could visit the tower to check, in turn, on the director. They could see at a glance how the inmates were doing. This arrangement is like Educational Testing Service's yearly set of SAT scores, which not only provide information about individual students for individual colleges, but also survey, through the statistics of means and standard deviations, the functioning of the educational system as a whole. Once such a prison is built and in operation, management and purpose float free. Others, not necessarily as gifted as the original architect or with different purposes, can step into the tower and run things. Parliament voted to build Bentham his prison, but George III in 1813 refused to sign a necessary document, perhaps because he had been irritated by some of Bentham's other writings. Parliament did pay Bentham £23,000 in compensation for his work, an early glimmering that the standardization of human affairs could be remunerative.

For industry, Bentham saw use of the cells as workshops for increasing productivity under central direction. For schools, he saw the cells as individual study rooms designed to prevent students from cheating and

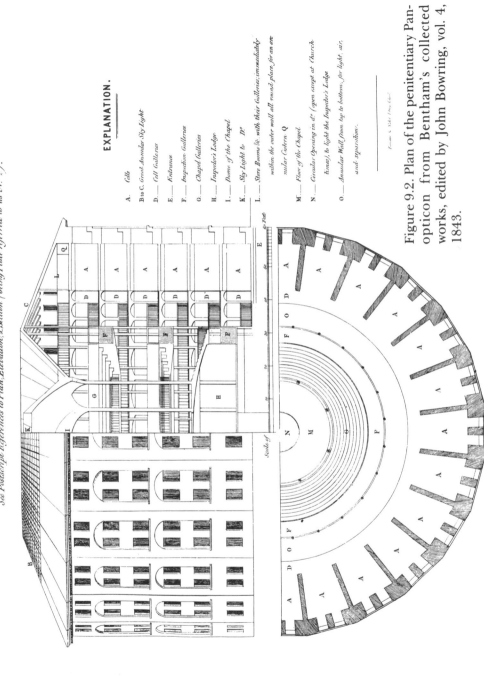

A General Idea of a *PENITENTIARY PANOPTICON* in an Improved, but as yet, (Jan.ʸ 23.ᵈ 1791), Unfinished State.

See Postscript References to Plan, Elevation, & Section (being Plate referred to as Nº 2).

## EXPLANATION.

A. ____ Cells

B to C. Great Annular Sky Light

D. ____ Cell Galleries

E. ____ Entrance

F. ____ Inspection Galleries

G. ____ Chapel Galleries

H. ____ Inspector's Lodge

I. ____ Dome of the Chapel

K. ____ Sky light to Dº

L. ____ Store Rooms &c with their Galleries; immediately within the outer wall all round: place for an annular Cistern Q

M. ____ Floor of the Chapel

N. ____ Circular Opening in dº (open except at Church times), to light the Inspector's Lodge

O. ____ Annular Well, from top to bottom, for light, air, and equilibrium.

Figure 9.2. Plan of the penitentiary Panopticon from Bentham's collected works, edited by John Bowring, vol. 4, 1843.

to deter rich noblemen from passing off as their own term papers purchased from others more gifted. Partitions would eliminate something desirable, however. Valuable learning can also take place directly between students. Now, we are considering here the great Jeremy Bentham, not some monomaniac, not some modern professional analyst. Bentham did see that his Panopticon had limits, even ludicrous possibilities. It was not the answer to everything. It could not serve for all of education. Indeed, it could not serve for any of the education of Rousseau's Emile, although it might serve to insure the virtue of Emile's intended bride, Sophie. In matters of science, the cells could help meet the condition, as Bentham put it, "that the subjects of the experiment be placed in circumstances exactly similar." Bentham opposed deception in experiments, although he saw possible uses—mixing two groups of children to see how they sort things out when one group had been taught that the moon is cheese and other falsehoods. Finally, in what he called his mood of *jeu d'esprit*-which Michel Foucault in his enlightening account of the Panopticon in *Discipline and Punish* unaccountably seemed to miss—Bentham sketched the benefits of the design for the economy-minded sultan keeping watch over his seraglio, with "the great saving it would make in the article of eunuchs." Mill in his essay on Bentham reminded us that Bentham was not always such a serious fellow.

## 3. Disturbing the Universe

The talent part, and on occasion the Nobel-prize-winning part, of science consists in discerning in nature recurrent happenings that others have missed. In 1894, during a brief period of work at the weather station atop Ben Nevis, highest of the Scottish hills, the young physicist C. T. R. Wilson observed one momentous morning a "glory." Under special conditions of light, an observer may see his shadow cast on a cloud with the head of the shadow looking as if it were surrounded by several colored rings. This is the glory. Wilson resolved on his return to Cambridge to study the optical phenomenon further, proposing to "imitate" it in the laboratory. The result was a piece of apparatus that another Cambridge researcher, the atomic physicist Ernest Rutherford, was to call "The most original and wonderful in scientific history."

To conduct an experiment, it is first necessary, however gently, to disturb the universe, that is to say, to fashion something, to arrange something. Before getting his glory, Wilson needed first to make clouds. Air always contains a certain amount of water vapor. Given a sufficiently rapid fall in temperature, some water vapor will condense out in droplets. A good way to lower the temperature of air is to let it expand rapidly, that is, let the pressure drop. Wilson fashioned a glass cylinder into which he set a piston and sealed the cylinder at top and bottom, forming a chamber above the head of the piston and a chamber below. He created the cloud in the upper chamber. The trick was to admit moist air to the chamber, then drop the piston rapidly, causing a rapid fall in pressure, causing the water vapor to condense out in droplets. The trick in dropping the piston rapidly was to connect the lower chamber by tube to a globe from which he had previously exhausted the air. When the valve in the tube was opened, the air rushed from the lower chamber to the globe, the piston dropped with the requisite velocity, and above the piston—condensation! Wilson summoned clouds at will, over and over again—the faster the drop, the denser the cloud. Wonderfully recurrent, total control!

The flame burns brightly, the fire leaps to fresh tinder. Interest in the glory was set aside, as Wilson explained in his 1929 Nobel address. In a rapid series of transformations, he found new purposes. Belief at that time was that condensation of vapor into clouds required the presence of dust in the air. Wilson produced clouds in a dust-free chamber. On what then does the water vapor condense? In 1895, Roentgen discovered X-rays. The following year Wilson trained them on his chamber—to produce condensation. His explanation was that the droplets formed on the ions left after the radiation had stripped away the electrons. A few such ions in smaller amounts are always present in the air, accounting for his creation of clouds under other conditions in dust-free air. Was there a better way to see, and preserve, observations of the effects of radiation? Wilson added lights and timing devices to his apparatus, to produce the now familiar photographs of streaks from "Uranium rays" and subatomic particles, like vapor trails left in the wakes of passing airplanes.

Here was striking confirmation for the then rapidly developing theories of subatomic particles. The Wilson cloud chamber became, as was once said, the telescope for these researches. For a long time, Rutherford was dubious that anything practical would come of such work. "Anyone who expects a source of power from the transformation of these atoms is talking moonshine," he said. But to disturb the universe was soon to take on new meaning. Today, forty-two years after the B-29 Enola Gay carried its payload to Hiroshima, both sides have the bomb, or rather 50,000 bombs between them.

## 4. Making People Behave

Bentham, to be sure, did want to apply the controls of physics to human affairs in some undefined, appropriate way—drop the ball bearing, get the bounce; open the valve, get the cloud. Modern behavioral science, so often scoffed at for its pretensions, has on occasion met the challenge, if not so nicely. In 1974 Stanley Milgram, of Yale University, reported in *Obedience to Authority* the extraordinary degree to which he could make ordinary people inflict pain on other ordinary people. Jerome Bruner, then of the Harvard psychology department, hailed the study as a major contribution to our knowledge of man's behavior. Roger Brown, also of the Harvard department, found the book to qualify as literature as well as science.

With funds from federal and private foundations, Milgram invited subjects, first students at Yale, then residents of Bridgeport who answered his ads, to assist for a few dollars in experiments on the effectiveness of punishment on rote learning. Taken by twos, subjects drew lots to determine who was to be the pupil and who the teacher. The pupil sat in a chair with electrodes fastened to his skin. The teacher sat before a console designed to administer punishment to the pupil in the form of electric shocks in graded amounts, from weak to mild to dangerous to "XXX." A technician in a laboratory coat explained to the teacher that if the pupil made a mistake in reciting the syllables, then the teacher was to administer shocks to him of increasing severity, according to a standard schedule, until he got it right.

The effectiveness of the design lay in its illusion. The true purpose was hidden. The teacher did not know that the shocks were not real, that the pupil was an accomplice of the technician, that the lots he drew were fixed, that the true purpose of the experiment was to examine his obedience to authority. Will the "teacher" go all the way to "XXX" as the "pupil" falters in his efforts to learn the syllables? or at some point will he refuse to follow orders? In the first series of subjects, the "pupil" was placed in an adjoining room, but could be heard at one point pounding on something. The result was that over half of the "teachers," twenty-six out of forty, went the full course to "XXX." The experiment was successfully replicated in cities in Germany, Italy, South Africa, and Australia.

Is this human nature in the raw? Milgram did not attribute his results to letting loose some innate sadism. Most participants who obeyed did so with obvious reluctance. But Milgram believed he had achieved a "cloud chamber" of total control. The closer the subject sat to the technician, the more obedient he became. The quicker the drop of the piston, the denser the cloud. And yet the encounter was of a very limited kind, not a matter of listening to one's doctor or lawyer and following his advice, but a one-shot exposure to naked command. The essence of the experiment was to deal with subjects by standardized procedures. There could be no discussion, no peeking under the hood of the shock generator to see where the wires went, no independent inquiries. The experiment no more tells us about the behavior of people in repeated encounters than a tiger pacing its cage in the zoo tells us about its behavior in the wild. Indeed, Milgram could not do his experiment in the "wild," in a society of repeated encounters between people. You can only deceive a person so many times, pull the chair out from under him so many times, before he declines the invitation to sit down. Milgram has exploited the fact that we already live in semi-Panopticons. This is the world of Adam Smith, the world of division of labor, in which people come to do a job for pay, with little knowledge of its purposes, with little involvement with their fellow workers.

As the experiment became widely known through magazine articles and the book itself, public revulsion put pressure on scientific groups to make rules against experiments based on deception. What is interesting is that nobody, neither a subject nor academic colleague repelled by the deceptions and naked commands, ever thought to stop the project by personal intervention, by personal distribution of knowledge, by standing at the entrance to the lab with a sign, "The shocks are fake!" There was no Mario, as in Thomas Mann's story, to shoot the magician who had tricked and humiliated him.

By another ingenious stratagem it did prove possible to obtain controls in social science to rival those of physics, but without deception. Volunteers agree to be assigned to one of two groups before the experiment begins. Only afterwards are they assigned randomly to a particular group. With $80 million from the federal government, the Rand Corporation, as reported in *The New England Journal of Medicine* of June 1984, compared health costs for fee-for-service systems with prepaid group practice, also known as health maintenance organizations (HMOs). In Seattle, 1,580 volunteers agreed to accept free care for three to five years in either system, then were assigned randomly to one of the two systems, controlling for health, age, sex, race, family size, and income. Results were useful. HMOs proved cheaper, and not because they were biased toward selection of healthier members, but because they utilized fewer hospital admissions.

The results were useful, but only as a kind of market research, applicable to a given place at a given time. The experiment did successfully predict the recent spectacular growth in health maintenance organizations. But that was for the old nonprofit HMOs. What about the new investor-owned HMOs? In a comment on the report in the same issue of the journal, Alain Enthoven asked, can these new HMOs "develop the kind of corporate culture that is compatible with high-quality care?" The difficulty here is that to answer that question would require another, say, $80 million for another round of market research. Unlike Wilson's cloud chamber or Milgram's chamber of horrors, the Rand study is not something easily transported to another site or, perhaps, even replicable after a lapse of several years. Conditions, HMOs, change. Other things do not remain equal, and trying to keep them equal is beyond the power of the experimenter.

## 5. Mass Production

From these special studies, turn now to industry and to efforts to make and control things on a large scale. For Adam Smith, in the eighteenth century, the way for manufacturers to increase productivity was by the division of labor—that is, by the division of manual tasks into elementary motions. This section offers a simplified, stylized, near mythologized sketch of the development of standardization in manufacture, from Smith to Marx to the founder of scientific management in America, Frederick Taylor, to the present, mounting contradictions in mass production. The sketch draws in good part on a recent book by Michael J. Piore and Charles E. Sabel titled *The Second Industrial Divide*. Adam Smith found that three workers in a pin factory produced more pins per day if one specialized in drawing the wire, a second in shaping the head, and third in shaping the point. These partial-pin makers perfected their skills faster and wasted less time shifting from one elementary motion, or set of elementary motions, to others than if each made whole pins. Unfortunately, as things turned out, this increase in efficiency was paid for in terms of an increased rigidity in manufacture. To increase or decrease production in response to an increase or decrease in the market now required hiring or firing workers in units of three rather than one.

As viewed by Marx in the nineteenth century, the division of labor had a profound impact not only on productivity, but also on the development of automatic machinery. To start with (or in the middle), there was the invention of a machine to replace an elementary motion. The yarn-spinning frame initially required the operator continually to move the carriage back and forth by hand, so as to stretch and twist successive rolls of cotton or other fiber. Then, in 1830, following a spinners' strike, the Manchester inventor Richard Roberts removed this chore from the operator and brought it under machine power, in his self-acting spinning mule. Replacement by machine of one elementary motion then created demand for, and subsequent invention of, other machines to replace other elementary motions. And the new mode of production spread to other industries. Marx wrote in *Capital*, "Thus spinning by machinery made weaving by machinery a necessity, and both together made the mechanical and chemical revolution that took place in bleaching, printing, and dying, imperative." But again efficiency had its price. The more special-purpose, automatic machines were introduced and the more they were connected in precise sequences, the more difficult it became for the whole system to turn around, to produce anything other than the initial products.

Late in the nineteenth century, Taylor, admired both by capitalists and communists (such as Lenin), extended the notion of special-purpose machinery to special-purpose people. Earlier in the century, in England, Charles Babbage had also begun thinking in this direction. The skills demanded of people in industry, Taylor believed, varied as much as their native abilities and training. It did not pay to have the smartest, handiest, most educated fellow do routine jobs. Let the most qualified do the most demanding work and the less qualified in descending order do the less demanding work. The mission of scientific management was to develop tests for manufacturers to enable them to sort people out properly. The mission was also to analyze in rigorous fashion the division of tasks into elementary motions. Of course, Smith and Marx appreciated human differences and job differences, but it remained for others to undertake that rigorous research—the time-motion studies of Taylor and Frank B. Gilbreth, the fatigue studies of Elton Mayo and others at the Hawthorne plant, Robert Yerkes's development of intelligence tests to identify officer material during World War I. Today, Milgram's experiments and the Rand study represent top-of-the-line work in the measure of man. They show how scientific such investigators can really get. There is no call anymore to suffer from physics envy.

Again new refinements brought new drawbacks. The very passivity of the worker essential to the efficiency of the whole system and for analyses undertaken by industrial psychologists posed problems. Jobs can be so narrowly defined and so repetitious and so boring that workers are diminished by them and do poorly even that work that is assigned them, as Smith already intimated. And jobs can be so remote from the function they serve that even when, far down the line, some other worker's life depends on the accuracy of a weld, the welder is no longer motivated to do his best work, as Marx suggested in his concept of alienation. Owners, managers, and heads of state are asking today how to get more involvement, commitment, initiative—even thinking—from workers. They are looking for other ways of dealing with people than from tower to the ring of cells.

## 6. Empathy

In its purest form, empathy has nothing to do with science. There are no controls, no click, click, click, click. This is the thesis of Elias Canetti, 1981 Nobel laureate in literature (and doctor of chemistry), in his essay on "The Writer's Profession," in *The Conscience of Words* and other writings. An empathic person does not collect people, like data, to arrange them side by side in an orderly manner. He does not regard particular individuals as so many pesky, nonrecurrent events, to be wished away in favor of classifications and norms. Empathy is an imaginative identification with another person, a kind of metamorphosis. One becomes another being, even as John Keats in the poem becomes the sparrow before his window "and picks about the grain." A wonderfully clear image of empathy and its consequences for power lies in an episode of the *Popeye* comic strip in which Olive Oyl has been stricken with the malady of "sympathetick pains." Popeye is battling his archenemy Bluto, only to discover that with each blow he lands, Olive Oyl, now suffering with Bluto, must also ("Oof!") double over in pain.

Empathy enables people to approach each other. Only by empathy can the powerful understand and help the powerless. In Dostoyevski's *The Brothers Karamazov*, Alyosha can help others because he does not "analyze from above." Alyosha had befriended the boy, Ilusha, and was seeking to give money to his father, the proud, hard-pressed, former captain, only to learn that earlier, in an altercation, Alyosha's brother Dmitri had insulted the captain grievously, and in front of the boy. Dmitri had pulled the "wisp of tow," the captain's miserable beard. To help the captain, Alyosha had to find a way to give him the money without seeming to "buy his honor." But in Dostoyevski's world to seek a strategem to help someone can be to humiliate him further—by the very presumption of making him the object of a stratagem, by "analyzing from above." Alyosha offers the money. The captain refuses the rubles,, grinding the notes in the sand beneath his heel. Alyosha, startled, soon realizes that this had to happen. The captain's pride assuaged, Alyosha is confident that a second try later will prove successful, and he is right. Alyosha sees himself in the captain, "We are all just the same as he is." That is why Alyosha is able to understand the captain and why that understanding is not cause for further insult.

It is precisely the lack of empathy, the phoney "We all have our moments of depression" that accounts for the devastating effect of Sir William Bradshaw, specialist in nerve cases, on the shell-shocked, World War I veteran in Virginia Woolf's *Mrs. Dalloway* (the quote is from what Bradshaw actually says). What Septimus encounters in the doctor's office is not someone who will listen to him, but someone exercising power— reflected in the low, grey motor car ready in front of the house, the title, the Harley Street address, and the carefully allotted office hours. The result of the interview is to speed Septimus on to his suicide. And empathy has its everyday instances. Coming into a room you might open a window for several "library rats" deep in a discussion, as Jean Paul Sartre suggested in *Search for a Method*. You find it too hot yourself. You sense that the "rats" are also uncomfortable, although so caught up in their discussion as not to take notice. You open the window to freshen things up. There are no controls here, yet there is a sense in which your inference might gain confirmation. One of the discussants might say "Hey, thanks."

If more than fictional examples are required, then consider some medical case histories offered by the empathic Dr. Oliver Sacks, in particular the case where the physician heals himself. A person who has lost a limb may continue to experience sensations as though it were still present. Sacks, in *A Leg to Stand On*, recounted his own recovery from a reverse situation, a scotoma. He had severely injured his leg and it was now healed and usable, but he no longer had any feeling of its existence. For him, the leg was gone. He could not move the limb because he did not feel it was there for him to move. Sacks' own doctor was very busy and not particularly sympathetic to his plight. Sacks described the problem in general terms in his earlier *Awakenings*, which concerned the "awakening," after fifty years of torpor, of victims of sleeping sickness through the remarkable drug L-DOPA. In cases of neurological injury or disorder, treatment requires a certain initiative on the part of the patient. He (or she) must effect a kind of integration between mind and body. There must be action, but the doctor's will, whether a command, a physical manipulation, or a chemical stimulation, will not do it alone. How is it to be done? How is the patient to be tipped into action?

Almost by accident Sacks began his own cure. Looking for diversion after long days abed, he asked a friend to bring him a tape recorder and some music cassettes. Mendelssohn's *Violin Concerto* was the only selection at hand. "Suddenly, wonderfully, I was moved by music," Sacks wrote, moved at first in spirit, then physically. At the beginning there was just a flicker, then painfully over an extended period, always with the concerto in mind, its rhythm and drive, Sacks came to walk haltingly with a stick. But the cure was not yet complete. That was accomplished another way, by a kind of practical joke (deception is not always bad). Sacks's friends knew he was fond of swimming. One of them, a physician, invited him to don trunks and to come to a pool where, suddenly, his stick snatched away, he was pushed in and challenged to a race. Sacks, outraged, found himself swimming easily and, on emerging from the pool, walking without a limp.

Empathy is a gift to humankind, like rational thought, and some people are more empathetic than others. Bentham, according to Mill, was particularly deficient in this department. "The faculty by which one mind understands a mind different from itself, and throws itself into the feelings of that other mind, was denied him by his deficiency of Imagination," Mill reported. Empathy, for Canetti, is an aspect of a more encompassing and enigmatic gift, that for metamorphosis, a general process of transforming anything into anything else. This gift is not metamorphosis in a scientific sense, something that can be studied experimentally with controls, like finding the hormones responsible for transforming caterpillars into butterflies. There is action but no periodicities, no parabolas, no trajectories—rather action as in myths, stories, and histories: transforming Narcissus into the flower, interweaving of fingers to make a basket into the construction of a basket of reeds, the wily warrior and seafarer Odysseus into an aged beggar on his homecoming, Saul into Paul on the road to Damascus, human-animal totems representing ancestors into their components of humans and animals—their descendents, the bone in Stanley Kubrick's film *2001* into weapon and then—tossed into the air—into orbiting satellite.

## 7. The Pierced and Thumbless Hand

What is the very opposite of the Panopticon, with its partitions and its inmates under central surveillance? Canetti, in *Crowds and Power*, drawing on primitive myths and narratives of travelers and anthropologists, presented the image of a primitive hunt. Ten to twenty men know each other well, know what they can expect of each other and of the animal they pursue. Eyes, arrows, and spears are directed outward toward the prey, the goal all can directly perceive. Here is a totally different basis for social relationships and the development of knowledge. The primitive hunting group is momentary, a matter of action, a shared concentration, a unit of communal excitement. "The feel of the pack is always stronger than the individual's sense of what he himself is apart from it," Canetti wrote. Distance between pack and quarry narrows for all of the hunters together. The pack produces a kind of "high," a kind of empathy.

After a successful hunt things are different. Now the stronger can take all. As a pack the hunters were united, seeking to slay the quarry that none could bring down separately. Now the hunters must separate, "never having developed," as Canetti put it, "the communal stomach which would enable them to feed as one creature." But in a common meal, each handed a piece of the slain animal, the pack has invented a rite to make up for this anatomical lack. This communion approaches, however distantly, a condition for which they all feel a need. The moment of unity is renewed. They eat together what they have caught together. They are joined by having all consumed parts of the same animal.

Conceptions of unity may include the prey as well. To depart from Canetti's schematic account, consider a remarkable doctrine of the Bering Sea Eskimos, that of the pierced and thumbless hand, as represented in motifs in ceremonial materials and hunting gear. Typical artifacts were exhibited some years ago at the Smithsonian Institution in Washington, D.C., gathered in the 1870s by Edward W. Nelson, who lived for four years among these people. One item is a dance mask to which are fastened, one on each side, two hands carved in driftwood, each with four fingers extended and a large hole in the palm (Fig. 9.3). William W. Fitzhugh and Susan A. Kaplan, in their book *Inua: Spirit World of the Bering Sea Eskimo,* explained the meaning of the motif. "The perforated hands signify the spirit's compassion for the animal he hunts, allowing some to successfully slip through his palms and return safely to their home in the sea." Lack of a thumb also makes grasping something more difficult. Once free, walruses, seals, and salmon can multiply and ensure prey for future hunts.

In his 1754 discourse on inequality, Rousseau also appealed to a primitive hunt as an instance of a joint effort, but foresaw a possibly earlier loss of unity in the joint undertaking. Savage society, for Rousseau, was intermediate between the state of nature and modern civil society. Suppose a hare were to cross the path of one of the hunters. He might be enticed from common pursuit of the deer to the individual pursuit of a prey which he could capture and eat alone. Elsewhere, however, considering the matter further, Rousseau allowed that a haunch of venison tastes better eaten in company than alone. The more spiritual Ralph Waldo Emerson forsook food in his essay "The Over-Soul," but offered another anatomical image, a communal circulatory system, to bring together his famous self-reliant spirits. The circulatory

Figure 9.3. Bering Sea Eskimo dance mask, without the feathers that were once mounted in the hoops (Catalogue No. 33107, Courtesy of the Department of Anthropology, Smithsonian Institution).

system is compared, in turn, to the global seas, "not an intersection is there anywhere in nature, but one blood rolls uninteruptedly an endless circulation through all men, as the water of the globe is all one sea, and truly seen, its tide is one." For Jimmy Boyle, once labeled "Scotland's most violent man," prison reform should begin, as he explained in *The Pain of Confinement: Prison Diaries*, with small groups of prisoners and guards sitting down and talking about the small events (like use of showers) in their lives, even having tea together.

Canetti, in *Crowds and Power*, distinguished other kinds of primitive packs. The war pack and its enemy, a second war pack, are out to vent on each other the same destruction. The lamenting pack forms when a group seeks to prevent the loss of a dying member, to hold him back because it needs his strength—or else seeks to propitiate him before he joins the possibly vengeful dead. The increasing pack seeks growth—protection of its members through an increase in numbers. It is inspired by the plentitude in nature of animals, fishes, insects, grasses, forests. Canetti sees the common meal following a hunt as an increase rite of a special kind, the people's minds are then filled with the requirements of future hunts. Certain Siberian groups treat the bear as a guest at the meal it provides and beg it to intercede on their behalf with its still living brethren.

Something in the nature of packs is imbued in American lore, in quilting bees, barn raisings, town meetings, wagon trains, cattle drives, volunteer fire departments, and the ubiquitous teams of today—football teams, A-teams, management teams, TV news teams, workers' quality circles. On the dark side, there are outlaw gangs, drug rings, cults, vigilante committees, and lynching parties.

## 8. Attack and Counterattack

The unofficial, front-line truces of World War I crystallized around meals. In *Trench Warfare: 1914–1918* Tony Ashworth thoroughly documented the way that truces were built on empathy among men of similar cultural backgrounds in similar predicaments, and led to internal struggles on both sides of trench fighters against command headquarters. Official war histories do note the well-reported Christmas Truce of 1914, arranged by soldiers at the front, but after that what Ashworth referred to as the live-and-let-live system of the trench fighters is largely ignored. Drawing on diaries, letters, reminiscences, and the literature of writers who had been at the front (Robert Graves, Herbert Read, Siegfried Sassoon, Wyndham Lewis), Ashworth showed that, alongside the carnage, local and durable truces were established up and down the line during the full four years.

Tommy and Fritz each made assumptions about the other's eating habits based on their own, and then acted on these assumptions. Tommy assumed Fritz was enjoying his breakfast, even as Tommy was. Hence, at breakfast Fritz would not shoot at Tommy, even as Tommy was too busy eating to shoot at Fritz. And, lo, if Tommy did not actually see Fritz eating, he had the evidence of a lull in the shooting during the accustomed mealtime. Behind the trenches on each side were the roads on which quartermasters brought up their ration wagons and water carts. It would have been a simple matter to shell the roads, but on the whole this was not done. Ian Hay of the 9th British Division said, "If you prevent your enemy from drawing his rations, his remedy is simple: he will prevent you from drawing yours." Tommy might just as well shell his own supply routes directly. What was going on here was an exchange of information through improvised signs and a strengthening of trust through shared experiences in repeated encounters. As one British trench fighter noted, We "had practically a code which the enemy well understood . . . [we] fired two shots for each one that came over, but never fired first."

Of course, this is not war. Indeed, it is very close to treason. Staff officers of the British High Command on visits to the front could hardly help but notice how quiet everything was and the unchallenged, occasional appearance of a German head above the parapet. The tower must get control of the cells. High command's first move was to improve sniping, to get those heads down, to destroy signs of trust, to kill more of the enemy. To this end, headquarters removed snipers from the authority of the local unit of command, the company, to that of a higher unit, the battalion. They professionalized the undertaking, sending snipers to newly established schools, where they were trained in teams of two, each serving as an observer for the other. Similar restructuring in organization—moving from local to more central authority and establishing monitoring procedures—was undertaken for the use of mortars, machine guns, and other major weapons. Where once several models of mortars were deployed, each with its own drill, one was selected and its production and use standardized. Instead of relying on apprentice-style learning in the ranks, the army began to teach the new technology and new drill from manuals in more special schools. Through centralization and standardization, headquarters proposed more forcefully to specify, and monitor, desired levels of fire.

The trench fighters struck back. The sharing of delicacies from home (food again) was one way the vulnerable trench fighters persuaded the gunners on their side to ease up on the enemy so that the enemy, in turn, would ease up on them. Snipers shot high and the action was reciprocated by snipers on the other side. Trench-mortar gunners fired into no man's land, or when they fired into enemy trenches, did so always at the same time and same place. Machine gunners fired evenly from left to right, not looping back at irregular intervals, making it less likely that they would catch unwary spotters. Musical machine gunners produced staccato bursts to represent popular music-hall tunes familiar to Germans who had worked in England, with answering choruses from machine gunners on the other side.

World War I was not only a struggle between the Allies and the Central Powers, not only a match between the technology and industry of the one side and that of the other, but also a war between trench fighters and high command, between the giving of commands and resisting them. Trench fighters and high command each developed their own knowledge systems. Local, underground, spontaneously generated knowledge—the live-and-let-live system—was rough and ready but good enough to save fighters' lives. Centrally directed, rationally developed, official knowledge was designed not only to increase fire power, but also to constrain the fighters to fight—the-kill-or-be-killed system. In the struggle between headquarters and the trenches, there was attack, counterattack, and escalation. An initiative by one side provided the necessity for a countermove by the other. The command wars are a worthy illustration of Foucault's concept of knowledge wars as developed in several of the essays in *Power/Knowledge*.

High command did finally introduce a tactic for which the trench fighters by war's end had found no answer. Night raids, a kind of coopted war pack ordered not locally but centrally, demanded a rapid sortie into no man's land to scout enemy positions. Previously, the authorities had demanded of the trench fighters that, as proof of their penetration of enemy lines, they bring back swatches of enemy barbed wire. The answer to this at one point by a British patrol was to stash a coil of wire just in front of their line. Now the authorities demanded that the troops return with enemy troops, either as prisoners or as corpses. There was no ready way to turn these commands into mock battle. Moreover, the more dedicated soldiers now had a chance to sway their fellows to more aggressive action. Violent and unpredictable, the raids destroyed the trust built by the gunnery rituals between official enemies. Returning fire was no longer a punishment for breaking a truce, two hits for one, but many hits to avenge a lost comrade.

## 9. Flexible Specialization

From Adam Smith's pin factory on, the demands of mass production were not the only factors driving technology. There was also the demand for production in small batches for rapidly fluctuating, fickle markets. An artist in the eighteenth century seeking to represent the clothing of different nationalities chose to depict the Frenchman naked, with only a pair of scissors. He was awaiting news of the latest fashion before preparing his attire. "We are the whipped cream of Europe," said an exasperated Voltaire. To produce fabrics in different patterns, not only for clothes, but also for tablecloths, bedcovers, and hangings, the choice in production was between hand-woven short runs or building a separate automatic loom for each pattern. Both were expensive propositions. How could technology help lower the cost of production? In the first decades of the nineteenth century, Joseph Marie Jacquard of Lyons, France, found the answer in the loom that bears his name, by coming up with a workable combination of several earlier developments. The basic mechanism is a series of perforated cards that serve to control the successive positions of the threads of the warp and so produce any desired pattern in the fabric. Change the cards and you get a new pattern. The procedure works much like the punched holes in a piano roll that control the successive striking of the strings to produce a tune. Change the piano roll and you get a new musical piece. Historically, music came first. Inspiration for the idea of the cards developed in part from the pegged cylinders used in music boxes.

Today, control technology is transforming military and civilian technology. Numerically controlled and fancier computer numerically controlled machine tools are direct descendents of the Jacquard loom, via the extraordinary twentieth-century achievements in electronics and in the mechanization of such mental operations as searching, sorting, and filing. A very simple example of a machine tool is the motor-driven grinding wheel the hardware man uses to cut a duplicate key using the original as a template. A very simple example of a program is to imagine the curve of the key punched into a tape as a series of $x$, $y$ coordinates and the tape then fed into a control unit to position the grinding wheel against the key blank. Starting in the 1950s, the U.S. Air Force supported a major effort by scientists at the Massachusetts Institute of Technology, working with a large computer, to develop programs and machines—so sophisticated that they operated along five, not three, coordinates—to cut dies for manufacturing complicated military aircraft. That was the military direction. Civilian use developed as a spin-off, although it is certainly possible to imagine, in some other universe, such uses developing directly. In the 1970s, the Japanese and others, building on military advances, began developing a less fancy control technology, easily programmed and suitable for the wide range of small-batch, metal-cutting tasks undertaken in the world's thousands of small and medium-sized job shops.

The development of automatic, special-purpose machinery was both caused by and the cause of division of labor. Some observers today believe that the new control technology will simply continue the trend, producing, as in the pin factory, a new line of specialties of decreasing work requirements—MIT scientist, systems analyst, programmer, machine tender. Piore and Sabel, in *The Second Industrial Divide*, on which this continued, schematic account draws, maintain to the contrary that what they call flexible specialization in machinery will be matched by flexible arrangements on the shop floor, requiring again workers who possess a general understanding of process. The military is the creature of much else besides the market, but on the civilian side, the driving force of small-batch production, resulting from volatile markets, demands broadly trained workers, who can quickly shift from task to task. Observers disagree over what is actually happening to machinists right now. Are they learning to combine special knowledge of metal working with new knowledge of writing the tunes for the machines? Or are new workers filling this need? Whatever the mix is or should be, machine tools represent a small part of contemporary developments in flexible production and, to use Marx's phrase, "variation of work."

Recent trends toward production in smaller batches include moves from mainframe computers to microcomputers; from blast furnaces to electric-arc furnaces; from petrochemical plants producing a few products by one process to what the director at Polaroid's specialty chemicals division likened to a set of "giant test tubes, arranged as in a huge laboratory to let you make whatever you want." Piore and Sabel see a pervasive flow from mass production for large, stable markets—growing increasingly less stable—to flexible specialization for smaller, volatile markets.

In 1919 the British neoclassical economist Alfred Marshall, in his *Industry and Trade,* gave the term "industrial districts" to loose associations (in the nineteenth and early twentieth century) of industries and shops, which, although competitive, gained from their contiguity. In their industrial "atmosphere," personal contact was important and idiosyncracy allowed a place. Examples, some mentioned by Marshall, included Lyon for silks; Sainte-Étienne for ribbons, hardware, and specialty steel; Solingen, Remscheid, and Sheffield for edge tools, cutlery, and specialty steel; and Philadelphia and Pawtucket for cotton goods. Drawing on Marshall and recent historical research, Piore and Sabel reported that small firms often developed new technologies without growing larger, while larger firms using sophisticated technology did not produce standardized goods. Considerations of economics mixed with considerations of community. Manufacturers, subcontractors, and employees met not only in the factory, but in church and civic organizations. In fickle markets, predictions sometimes went awry, and people in these three groups sometimes found themselves in each others' positions, which affected how they treated each other. Firms and municipal governments sponsored vocational schools and research establishments for the benefit of all. At Sainte-Étienne, firms could compete, but not in sweat labor, not by demanding extra hours of workers. The socialist city government controlled the length of the workday by regulating the hours at which the municipal power plant supplied current to the looms.

Alternate forms of production also had their idealistic and romantic partisans. In the nineteenth century, Pierre-Joseph Proudhon regarded competition and productive association as complementary, to the scorn of Marx. But Proudhon had an advantage that academic thinkers lacked—first-hand experience as an artisan and the opportunity to observe the semi-secret world of trade fraternities and mutual-aid societies. Perhaps he was in a better position than Marx to appreciate how social bonds functioned in the workplace. In turn-of-the-century America, Terence Powderly, of the Knights of Labor, with its once secret membership and secret meetings, drew on his experience as a machinist in the sophisticated shops of Pennsylvania. His master had been apprenticed for his training to George Stephenson, the early builder of locomotives. A man of deepest fellow feeling and a believer in a kind of primitive Christianity, Powderly saw the factory as but another community. He sought to establish systems of what, in *The Path I Trod,* he called "earnings sharing" and "management sharing," which sound like some contemporary proposals for reform, earnings sharing being a shade more radical than profit sharing.

For Piore and Sabel, mass production is facing increasing rigidities in manufacture and making increasing demands on governments to maintain stable market, a la Keynes. Under these evolving conditions, flexible specialization, attuned to short-run, volatile demands, may prove more efficient than mass production, giving us the second industrial divide of the title of their book. The authors look to new versions of industrial districts in the United States, Asia, and Europe, where, as in Prato, Italy workers modify even new machines to perform special tasks for local needs. The bottom line: rising productivity and technological advance are not necessarily synonymous with standardization and centralization.

## 10. Pedagogical Wars

During the heyday of the educational reforms in the 1960s, many of the innovators sought a craft approach to improvement. They wanted to be teachers, or rather master teachers, to reconsider what is worth knowing and to find out how to teach it—by working with real children for an extended period in real classrooms—and then to put the results into the hands of other teachers and other students. A special hope of MIT physicist Jerrold Zacharias, a leader in curriculum reform, was to teach in arithmetic, not only the multiplication tables, but also a full understanding of why, when you multiply two negative numbers, you get a positive number. The task for innovation was to make the understanding of signed numbers more than just rote learning and more than just something for the elite—a usable tool for all students.

Against such simple but difficult to achieve ideas were arrayed several powerful forces, as I was able to see from my vantage point as assistant to a government panel on educational research, in the Office of Science and Technology, during the Kennedy and Johnson administrations. The first opposing force was the tendency of curriculum innovators themselves to become a little too timely and clever. They sought to be virtuosos in bringing the latest scholarly advances to the earliest possible grades. Secondly, and more fundamental, was the pressure on the innovators by the private and government agencies paying for these endeavors for proof of the efficiency and efficacy of the new materials. Not only did the innovators, the master teachers, have to invent new approaches, hardly yet knowing what the possibilities were, they were supposed to set up experimental and control groups to demonstrate that what they were doing was cheaper and better than what was already in the schools. Thirdly, the school authorities, those figures in Bentham's tower, who were supposed to use the results, were not, for the most part, all that interested in why $-2 \times -2 = +4$. What they wanted were guaranteed methods to achieve foreordained results. The one thing invariably called for by educational administrators, school or college level, was the definition of a good teacher—his or her key characteristics. Once armed with the definition administrators could then identify, and schools of education could produce, teachers with those characteristics, and the job of raising student performance on standardized tests was just about done. Turn the valve, make it rain.

From the start, the Teachers & Writers Collaborative in New York City, practically the only such 1960s effort still surviving, refused the demands of the U.S. Office of Education for experimental and control groups. To their great credit, the poet Muriel Rukeyser and others in an early group sent the grants officer packing. They did not, however, get the sum of money they requested. Earlier, the National Science Foundation, in its initial support of the new high school science courses, had made no such demands for proof. Perhaps first-hand experience with experimental and control groups in the natural sciences had made NSF grants officers more dubious about their easy use in educational research. Teachers & Writers did manage to patch together support from various sources, year by year. Well-known writers associated with the effort lent it a certain credibility. Robert Silvers, editor of *The New York Review,* was chairman of the board.

Some early meetings of novelists, poets, playwrights, and essayists, held under the auspices of the Office of Science and Technology, had explored the idea of published writers teaching writing in ghetto schools. The idea was to involve creative writers in educational tasks just as research scientists earlier had been involved in preparing the new science courses. A more extended conference of writers and teachers, chaired by Herbert Kohl, who was soon to publish *36 Children* (1967) about his own experiences teaching writing in Harlem, led to the formation of the Teachers & Writers Collaborative. The writers were troubled by what they took to be an overemphasis on neatness, proper sentiments, and formal correctness; they thought they could bring authenticity of feeling and experience to the schools instead. Having wrestled with the demands of writing themselves, they felt they had something special to offer in helping others to put down on paper what they wanted say. "I would ask [the students] the questions I might ask myself if I were the author," writer Alan Ziegler was later to explain in describing (in Lopate's book noted below) how he proceeded. Of course, some teachers were already succeeding where the writers were only trying, hence the teachers in the collaborative.

Philip Lopate, in his passionate *Journal of a Living Experiment,* takes up the tale here. In the opening chapter, he found the suggestion at the earlier meetings by the Office of Science and Technology representative, that writers keep public diaries, as phrasing the writer's obligations to funding agencies "in terms that would not be inimical to their craft." For Lopate, emphasis was always on what he called "the devilishly local," particular children's knowledge of particular streets, in contrast to official, universal knowledge of socioeconomic indices. Technology had a role in the use of copying machines to reproduce students' work for other people to read—teachers, program evaluators, and other students—rather than in the use of optical scanning equipment to read responses to questionnaires and multiple-choice tests.

At the beginning, some of the writers and teachers saw a chance to fight the Vietnam War right there in the New York City School system. There was present, as seen by the writers, the same oppression, the same refusal to recognize the value of other cultures, the same crushing of local authority. And some writers were disconcertingly successful in establishing rapport with students, in starting an unofficial, counter-curriculum of writing that drew on rock music, graffiti, "the dozens," black rhythms, and disc-jockey rap. It was not long before school principals, who, after all, were not required to welcome these visitations, ceased to do so.

A second direction, emphasizing elementary rather than high school, reached its best known expression in the contributions of poet Kenneth Koch of Columbia University. Trying out all kinds of approaches in school classrooms, Koch evolved some techniques that led kids to write in ways that caught his professional ear as poetry, even when written as prose. He told Lopate, "I had people write poems about their dreams. I said: 'Dream, and write a poem about it. And also bring me a prose account of the dream.' I didn't know what was going to happen. But in almost every case the prose account was better poetry than the poetry account, and this was a wonderful way to show them that it was better to be particular, to mention names." Using the journal that Teachers & Writers had required him to keep, Koch then wrote up his approaches, publishing the experiments and results to national acclaim in *Wishes, Lies, and Dreams* and *Rose, Where Did You Get That Red?* Elated by a sense of discovery, Koch explained in Lopate's book: "I was very excited by what the children wrote. I don't know, I think I was excited the way people say they are when they make scientific discoveries. I thought I'd been fooling around in the laboratory and all of a sudden there was this cloud of pink smoke, which was really great. I thought everyone ought to know about it."

Which is just right as long as the results are available to be picked up by other teachers on a voluntary basis, leaving them free to try out further things on their own—which already would begin to redefine the profession. The trouble was, as Koch's work gained acclaim, ambitious administrators simply seized on it as a new curriculum to be imposed on teachers. On visiting schools, Lopate found bulletin boards everywhere suddenly filled with the wish poems, the lie poems, the dream poems, "like the civil examinations in ancient China where everyone had to write a poem on the same subject." Lopate proceded a third way. Limiting himself to one school, under the aegis of a sympathetic principal, he introduced what he called a team approach, a kind of pack in a system less concerned with control, but not co-opted, devoting efforts to experiments in that school. The four members of the team developed ideas for their school in its circumstances, taught children, met with other teach-ers, but did not seek to develop approaches for distant use, or repeated use, year after year. This project also could be replicated, but in a different way. It would be in the form of establishing other teams of writers—or perhaps teams of artists, film makers, composers, mathematicians—in other schools, under the aegis of other principals, on a voluntary basis. Even teaching signed numbers can have a local component: in Washington, D.C., let the Capitol be zero, then 2nd Street East is −2 and 2nd Street West is +2.

## 11. The Hacker Ethic

The hand of science draws strength from established power and fashions the basis of new power. To prove, if you do X, then you get Y, science must disturb the universe—must fashion a change and must fashion a way to hold other things equal. This requires the modest power of Wilson at Cambridge to seal pistons in cylinders; the more extensive power of Milgram to summon forth people out of the urban mass and then dismiss them when no longer needed; the still greater power of generals, corporation executives, educational administrators, and heads of government agencies to develop technology and arrange people in an orderly fashion—both to carry out their purposes and to experiment with better ways of doing so. Now, very often the necessary power for science cannot be fully achieved. Then the incomplete experiment and results are regarded as just a way station. The demand to know is the demand for greater power over things and people, power which the figures in the tower may find it in their interest to provide. Only then can science fully understand the phenomenon in question. If there is hesitation by some, the history of science and technology teaches one thing for sure, what Bentham I, with his *jeu d'esprit,* will not do, Bentham II, his successor, will.

The nightly invasion in the late 1950s and early 1960s of the MIT computer laboratory by the original software hackers and nerds is affectionately described by Stephen Levy in *Hackers*. With the connivance of several highly placed and highly unusual administrators and professors, any genius (as judged by those already there), whether a neighborhood twelve-year-old or a freshman flunking out, could join the pack. But there was an ethic. Hackers were there to improve the machines and for their own edification. Every paper tape produced went into the drawer, an actual drawer. Everyone was free to appreciate and use everyone else's "hacks." Later, as work grew more sophisticated, all agreed to foreswear the use of passwords, to keep access to their files open. This was a beautiful arrangement, but fragile. The whole setup was supported by the Defense Department—again war, or the preparation for war, crops up to assist the advance of things scientific and technical! The TX-0, PDP-1, and PDP-6 came without much software. Hackers were the foot soldiers developing the machine languages to underlie the higher-level programming languages. But DOD could not overlook indefinitely irregularities in the administration of their program, especially this matter of security, of access to files and computers.

What is more, the notion of free programs became hard to sustain once the new software became worth money to owners of computers. Conditions at the computer lab changed. Some hackers went elsewhere, some pretended not to see what was happening, some thrived, some were heartbroken.

The hacker ethic is the traditional ethic of scientific inquiry, no secrets, no holding back, building on the findings of others. But we are now in an era when a discovery in purest mathematics can have immediate implications for the designing and cracking of military codes, when observations from satellites of the earth's geology can immediately disclose good places to hide submarines. Start with cloud chambers, end with mushroom clouds. The time-lapse is shortening, the distinction is disappearing. There is today an uncanny identity between controls in science and controls in human affairs: the perfection of one is the perfection of the other. For a scientist to commit himself or herself to put everything in the drawer, in the communal stomach, and to work professionally only with colleagues who do likewise, is to make a commitment affecting that person's entire life. But only then will he not be a hypocrite when he justifies his work on the grounds of love of truth, love of a neat hack, following the argument wherever it may lead. Only then can he claim to be the graceful figure deserving the torch in Rousseau's allegory.

## 12. Anti-Science

Divinely local knowledge, unofficial knowledge, seat-of-the-pants knowledge, empathic, participatory knowledge—none of these seek the perfection of proof. Proponents of such knowledge do not have the necessary power or resources, nor do they want them. These efforts are not part of the project of science. They are anti-science in the sense that they are against the project of science, against seeking everywhere that totality of experimental controls. The term "anti-science" is appropriate because, from the perspective of science, if control is not total, if other things are not held equal, it is not science, but at best a way station. Yet proponents of anti-science are not compelled to embrace superstition. Barn-raisers can go on putting up barns. Hunters in a pack may discern each others' character and improve their knowledge of the flight pattern of their quarry. We can all go on using aspirin, electroencephalography, and Cuisinarts.

No implication is intended here that all unofficial knowledge is necessarily selfless and for human betterment. To what has been said of war packs and lynch mobs could be added much about contemporary terrorist gangs and civil strife. "Anti-science" is used in the same sense as "anti-hero" in literature. There is still a protagonist but he is not larger than life. An anti-hero recognizes that the very controls necessary for science to achieve its recurrence of the same event may mean constraint for him. He is among the elements destined to be held constant, to be placed alongside other elements in orderly fashion.

There is nothing on this earth quite like the scorn in high scientific circles heaped on anyone appealing during the course of an investigation to empathy, to measures not amenable to further refinement. Some investigators are renowned for ingenuity in experimental design, but certain others for a talent for empathy—Sandor Ferenczi in analysis, Alexander Luria in neurology, Bruno Bettelheim at his school for autistic children, the Swiss zoologist and zookeeper Heini Hediger with animals. But such efforts at understanding depend for replication on that special person. Where is the valve that anyone can turn? At the end of *A Leg to Stand On*, Sacks expressed growing frustration as he recounted how one's every empathy initiative becomes in turn the subject of someone else's attempt at mechanization.

Simone Weil, in her 1940–1941 essay on *The Iliad*, wrote of the "marvelous indifference" with which the strong can regard the weak. From the tower they can see no resemblance between themselves and the occupants of the cells. They have no time for stories. And few technical persons are ever prepared to see themselves as the subject of Hawthorne's strictures in the entry for 1844 in his *Notebooks*:

The Unpardonable Sin might consist in a want of love and reverence for the Human Soul; in consequence of which, the investigator pried into its dark depths, not with a hope or purpose of making it better, but from a cold philosophical curiosity—content that it should be wicked in whatever kind or degree, and only desiring to study it out. Would not this, in other words, be the separation of the intellect from the heart?

No one thinks he is Bentham II.

## 13. The Giant

In one of the delusions of that poor madman Daniel Paul Schreber, his case celebrated in the psychoanalytic literature from Freud's essay onward, a giant comes to absorb a crowd of tiny men who, like so many insects or bats, had been constantly fussing about him. This fantasy is reminiscent of the frontispiece of Thomas Hobbes's *Leviathan* (1651), which depicts in its upper half a giant whose torso and limbs are fabricated out of a multitude of tiny men, assembled in an orderly manner, attention directed upward toward the crowned head (Fig. 9.4). Hobbes sought what Foucault in *Power/Knowledge* described as "the distillation of a single will from the particular wills of a multiplicity of individuals." The distilled will is the heart, or rather, the head, of the giant. Each of the midgets in the multitude possesses a modicum of power—for Hobbes, power is a commodity that can be traded—and they transfer this power to the sovereign. Each midget does so under the condition that all the other midgets do likewise. This is the social

Figure 9.4. Frontispiece to the first edition of Hobbes's *Leviathan*.

contract. The giant wields a sword in his good right hand to ensure compliance with the contract, to prevent escape from his body of the tiny figures, and so prevent a return to the condition of all fighting all, which Hobbes saw as being to the detriment of all.

The thinkers stressed in this essay, Foucault and the lesser-read and cited Canetti—and Friedrich Nietzsche could have been added—looked on power differently. Rather than analyze the distillation of wills, these thinkers focus on the crowd of bodies which have become peripheral subjects as a result of the effects of power. For these thinkers, power is not a separate something that can be traded like a commodity. Rather it exists only as exercised, only in action, as in the action into which Sacks was tipped to effect his final cure. Power circulates through the arteries of the giant to the capillaries. And what are the capillaries but the familiar human spaces of board rooms, shop floors, neighborhoods, battlefields, homes, and research laboratories? Hobbes asked by what right one person got to tell another what to do, and his answer was, by virtue of the social contract. Foucault and others now ask instead, how does one person get another to do his will? Canetti sees in Schreber's image the mechanism of subjection—the diminution of men. Reduction in size starts with simple gestures, postures (some standing while others sit or kneel or bow), seating arrangements, jokes, time-motion studies, questionnaires (some can ask, others must answer)—action in the capillaries. Instead of a distillation of wills, the giant is seen as the incorporation of souls.

Two brief digressions before concluding will be helpful. Ever since Achilles, at certain moments in the exercise of power, those in charge have found it hard to distinguish between the enemies without and their own subjects—Achilles, whose dream of comradeship was that all his troops should perish in the conquest of Troy so that he and Patroclus alone would share the glory. Hobbes distrusted the individual conscience, hence his elevation of the sovereign. We distrust authority, hence the search for ways to keep open access between people, such as that opened by the gods between Achilles and Priam.

Milan Kundera, in the 1982 preface to his *The Joke,* asked ironically why it was banned in 1968 (one year after publication) in Czechoslovakia. After all, he said, it was "*merely* a novel." The answer, as he explained in his essay, "The Novel and Europe," is that what novels offer is "the wisdom of uncertainty." By its mere existence, its unauthorized authorship, a novel expresses resistance. Novels cannot be used by superior forces. There are no results, no valves to turn, no final interpretation. Uncertainty has its strength.

What is the Panopticon, of which perhaps too much has already been made, but the giant become rationalized and mechanized, with the tower as its head and no space for pesky insects and bats. If never built in stone as designed by Bentham, the Panopticon exists today in the centralization, standardization, and normalization that characterizes so much of our industrial and scientific life. In the age of knowledge complexes, perfection of proof has become perfection of the Panopticon. Yet some people are not all that ready to become Lilliputians. And some Lilliputians may seek to transform themselves back into full-sized men and women. Against the question "how does one person get others to do his will?" may be posed the question "how do others come to resist that will?" Local, unofficial, grass-roots knowledge can be a precursor to the perfection of proof, but it can also oppose such perfection. There is attack, counterattack, and escalation. Opposing systems of knowledge develop as each side advances to match the advances of the other—in production wars, command wars, pedagogical wars. Struggles are pervasive, and now we can look forward to the war of the genes—the search for perfect genes via genetic engineering versus the uncertain determination of characteristics of offspring through choice of spouse by what used to be called, to rightly emphasize a different causality, personal chemistry.

And yet there is a saving lack of symmetry in these wars. Writers in the schools did not want to be superintendents. Hackers were not seeking big bucks. Advances in flexible specialization did not depend on enlarging the market. Trench fighters were not striving to be generals. And General George Washington was actively striving not to be king, as Gary Wills so ably demonstrated in *Cincinnatus: George Washington and the Enlightenment*. Like the Roman hero and Rousseau's ideal of the lawgiver, Washington studied how to turn over the power to others, to retire to his place in the country. Anti-science does not seek to occupy the tower, but rather to knock out partitions for common rooms and to establish escape routes. The result is the architecture of communal stomachs and pierced hands.

# Bibliography

Ashworth, Tony. *Trench Warfare,, 1914–1918: The Live and Let Live System.* New York: Holmes & Meier, 1980.

Bentham, Jeremy. "Panopticon; or, the Inspection-House." *The Works of Jeremy Bentham.* Vol. 4. Edited by John Bowring. 1843. Facsimile reprint New York: Russell & Russell, 1962.

Boyle, Jimmy. *The Pain of Confinement: Prison Diaries.* London: Pan Books, 1985.

Canetti, Elias. *Crowds and Power.* Translated by Carol Stewart. New York: Seabury Press, 1978.

———. "The Writer's Profession." *The Conscience of Words.* Translated by Joachim Neugroschel. New York: Seabury Press, 1979.

Dostoyevsky, Fyodor. *The Brothers Karamazov.* Translated by Constance Garnett. New York: Random House, Modern Library.

Emerson, Ralph Waldo. "The Over-Soul." *Essays by Ralph Waldo Emerson.* New York: Thomas Nelson & Sons.

Enthoven, Alain C. "The Rand Experiment and Economical Health Care." *The New England Journal of Medicine,* 7 June 1984.

Fitzhugh, William W., and Kaplan, Susan A. *Inua: Spirit World of the Bering Sea Eskimo.* Washington, D.C.: Smithsonian Institution, 1982.

Foucault, Michel. *Discipline and Punish: The Birth of the Prison.* Translated by Alan Sheridan. New York: Random House, Vintage Books, 1979.

―――. *Power/Knowledge: Selected Interviews and Other Writings 1972–1977.* Edited by Colin Gordon. Translated by Colin Gordon, Leo Marshall, John Mepham, and Kate Soper. New York: Pantheon Books, 1980.

Hawthorne, Nathaniel. *The American Notebooks.* Edited by Claude M. Simpson. Columbus: Ohio State University Press, 1972.

Hobbes, Thomas. *Leviathan Or The Matter, Forme and Power of A Common Wealth Ecclesiasticall and Civil.* 1651. Facsimile reprint. Menston, Yorkshire: Scolar Press, 1969.

Koch, Kenneth. *Wishes, Lies, and Dreams: Teaching Children to Write Poetry.* New York: Harper & Row, 1971.

―――. *Rose, Where Did You Get That Red? Teaching Great Poetry to Children.* New York: Random House, Vintage Books, 1973.

Kundera, Milan. *The Joke.* New York: Harper & Row, 1982.

―――. "The Novel and Europe." *The New York Review of Books,* 19 July 1984.

Levy, Stephen. *Hackers: Heroes of the Computer Revolution.* Garden City, New York: Anchor Press/Doubleday, 1984.

Lopate, Philip, ed. and commentator. *Journal of a Living Experiment: A Documentary History of the First Ten Years of Teachers and Writers Collaborative.* New York: Teachers & Writers, 1979.

Manning, Willard G., et al. (Rand Corporation group). "A Controlled Trial of the Effect of a Prepaid Group Practice on Use of Services." *The New England Journal of Medicine,* 7 June 1984.

Marshall, Alfred. *Industry and Trade.* London: Macmillan, 1919.

Marx, Karl. *Capital.* Vol. 1. Edited by Frederick Engels. Translated by Samuel Moore and Edward Aveling. New York: International Publishers, 1967.

Masters, Roger D. *The Political Philosophy of Rousseau.* Princeton: Princeton University Press, 1968.

Milgram, Stanley. *Obedience to Authority: An Experimental View.* New York: Harper & Row, 1974.

Mill, John Stuart. *Utilitarianism, On Liberty, Essay on Bentham.* Edited with an Introduction by Mary Warnock. New York: New American Library, 1974.

Piore, Michael J., and Sabel, Charles F. *The Second Industrial Divide: Possibilities for Prosperity.* New York: Basic Books, 1984.

Powderly, Terence Vincent. *The Path I Trod: The Autobiography of Terence V. Powderly.* New York: Columbia University Press, 1940.

Rousseau, Jean-Jacques. *A Discourse Upon the Origin and the Foundation of the Inequality Among Mankind.* The Harvard Classics, vol. 34. New York: P. F. Collier & Son, 1910.

―――. *Discours sur les Sciences et les Arts.* Edited with Commentary by George R. Havens. New York: Modern Language Association, 1946.

Sacks, Oliver. *Awakenings.* Rev. ed. New York: E. P. Dutton, Obelisk, 1983.

―――. *A Leg to Stand On.* New York: Simon & Schuster, Summit Books, 1984.

Sartre, Jean-Paul. *Search for a Method.* Translated with an Introduction by Hazel E. Barnes. New York: Random House, Vintage Books, 1968.

Weil, Simone. "The *Iliad,* Poem of Might." *The Simone Weil Reader.* Edited by George A. Paniches. New York: David McKay, 1977.

Whitehead, Alfred North. *An Introduction to Mathematics.* New York: Henry Holt, 1911.

Wills, Gary. *Cincinnatus: George Washington and the Enlightenment.* Garden City, New York: Doubleday, 1984.

Wilson, Ch. Th. R. "On the Cloud Method of Making Visible Ions and the Tracks of Ionizing Particles. In *Les Prix Nobel en 1927,* edited by V. Carlheim-Gyllensköld et al. Stockholm: Imprimerie Royale, P. A. Norstedt & Söner, 1928.

Woolf, Virginia. *Mrs. Dalloway.* New York: Harcourt, Brace, 1925.

# 10

# Conclusion: A Manifesto of Reconstructive Knowledge

## MARCUS G. RASKIN

The knowledge worker at the end of the twentieth century can discover the insight of Cratylus. The world— that is, the world we communicate about—is transformed by description of it. Knowledge workers shape the social organization in which our inquiries about nature take place. And our cognitive understandings of the world are manufactured, indeed, usually *man*-ufactured. This being so, what can knowledge workers, men and women, do and be aware of once they comprehend their own power and prejudices as these relate to the terrifying situation in which humankind finds itself?

We are best advised if we begin by embracing modesty and limits rather than the modern belief in endless frontiers to conquer. We are required to be aware that (a) empirical descriptions are limited. They are like photographs that give a momentary appearance of *vérité*. But that truth or "fact" is invariably much less than what meets the eye. The camera is limited to what the eye sees for a specific moment and the developer chooses to develop. Similarly what we see and how we describe the world is filtered through the researcher's screen of preconceptions, needs, and the social framing system in which a particular piece of research is conducted and considered valid. While the assumption is that scientific laws are "true," more precisely they are *valid* according to an undefined or unanalyzed set of social propositions which are brought to the experiment or inquiry. It is also true that once the "matter" is described, those who describe it—and the rest of us—reciprocally are defined by the material object described. We see the object in a new way, and the new way of seeing the object results in the formation of social structures which are meant to match the new way of seeing the object. Thus, for example, the medical decision that particular symptoms exist as a disease syndrome results in a new form of social organization as for example, Fleck shows in the case of syphilis.[1]

(b) Our conception (that is, humanity's conceptions) of scientific laws changes under different conditions according to what people see and choose to see. Just as matter itself changes through time, so knowledge workers see different aspects to matter; physicists "construct" subatomic matter in continuously different ways. The result is that even in physics there is a social reality, admittedly constructed, which impinges upon physical reality. Yet physical reality also demands its reciprocal price, for now it demands that once discovered it no longer remain inert. Instead it plays an active role in our social organization. Thus, Einstein's $e = mc^2$ soon made demands on how his contemporaries organized their governments and enemies alike.

(c) Over the long run, scientific knowledge tends to yield different emphases according to the gender, class, and race of knowledge workers. This fact should be included in terms of its relevance to the inquiry under consideration so that it is weighted in the judgment process by other knowledge workers. This will help us obtain the most reasoned analyses and explanations of empirical data and conclusions from such data. It will help in the creation of sciences that relate matter and human beings to one another within the inquiry itself.

(d) It follows that even if we were to widen the screen of consideration, thereby moving from a problematic mode of inquiry to a dialectical or organic mode, we must still recognize that the possibilities of proof are limited. The reason is that in the last analysis proof is a subjective sentiment overladen with social fashions which emphasize one type of "proof" over another at any particular historical time, for differing human needs and purposes. It would appear that David Hume's objections about cause cannot be transcended in any specific discipline or subspecialty of knowledge.

In sociological terms the dominant class seeks to develop knowledge skills according to its needs. For example, conservatives "set up" sociologists to do experiments which reinforce the idea of nonredistribution of income. The problem for oppressed classes is that they do not have the power, or the resources and institutions, to redefine the knowledge project of the society to include their needs and understandings of the world. The fundamental importance of American pragmatism and socialist thought was that, notwithstanding the inherent conservatism of the universities, the work of thinkers such as Dewey and Marx produced whole new agendas on inquiry which included concern for the oppressed classes.

(e) The human crisis around survival in every sphere of our existence (that is, from problems raised by the possibilities of nuclear annihilation to toxic poisoning of the atmosphere, to outrageous inequalities between rich and poor to possibilities of world famine and lingering totalitarianism) creates the ethical need for knowledge workers continuously to analyze their conscious and unconscious decisions any of which may doom future generations. It is only recently that some knowledge workers, including scientists, have begun to see themselves as trustees for future generations.

One way to serve as good trustees is through a rethinking of the meaning we give to facts and values. Another is for knowledge workers to comprehend clearly the limits and lacunae of their respective disciplines, including unproved assumptions which underlie them. Knowledge workers need to introduce a radical and continuous consideration of human location points (values) as they relate to the definition of the scientific project and of its situational setting beyond the laboratory—and including the supposedly irrelevant aspects of the laboratory. Values themselves are location points. That is to say, they are socially designated places which may, or may not, relate to motion points—that is, structured cognitions of the past which we believe govern our technical and social understanding of the world. Obviously, location points are also in continuous flux; and while their place seems to be less fluid, they too give way through time. Nevertheless, except through external turbulence, location points are less likely to change since they are the props of behavior for cultural and social systems which indeed may outlast any particular political revolution.

Why would we now want to call facts and values "location" and "motion points"? The words *fact* and *value* do not tell us of their transient character and their interdependent links. Values and facts come with the baggage of solidity, which for most people not involved in inquiry appears unchanging and cumulative. They do not carry with them the idea of fields of relationships which are in continuous flux and which must include those doing the inquiry as well. If we posit the image that facts should be thought of as motion points and values as location points, both hovering around one another and indeed complementary to each other, we are able to see their fluid and changeable character. If we accept this characterization of facts and values, it furthers the creation of a mode of dialogue and meaning to objectivity which include the relevance of subjective understandings and those impinging social relationships and language uses which shape reality.

The creation of continuous dialogues (and forums for them), operating in nonhierarchic ways and free-wheeling in character, allows for the consideration of seemingly nonrigorous questions, such as human consequences and subjective feelings.

Such dialogues are not thought relevant to the discussions which take place in and around particular disciplines of knowledge. The consequence of this attitude is that the acquisition of knowledge and the modes of inquiry that are fashioned are not critical in the sense that they are not self-analytic and do not help in the task of framing and delimiting our multiple human social problems. They are power oriented, with the powerful framing questions and dictating answers through institutions which at first appear autonomous and neutral but which in social reality operate as factories for the holding companies of power. The result is that, without critical and reconstructive analysis, knowledge is used as the stabilizer of the ongoing social system. It is, as I have pointed out in *Being and Doing*,[2] colonizing in its effect. Yet there are contradictions.

Despite all the attempts at propping up old style authority and fundamental explanations of cause, the present period is one of indeterminacy. It should not be a surprise that this sentiment finds its way into the very foundations of the knowledge enterprise itself. For example, in the United States (in part as a result of political and social movements that seek the extension of personhood and dignity, and partly because of the revolutionary character of technology) various thinkers and movements want to locate humankind on a path marked by beliefs, logics, methods, and discourses which challenge those ideas that buttress the comfortable notion that institutions and assumptions are "settled" without need of challenge, reformulation or reconstruction. Indeed, the profound intellectual program of John Dewey was intended to open such inquiry at our universities. The realities now are different. Universities and academic disciplines alike are strangling under two needs.

One is the requirement of ever-increasing capital investment for experiment and maintenance and the other is the conventionalist grip of false "rigor." In the first case inquiry has fused with technology, and the illusion is created that the more funds are spent on equipment the more likely scientific ends will be served. The second problem of university disciplines is the continuing quest for rigor. For conventionalists, rigor is the armor plate against fraud, against upstarts, and against the Right. Its proponents are strong believers in the scientific method, although when they are pressed on the character of that method, or on the meaning of the facts and theories gathered through that method, one finds that the proofs are more likely to come back to subjectivism and guild or peer authority. Much of the power of this position rests on capturing the idea of objectivity for its armor. Its adherents deny that value judgment and presuppositions affect their experiments or data. There is a religious belief in the truth value of "facts" and empirical research without much (if any) attention paid to how a fact becomes one or what its hidden determinants are. Curiously, while facts are presented as holy, the guild assumption in the social and physical sciences is that facts have little lasting weight. To think otherwise would of course disrupt the modern process of inquiry. Thus, the believers in empiricism know that the historic facts in any discipline of knowledge a generation later are often categorized as the artifacts of an earlier generation because they are viewed through a different material and ideational lens. Whether the proponents of rigor and objectivity follow the principles of induction or the style of falsifiability (which remains fashionable) there is agreement between their respective advocates that values are to be treated as exogenous to the consideration of the experiment or inquiry even though the experiment or inquiry is a deep reflection of either the society's needs, or the needs of a particular grouping within the society, usually that group which has amassed power. At the universities the conventionalists are fearful of widening a particular inquiry beyond a narrow boundary.

Is there a reason for the fear that other methodologies would have to be adopted?—methodologies which include, as it were, a methodology of ends and therefore consideration of questions far beyond any specific discipline into the nature of the society itself and practical theories of action? The intellectual fear is that if any particular question under inquiry is not limited and not framed as a problem, the scientific project will be utterly transformed. This fear, of course, has its roots in reality. But it begs the question which now has to be asked: why shouldn't the scientific project be transformed? Politically scientists hold to the view that what a scientist does as a citizen is different or irrelevant to what he or she does in the study or laboratory. It is also held that while some may argue one way or the other on questions of value, there is an accepted system of proof—standards and means to tell the true from the false in the scientific program. This system stands against the onslaught of those who approach science with their own political and intellectual agenda. For the conventionalist model to be believable there must be a shared sense of illusion about reality and cause. Scientists need to accept the profoundly religious notion that there is a uniformity to nature which excludes humankind's operations in and on it. Yet since the eighteenth century what is uniform is not nature but humanity's need to use and conquer it. We are inclined to accept surface explanations and relationships as the sound ones. For understanding nature we are less likely to look at cause and more likely to adopt words and concepts which are verbally and logically consistent and coherent. We hope that by adopting a coherent picture of nature it will not be obvious or necessary to transform the social structure under which we make judgments about nature. In our time, a phrase so pregnant with social meaning as "it works" becomes the pragmatic proof of the inquiry or the scientific and technological phenomenon under consideration.

Those of a politically liberal cast of mind may be counted on to champion this point of view, for it has within itself an authority pattern of proofs and verifying systems through technology which are justified in economically functional terms and terms of immediate utility. The "it works" mentality plays to several audiences simultaneously. The first is those who are involved in paying for the research inquiry. The second is the state. The third is the group of knowledge workers who are competing within the same frame of reference and who have adopted the same language system of description. The fourth (in the United States) is the media, both the lay press and the scholarly journals. The success of "it works" thought is that it appears to be scientific, but functions in thoroughly political ways, favoring and reinforcing the pyramidal authority of society. This method in the United States has been championed throughout the twentieth century by a vulgar pragmatic scientism which encourages everyone to emulate "scientific methods" divorced from ends in ways that John Dewey, late in his life, thought reprehensible.

Social scientists were called upon to adopt the ways of the natural scientists in conception and execution. But an irony within democracy is that pluralism and scientific dominance are contradictory. The assumption that the so-called scientific explanation is the correct one leaves much to be desired, especially when we come to reconstruct the actual modes by which facts and theories are determined in the sciences. For nonscientists it is hard to face up to the reality that scientific theories are themselves by nature faulty and incomplete. (Indeed, this recognition is the strength of science.) The growth of scientific knowledge by contradicting other scientific knowledge is the dogma and the strength of the system. But it is not clear that any one scientific theory is better than a religious/scientific theory of explanation. This must be one reason why Isaac Newton kept a set of books on the religious and the occult, attempting to explain the existence of God, the unity of the universe, and other metaphysical questions.

In our time we have been treated to the continuing tension between religion and science but without clearly understanding why there should be such a contradiction. Let us take even the most pedestrian case. Darwinian theory, for example, may be more satisfying to one group of people whereas creationism may be more satisfying to another group. The capacity of either theory to predict the future evolution of humankind is notoriously restricted, and their respective capacities to reconstruct the past out of fragmentary evidence can only be partially satisfying to anyone. Without facing the fundamentally limited character of what we know of nature and without acknowledging that how we "construct" nature is utterly involved with the dominant styles of political behavior at one particular moment, we miss the clear interlinks between that which we cause to be seen and our cognitive constructions of what and how we look at things. The dominant political attitudes and world views decide the character of the experiment and, as Koyre points out, the meaning of it. This view rejects the idea or possibility of Cartesian and Kantian objectivity, both of which assert a knowledge of mind separate from body and a means of protection of mind behind the walls of academic or bureaucratic life which ostensibly is autonomous in the inquiry and expression of knowledge. Such views may be criticized from a reconstructive stance, pointing to future struggles which may emerge in centers of thought. Some people will be puzzled as to why certain scientists, for example, will side with the establishment center in debates where one might have thought they would have dissented. It is because they have construed "freedom" for all the professional members of the university and guild as a vested interest rather than as a project whose ends might foreclose the freedom of others. For example, SDI research might both cause nuclear war and commit the vast majority of scientists to frame their researches according to Defense Department specifications because, as Willie Sutton, the bank robber said, "that's where the money is."

This would tend to explain a split among scientists on issues one would have thought liberal-minded scientists would have agreed on. On one side was the grass roots attempt to move nuclear war research out of Cambridge, Massachusetts because of its potential negative consequences to free inquiry, while the other claimed the research to be immoral. In the political struggle between both sides, established scientists who fear and loathe the arms race and nuclear war could not bring themselves to change the character of their intellectual research enterprise or the nature of the university which housed them. Thus, they supported military and corporate groups who successfully argued for the continuation of war research under the flag of academic freedom.

In 1975 at Asilomar, California, biological scientists courageously pointed out the possible negative effects of continuing phage experiments with *E. coli*, the bacteria most commonly found in our intestines. Their concern stimulated nonscientists, who concluded that they had a right to enter into decision making (even though they were merely grassroots citizens) with scientists on the implications and possible consequences of their research. Scientists withdrew their doubts about the research as they witnessed an "invasion of the townies," who questioned two pieces of scientific armor, namely peer review and federal standards that were propounded by fellow scientists inside the bureaucracy. It was no mystery as to why scientists favored the bureaucratic approach to regulation, if there had to be any regulation. Academic scientists would be able to influence the various boards where scientists often sit in the dual role of judge and claimant. Of course by the middle seventies there were eighty-six laboratories that wanted to do DNA research and no fewer than nine pharmaceutical companies. Academic scientists sought to continue their work on genetic engineering, exchanging genes from one species to another, perhaps increasing, according to George Wald, the chances for new types of cancer as well as contagious disease especially among newborns and those who have sterile bowels as a result of antibiotics.[3] While in the early seventies there was concern among genetic scientists about whether scientists should be in the business of redesigning living things or "whole complex organisms," that concern has waned both on the part of scientists and government regulators. "Sweetheart" arrangements with business firms which now pay directly for the salaries of professors and in exchange own their scientific output are surrounded with the ideological armor that scientific method and rationality cannot and should not include the ends or purposes of the activity. In the context of the so-called technology of gene splicing, the three horsemen of social legitimacy, bureaucratic authority, and guild accreditation teamed up with the profit motive and military "requirements" to dictate the scientific program within the laboratory. Even more important, these phantoms become the guardians to decide what is thought of as rational and prudent public policy.

Because of the dangers which may threaten laboratory technicians, their families, or the population at large, conventionalists might favor administrative and regulatory limits on the activities of the scientist in the laboratory. But these limits should also be judged in terms of the nature of freedom and control in the society. Indeed, from the aspect of political freedom we will find that it will make far more sense to proscribe certain types of experiments just because carrying them out will require enormous controls over the laboratory and new forms of policing of the laboratory, the university, and society. These policing systems add of course to the hierarchic and bureaucratic nature of society, in which new controls have to be implemented to reduce physical danger. Presently continuation of such experiments is thought to be the inherent right of the scientist and the corporation under the theory of academic and business freedom. But the nature of the experiments and their implications are control formulations. That is, they are concerned with control over the future of humankind. It should not be surprising that regulatory and police controls will accompany them. Given this likelihood, from the position of ensuring democratic freedom, certain experiments should be terminated just because their effects will be to diminish the exercise of social freedom.

The Right is only tangentially concerned with social freedom. Its relation to the knowledge project is to ensure the protection of political authority with the reinforcement of settled accepted knowledge and the shaping of new knowledge to the exercise of power as it exists for the few against the many. The Right has also hurled its missiles at the carefully crafted citadel of the established sciences. There are distinct but overlapping strands to the rightist attack. For example, there is the work of political thinker Leo Strauss, who criticized the social sciences and empiricism from the standpoint of platonic elitism and the tyranny of the text as interpreted by the teacher or authority figure. For Strauss, education is a waste of time for most people because it is only the few who can or should be educated beyond a particular task. Other quarters in the Right hold that science must never contradict the plan of the creator, for the creator has specific views of harmony, stability, and hierarchy, all of which manifest themselves in an ascendant order of nature with man the highest creature and in a harmonious society where the rich, wellborn, and powerful are to retain societal control from one generation to the next. According to this view, nature's forms are copies of the master forms for which the Creator has made noble man (as distinct from woman) responsible.

For the Right, scientific work is the practical means to prove the importance of idealism over materialism. It embraces essences at the expense of the human being—a recipe for modern-day totalitarianism.

The belief in fixed essential forms of course has a long history in philosophy and social thought. Platonists have had the disturbing habit of yoking knowledge to reactionary power in order to protect class privilege. Essential forms and eternal truths are the ideological wrapping for any class that does not want to analyze itself and its purposes. The cultural war which is being waged by the various rightist groups from Reverend Sun Myung Moon to the neoconservatives of the Irving Kristol stripe is meant to assure that the scientific project fulfills capitalist and military needs. Whether this is consciously stated, as in the case of Moon and his acolytes, or understood without the formal contract being written among the parties of the Right (as in the case of the relationship between former socialists turned troubadours for capitalism and militarism and the less prudent leaders of the national security state), their roles are clearly defined as justification and defense of the State and Capital.

In science we have had the political/scientific work of Teller on the hydrogen bomb and that of his disciples pushing SDI. Earlier we were treated to the work of missile and hydrogen bomb computation by John von Neumann. These men not only have supplied the advertising brochures for the state, they supplied the missiles themselves. It should not be surprising therefore that Reverend Moon has been able to rally some Nobel laureates to his cause. While Galileo was not prepared to kneel before Cardinal Bellarmine and the Catholic church, it seems that some of our more creative scientists, including Eugene Wigner, are prepared to share their visions of God and immaterial reality with Moon. (I might add at this point that criticism of Moon is not meant to endorse the government's miscarriage of justice in his tax evasion case.) Given the political realities behind the positions taken by our scientists and many of the professoriat, the question to pose is whether or how the terms of the reconstructive program would change the nature of the scientific project, bringing it into line with the rather attractive idea that knowledge workers are trustees for nature and civilization, and for unborn and unseen generations.

It is obvious that a massive psychological shift willl have to occur among knowledge workers, and especially scientists, to get them to realize where their experiments or the products of their experiments are presently located in the current social situation, thereby getting ourselves to relocate their inquiries, their purposes, and the nature of what they are trying to explain. In recent years one scientist frightened for civilization, the physicist Charles Schwartz of the University of California at Berkeley, has urged that physicists stop teaching physics of any kind so that the fundamental knowledge base of that discipline would not be used as a dagger at the throat of humanity.[4] But perhaps this step does not have to be taken. Instead, it should be possible to formulate computer programs relating social and ethical considerations to the experimental process and giving the knowledge worker/scientist guides, questions, and symbols for discourses so that they become aware of the implications of what they are doing. These discourses would, of course, be publicly debated. If knowledge workers open the doors of their laboratories and buildings to outsiders for dialogue about their work (why they are doing what they are doing), science and technological application will improve because questions not otherwise asked will be asked and the vibrancy of the scientific project will be that much greater. But these questions are to be asked by new players in the task of inquiry. It requires that the most improbable now participate in the dialogue of the laboratory to determine effects from personal health to telos, ultimate purpose. Such a change in the project of science will necessitate that our knowledge workers acquire independence and new relationships beyond those established between the funding nexus of the military and the great corporations on one side, the university playing a brokerage role in the middle, and knowledge workers on the other side. They will have to relate to constituencies and groups coming to consciousness, having struggled for new modes of liberation and egalitarian interdependence whether in Poland, among people in the Third World, or among women and workers in the United States. But these groups must seek and sustain this consciousness from one generation to another. If this occurs, the likelihood of reconstruction and liberation being sustained is much greater. The system of pyramidal control is progressively effective with human beings unless they can be totalized and infantilized so that they learn only particular things which are "performative functions," while ideas of what they do—consciousness of their situation—are pushed into the recesses of the unconscious, replaced by corporate or state dream fantasies.

Similarly, the handling and abuse of nature as a thing rather than a generative process is also bound to failure, for it assumes that rationality, compulsion, and control are inseparable. At some future time my view may be proved wrong if ultimate forms of compulsion are used successfully to protect colonizing domination without a liberatory consciousness being sustained. On the other hand, my view may be wrong if ultimate forms of liberation surpass my vision so completely that my views can only be seen as part of the old order, however important as midwives to an era of freedom.

But for our time there is enough empirical evidence to support those like myself who hold that the limits of domination are and will be continuously broken. One may look at the bewildered expressions on the faces of scientists in the space program or white racists in South Africa, or Kremlin bureaucrats as they contemplate resistance to their work or policies. I am aware that my view may only be correct as a myth which can be contradicted with other examples, but it is a profoundly important myth-finding which sustains the human attribute of the need for freedom and the necessity of escaping the organized mass murder of nuclear war. This modern myth carries with it an ensemble of operational truths upon which humane scientific and political endeavor can be conducted. This myth requires the reconceptualization of values to location points so that we may recenter ourselves, judging what we may do as human beings in our personal lives, work, and social role functions. We will open up hidden and seemingly unrelated questions which are central to the experiment or scientific inquiry that is under consideration. Through this process, framing questions will be asked which are meant to unravel hidden relationships so that ethical and empirical judgments can be made—questions which will transcend present capitalist definitions of profit and productivity.

Framing questions may deal with every issue from the anthropology of the laboratory and its internal social structure to the contradictory evidence which is discarded (and why) to the economic structure which supports the project to the epistemological underpinnings of both the social structure and the operations of the scientist, including determinants and modes of reporting experiments and inquiries which frame their future meaning and relevance to other scientific inquiries. Substantively, it includes the reanalysis of chemical and biological processes that comprise modern technology so that a clearer understanding of genetic and medical effects on present and future generations may be known.

Who are now the audience and the creative actors of scientific inquiry? The explosion of research has made it necessary for most scientists themselves to be passive audiences, taking on faith or without skepticism the mixed results and ambiguity of scientific inquiry. The greater the ambiguity (and the more obvious it is that knowledge and scientific inquiry are utterly determined through the institutions of the society) the more we will hear about the objectivity of science and the need for it. But the onslaught against objectivity now has a psychological component. Is there not a role that the unconscious plays in scientific and technological work? Park Teter has posed a direct challenge to objectivity by insisting on the importance of the unconscious and the "collective unconscious" as a fundamental dynamic in framing what we say and how we describe the physical events of the universe. Metaphoric conceptions of reality by scientists have three purposes. First of all, because scientists use and create specialized symbols as well as everyday language in their descriptions of physical reality, it is not surprising that phrases which have multiple meanings find their way into scientific description. Indeed, one might go further and wonder whether what we describe to each other is always only emblematic and ambiguous. Each mind brings to someone else's analysis its own meaning which is then added to the group's meaning. It is also obvious that literary or aesthetic descriptions play an important part in the manner the great scientists of the early twentieth century looked at the world. Teter thinks Bohr embraced complementarity because of a wish to have a happy complementary marriage. While this may appear to be far fetched it should be noted that the sociologist Lewis Feuer argued that the conception of complementarity was an age old literary myth which surfaced in Danish literature. Supposedly it was this idea of complementarity which gave Bohr the metaphor picture to be described iconically and mathematically in physics. In comprehending the deep means by which we project our human yearnings onto nature we must conclude that any epistemo-logical and logical rigor can only be helpful through inclusion of the seemingly irrelevant rather than through methods of exclusion which deprecate the evidence that doesn't fit or presses evidence (humanly derived) and theories (humanly constructed) into a procrustean box of formal logic. For generations, conscious efforts were made in Western science to split material data and events into a constructed reality which recognized primary data while decreeing that certain data, color, taste, for example, were secondary to measurement and sight. But a recon-struction of knowledge may require a reexamination of the categories of "primary" and "secondary." There is little doubt that the development of science suffered when it consigned as secondary those attributes of materiality which give a "thing" special meaning to the observer beyond that of size and shape. Teter's thesis opens for further inquiry the question of whether there is an unconscious and how much of our "rational" thought processes begin there. When science appeared to be related directly to what could be "touched" and the instruments made appeared to put the observer directly in touch with reality, it might have been easier to refute or embrace Teter's thesis. But methods of physics have removed us from what can be directly observed although physicists now produce what they cannot see. What they make can only be understood from its effects. Surely this situation creates a critical ethical question. It is a public political and ethical issue, not one which remains in the recesses of a supposed unconscious.

The process by which we can begin to have insight into our own cognitive and ethical capabilities is not an individualistic activity, nor one which centers only on studying the individual. Rather it is through the group, which allows the encouragement of the discussion of ends. The group in this case ranges far beyond the so-called peer group to include those whose contributions express different forms of rationality than that applied in the scientific project. The character of reconstructive knowledge emphasizes the dialogic nature of inquiry within the group.

The dialogic method brings into being questions hitherto thought to be irrelevant or nonexistent. Dialogue defies the rigorous boundaries of logic, which sets limits against questions that are not to be considered in an integrative way for any closed scientific program. Any question can be asked, any response given, any set of sounds and signs traded which are at once complementary and simultaneously antagonistic. That is to say, the dialogue creates new understandings and relationships while allow-ing for a set of inquiries which will cause the person and group to rethink their methods, conclusions, or views.

The development of computer language related to specific activities of organizations, whether the military or airlines, creates the appearance of a right and wrong way, in which one's understanding or meaning cannot be queried and the language used under the guise of "rigor" denies a mode of challenge and reinvention. As a way of proceeding, the closed system of knowing (wherein the answers are already known and applied as in certain forms of logic or particular strands of ideological politics) is to be eschewed. Curiously, the value of openness is both reinforced and contradicted by present scientific methods. Science proceeds on the assumption that there is a Truth to be known and taught, while its methods assert that any specific truth, what Arendt refers to as a string of verities, can be overthrown. The assumption of such thinkers as Leibniz and Chomsky is that truth rests in the human mind. Mathematics, for example, is supposedly compelling and self-evident, independent of any facts and any specific place. Chomsky thinks the same about structures of grammar, which supposedly generate language.

But what is compelling and self-evident must finally come back to a human sense of identity with the other, and that human sense of identity can be known only within history, within the actions, experiments, and human "doings" of groups. We then come full circle and realize that since any Truth from mathematics, any fact from physics or biology, can be known only through social endeavor, whether in the shaping of evidence or the intuitions of the mind, the question of ends is directly involved either consciously or unconsciously. Teleology and ethics (the construction of ends) raise the issue of fixed beliefs from which the knowledge worker must judge the validity of his or her work. Where should the knowledge worker turn for guidance concerning these questions? Hegel complained about philosophy first being the handmaiden of religion during the middle ages and then science after the Enlightenment. Our problem now is that philosophy itself fails to determine how it will ask and resolve questions of ends. There is a compromise which can be reached. The task of philosophy is to ask "dumb-dumb" questions, that is, questions which others are too expert or too socialized in a particular discipline, craft, or technology to ask. They are questions which can now be asked because political and social transformation has brought forward new groups (formerly invisible) to ask questions. Note, for example, the effects on inquiry which women knowledge workers have in the natural and social sciences (Evelyn Fox Keller and Ruth Brandwein, for example.) For knowledge workers a different type of responsibility opens up which changes the definition of rigor. Nothing is thought of as irrelevant or without effect and relationship. By beginning from this proposition, what is to be eliminated or delayed for consideration, what is thought of as trivial both in the natural and social sense, is presumed (but with a rebuttable presumption always in reserve) to be interrelated either in the sense that one affects the other or in the sense that it is the same phenomenon which is being studied.

This point of view cannot be "proved" absolutely. I adopt it as my myth-understanding of the universe and the world for political reasons having to do with the question of ends. Parenthetically, there is nothing to suggest that the other heuristic system or myth structure, which assumes separation and the metaphysical direction of sequencing, is anything more than a convenience, listing one thing at a time (as if we know what time is and what a thing is except by social agreement), or that it helps us understand more or explain the universe more clearly. Obviously, to live is to do more than one thing at a time. We breathe, move, think, write, and listen to music all at the same "time." Thus, our biological capacities demand that we do more than one thing at a time, say, for example, breathe. The organic interrelationships within us, which appear to require multiple, simultaneous, and complementary functioning, are a powerful explanatory myth and ritual structure that also begin to specify certain ethical requirements of relationship to others. It may not be too far-fetched to say that ethical requirements grow out of a sexual sense of incompleteness which translates into curiosity, wonder, the need to uncover, and make naked the Other— whether nature or human beings. But the need to compel and uncover is not invariant in human beings or in the nature of reality. What is present in human beings is their sense of incompleteness.

Myths of incompleteness are often sexual myths. The Greek myth of the Androgyne is an example of the attempt on the part of man and woman to reconnect themselves as one but as complementary to each other in a nondominating way. But when translated to social relationships, the wholeness must first stem from separation so that awareness of the other as more than a slave or dependent is made manifest when the relationship is reordered. I conclude that it is egalitarian interdependence which people seek and which has powerful explanatory value of the "natural" world and human relationship to it.

Dominance, hierarchy, and control of one atom or molecule over another, and of one individual or group over another, is not a necessary relationship but a contingent social one, dependent on how we decide to see, describe, and act on relationships whether within the atom or in society. One should not forget that our empirical evidence is probabilistic, dependent as well on assumptions about number, behavior, and the universe which are brought to the inductive computing table by those computing. Two questions remain to be considered. Those skeptical of reconstructive knowledge will wonder why, if the modern world is made by human beings through their description of it (and that therefore knowing whether or not there is a reality is beside the point), we bother to seek the elixir of ultimate phenomena.

My answer is that basic atomic structures are merely one way of describing the world. The atomic formulation does not help us look at "wholes" but forces us to look at what we think of as smaller and smaller parts. Alfred North Whitehead complained in *Science and the Modern World* that scientific knowledge had been faulty since the days of Newton because it did not include ethical concerns.[5] If the content of our scientific thought is just another way of describing a part of the world, one which is invented through language description, there are special demands which we must place on ourselves because our description of the world then dictates the social relationship which emerges. Obviously, the naming of things and use of language describes the mode of human struggle which emerges between us. David Bohm points out that in ancient Greece, "The school of Parmenides holds that space is a plenum. This view was opposed by Democritus, who was perhaps the first seriously to propose a world view that conceived of space as emptiness (i.e. the void) in which material particles (e.g. atoms) are free to move." Bohm goes on to suggest that "what we perceive through the senses as empty space is actually the plenum, which is the ground for the existence of everything including ourselves."[6] In a period of social turbulence and visions of the armageddon screaming out from humankind's behavior, the myths of Bohm and Parmenides may be helpful as a social thought system which emphasizes density, similarity, and then interdependence. Such a myth system leads to the political issue which starts from class struggle and attempts transcendence of it. The modern myth of Marxism has sought to transcend class struggle through revolution and civil war, just as fascism continues its pretensions at universality claiming that bourgeois and military officer classes hold the key to universal meanings. A reconstructive formulation builds on an active, nonviolent discourse throughout the society which seeks egalitarian interdependence and liberation in social relationships and the realization that scientific endeavor is to be subordinated to the question of ends, taking as its natural text the fullness of the universe.

Reconstructive knowledge depends on the generation of discourse and the fashioning of actions which transform the relationship of knowledge to the distribution of power in society. Thus, for example, in the latter case imagine groups of professors and students staging knowledge events which prove that knowledge is a shared good among people and is not for the purpose of distributing class position. Suppose knowledge events were staged which interrupted business as usual. Examples might be making public the answers to SAT examinations, or telling people who are to be subjects in psychological experiments that the experiments are predicated on deceiving them or that the knowledge gained from any particular experiment is not a truth, but a provisionality to be constantly contradicted by a new fashion, or that the inventions and production of the microchip, food additives, and so on, have serious consequences for the user and the unaware worker. Suppose scientists began speaking out on the incredible waste of time and money which now goes into finding new chemical compounds which if discovered would have profoundly dangerous consequences. And suppose outer space is not empty but a plenum of virtual fluctuations, correlated over vast distances yet subject to disruptions which might trigger deleterious effects. Or suppose we adopt Goldhaber's rule that space-time points in field theory be thought of as real events both in the Soviet Union and the United States.

How should we generate discourse on such matters? Those who are dissatisfied with the canons of their discipline because of their inherently soggy assumptions, or are despondent over the nexus between particular kinds of knowledge/myth generation and power, or women and Third World people who have been left out of the scientific project, should now consider questions of science and social science, introducing into them their own subjectivity. In so soing these groups will transform the organization and program of the disciplines of knowledge. They will want to initiate their own set of questions to illuminate their own discipline and to show what the actual determinants are for the assumptions of their discipline.

They will be prepared to present the questions that are not now being asked. And they—we—will be prepared to organize study action groups across disciplinary lines in our places of work to allow knowledge workers to rethink the knowledge project: asking whether the way their own work as formulated can or would have the effect of yielding catastrophe or, contrariwise, the type of understanding which assures the existence of a future for humankind with a path for liberation from oppression.

The reader by this time is aware that this book serves as a manifesto to initiate new forms of inquiry and new objects of inquiry, seeking to fit the means of study into the larger framework of ends and consequences. Its underlying program is to sustain and systematize liberation by transforming our epistemological framework, a framework which Kuhn rightly points out is so socially dominant that we think of it as the real reality. The cracks in the reality structures of our disciplines require an analysis of propositions of ethics—and the forging of a heuristics, that is, a set of provisional myths—that will bring together social harmonies premised on liberation. Ludwik Fleck has pointed out in his classic analysis of syphilis that even within relatively recent times

Astrology was the dominant science and religion created a mystical frame of mind. Together these produced that sociopsychological prevailing attitude which for centuries favored the isolation and consistent fixation upon the emotive venereal character of this newly determined disease entity. The stigma of fatefulness and sinfulness was imprinted upon syphilis—a stigma which it still carries within large sectors of the public.[7]

(In our time a Rightist religious stigma also applies to those with AIDS.) Since the eighteenth century, physics took the place of astrology as the guiding scientific belief. At first it sought cause and then the removal of cause, favoring instead probabilistics. But the issue, as this manifesto has argued, is the development of the ethical scientific framework as the means of judging and rejecting. This framework needs "words" and "symbols." Our task is to unpack their meanings, placing them into a social context of reconstruction, showing how there is no separation between different modes of inquiries, that a common field of endeavor is to be formulated which relocates our inquiries in new attitudes towards nature which also foster a common liberated humanity.

The question persists: Where do we find our "ethics," and what ethics? In his preface to Frantz Fanon's the *Wretched of the Earth*, Sartre points out that no professor of ethics that he knew was prepared to take a bop on the head for the oppressed.[9] This may be a bit of hyperbole but only slightly so. The ethics which we apply usually come from our family, the laws and regulations of the nation state, and the guild of our profession. Schools and churches act as the purveyors of past ethical practices, which are often class bound, antirational, and antiempirical. They are proscriptive rather than liberatory. At first glance one would think that the type of ethics we now need is proscriptive. But proscriptive ethics should apply only to the dominating classes. It is they who must learn their limits. What of those who are the powerless and who now need a way of defining reality so that they can live in that reality in dignity and liberation? The great fear of the Western and state socialist nations is that such nations as Libya might obtain modern military technology, even nuclear weapons. "What if Khaddafy gets the Bomb?" is the cry of the national security manager during the eighties, just as the nineteen fifties had a similar cry, "What if Nasser got the Bomb?" To the West these men are metaphors for the uncontrollable in history, and the fear is that they will use the conquered elements of science and nature for their uncontrollable purposes. This view, especially popular in the United States, is the analogue to the question: "Suppose the American Indians got nuclear weapons?" The fear is that the oppressed will act vengefully, especially given the oppressive circumstances under which they were forced to live. Such root fears are more at the center of colonizing politics and the scientific project than wonder. The project of reconstructive knowledge, on the other hand, becomes the means of rearranging the world in ways which take account of fears and formulations, moving beyond the oppressive and coercive while finding the desire within human beings to forego the framework of domination. An ethics of reconstruction builds on the incompletely developed human attribute of empathic invariance, which fosters justice and liberation with others. The search for such a capacity in individuals and groups is part of the modern social scientific program.

At the beginning of the twentieth century, the anarchist thinker Kropotkin recognized the heuristic conception of oneness and interdependence and what must surely be present in our very being, an empathic invariance, a capacity within all of us for each other. At the end of World War II the great sociologist Pitrim Sorokin had established an Institute for the Study of Altruism at Harvard. This "nonsense" was moved aside in favor of Cold War studies and studies which can only be described as exercises in the imperial mode. It is not too late to begin studies of altruism and empathic invariance. It is not too late to initiate study groups whose responsibility is for the development of an ethics for political liberation. Nor would we be mistaken in reorganizing our corporate forms to take into account a feminist rather than a patriarchal consciousness. This would help in recognizing that the locus of new knowledge must find a moral discourse in our day-to-day language and scientific inquiries. A continuing discourse by knowledge workers bent on reconstruction of their disciplines could have the effect of shaking off the death instinct from humanity. This will be accomplished by transforming the objects of study and shifting our gaze to different realities that are there and are far more important to humanity. Many of our specialized disciplines of knowledge will have to be treated either as literary residues of the past or as instrumental descriptions required by the powerful to continue their power over history. And similarly, religion cannot escape the new dialogue which lifts the veil of holiness from those who mask coercion in the name of religious duty. Finally, knowledge and especially scientific workers are to extend the boundaries of concern in the problems we study to include the "secondary," "irrelevant," "trivial," and "subjective." We are to incorporate the subjective in our work, stating it honestly and examining it accordingly. By finding the human in our activities and inquiries we will be helping ourselves through dark times to see and act in new ways. To do so will require a new heuristic: that the distinctions between objective and subjective have been overstated, that new forms of symbolic logic and notation to take account of the subjective and the objective are necessary, that the claims of universality of science are only valid when they include an analysis of the social system which produces the "scientific law," and that the separation of "ought" principles from "objectivity" merely masks the framework and process of science, which surely are no longer to be exempt from the analyses and comment of "outsiders."

In the eighteenth century the encyclopedists paved the way for political and intellectual transformation. In our own time knowledge workers can also accomplish this end by forming themselves into groups for study to redefine the program and purpose of inquiry. There is no reason that the "last ding dong of civilization" has to sound in this generation. But to avoid it requires the use of mind and political energy. The development of a new encyclopedia, one which seeks to recount the profound reconstructive changes that have occurred and those which are still needed as we approach the twenty-first century could be an important organizing instrument that relocates the questions of wonder and concern of humankind to the joint project of liberation.

Humankind yearns for such a possibility. A beginning in this direction can be made by breaking down the barriers of specialization at universities and within academic guilds, by meeting in small groups to determine those knowledges and inquiries which will not deny humankind its future. It is time to begin.

## Notes

1. Ludwik Fleck, *Genesis and Development of a Scientific Fact,* trans. Fred Bradley and Thaddeus J. Trenn; ed. Thaddeus Trenn and Thomas Merton (Chicago: University of Chicago Press, 1979), 3.

2. Marcus Raskin, *Being and Doing* (New York: Random House, 1971).

3. George Wald, testimony before Subcommittee on Scientific Research Technology, Science and Policy Implications of DNA Recombinant Molecule Research (Washington, D.C.: Government Printing Office, 1971), No. 24, p. 72.

4. Charles Schwartz, "Proposed Physicists' Experiment to End the Nuclear Arms Race," presented at University of California, Berkeley, March 27, 1985.

5. Alfred North Whitehead, *Science and the Modern World* (New York: Macmillan, 1925).

6. David Bohm, *Wholeness and the Implicate Order* (London: Routledge & Kegan Paul, 1980), 191–192.

7. Fleck, *Genesis and Development of a Scientific Fact.*

8. Frantz Fanon, *The Wretched of the Earth,* preface by Jean Paul Sartre (Harmondsworth: Penguin Books, 1963).

# Index